COME, YE CHILDREN

taken from Psalm 34:11
"Come, ye children, hearken unto me:
I will teach you the fear of the Lord."

A Bible Storybook
for Young Children
by Gertrude Hoeksema

Illustrated
by Jeff Steenholdt

*R*eformed Free Publishing Association
4949 Ivanrest Avenue, S.W.
Grandville, MI 49418-9709

by Gertrude Hoeksema
Illustrated by Jeff Steenholdt

© 1983
by Reformed Free Publishing Association
Second Printing 1998

PRINTED IN THE UNITED STATES
OF AMERICA

For Information, address:

Reformed Free Publishing Association
4949 Ivanrest Avenue, S.W.
Grandville, Michigan 49418-9709
(616-224-1518)

Library of Congress Catalog Card #: 83-51588
ISBN 0-916206-27-0

To
my
grandchildren

Preface

With trembling hand I have set down these one hundred ninety-eight Bible stories, echoing David's words, "Come, ye children, hearken unto me: I will teach you the fear of the Lord." It is to very young children that I have directed this book, children of the approximate ages of four to eight years. Because it was not merely **stories** I was setting down, but because it was the **fear of the Lord** I was teaching, I tried to take particular care to use a simple, direct style and words young children would understand. When some of Scripture's more difficult concepts entered the narrative, I explained the concept in vivid picture language, at their level of understanding.

Central to the contents of these stories is the **fear of the Lord.** For that reason I have closely followed the Scriptural narrative and the stories are, I believe, Biblically accurate. When I wrote them, I used not only the one passage which told the story proper, but searched through the whole of God's Word for other references or commentaries on that particular incident. I did that, of course, because the Word of God is one whole, and Scripture interprets itself. That is the reason, too, that I did not write a series of separate "Bible stories." Each story is written as a part of a whole, the whole being the revelation of the whole counsel of our great God and Father to His people through our Lord Jesus Christ. In that our young children also share.

It has been said that one cannot write Bible stories without interpreting them, without applying them, and without teaching the fear of the Lord through them. I believe that. Throughout this book I have tried to show to the children who will listen to these stories that the Bible is **one whole.** Therefore, no matter what story we hear, we are always learning the fear of the Lord. Especially I have stressed the covenant idea: that God has worked out His purpose and fulfilled His promise through the line of believers and their children. In order that our young children in these last days will always know that the stories of the Bible are for them, as children of believing parents, and that the stories will touch them each day, I have added, under the title **REMEMBER,** the key to the spiritual application of each story which they can carry away in their little hearts.

The artist, Jeff Steenholdt, and I have tried to blend the nature of the illustrations to fit the style of the stories. The reader will find that the illustrations in this book are different from those in other Bible story books. Because we do not know the facial features of any of the Biblical characters, we have purposely eliminated direct facial views of any of them. Instead, Jeff has tried to capture, not only the authenticity of the landscapes and clothing of Biblical times, but also the positive element of each story, and has inserted it at the proper place in each story. He has done this with reverence, without prying into the spiritual, which cannot be seen, but by helping young children, who need pictures, to remember the heart of each story.

It is our prayer that this book may be used in the fear of the Lord and to His glory.

Contents

1. God Makes Light
   Genesis 1:1-5. 25

2. God Makes the Sky and Plants
   Genesis 1:6-13. 27

3. God Makes the Sun, Moon, and Stars
   Genesis 1:14-19. 30

4. God Makes Fish, Birds, and Animals
   Genesis 1:20-25. 33

5. God Makes Adam and Eve
   Genesis 1:26 - 2:25 36

6. Adam and Eve Fall Into Sin
   Genesis 3. 39

7. Cain and Abel Offer Sacrifices
   Genesis 4:1-15. 41

8. Enoch Walks With God
   Genesis 4:16 - 5:24 44

9. Noah Builds the Ark
   Genesis 6. 47

10. God Sends the Flood
    Genesis 7, 8, 9. 50

11. The Tower of Babel
    Genesis 9:18-29; 11:1-9 53

12. The Story of Job (1)
    Job 1. 55

13. The Story of Job (2)
    Job 2 and selected passages. 57

14. God Calls Abram
    Genesis 12. 60

15. Lot Leaves Abram
    Genesis 13. 62

16. Ishmael is Born
    Genesis 16. 65

17. Three Angels Come to Abraham
    Genesis 18. 68

18. God Destroys Sodom and Gomorrah
    Genesis 19. 71

19. Isaac is Born
    Genesis 21. 74

20. Abraham Obeys God
    Genesis 22. 77

21. Isaac Gets a Wife
    Genesis 24. 79

22. Esau Sells His Birthright
    Genesis 25:27-34. 82

23. Isaac Blesses Jacob
    Genesis 27. 84

24. God Comes to Jacob at Bethel
    Genesis 27:41 - 28:22. 87

25. Jacob Stays With His Uncle Laban
    Genesis 29, 30. 89

26. Jacob Leaves His Uncle Laban
    Genesis 31. 92

27. Jacob Goes Back to Canaan
    Genesis 32, 33. 95

28. Joseph is Sold
    Genesis 37. 98

29. Joseph is a Slave in Potiphar's House
    Genesis 39. 101

30. Joseph Tells the Dreams of the Butler and Baker
    Genesis 40. 103

31. Pharaoh Dreams Two Dreams
   Genesis 41 105

32. Joseph's Brothers Visit Egypt
   Genesis 42 108

33. The Brothers Visit Egypt Again
   Genesis 43 111

34. "I Am Joseph"
   Genesis 44 - 45:15 113

35. Jacob's Family Moves to Egypt
   Genesis 45:16 - 50:13 (selected passages) 115

36. Three Hundred Dark Years
   Genesis 50:14-26; Exodus 1 118

37. Moses is Born
   Exodus 2:1-10 121

38. Moses Runs Away to the Desert
   Exodus 2:11-22 124

39. God Visits Moses in the Burning Bush
   Exodus 3 127

40. Moses Talks Back to God
   Exodus 4 130

41. Moses and Aaron Come Before Pharaoh
   Exodus 5:1 - 7:13 132

42. God Sends the First Three Plagues
   Exodus 7:14 - 8:19 135

43. God Sends Plagues Four, Five, and Six
   Exodus 8:20 - 9:12 137

44. God Sends Plagues Seven, Eight, and Nine
   Exodus 9:13 - 10:29 139

45. God Sends the Last Plague
   Exodus 11, 12 142

46. Israel Goes Through the Red Sea
    Exodus 13:17 - 14:31 144

47. Israel Travels Through the Desert
    Exodus 15, 16. 147

48. God Gives Water From the Rock
    Exodus 17. 150

49. Israel Comes to Mount Sinai
    Exodus 19, 20. 153

50. Israel Worships the Golden Calf
    Exodus 32. 156

51. The Israelites Build the Tabernacle
    Exodus 25 - 30 (selected passages) 159

52. Two Sins at Sinai
    Leviticus 10:1-7; 24:10-16 162

53. The Israelites Complain in the Desert
    Numbers 11. 164

54. Miriam Sins
    Numbers 12. 166

55. Moses Sends Out Twelve Spies
    Numbers 13, 14. 168

56. Korah, Dathan, and Abiram Rebel
    Numbers 16. 171

57. Moses Sins
    Numbers 20:1-13 174

58. God Sends Fiery Serpents
    Numbers 20:14 - 21:9. 177

59. The Story of Balaam (1)
    Numbers 21:21 - 22:21. 180

60. The Story of Balaam (2)
    Numbers 22:22 - 24:25. 183

61. Two Spies Go to Jericho
    Joshua 1, 2 186

62. Israel Crosses the Jordan
    Joshua 3, 4 189

63. The Walls of Jericho Fall Down
    Joshua 6 192

64. Achan Sins
    Joshua 7 195

65. Israel Wins the Victory at Ai
    Joshua 8 197

66. The Gibeonites Trick the Israelites
    Joshua 9 200

67. The Sun Stands Still
    Joshua 10 203

68. The Last Days of Joshua
    Joshua 24, Judges 1:1-15 206

69. Ehud, the Left-handed Judge
    Judges 3:12-30 209

70. Deborah and Barak Judge Israel
    Judges 4, 5 212

71. God Calls Gideon
    Judges 6 215

72. Gideon Wins the Victory by Faith
    Judges 7 218

73. Jephthah Keeps His Promise
    Judges 11 221

74. The Story of Samson (1)
    Judges 13, 14 224

75. The Story of Samson (2)
    Judges 15 227

76. The Story of Samson (3)
   Judges 16 230

77. Naomi and Ruth
   Ruth 1, 2. 233

78. Ruth and Boaz
   Ruth 3, 4. 236

79. Samuel is Born
   I Samuel 1. 239

80. The Philistines Take Away God's Ark
   I Samuel 2, 3, 4. 242

81. God's Ark Makes Trouble for the Philistines
   I Samuel 5:1 - 6:12. 245

82. Bethshemesh and Mizpeh
   I Samuel 6:13 - 7:12. 248

83. Israel Asks for a King
   I Samuel 8, 9. 251

84. God Gives Israel a King
   I Samuel 10. 254

85. Saul Helps Jabesh-Gilead
   I Samuel 11. 256

86. The Lord Saves Israel Through Jonathan
   I Samuel 14. 259

87. Saul Disobeys
   I Samuel 15. 262

88. Samuel Anoints David
   I Samuel 16. 265

89. David Kills Goliath
   I Samuel 17. 268

90. David and Jonathan
   I Samuel 18. 272

15

91. Saul Tries to Kill David
   I Samuel 19 275

92. David and Jonathan Meet
   I Samuel 20 278

93. Saul Chases David
   I Samuel 23, 24 281

94. David and Nabal
   I Samuel 25 284

95. David Saves Saul's Life
   I Samuel 26 287

96. Saul Goes to the Witch of Endor
   I Samuel 28 290

97. Saul Dies in Battle
   I Samuel 31 293

98. David Hears News of the Battle
   II Samuel 1 296

99. David Brings Back the Ark
   II Samuel 6 299

100. David Wants to Build God's House
   II Samuel 7, 9 302

101. David Sins
   II Samuel 11, 12 305

102. Absalom Rebels
   II Samuel 15:1 - 17:24 308

103. The Sad Battle
   II Samuel 17:27 - 19:8 311

104. David Numbers the People
   II Samuel 24; I Chronicles 21 314

105. Solomon is Made King
   I Kings 1 317

106. King Solomon Dreams a Dream
    I Kings 3; II Chronicles 1. 320

107. King Solomon Builds the Temple
    I Kings 6, 7; II Chronicles 2. 323

108. The Queen of Sheba Visits Solomon
    I Kings 9, 10 326

109. The Last Part of King Solomon's Life
    I Kings 11 329

110. Rehoboam is Made King
    I Kings 12; II Chronicles 10. 332

111. Jeroboam Teaches Israel to Worship Idols
    I Kings 12:25 - 13:32 335

112. The Prophet Elijah and King Ahab
    I Kings 17 338

113. Elijah at Mount Carmel
    I Kings 18 341

114. Elijah Runs to the Desert
    I Kings 19 344

115. Ahab and Naboth
    I Kings 21 347

116. King Ahab Dies
    I Kings 22:1-40 350

117. God Sends Fire From Heaven
    II Kings 1 353

118. Elijah Goes to Heaven
    II Kings 2 356

119. Israel Goes to War With Moab
    II Kings 3 359

120. Three Wonders
    II Kings 4 362

121. Naaman is Healed
    II Kings 5 365

122. God Makes the Syrians Blind
    II Kings 6:1-23 368

123. The Syrians Surround Samaria
    II Kings 6:24 - 7:20 371

124. Jehu is Made King
    II Kings 9 374

125. The Last Days of the Kingdom of Israel
    II Kings 13, 17 377

126. God Calls Jonah
    Jonah 1, 2 380

127. Jonah Preaches
    Jonah 3, 4 383

128. Trouble in Hezekiah's Time
    II Kings 18, 19 386

129. Hezekiah's Sickness
    II Kings 20 389

130. King Manasseh Rules in Wickedness
    II Kings 21 392

131. The Last Days of the Kingdom of Judah
    II Kings 24, 25; Jeremiah 38 395

132. Daniel Lives in the King's Palace
    Daniel 1 398

133. Nebuchadnezzar Dreams a Dream
    Daniel 2 401

134. The Three Friends in the Fiery Furnace
    Daniel 3 404

135. Nebuchadnezzar Dreams Another Dream
    Daniel 4 407

136. The Fall of the City of Babylon
   Daniel 5. 410

137. Daniel is Thrown to the Lions
   Daniel 6. 413

138. Some of God's People Go Back to Their Own Land
   Ezra 1, 2, 3 417

139. Esther Becomes Queen
   Esther 1, 2. 420

140. Trouble for the Jews
   Esther 3, 4. 423

141. The King Honors Mordecai
   Esther 5, 6. 426

142. The Jews Are Saved
   Esther 7-10 429

143. Ezra and Nehemiah Help God's People
   Ezra 7, 8; Nehemiah 1, 2. 432

144. The Angel Visits Zacharias
   Luke 1:5-23 435

145. John is Born
   Luke 1:24-80 438

146. Jesus is Born
   Luke 2:1-20 441

147. The Wise Men Come
   Matthew 2:1-15. 444

148. Jesus as a Child
   Matthew 2:16-23; Luke 2:40-52. .447

149. John Baptizes Jesus
   Matthew 3:13-17; John 1:19-34 450

150. The Devil Tempts Jesus
   Matthew 4:1-11; Luke 4:1-13. 452

151. Jesus Works His First Miracle
John 1:35 - 2:11 455

152. Jesus Goes to the Passover Feast
John 2:12-25. 458

153. Jesus and the Samaritan Woman
John 4:1-42. 462

154. Jesus in Galilee
John 4:43-54; Luke 4:14-30 464

155. The Miracle of Catching Many Fishes
Luke 5:1-11; Mark 1:16-20 467

156. Jesus Heals the Man With a Devil
Mark 1:21-35; Luke 4:33-41 470

157. Jesus Heals Two Men
Mark 1:40-45; Luke 5:12-26 473

158. Jesus Calls Levi and Heals a Man With Palsy
Mark 2:13-17; John 5:1-20 476

159. Jesus Teaches About the Sabbath Day
Matthew 12:1-13; Luke 6:1-16 479

160. The Centurion's Servant and the Widow's Son
Luke 7:1-17; Matthew 8:5-13 482

161. Simon and the Woman
Luke 7:36-50; Matthew 12:22-31 485

162. The Parable of the Four Kinds of Soil
Matthew 13:1-23; Mark 4:2-20 488

163. Jesus Stills the Storm and Heals the Man With Devils
Mark 4:34 - 5:20; Luke 8:22-40 491

164. Jesus Raises Jairus' Daughter
Mark 5:21-43; Luke 8:41-56 494

165. Jesus Heals Two Blind Men and Sends Out the Disciples
Matthew 9:27 - 10:22; Luke 9:1-6 497

166. The Death of John the Baptist
    Matthew 14:1-13; Mark 6:14-32...........................500
167. Jesus Feeds the Five Thousand and Walks on the Water
    Matthew 14:13-33; John 6:1-21 503
168. Two More Miracles
    Matthew 15:21-31; Mark 7:24-37 506
169. Jesus Feeds Four Thousand People and Heals a Blind Man
    Matthew 15:32-39; Mark 8 509
170. The Transfiguration
    Luke 9:28-42; Mark 9:1-29...............................512
171. The Tax Money and the Ten Lepers
    Matthew 17:24-27; Luke 17:11-19.........................515
172. Jesus Visits Bethany and Heals a Blind Man
    Luke 10:38-42; John 9..................................518
173. Jesus Raises Lazarus From the Dead
    John 11..521
174. Jesus and the Children, Jesus and the Ruler, Jesus and Zaccheus
    Mark 10:13-31; Luke 19:1-10............................524
175. The Royal Entry
    Mark 11:1-11; John 12:1-19.............................527
176. In the Upper Room
    Matthew 26:17-35; John 13:1-30 530
177. In the Garden of Gethsemane
    Mark 14:22-41; Luke 22:5-46...........................533
178. Jesus is Captured
    Luke 22:47-54; John 18:1-14...........................536
179. The Trial of Jesus
    Matthew 26:57 - 27:30; John 18:28 - 19:12.............539
180. Jesus is Crucified
    Mark 15:21-32; Luke 23:26-38..........................542

181. Jesus Dies
     Luke 23:39-56; John 19:25-42 545

182. Jesus Arose
     Matthew 28:1-15; John 20:1-10 548

183. Jesus' First Appearances
     John 20:11-18; Luke 24:13-35 551

184. Jesus Appears to His Disciples
     Luke 24:36-53; John 20:24-25; 25 555

185. The Day of Jesus' Ascension and the Day of Pentecost
     Acts 1, 2 558

186. The Healing of the Lame Man
     Acts 3, 4 561

187. Ananias and Sapphira Sin
     Acts 5:1-11 564

188. The Rulers Stone Stephen
     Acts 5, 6, 7 567

189. The Story of Philip
     Acts 8 570

190. God Converts Saul
     Acts 9:1-31 573

191. The Church Grows and Spreads
     Acts 12 576

192. Paul's First Missionary Journey
     Acts 13, 14 579

193. Paul's Second Missionary Journey
     Acts 16, 17, 18 582

194. Paul's Third Missionary Journey
     Acts 19 585

195. The End of Paul's Third Missionary Journey
     Acts 20, 21, 22 588

196. Paul's Trial

Acts 23, 24, 25, 26 591

197. The Shipwreck

Acts 27 594

198. Paul Comes to Rome

Acts 28 597

God Makes Light

What did you have for breakfast this morning? Toast and jam? Or a bowl of cereal with milk? What did you have for lunch? A sandwich and soup? Did you say, "Thank you," to your mother?

When you eat the good breakfast your mother makes for you, do you ever ask her where your toast and cereal come from? If she tells you she bought it at the store, do you ask her where the store gets it from? After she tells you the store buys the bread from the bakery and the cereal from the cereal factory, do you wonder how they make the bread and the cereal? Then your mother tells you that bakers need the wheat and the corn and the oats that grow in the farmers' fields to make bread and cereal. She tells you that the farmer plants the seed in a field that God made; God sends His rain and His sunshine and makes the wheat and corn and oats grow, so that the baker and cereal maker can make bread and cereal for you and your family.

Your mother might tell you, too, that God made the trees that the carpenters used for the boards to build your house, and God gave the sand that goes into the cement. Your mother will tell you that everything we have comes from God. Yes, everything comes from God! Would you like to hear how God made everything?

Long ago, in the beginning, God was there. God always was. He has no beginning and no ending. We call Him **eternal**. That is very hard for us to understand, isn't it? God is holy and pure and perfect, and without any thought of wickedness in Him; and because He is holy and pure and perfect, He knows

what is best. We call Him **wise**. And God is so great that He has all the power.
He knows what is best and He can do what is best.

Do you know what God in His greatness did? He made the world. First,
the world was not there, and then the world was there! How could that be?
The earth where we live and the heavens where God lives came because God
spoke. His powerful Word called the heavens and earth to be made. When God
told the heavens and the earth to be made, we say that He **created** them.

But God's world was not finished the minute He spoke. Many things, like
water, sand, and air, were all mixed together. And the world was dark, pitch
dark, black dark, thick dark. God wanted a world that would be light and alive,
so God's Spirit sat over the dark world. You know what happens when a hen sits
over her eggs for many days, don't you? They hatch into live little yellow
chicks. God's Spirit sat over His world to make a **living** world. Nothing can live
in a black, dark world, so God said, "Let there be light." And there was light —
for a whole day. In the evening God made night, and that was the end of the very
first day. God saw that His light was good. Do you see the good light that God
makes every morning of every new day?

REMEMBER:

God is light. When we look outside and see the beautiful, bright daylight He
has made, we will know that it is a picture of the light of our great God.

God Makes
the Sky and Plants

On a bright, warm, summer day, do you like to lie on your back in the grass and watch the sky? Do you see the clouds slide past? Do you ever try to look as high as you can, **right into** the sky? Do you wonder whether God is behind that blue sky?

We remember that everything comes from God. On the very first day, God made the light. On the second day, He made the sky, the blue sky we see every day. What do you think the world looked like before God made the sky? The earth and the water and the air and the sky were all mixed together. Then God spoke the Word of His great power, and He **separated** the waters of the sky from the waters of the earth. Do you know what **separate** means? When your mother cracks an egg and puts the yolk into one bowl and the white into another, she **separates** the egg. She pulls it apart.

God pulled the waters of the sky apart and stretched them out on top of the earth. God stretched the sky thin, like a beautiful blue curtain on top of us. We say that the name of that beautiful blue curtain is the sky.

The next day God separated some more. The land and the water on the earth were still mixed together, and there was not a dry, hard place for anyone to stand. Then God told the waters to come together to one place, and the dry

land appeared. God pulled the waters into little brooks and streams, and big rivers and lakes, and oceans, too.

If you could have stood on the dry land on the day that God made it, all you would have seen would have been sandy ground, brown and bare. God's dry land was not finished yet! It needed grass and flowers, corn and wheat, bushes and trees, and all the different kinds of plants you can think of. God did not plant tiny seeds, and then wait and wait for them to grow. He made the plants and trees big, already grown up.

If you could still be standing on God's earth after He told the plants to come, you would have seen the whole earth become beautiful and green with all the hundreds of plants and trees that God wanted on His earth, and the red and yellow and orange and purple flowers already blooming.

When you want a plant to grow, you need a seed and plenty of rain and sunshine. Then you must wait and wait for it to grow. But God did not create His plants that way. All God's plants were there the very minute God spoke His Word. We call that a great **wonder**. God saw that His wonder was good.

REMEMBER:

Plants need light in order to live. That is why plants turn themselves to the light. God's children are like plants, for they, too, turn to God's light so that they may live. Where can we find God's light? In His Word, the Bible.

God Makes the Sun, Moon, and Stars

What kind of weather do you like better: cold, rainy weather, or warm, bright sunshine? When it is the day for a picnic, do you run to your bedroom window early in the morning to see whether the sun is shining and do you hope that the sun will make the weather warm and beautiful for your picnic? God makes the sun shine.

On the fourth day, God made the sun and He put it in the big blue sky that He stretched out like a curtain over the earth. God made the sun to be a **holder** for the light that He had made on the very first day. In our homes we have light holders, too. We call them **lamps** and we can switch them on and off whenever we wish. But God's great light holder, the sun, always holds the light. It never goes off.

God made the sun very big and very hot. He made it bigger than our earth; and then He set it far away from us in His heaven, so that it cannot burn us up. He made it just warm enough to make the trees and flowers and our gardens grow.

Every day the sun tells us what to do. In the morning, when it comes up, it tells us to get up, for a new day is starting. When the sun sets at night, it tells us that it will soon be bedtime. When the sun tells us what to do, we say it **rules** us. God's sun rules us by telling us what kinds of clothes to wear: for in the wintertime, when it does not shine so brightly, it tells us to put on warm jackets and mittens. In the warm summertime, it tells us to get out our swimming suits, because it is warming up the lakes and pools.

God made the sun to shine during the day, and He made holders for the light to shine at night, too. We call them the moon and the stars. If you go outside on a dark night, try to find the moon. It catches the bright light of the sun and shines it back down on our dark world. The moon is just a mirror of the sun and we can see the sun's light in the moon just as we can see ourselves in a mirror.

When the Lord set the stars in His heavens, He set them very far away from the earth. God's stars are really very big, many of them bigger than our earth, but they are so far away that they look like tiny, sparkling dots in the sky. God made **millions** of those beautiful stars, more than we can count, and put them in patterns in the sky. Do you know why? Because He wanted His world to be great and beautiful and He wanted His great and beautiful world to praise Him. When we look at God's wonderful sun, His moon, and His stars, we must remember to praise Him, too.

REMEMBER:

The lights in the sky are pictures of Jesus. Sometimes the Bible calls Jesus "the **Sun** of righteousness" and "the bright and morning **Star.**" Jesus is the Light of the world because He saves His people from their sins.

God Makes Fish, Birds, and Animals

Have you ever thought what our world would be like with plants and trees, sun, moon, and stars, but with nothing that can run or hop? Can you think what it would be like to play in a pond without any frogs to catch, to have a garden without ever seeing a rabbit, to go to a farm without horses or cows, and to see trees and no birds flying to them?

On the fifth day, God spoke with His powerful Word to the waters of the earth and told them to bring out things that moved: fish and birds; and the waters obeyed God's Word. Our great God wanted His earth to have many, many fish and birds, such a great plenty and so many different kinds that His earth would never run out. He made the tiny silver minnows, the middle-sized trout and salmon, and the huge sharks and whales; and then He made one rule for them all: to stay alive, they must always be in the **waters** God made. If they tried to live on land, they would die. That is God's rule for the fish.

God called the birds out of the water, too. Did you know that birds are something like fish? Many of the birds God made are water birds, and can swim. Think of the ducks and the sea gulls. Most birds can fly, for God gave them perfect wings, and told them to live in the air and make nests in the trees. That is God's rule for birds: to live in the air. If they try to swim under water, they will die. Would you like to know why God made the birds? To make His earth beautiful. He painted their feathers such beautiful colors! Only a wonderful

God could paint them that way! God made the birds to sing praise to Him, too. When you hear a bird sing, remember that it is singing its Maker's praise.

On the sixth day, God spoke His powerful Word to the **earth** and called all the animals that moved out of the earth. He made three kinds of animals: the wild animals that live in the forests and jungles — like lions, bears, elephants, and zebras; the tame animals that live on farms or are pets — like sheep, horses, dogs, and cats; and the small animals that creep along the ground, which we call **bugs** — like ladybugs, beetles, grasshoppers, and caterpillars.

When God made the fish and the birds and the animals, He made them know just how to make their homes and how to take care of their babies. When you see a mother robin feed her baby robins, think that our wonderful God taught the mother robin just how to take care of her babies. God told all the fish, the birds, and the animals to have many babies and grandbabies and great-grandbabies because He wanted His creatures all over the earth.

Then God **blessed** the earth and all that He had made in it. That means He showed **kindness** and **goodness** to His world. God saw that it was good, and He liked it.

REMEMBER:

God likes to use pictures of His animals when He tells us about Jesus, too. God calls Jesus a **Lamb** Who died for us and a **Lion** Who is our King.

35

God Makes Adam and Eve

God's earth was almost finished! It looked so beautiful with the trees and flowers, fish and birds, and all the animals God had made. But something was missing: someone to take care of God's earth. God said He wanted someone **wonderful** to take care of His earth, a **man** who could think and talk and do God's will, a man who would be **like** God Himself. So God made a picture of Himself, only a little, weak picture. That picture was a man.

Do you know how God made the first man? He took dust from the ground and formed it into a man, and then He breathed His own breath into that man, and he became alive. God called that first man Adam.

Then God gave Adam a home in a wonderful garden He planted. In this garden were many beautiful trees with all kinds of food for Adam to eat. God made rivers in this garden, and very special, precious stones, and gold; and He told Adam to take care of his wonderful, perfect, new home. The name of the garden was the Garden of Eden.

Animals lived in the garden, too, and God told Adam to give names to all the animals. When God made all the animals to come to Adam to get their names, Adam knew just what to call them. The animals came to him two by two: a father and a mother sheep, a father and a mother monkey, a father and a mother dog, until there were no more animals left to have names. And then Adam felt very sad. Do you know why? Because all the father animals had mother animals and the mother animals had father animals, and they were so happy together. But Adam was all alone, and he couldn't even talk with anyone.

God knew how lonely Adam was, and He knew that Adam needed a helper, a wife. As Adam sat there, feeling sad and alone, God made him sleep very soundly. While he was asleep, God took one of Adam's bones, his rib, and from it made a beautiful lady, his wife. Can you think how happy Adam was to wake up and see his helper, his wife? Her name was Eve.

Then God told Adam to be the king of God's earth, to rule over it and to take care of it and to use it. And He told Adam and Eve to have many children and grandchildren and great-grandchildren to live on His earth, for God gave His earth to His people as a present.

The beautiful Garden of Eden where Adam and Eve lived was perfect. Nothing in it died, and there was no evil in it; and Adam and Eve didn't do anything wrong, for there was no sin in the garden. Every day they talked with God.

Now God's wonder of creation was almost finished. He made only one more special day of creation. That was day number seven. God made that day a special day of rest. God did not just sit and do nothing, but He looked at His wonderful world and enjoyed it and blessed it. And God told Adam and Eve and us to have a special day of rest every seven days, too. He taught Adam and Eve and us to worship Him and praise Him and sing to Him on our day of rest. Our special day to praise God is Sunday.

REMEMBER:

God made **us** to be little pictures of Himself, too. Do we try to live as God wants His little pictures to live?

Adam and Eve Fall into Sin

When you have been naughty and your parents make you sit on a chair, have you ever thought, while you sat there, what it would be like to be perfect? Always to do exactly what your daddy and mother say, always to do what God wants you to do, never to say bad things? Adam and Eve were perfect in the Garden of Eden.

In the middle of the garden, God had planted two trees. Their names were **the tree of life** and **the tree of knowledge of good and evil.** The tree of life would make Adam live, and God told him to eat all the fruit he wanted from it, but God told Adam not to eat of the tree of knowledge of good and evil, for then he would surely die. Adam obeyed God. Eve knew about the two trees, and she obeyed, too.

But one day trouble came to the Garden of Eden. The devil came to Eve. Who was he? Once upon a time he was one of God's good angels in heaven, one of the highest of all the angels; but he was not satisfied to be an angel. He wanted to be like God, and that was a terrible sin. God threw him and his helper-angels out of heaven into hell, an awful place of fire and punishment, where there is always suffering.

The devil did not always live in hell. God let him walk on the earth, too. Do you know how he came to Eve? He put himself inside a snake and talked to Eve through the snake's mouth. Purposely the devil asked a wicked question about God. He said, "Hath God said, Ye shall not eat of every tree of the garden?"

39

Eve's answer was not quite right, either. She said, "We may eat of the fruit of the trees of the garden."

But when she told about the tree of knowledge of good and evil, she said they might not even **touch** it. The last part was not true. God did not say anything about not touching the tree.

Then the devil told a wicked lie. He said, "Ye shall not surely die." Eve should have looked at the tree with obedient eyes, but she began to look at it with sinful eyes. She reached out her hand, took some fruit, ate, and gave Adam some, too. Now they both had sinned.

The first thing they noticed was that they had no clothes on. When their hearts were perfect, they did not have to cover their perfect bodies; but now they saw their nakedness with their sinful eyes. Eve sewed fig leaves together to cover their bodies. Then God came to talk with them, and they were both ashamed and hid away. God found them and kept asking them questions: "Who told thee that thou wast naked? Hast thou eaten of the tree?"

Adam, with his sinful heart, blamed Eve and said she gave him the forbidden fruit to eat. He said it was Eve's fault.

When God asked Eve, "What is this that thou hast done?" she blamed the snake with the devil inside him. God **cursed** the snake and punished him. God's punishment for the snake was that he would crawl on his belly in the dust all his life.

God told Adam and Eve that they would have trouble and sickness and pain in their lives, for from now on they would live in a sinful world, with sinful hearts. But didn't God say they would surely die if they ate the fruit of the tree? God did not make them drop dead and stop breathing right there in the Garden of Eden. What did God mean, then, when He said, "You shall surely die if you eat the fruit of the tree"? It meant that they would live **away** from God's face; for the Bible says that to live away from God is **death.**

How sad Adam and Eve were! But God did not leave them in their terrible sadness and death. He gave them a promise. Some day He would send a Savior, the Lord Jesus, Who would crush the devil's head and would save them from their sin and death.

God made clothes for Adam and Eve from the skins of animals. Do you know why? When God killed the animals, He was making a picture of Jesus, Who some day would die for their sins. Adam and Eve had to learn to kill animals and bring them as sacrifices to God as pictures of Jesus, Who would die on the cross for them.

REMEMBER:

Because Adam and Eve sinned, we are born sinful, too. The promise of Jesus to die on the cross is for **us,** too. He saves all His children from their sins.

Cain and Abel
Offer Sacrifices

After Adam and Eve had sinned, they could not stay in the perfect Garden of Eden anymore. The Lord chased them out and He set angels with fiery swords to guard the gate so that no one could get back into the garden.

Now Adam and Eve did not live in the garden where they had been perfect and happy. Now they had to plant their own seeds and grow their own food from the hard ground. Often they must have felt very sad and sorry, and probably very tired. The Bible does not tell us how they made a house and furniture and clothes. But don't you think God took care of them? For they were His children.

One day God brought happiness to their lives. He gave them a baby boy, and Eve named him Cain; and soon afterwards God gave them another baby boy, whom they called Abel. Eve did not have a beautiful cradle nor soft, white blankets for her babies as our mothers have, but she probably made them beds of straw or hay and covered them with the skins of animals for blankets.

Feeding their children and keeping them warm was not the most important thing for Adam and Eve. Do you know what was much more important? They wanted to teach their boys about God. Adam and Eve must have often sat down with their boys, just as our daddy and mother sit down with us, and they must have told them stories about the beautiful Garden of Eden and about the snake and the devil and about their terrible fall into sin. The best story was the one of God's great promise to send them a Savior, Jesus, Who would take God's anger away by dying for them and making a bright pathway into heaven for them. That was a happy story.

Then Adam and Eve would teach the boys how to make an altar, probably of stones piled on top of one another, and how to bring a gift — a present — to God. It had to be the right kind of gift: a lamb that was killed, and whose blood ran down the stones of the altar; for that lamb was a picture of God's Lamb, Jesus. They taught their boys to bring **themselves** as offerings to God when they prayed on their knees at the altar and promised to love and obey God.

As Abel grew up, he listened to his parents and took a lamb from his flock of sheep, and with faith and love in his heart came to God with a picture of Jesus and Jesus' blood.

Now watch Cain take an offering to God. He was a farmer, and he took some of the crops that grew in his fields as a gift on his altar. Do you know what Cain was saying to God when he did that? He was saying that he did not need a

41

lamb, a picture of Jesus. He did not need Jesus to save him. He would bring something that he grew all by himself. Cain did not come to God in faith and love, and he did not want to be saved by Jesus' blood.

God liked Abel's sacrifice, but He hated Cain's. How did they know? God probably told them by a voice. Cain should have been very sorry for his sin. Instead, he became angry. He was angry with God! He knew he could not touch the holy God, but he could hurt Abel, who loved God. One day, when they were in the field together, Cain killed Abel. We do not know how. There lay Abel, cold and still and dead.

But Cain was not sorry. When God asked him, "Where is Abel thy brother?" he said, "I know not: Am I my brother's keeper?"

The Lord saw Cain's sin and his lie, and gave him a punishment: God **cursed** the ground so that it would not grow food for Cain; and he would have to wander from place to place on the earth. Cain was so wicked that he talked back to God, and said, "My punishment is greater than I can bear." He said it would never work, anyway, because everyone would try to kill him because of his sin. So God put a mark on Cain — we do not know what kind of mark it was — so that no one would kill him. And Cain wandered over the earth the rest of his life.

Do you know who won the victory? Abel did. He was the first man who went to heaven to be with the Lord. He is in heaven now.

REMEMBER:

Adam and Eve taught Cain and Abel all about God just the way our daddies and mothers teach us. We do not have to bring gifts of lambs on altars anymore. We bring gifts of faith and love in our **hearts** when we worship our God in church.

Enoch Walks With God

After Cain killed Abel, he moved with his wife to the land of Nod, away from the other people on the earth, and built himself a city. Now Adam and Eve lost both their sons. Abel was in heaven, and Cain lived far away — a wicked murderer.

God remembered Adam and Eve and gave them another son in Abel's place. They named that son Seth. When they taught Seth about God's love and God's promise, God put faith in his heart, and he believed; and Seth loved and served God, just as Abel had. We call him "God-fearing." After Seth grew up, he married a wife, and the Lord gave them children and grandchildren and great-grandchildren who feared the Lord, too. Finally, a special boy was born. He was the sixth grandson from Adam, and his name was Enoch. Do you know what was so wonderful about this? Adam was still living when Enoch was born. God let people live very long lives in those days, and Adam lived almost a thousand years. Nowadays hardly anyone lives to be even a hundred years old. Adam was old by the time Enoch was born, but he could still take him on his lap and tell Enoch all about God and His wonderful creation and teach him how to serve the Lord.

Do you know what was wonderful about Enoch when he grew up? He became a preacher. He called God's people together to worship Him and to pray to Him and to offer sacrifices on altars. Not very many people came to listen to Enoch, because there were not very many people on the earth who loved God and wanted to come to church to serve Him. Oh, there were a lot of people on the earth by this time — thousands and thousands of them — but they were all wicked. They hated God and God's people. Enoch preached to the wicked people, too.

Shall we take a look at those wicked people on the earth? They were born from the children of Cain and they hated God and loved the devil, just as Cain did. God let these men live very long lives, too, almost a thousand years. He gave them strong bodies and good minds, and these people from the family of Cain used their bodies and minds well. They worked hard! They wanted to be great men in the earth! They thought of all the great things they could make. They became very rich men, but they didn't give any of their money to God or His church; they learned how to make beautiful instruments to play all kinds of music, but they did not play songs of praise to God; and they made tools to use on their farms and to use in fighting, but they did not use them to God's glory. These wicked people from Cain's family used them all to sin. They wanted only to have a good time and to please themselves and the devil. They did not have time to serve God.

And Enoch said to them, "Repent! Be sorry for your sins! Bow on your knees and pray! Offer a lamb, a picture of Jesus, to God! And if you don't, God will come with His angels to punish you!"

Do you think those wicked people listened to Enoch? Oh, no! They told him to stop preaching and to go away. Their hearts were hard and they would not listen.

Do you think that Enoch stopped preaching then? Oh, no! He kept warning them that God would be angry with them. He kept telling them that everything they did was very wicked and that their words of cursing against God were terrible sins and that they must turn their lives around and love and serve the Lord.

The more Enoch preached, the more angry the wicked people became. They poked fun of Enoch because they hated the God he preached about. Finally, they even tried to kill him. But they could not find him. Do you know why? God took Enoch right to heaven, safe from all his enemies. He did not even have to die first. Enoch lived only three hundred sixty-five years on this earth, but he will live forever in heaven. When he was preaching on the earth, he was walking with God. He is walking with God in heaven now.

REMEMBER:

We do not want to be rich and great in **this** world when we grow up, for this world is not really our home. We want to be loving children of God who are looking for our home in heaven.

Noah Builds the Ark

Do you know that it is easier for us to be naughty and to do wrong things than it is for us to be good and do the things God tells us we must do? Do you know why? Because our hearts are so very wicked. The hearts of the people in Enoch's time were very black with sin and wickedness. Let me tell you about it.

After God took Enoch to heaven, the people of Cain's family were not sorry for their sins, but kept on doing more and more wickedness. They stole other people's property, they killed people they did not like, and they tried to do all the evil they could to God's people. Many of God's people died and there were not very many of them left on the earth. No one could feel very safe in those days. And it **looked** as if the people from Cain's family were getting stronger and greater. It **seemed** as if they could think up more and more wicked things to do, and that God was just letting them go. But He wasn't. When their wickedness filled the whole earth, He said: "That's enough."

Right in the middle of this sad story of their wickedness the Bible tells us about Noah, one of the great-grandchildren of Enoch. Noah was looking for something. He looked hard for it. Do you know where he looked? Into the eyes of the Lord. Now, we know that we cannot really see into the Lord's eyes, for He is in heaven. But we, too, with Noah can look into His eyes by listening to His Word, and by praying and singing to Him. And when Noah looked into the eyes of the Lord, he found what he was looking for. He found **grace** — that means he found God's love and His mercy. It means that he found God to be His friend.

Noah was God's friend, and God told Noah His secrets. These were some of the secrets God told Noah: that in one hundred twenty years He would send a

flood to destroy the whole world and everyone in the world except Noah and his family. He would save Noah and his family in a large boat, called an ark.

Then Noah had to **work** on God's secret, for God told him to get busy and build that big ark. The ark was a very long boat, about as long as seven houses in a row, and it was three stories high, with only one door in it, and with windows around the top story. God told Noah that after he finished building the ark, he must fill it with food — food for animals, too — for a long, long stay in the ark.

Noah did not have to keep God's secret to himself, for God wanted Noah to tell all the people on the earth that in one hundred twenty years He would send a flood over the whole earth, and they all would drown. While Noah was building the ark, he preached, too. He preached the same kinds of sermons that Enoch did with words like these: "Repent! Be sorry for your sins! Turn to God and serve Him! If you don't, God will send a flood to destroy you!"

Do you know what the wicked people did? They laughed. And they made fun of Noah. We call that **mocking.** God had never yet made it rain on the earth, because He had watered the ground with a mist — something like fog. So the people laughed, and said it had never rained before and it never would rain. They made fun of the huge boat that stood on dry ground, far away from any water. They did not believe Noah, and they did not believe God.

Seven days before the flood came, God told Noah and his wife and his three sons and their wives to go into the ark. There was still no rain. There they sat, in a big boat in the middle of the dry land, with all the wicked people mocking them. It seemed so foolish for Noah to build the ark on dry land and then to sit in it. But Noah **believed** God; and he waited for God to send the rain.

REMEMBER:

When Noah looked into the eyes of the Lord, the Lord told him His secrets. When we look into the eyes of the Lord He tells us His secrets, too. What secrets does He tell us? He says, "I love you, even though you are so sinful, for you are my child, and I have sent Jesus to take away your sins and bring you to heaven after you have finished living on the earth."

God Sends the Flood

When Noah and his family sat in that very big ark in the middle of dry land, and when all the wicked people mocked and poked fun of them, it seemed as if they were sitting there **all alone** against the whole wicked world. But they weren't alone at all. God was right there, taking care of them. And He would take care of them with a great wonder. Our story is about that wonder.

Before God sent the rain, He sent animals to the ark. Noah did not have to run out into the fields and woods and hunt for them and call to them. Oh, no! God just sent them two by two, the father and the mother animals, from the smallest chipmunks to the biggest elephants. Even the fierce, wild animals like the lions and tigers walked quietly two by two into the ark. They did not eat the smaller animals and they did not try to get away. That was a great wonder. The wicked people saw how the animals obeyed God, and they could see that it was a great wonder, but they would not turn their wicked hearts from their sins and be sorry before God.

After all the animals were in the ark, God shut the door of the ark, and then God stayed right there at the door of the ark to keep Noah and his family safe. For Noah was not going on a nice boat trip. He was going through a terrible flood that would shake the whole earth.

Then God made it rain for the first time. Do you think the wicked people were afraid when they saw that Noah's words about the rain came true? I think so. They became more and more afraid, for God made the rain fall for forty days and forty nights without stopping. God's rain was not like the rain we get now, when it falls lightly, or even when it bursts down in our very worst storms. It was much worse! God broke the earth open and sent up fountains of water out of it, and made the windows in heaven, on top of the clouds, open up and pour water down on the earth. And God destroyed that whole old world and made another world, a new world. Everything and everybody in the whole first world died, except Noah and his family.

Shall we look into the ark and see Noah and his family? They were not afraid but trusted God to carry them safely over the big waves of the flood; for Noah and his family were God's children, His church, and they worshipped Him in the ark.

For one hundred fifty days the ark floated on the waters, and then God made it rest on the top of a mountain. But they could not get out right away, for

the whole earth was still covered with water. God made them patient and happy to wait in the ark.

While they waited, God made a wind blow to dry up the waters. After the wind blew for forty days, Noah wondered whether it was almost time to leave the ark. So he sent out a raven from the window of the ark, and then waited to see if it came back. The raven was a strong black bird and could eat the dead bodies of the drowned animals. The raven did not come back. It could live on the earth now.

After seven days, Noah sent out a weaker bird, a dove, who needed trees with leaves on them in order to live, and then he waited to see if the dove would come back. It did, and Noah put his hand out of the window and took the dove back into the ark. The dove could not find leafy trees to live in yet.

After another seven days, Noah sent the dove out again, and waited to see if it would come back. Sure enough, it did! But what was in its mouth? An olive leaf. Now Noah knew that some of the trees had leaves.

After still another seven days, Noah once more sent out the dove, and this time it did not come back. Noah knew that now there were trees with leaves and

that there was dry land so that the dove could live on the earth again. Noah and his family had to stay in the ark two months longer, and then God told him it was time to leave.

He took off the covering from the ark and saw the dry land instead of water all around them — the first time in a whole year. How happy Noah and his family and all the animals must have been to run on dry land again! Noah was so happy and thankful that the first thing he did was build an altar to God and he offered sacrifices of animals to Him. As the blood of the animal ran down the altar, Noah was making a picture of the blood of Jesus, Who saved him and his family.

God liked Noah's sacrifices and promised that He would never again destroy the whole world with a flood; and He gave Noah a sign in the clouds, the sign of the beautiful rainbow. It was a sign to Noah that God would keep His promise. When we see a rainbow in the clouds, it is a sign to us, too, that He will never again destroy the world with a flood, and that He will always send the seasons of the year: spring and summer and fall and winter. Will you think of Noah the next time you see a rainbow?

REMEMBER:

When Noah was in the ark, God guarded Noah's door and kept him safe. God guards our doors, too, the doors of our homes and of our bedrooms when we sleep. We are always safe with Him.

The Tower of Babel

Only eight people, just Noah and his family, lived on the new earth after the flood. Where were all the wicked people who had mocked Noah? Where was all their money and where were their treasures? Where were the beautiful musical instruments they had made? They were all gone, destroyed by the flood. But **wickedness** was not gone from the earth. It never is. Our story will tell about great wickedness after the flood.

Noah and his family went to work after the flood. Noah planted rows and rows of grapes. We call it a vineyard. When the grapes were ripe, he crushed them and made wine. Then he drank the wine — too much of it — and it made him drunk. That was very wrong of Noah for, though he was one of God's dear children, he sinned, just as you and I do.

Noah's son Ham laughed at his father when he was drunk and lying naked in his tent. Ham was glad that his God-fearing father had sinned because Ham did not love God. He loved sin, and mocked his father. That was a shame, wasn't it?

But Noah's other boys, Shem and Japheth, who loved the Lord, were sorry that their father sinned, and walked backwards into Noah's tent and covered him with a coat.

When Noah awoke from his drunkenness, he knew what had happened, and he cursed Ham and the children who would come from Ham. That means they would be wicked and have no blessing from God. Then Noah talked about Shem. He would be a special boy, and his children would be a special people, for **Jesus** would be born from Shem's family. Noah had beautiful words for Japheth, too. He told that Japheth and his children would share Shem's blessings, and that Jesus would be **their** Jesus, too. We are children from Japheth's family, and Jesus is **our** Jesus. Noah did not say all these words by himself. God talked through Noah.

Shall we take a look at Ham's family, the people who did not love the Lord and would not obey His commands and who had no blessings from God? God had told all of Noah's sons to spread out over the whole earth and to live in all the parts of it. Ham's family said, "No." They disobeyed God. This is how they did it: they listened to Nimrod. Nimrod, the grandson of Ham, was a strong, brave man, who hunted the wild animals that were running over the earth and scaring and killing the people. The people of Ham's family liked Nimrod for that.

Nimrod had a plan. He led them all to a nice, flat place, where they could stay together and build a strong city and be safe. In this city they would build

a great tower which would reach to the sky. They said they would be a great, strong people, who would live without God. They wanted to put their trust in a tower instead of in God; and they did not want God's people to trust in Him either.

Then God stepped in and stopped them. Until this time, everyone spoke the same language and everyone could understand everyone else. Suddenly, God made different languages, so that they could not understand one another, and they did not think the same way, and they began to quarrel and fight, and they could not work together anymore. They could not stay together anymore either, and their tower was never finished. God **made** them obey His command to scatter over the earth. That was the day God made the different kinds of people, the blacks, the whites, the Chinese, the Indians.

The tower was called the Tower of Babel, and it means a **noise**, a **mix-up**. God made the mix-up, and He won the victory over the wicked. He always does.

REMEMBER:

People who do not love God like **this** world very much, and would like to stay here always. God's children do not. They want to go to their beautiful home in heaven.

The Story of Job (1)

Far away to the East in the land of Uz lived a great and rich man who probably came from the family of the God-fearing Shem. This rich man's name was Job, and he loved the Lord with all his heart. Job showed the love of God in the way he lived: he helped the poor people and the blind; and he was kind to those who had no fathers and mothers. He showed his friends how to serve God with all their hearts.

God blessed Job with ten children, seven boys and three girls; and He gave Job thousands and thousands of animals: sheep, camels, oxen (something like cows) and donkeys. Job was the greatest man in the land of the East. He taught his children to fear and love the Lord, too. And when they had a little party together, Job offered a sacrifice of a lamb on an altar for them, a picture of the sacrifice of Jesus on the cross; and Job prayed God that He would forgive his children for Jesus' sake if they sinned at their party.

Many people came to Job when they had trouble and Job helped them. They could trust him because he lived close to God. Would you have liked Job? I think you would have liked him very much.

Now we will leave Job for a moment and see what was happening in heaven. Oh, we cannot **really** see into heaven, for our eyes are so very sinful; but the Bible tells us about it and gives us a little peek into heaven. Aren't you glad?

The angels were standing in heaven before the Holy God when Satan, the wicked devil, came to stand before God too. Do you remember that Satan was once a good angel, before he sinned and wanted to be like God? Now Satan's home was in hell but he could still stand before God in heaven.

God asked Satan where he had come from and Satan answered, "From walking up and down in the earth."

Then God asked Satan whether he had noticed Job, a man who tried hard to do the right and who hated evil, because he loved God so much.

Satan had a wicked answer. He said, "Doth Job fear God for nought?" Satan meant that it was **easy** for Job to serve God because God had blessed him and made him rich. "But," Satan said, "put forth thine hand now, and touch all that he hath, and he will curse thee to thy face."

That was a terrible thing for Satan to say. He said that Job served God only because God gave him such nice things. Now Satan wanted God to let him take it all away. Do you think God let Satan do that? Yes, He did.

We will go back to Job's house now, and see how Satan took everything away from Job. Watch as one of the servants shouted to Job that some wicked men killed all the donkeys and the oxen and the servants who took care of them and that he was the only one who got away.

While he was talking, another servant came, and said that fire from heaven burned all the sheep and the servants and that he was the only one who got away.

While he was talking, another servant came and said that wicked men took all the camels and killed the servants and that he was the only one who got away.

While he was talking, another servant came and said that all Job's children were eating at their oldest brother's house when a great wind struck the house and it fell on them and they all died and that **he** was the only one who got away.

Poor Job! He tore his coat and shaved his head to show how sad he felt, and then he fell down on the ground and **worshipped** his God. He said beautiful words, too: "The **Lord** gave, and the **Lord** hath taken away; blessed be the name of the Lord."

REMEMBER:

Everything comes from God, even sadness and trouble. Job did not know why God sent sadness and trouble to him. But he knew that God loved him. We know that, too.

The Story of Job (2)

We will be glad that this part of the story of Job starts with another little peek into heaven; and when the Bible lets us take another peek, we will know that Job's loving Father is still watching over him, even though He let Satan take everything away. Job's loving Father is God.

On this day, God's angels were standing before God's holiness again, and Satan came, too. Again God asked Satan where he had come from and Satan answered the same way: "From walking up and down in the earth."

Right away the Lord talked about Job and said something like this to Satan: "Have you watched Job? Have you seen how he worships Me with a perfect heart even though you asked Me to let you take everything away from him? And Job didn't do anything bad to deserve it!"

But Satan had his wicked answer ready for the Lord. He told the Lord that Job was still strong and healthy. "But touch his bones and his flesh," said Satan, "and he will curse Thee to Thy face." Satan wanted the Lord to let him make Job very sick. Do you think the Lord let Satan do that terrible thing? Yes, He did; only Satan might not kill Job.

Let us go to find Job now. Oh, there he is, sitting in the dirty ashes outside the city. We can hardly see that it is Job, for he is full of sores all over his body

and they have made his face and his body all swollen. They itched so badly that he has had to take a piece of a broken flower pot and scratch his awful sores with it. Those sores smelled so terrible that he had to live away from other people, outside the city. Those sores hurt so much that they gave Job high fevers and bad dreams. Poor Job had a dreadful sickness. It could have been the worst kind of leprosy.

Job's wife did not help him at all. When she saw that he had the worst kind of sickness, she said, "Curse God, and die." That was a wicked thing to say, but Job gave her a beautiful answer: "What? Shall we receive good at the hand of God, and shall we not receive evil?" He was scolding his wife by saying these words and he was thanking God for his sickness, even though he did not know why God was sending it.

Then three of Job's friends came to visit him. Job's sickness was so awful they did not even know him and they were so surprised that they did not say one word for seven days.

Then they talked but their talking didn't make Job feel any better. Do you know what they said? Something like this: "You must have done something very, very bad, and now God is punishing you for what you did." Do you believe what those three friends said? Job didn't believe them, either.

Job said words like these: "How can I find words to answer **God**? I don't know why God sent all this trouble to me, but I know He is my good and loving Father."

Oh, Job complained sometimes, and cried. Wouldn't you? He even said that God didn't care what happened to him, and he wished that he would die. But then he quickly said that if he **did** die, Jesus would save him and take him to heaven.

Poor Job! He did not want to wait for God to make him better. He begged God to answer him and take away his troubles. Suddenly God came to him in a big whirlwind and talked to him. Do you know what God talked about? How great He is! He asked Job ever so many questions, questions like this: (See if you can answer them, too.)

Where were you when I made the earth?

Who stopped the waters of the lakes and the oceans on the shores, just as if they had doors?

Did you make the snow and the hail?

Who makes the path for the lightning and thunder?

Who is the Father of the rain?

Who can count all the clouds in the sky?

Did you make the horse strong?

Do you tell the eagles where to fly and where to build their nests?

After God was finished with His questions, Job saw how great and wonderful his God is and Job felt so small, so very, very tiny. Do you feel tiny now, too? Job said he would put his hand over his mouth because God is so great. Now Job would not grumble and complain to God, for God knew what was best for him all the time. Job prayed that he was very sorry.

God heard him and made him all better and gave him back twice as much as he had before: twice as many camels, oxen, donkeys, and sheep; and ten more children, seven boys and three girls, the most beautiful girls in all the land. After that Job lived one hundred forty more years.

REMEMBER:

Job did not know what was good for him. God did. We do not know what is good for us, either. God does. He is our dear Father, and sends everything to us because He loves us.

God Calls Abram

Did you ever have to move away from your house and go to live in a new one? We do not always like to move away from the house and yard we like so well and from the friends we play with and go to a house and yard that is new and strange and find new friends, do we? But what if we had to move far, far away, without our daddy and mother, leave everything at home, and not even know where we were going? That is what Abram had to do.

Abram lived with his wife, his father and mother, and all the rest of his family in the land of Ur. They came from the family of Shem, who loved the Lord. Abram and his family loved the Lord, too, and worshipped Him and built altars to sacrifice lambs to Him. They were happy in the land of Ur and God had blessed them with good homes, many animals, and much money. Abram was a rich man.

Then God came to Abram and asked him to leave his family and friends and go to a land that God would show him. Abram did not even know where it was! Do you think that Abram was unhappy about that? Do you think he talked back to God? He could have. He **could** have said to God, "I am happy here. Everyone I love lives here. I do not want to leave them. And how can I get my hundreds and hundreds of animals to another country? Besides, I am an old man, seventy-five years old, as old as a grandfather, too old to move now."

But Abram did not say any of those things. He said, "All right, Lord." And God promised Abram, "I will bless thee, and in thee shall all the families of the earth be blessed." That meant that Abram's people would be God's people.

Abram obeyed God and took Sarai his wife and his servants and his animals with him. His nephew, Lot, wanted to go along, too, and together they traveled where God told them to go. They **believed** God's words. We call it **faith.** It was not easy for Abram and his family to travel, for they had no cars in those days, and they had to walk or ride on the backs of their animals. They piled every-thing they needed, their clothes, blankets, food, and dishes on the backs of animals, too. All the animals, even the babies, had to walk. At night they put up their tents so they could sleep.

When they came to a river it was not very easy to cross that river. They had to find a shallow place so that their animals could cross without drowning. Some of the baby animals could not walk across, and the servants had to carry them in their arms.

At last they were in the land that God had promised them. Do you think it was all empty, waiting for Abram? Oh, no! It was filled with wicked people, people who served idols and hated God. Don't you think that Abram felt like a poor, helpless sheep in the middle of wolves?

60

This is what Abram did: he and his family set up their tents and Abram built an altar and offered a lamb on it, a picture of Jesus, Who would take their sins away. He let all the wicked people see that his God was the **Lord**. Abram moved up and down the land, showing the people that **he** worshipped God.

This whole land belonged to Abram, and God promised to give it to Abram's children and his grandchildren. But Abram had no children and his wife, Sarai, was as old as a grandmother already. Could she still get a baby? Abram believed God's word. He had **faith**.

The name of this land was Canaan and it was a picture of heaven. Though it all belonged to Abram, he never built a house there. He always lived in tents and moved from place to place in the land. Why did he live in tents? Because he was making a picture by living in tents. This land was only a **picture** of heaven. He was not going to live in this land always and a tent was good enough to live in. His tent was a picture that told all the wicked people, "I am not staying in Canaan forever. I am looking for a better land, for a heavenly land where God is."

REMEMBER:

We live in houses now, not in tents. But our lives make pictures, too. We say, "We are not going to live here always. We are going to heaven, too."

Lot Leaves Abram

This story is about trouble, about a quarrel between the servants of Abram and the servants of his nephew, Lot. How do you think the trouble started? How does trouble start between you and your friends? You both probably want the same things and you won't take turns because both of you are being stubborn, thinking only of yourselves. That was the way the trouble with the servants of Abram and Lot started, too.

After they had lived in the land of Canaan for a while, Abram and Lot became even richer than they were before. The mother sheep had baby lambs, the mother cows had baby calves, the mother goats had baby kids, and then there were twice as many animals as there were before. God blessed Abram and Lot with all these good things because they were pictures of God's blessings of salvation in their hearts. They thanked God for all His goodness and they were happy.

But Abram and Lot did not stay happy. They had to settle a quarrel. Now they had too many animals, and there was not enough grass and water for all of them. The servants who took care of the animals had trouble. Lot's servants wanted more land and better land for **their** animals, and Abram's servants wanted more land and better land for **their** animals. They did not speak kindly to one another. They used hard words. And soon they probably had their fists in each other's faces.

Abram and Lot heard about it and Abram went to Lot and said, "Let there be no strife between me and thee and between my herdmen and thy herdmen; for we be brethren." Brethren are brothers. Abram and Lot were brothers **in the Lord.**

Abram had an idea. He told Lot the land of Canaan was big enough for both of them and he asked Lot to look it over and take what he wanted. If Lot went to the right, Abram would go to the left; and if Lot went to the left, Abram would go to the right. Lot looked at the land down by the Jordan River. It was rich and green, the best land in the whole country. Lot chose the best for himself. Be careful, Lot! Near that good land are two very wicked cities, called Sodom and Gomorrah.

What do you think about Lot? Should he have chosen those rich, green pastures near those two wicked cities? Lot should have stopped to think first. He should have remembered that God gave all the land of Canaan to **Abram**. But Abram had not grabbed it all and he did not build a big palace on it and rule over everyone. No, he lived like a stranger, in a tent. Lot should have remembered that Abram was older than he was, and should have let Abram choose first. But Lot chose that land with his **eyes**, not with his **heart**. He wanted the best he could get in **this** world. He was greedy. Lot should have remembered that when he walked away from Abram he was leaving God's altars and God's worship. Lot was running away from God's church, because Abram and his family were God's church. And what did Lot choose instead? The wicked city of Sodom, a picture of hell.

Poor Lot! He **thought** he was getting the best, but he was getting the worst. Lot was still one of God's own children, but he served God with a poor, weak heart. He did not love God enough to do what was right.

Do you think Abram was sad to see Lot and his family leave? I think so. But God came to talk with him and made him feel better. He asked Abram to look in all directions — to the north, to the south, to the east, and to the west. God promised to give all that land, as **far** as he could see, to Abram's children; and God promised to make his children and grandchildren as many as the specks of dust on the earth. Could we count all the specks of dust on the earth? No, we couldn't. That is as many children as would be in Abram's family. But Abram was growing older and he had **no** children, not even one.

REMEMBER:

Lot cared more for green pastures for his animals than for God's altars and God's church. We must never be like Lot. God and His church must always come **first** for us.

Ishmael is Born

Many years went by. Abram and Sarai kept on living in the land of Canaan, which God had given to Abram. They kept on waiting for the baby God had promised. But they **still** had no baby. Then God came to Abram and said, "I am thy shield, and thy exceeding great reward." That meant, "I will take care of you and I will bless you. I am your Friend and your Savior. Jesus will come! He will be born from your family."

Abram asked God, "What wilt Thou give me?" He had a very good **servant**, but no **son**. How could Jesus be born from his family?

God promised once more: "You will have your own son," and He took Abram to see all the stars in the sky at night, and promised him as many children as the stars.

Abram believed God. But, when God did not hurry and give Abram and Sarai a baby boy, it was hard for them to wait. It is hard for us to wait, too, when we know that something is going to happen, isn't it? Sarai, especially, was impatient. She believed God and yet she was worried. She was too old to have a baby! But, wait, she had an idea! Maybe she and Abram could help God along. Do you think God needs any help? No, not our great God. But Sarai was still thinking and she decided to do things her own way. She would take her maid Hagar and ask Abram to marry her. Probably God would give Abram and Hagar a baby, the baby they were waiting for. Sarai was not trusting God very much. Her faith was not very strong right now.

Would Abram do it? Would he marry Hagar? Yes, he would. He was ready to help God along, too. Right now, his faith was not very strong, either. He married Hagar. Now he had two wives, and God had said that a man must have only one wife. When Hagar knew that she was going to have a baby, she was proud. She looked down on Sarai and would not obey her anymore. She thought she was better than Sarai.

Poor Sarai went to Abram with her trouble and asked what she should do about Hagar. Abram told her to do as she pleased. Sarai was stern to Hagar and spoke hard words to her, such hard words that Hagar ran away. She ran away to the desert, a hot, dry, sandy part of the land; and she sat down by a well of water in the desert. There the angel of the Lord found her. Do you know what he called her? "Hagar, Sarai's maid!" That was a scolding. For Hagar, Sarai's maid, had run away. The angel told her to go back to Sarai and obey her. The angel had a promise for Hagar, too. She would have a baby boy, and from that boy would come a great nation of people, but **not** the special people God had promised to Abram. The angel named Hagar's baby **Ishmael.** Hagar listened to God's angel and went back to Sarai. Before she left the well, she said, "Thou God seest me." She could run away from Sarai, but she could not run away from God.

After Hagar came back to Sarai, God gave her a baby boy and she called him Ishmael, as the angel had said. But Ishmael was **Hagar's** boy, not **Sarai's** boy. Ishmael was not the promised boy, for God had promised that **Sarai** would have a baby. Ishmael grew up to be thirteen years old, and Abram and Sarai had no baby. They were still waiting.

Once again God came to Abram with beautiful words. God promised to make His **covenant** with Abram. That means God promised to be Abram's friend and to make him the father of many nations, and to be the God of Abram and his children. God changed his name to **Abraham**, which means "father of many nations," and God changed Sarai's name to **Sarah**, which means "princess," and He promised to make her the mother of many nations.

Do you know how old Abraham was now? Ninety-nine, one year less than one hundred; and Sarah was ninety years old. What do you think Abraham did when God said that they were still going to have a baby? He laughed. And he said, "Shall a child be born to him that is a hundred years old, and to Sarah, who is ninety years old?"

God answered that next year Sarah would have a baby. That would be a great wonder. Abraham believed God.

REMEMBER:

Hagar said, "Thou God seest me." She knew that she could never run away from God. We know that, too. God watches us, and takes care of us, and keeps us safe. He sees when we are naughty and sneaky, and He sees and hears us when we are sorry and pray to Him to forgive us.

67

Three Angels Come to Abraham

The land of Canaan was hot. In the early part of the afternoon, when the sun shone very hot, no one could work. People rested in their tents. As Abraham was sitting in the doorway of his tent, he saw three men coming. Abraham ran to meet them and bowed to them and begged them to do him a favor — to stop to rest and eat at his house. Abraham was so eager to serve them!

The three visitors stopped at Abraham's tent, and he hurried to take care of them. He brought water to wash their hot, dusty feet — for people wore sandals in that hot country — and then he ran to ask Sarah to make some little loaves of bread. Next he found a young calf and told his servant to cook some of its meat. After the bread and meat were done, he brought them butter and milk, and the meal was ready.

Abraham did not sit down to eat with his visitors. He stood under a tree, to talk with them and to serve them if they needed help. He was so glad he had company! As he looked at his visitors, he started to think that they were not just ordinary men. They were special visitors. Were they, maybe. . . even **angels?** Yes, they were. God made them look like men. That is a wonder. But one visitor was not an angel. He was the Son of God, the One Who would come into the world as the baby Jesus. But today He looked like a man. Abraham was serving dinner to the **Lord!**

Around Abraham's tent were other tents: Sarah's tent and Hagar's tent and the servants' tents. Abraham's visitors looked around and said, "Where is Sarah thy wife?"

Abraham answered, "In the tent." Abraham was not surprised that they knew Sarah's name. Wasn't one of the visitors the Son of God, Who knows everything?

Then his visitor, the Son of God, told him some wonderful news: in a very short time Sarah would have a baby boy.

Do you think Sarah heard the news? Shall we see if we can find her? Oh, there she is, hiding quietly behind her tent door, listening to everything the visitors said — just as we like to peek and listen when our parents have company. Sarah had heard the news that the Lord told Abraham, and she laughed. She could not believe **that!** She was too old! Older than most grandmothers! And yet — what if — what if the Lord would make a wonder happen?

The Lord knew that Sarah laughed. He did not have to turn around to

see her. He knows every-
thing, and He asked, "Wherefore did Sarah laugh? Is anything too hard for the
Lord?"

Then Sarah was scared
and she told a lie, "I laughed
not;" and the Lord had to
scold her and say, "Nay; but
thou didst laugh."

Abraham's visitors
stood up then, and the two
angels walked on toward the
wicked cities of Sodom and
Gomorrah, where Lot lived. The Lord stayed behind to talk with Abraham, for he had more news. This news was not very happy. The Lord would not hide from Abraham, His friend, what He was going to do. He was going to destroy those wicked cities.

Suddenly Abraham was very worried. Lot lived there, and Lot was righteous. That means he feared God, that he was one of God's children. What

69

would happen to Lot? So Abraham asked the Lord, "Wilt Thou destroy the righteous with the wicked? If there are fifty righteous in the city, wilt Thou not spare the place?" **Spare** it means to **save** it.

The Lord answered, "If I find in Sodom fifty righteous, then I will spare all the place for their sakes." But there were not fifty.

Abraham asked another question, "If there are forty-five, wilt Thou destroy the city?"

The Lord answered, "If I find forty-five, I will not destroy it." But there were not forty-five righteous people.

Again Abraham talked. "If there are forty?"

The Lord answered, "I will not do it for forty's sake." But there were not forty righteous people in the city.

Then Abraham wondered whether he were begging the Lord too much. So he said, "Let not the Lord be angry. If there are thirty?"

The Lord answered, "I will not do it, if I find thirty there." But there were not thirty.

Once more Abraham asked, "If there are twenty?"

The Lord answered, "I will not destroy it for twenty's sake." But there were not twenty.

Abraham asked just once more. "If there are ten?"

And the Lord answered for the last time, "I will not destroy it for ten's sake."

There were not even ten righteous people in those two big, wicked cities. Yet the Lord had promised that He would not destroy the righteous with the wicked — not even **one** righteous man. What would happen to righteous Lot now?

Then the Lord went away and a sad Abraham went back home. Do you know why he was sad? Because righteous Lot was living in such a wicked city and Abraham did not know what would happen to him.

REMEMBER:

The Lord asked Abraham, "Is anything too hard for the Lord?" Abraham and Sarah knew that the answer was, "No." We know that answer, too. God made everything, He made us, and He will always love us and do what is best for us. Aren't we glad He is our Lord?

God Destroys
Sodom and Gomorrah

When Lot had left Abraham for the lovely green pastures near Sodom and Gomorrah, he was not interested in those wicked cities. He would live in tents on the rich green grass. Shall we watch Lot to see what happened? He had moved nearer and nearer and nearer to those cities. Soon he was living right outside the city of Sodom. Look! Where is he now? Right **inside** the city, living in a house. He is a rich man now, and a house is much nicer to live in than a tent. Lot's children are growing up in wicked Sodom.

That is where the two angels who visited Abraham found Lot — **in** the city of Sodom, sitting at the gate, helping to rule the city. He was quite an important man in Sodom already. It was evening when these two strangers came and Lot begged them to come to his house. He, too, just like Abraham, was eager to serve them. Besides, Lot did not want the two visitors to go to the homes of any of the wicked people of Sodom.

At first the visitors said no to Lot, but he kept asking them, and then they came in. Lot had his servants make a big dinner party for them. Remember, Lot was a very rich man.

Then it became dark. Darkness is the time wicked people do their wickedness. The darkness of Sodom was **full** of wickedness. Soon wicked men stood all around Lot's house, shouting for Lot to send his visitors out to them. They wanted to treat the two men badly and hurt them.

What an awful thing to do! Lot could not let that happen! So he went outside the door to talk with his wicked neighbors from Sodom. He told them not to be so wicked. But the men became very angry with Lot and they rushed at him and pushed so hard the door almost broke down. Don't you think Lot must have been scared?

Just then the two visitors reached out their hands and pulled Lot safely into the house. And a wonder happened. The Lord made those wicked men blind and mixed up in their minds so that they tried and tried, but they could not find the door of Lot's house. The Lord would not let them get in.

By this time Lot knew who his visitors were. They were **heavenly** visitors, angels to help him. Quickly they told Lot and his family that God would destroy the cities of Sodom and Gomorrah.

The angels told Lot to tell his daughters who had married husbands from the wicked city of Sodom to hurry and run out of the city to save their lives. But Lot's daughters and the men they married loved Sodom, and they poked fun of the words of the angels. They would not leave. Even Lot would not hurry out of Sodom. While he took his time, the angels had to take his hand and the hand of his wife and the hands of his two youngest daughters and lead them out of the city; for the Lord loved Lot and was kind and merciful to him.

When they were outside the city of Sodom, the angels told them to run for their lives, to run to the mountains! But Lot complained that it was too far to run. Might they go to the little city of Zoar?

The angels said it was all right. But they must hurry and not turn around to look back at those wicked cities.

By this time the night was over and the sun was coming up; and the Lord, in His anger against those cities, made a rain of fire and brimstone — a kind of salt — on the cities.

Lot's wife was sad. In her heart she loved Sodom, and she **had** to see what was happening to everything she loved. She disobeyed the angels and turned around, and God showered her with the fiery salt, so that she died and became a pillar of salt.

Poor Lot! Almost everything he loved was gone: his pastures, his animals, his riches, his married children, and his wife. And it was all because he liked the good things of **this** world too much.

Now all he had left were his two girls. He had God, too. God saved Lot. He always saves His people.

REMEMBER:

Lot had many treasures. Treasures are riches. Treasures are things we like the best. Sometimes Lot forgot his best treasures, his treasures in heaven. Do **we** have **our** treasures in heaven, where Jesus is?

Isaac is Born

It was almost time now! God had promised and promised that special baby boy, and Abraham and Sarah had waited and waited for His promise to come true. Sometimes they could hardly wait, but God was not in a hurry. He would give them a baby at the **right** time. Now it was time for God to make His promise come true.

Abraham was one hundred years old now and Sarah was ninety years old, but they remembered God's words, "Is anything too hard for the Lord?" Sure enough, God made a great wonder and gave them a baby boy, whom they named **Isaac.** Isaac means **laughter.** Once Sarah had laughed because she did not believe the words of the Lord. That laughter was wrong. Now Sarah laughed because her heart was spilling over with praise and thanks to God for her new baby. That laughter was the right kind. Do you like the name **Isaac — laughter?** Abraham and Sarah did.

What happy days they must have had with their special little boy. They must have loved him so much, most of all because God would bless him, and God's people would be born from his family. Isaac was not one bit like his older brother, Ishmael. Ishmael was a strong, healthy boy, who liked to live outside and hunt. Isaac was not strong, but a small, weak boy, who had trouble with his eyes. When he was older, he would become blind.

Abraham and Sarah took such good care of Isaac, and soon he was old enough to take care of himself: to eat by himself, to dress himself; and Abraham made a big party to celebrate. Now Isaac was growing up! But they did not have a good time at their party. Do you know who spoiled the party? Ishmael. He was a much bigger boy, almost grown up, and he mocked Isaac at the party. He poked fun of Isaac and tried to hurt him. Why would Ishmael do that? Wasn't he Isaac's brother?

Ishmael mocked Isaac because he hated him. He pulled up his nose at Isaac because Isaac was God's child, because Isaac was the promised boy, and because Isaac had the love of God deep down in his heart. Ishmael did not love the Lord in his heart. Ishmael liked to do just as he pleased, and he didn't care if he was sinful. In his heart, Ishmael was not one bit like Isaac.

Sarah had her eyes wide open. She saw that Ishmael was poking fun of Isaac and trying to hurt him; and Sarah hurried to Abraham and asked him to send Hagar and Ishmael away and not let them come back. Send them away? Oh, Ishmael did wrong, but was it bad enough to send him away from home forever?

Shall we see what Abraham said about it? He felt sad when Sarah asked to send Hagar and Ishmael away, for he liked Ishmael. Then he did the right thing. He asked God what to do. God told him to listen to Sarah and send Ishmael and his mother away. Ishmael did not love Isaac and he would not love Jesus Who would be born from Isaac's family, for he did not have God's love in his heart; and God did not want him to grow up with Isaac.

Now Abraham had to do a sad thing. Early the next morning he gave Hagar food and water and sent her and Ishmael away to the desert. They walked and walked in the hot, sandy places, stopping to take drinks when they were thirsty, until Ishmael wanted a drink and there was none left in the water bottle. And there was no water for them in the desert.

Now he would die, Hagar thought, because a boy cannot live very long without water. She put him down under the shade of a little bush and turned her face away and cried. She was so sad because she was sure that her son would die.

Then she heard a voice saying, "What aileth thee, Hagar?" It was God's angel again. The angel told her that God had not forgotten her and Ishmael. He had heard Ishmael crying. Then God opened her eyes and she saw a well of water. It was a wonder that God had made for her! Can you think how happy Hagar was to fill her bottle with the nice, cool water, and bring it to her thirsty boy?

Ishmael grew up in the desert and became a strong hunter with a bow and arrow.

REMEMBER:

Isaac's name means laughter. There are two kinds of laughter: the wrong kind and the right kind. When **we** laugh, shall we ask God to make us laugh the **right** way, because we are so happy that He is our Father?

Abraham Obeys God

When Isaac grew up a little more, God came to Abraham and asked him to do a very hard thing — the hardest thing in all his life to do — harder even than waiting for Isaac to be born. This is what God said, "Take now thy son, thine only son, whom thou lovest, and offer him for a burnt offering."

Was Abraham hearing God's words right? God said, "Take your only son" — he had waited one hundred years for him. God said, "your son, whom you love" — he loved Isaac more than anything else in the world. God said, "offer him for a burnt offering" — he would have to take a knife in his own hand and kill his own son with it. Maybe Abraham would tell the Lord he could not do that. Do you know what Abraham did?

He got up early the next morning, made some of his donkeys ready for a trip, and started out with two of his servants and his son Isaac; for God had said he had to offer Isaac on a mountain far away. He did just what God told him to do. It took three days to reach the mountain. Abraham had three whole days to think about the hard thing God had asked him. He must have said to himself, "How can my children be as many as the stars of the sky, if I must kill my only son?" Or, "Maybe the Lord will let me find a lamb to offer on the altar when we get there." Or, "Maybe the Lord will raise Isaac from the dead if I must kill him." Abraham **could** have changed his mind and turned around and gone home, and said, "No, Lord, I can't kill my only son."

But Abraham kept traveling toward the mountain. I don't think he talked very much those three days, do you? How could he tell Isaac what he had to do? God was making Abraham choose between his dearest son Isaac and his great love for God. Would Abraham choose Isaac or God? Whom did he love most? Abraham loved God above everything, and he obeyed God, but he could not understand why he had to do such a hard thing.

When they were near to the mountain, Abraham left his donkey with the two servants and he told them that he and Isaac would go on alone to worship God. Then Isaac noticed something was wrong. He knew how to worship God: build an altar, put wood and fire on it, and offer a lamb. They had the wood and carried some coals of fire, probably in a little pot, but he asked his father, "Where is the lamb?"

Abraham told him that God would take care of it. Abraham trusted God, but don't you think his face became more and more unhappy, and it was hard for him to drag his feet up the mountain?

When they were at the top of the mountain, Abraham built an altar, laid the wood on it, and took his dear son, and tied him on top with ropes. Isaac did not kick and scream and fight. Quietly he obeyed his father Abraham and his Father God. As Abraham raised his knife, the Lord, the Son of God, called to him, "Abraham, Abraham."

Oh, how glad Abraham was to hear that voice! What a relief that he could answer, "Here am I."

The Lord told him not to kill his son for, he said, "Now I know that thou fearest God." God always knew that, for He knows everything. But Abraham had to **show** how much he loved God by doing this hard thing.

In a bush nearby, Abraham saw a ram (a father sheep) caught by his horns; and he offered the ram on the altar instead of his son. The ram was a picture of Jesus, Who was God's Sheep Who would die, just as the father sheep had died. Abraham did not have to kill his son Isaac, for God would offer up His Son Jesus to die on the cross instead, for the sins of all His people.

REMEMBER:

Can you think how much Abraham loved his God? So much that he would kill his own son when God asked him to? How much do **we** love God? Do we think about Him every minute of the day, even when we play, or when we are naughty? No, we don't. Ask God to help us love Him more.

Isaac Gets a Wife

As Isaac grew up to be a man, Abraham and Sarah became older and older. When she was one hundred twenty-seven years old, Sarah died. It is not so sad when God takes His people to heaven, especially when they are old and tired. But Isaac had always stayed close to his mother and he was lonely now. He was almost forty years old already and usually people get married before they are forty years old. But not Isaac. He did not even try to find a nice girl to marry.

Abraham was worried. He remembered God's promise to give him as many children as the stars in the sky. Isaac must get married and have children so God's promise could come true. Abraham called his servant Eliezer, who feared God, to help him find a wife for Isaac. They could not look at any of the girls who lived in the land of Canaan, for those girls were wicked and served idols. Abraham would have to send Eliezer his servant back to the country from which he had come. Quite likely he would find a girl who loved the Lord there.

The servant Eliezer promised Abraham that he would try to find a God-fearing girl and bring her back with him; and he set out with ten camels to carry the things they would need for the trip and the presents for the girl he wanted to find. It was a long trip but at last they came to the city where Abraham's relatives — his cousins and his nephews and his nieces — lived. Outside the city was a well of water, and people from the city had to let down water pitchers in the well to get water for themselves and their animals.

As Eliezer came closer to the well, he knew **he** could not choose a wife for Isaac. **God** would choose, for God was leading him. But how would he know? He would ask God for a sign. So he prayed and asked God for this sign: when the girls come to the well to get water for their sheep, and I say to one of them, "Let down thy pitcher that I may drink," and if she says, "Drink, and I will give thy camels drink also," let that be the girl God chooses for Isaac.

Before Eliezer finished the words of his prayer, a girl with a beautiful face came to the well with her water pitcher. Eliezer ran to meet her. Would this be the girl? Eagerly he asked her for a drink. What would she answer? Listen: "Drink, my lord," and when he finished drinking, she said, "I will draw water for thy camels also."

Eliezer watched her as she gave his camels water. This **must** be the girl! The Lord had shown him already! He took golden bracelets and put them on her arms and a chain of gold for her forehead and then he asked her who she was. Her name was Rebekah, and she was one of the relatives of Abraham. How happy Eliezer must have been. He showed how happy he was by bowing his head and thanking God; and he said some beautiful words, "I being in the way, the **Lord** led me." Then Rebekah invited Eliezer to go home with her, and there Eliezer met Rebekah's father Bethuel and her brother Laban.

What an excitement there must have been at Rebekah's house! Some servants were taking care of the camels. Others were getting the dinner ready. Laban, Rebekah's brother, did most of the talking. He told the servant Eliezer to come in and eat, but Eliezer would not eat until he told his story, his story about how God blessed Abraham with a special baby boy, how that special boy grew up and needed a wife, and how Abraham had sent Eliezer to find that wife. Then came the interesting part, when he had asked God for a sign at the well — to have the girl **He chose** say, "I will draw water for your camels, too," and Rebekah had said it.

Rebekah's father and her brother said, "Behold, Rebekah is before thee, take her, and go, and let her be thy master's son's wife." Eliezer was so happy he thanked the Lord again, and brought out golden jewelry for Rebekah and her family. Then they ate and drank and talked for a long time.

The next morning Eliezer wanted Rebekah to go back with him. Rebekah's family asked him to wait about ten days, so Rebekah could get ready, but Eliezer wanted to go right away. They decided to ask Rebekah. She said, "I will go." Rebekah knew the Lord was leading her. Now she would marry Isaac, whom she had never even seen. But she wasn't afraid. She trusted the Lord.

It was evening as they came close to Isaac's home, and she saw a man walking in the field. When she asked Eliezer who it was, he told her it was Isaac. Quickly, she put a heavy veil over her face — they did that in those days — got off her camel, and met Isaac. She became his wife and he loved her and he was not lonely anymore.

REMEMBER:

Eliezer said, "I being in the way, the Lord led me." God leads us, too. He led us to be born in our mother and father's family, He leads us when we go to school, and He will lead us all our lives until He leads us to heaven.

Esau Sells His Birthright

The Lord let Abraham become a very old man. When he was one hundred seventy-five years old, he died and went to heaven, where he could be with Sarah and Noah and Enoch and Abel and all God's children who had died before him.

Isaac lived happily with his wife Rebekah for twenty years, but in all that time God did not give them a baby. They prayed very hard to the Lord and asked Him for a baby. The Lord listened and said now was the time He would keep His promise. God told Rebekah she would have not one baby, but two. We call them twins, and these twins would be special. God told Rebekah all about the twins before they were born.

In those days the twin who was born first would get special blessings. The oldest son in the family always did. The oldest one would get twice as much of his father's money and animals and in Isaac's family the oldest one would become the great nation from which Jesus would be born. It is called the "birthright." Can you remember that?

That is the way it **usually** was. But **this** time, the Lord told Rebekah it would be just the other way around. The twin who was born first, the stronger one, would **not** get twice as much and he would **not** become the nation of God's special people. The twin who was born second, the weaker one, would get the birthright blessings. The weaker one would rule over the stronger one. It **seemed** as if God was working backwards, but He wasn't. He always knows the best way.

Then the twins were born. The first one had red and hairy skin, and his parents named him **Esau**, which means **red**. The second one was holding on to his brother's heel when he was born. He could not talk yet, of course, but it seemed as if he was trying to say, "Let **me** be born first." His parents named him **Jacob**, which means **heel-holder**.

As the twins started to grow up, they were so different from each other. They did not look at all alike on the outside. Esau was an "outdoors" boy. He was brown from the sun and strong from going hunting in the woods, and he was always ready for a good time. Jacob was an "inside" boy. He had smooth, pale skin, for he liked best to stay in the tent and talk with his mother. He was a quiet boy who liked to sit and think.

The twins did not look alike on the inside, either — in their hearts. In his heart, Esau thought about animals, about being a brave hunter, about cooking delicious roasted meat from the animals he killed, and bringing it as a special treat to his father. He liked fun in **this** world. He did not think about God very

often. He did not care about sacrificing lambs on the altar. Jacob was interested in worshipping God and in His promises. He loved to stay quietly near his mother's side. Don't you think he would beg her, "Just one more Bible story, Mother?"

Esau was his father's friend. Jacob was his mother's friend. Who do you think was **God's** friend? Jacob, the weaker brother.

One day, when Esau was out hunting, Jacob cooked some delicious brownish-red beansoup. The Bible calls it "pottage." He probably cooked it in a pot over an open fire, and, oh, it smelled so good. Just then Esau came home from his hunt, very hungry and thirsty. The first thing he said was, "Feed me with that same red pottage."

Jacob was not ready to **give** the soup away. He would **sell** it. Listen to what he said: "Sell me thy birthright." Jacob wanted to get the special blessings. He wanted to become the great nation God had promised. He wanted to be one of the grandfathers of Jesus. And he wanted Esau to sell all of that for a bowl of soup. It was wrong of Jacob to do that.

What did Esau answer? He said he was going to die sometime anyway, and that would be the end of everything. He was not interested in Jesus, the Savior. He would rather have a bowl of soup in his stomach. So he ate and drank, rose up and went his way, and did not care about his birthright.

REMEMBER:

The way God works is so different from our way. **We** always think that the strongest one wins. **We** like to be the strongest and the first. **God** says He likes to work through His weak children, so they will get all their strength from Him.

Isaac Blesses Jacob

Isaac was not very strong when he was a boy, and he was not a very strong man. When he became old, he was not strong at all. He was weak and blind and had to lie down in his tent. He thought he would soon die. Before he died, he had to give the blessing to his son. Do not forget that, in those days, when fathers blessed their sons, **God** spoke through their mouths, and their sons **would** be blessed.

Isaac knew which son should have the blessing. Had not God told Rebekah, before the boys were born, that the second son, the weaker one, would rule the first son, and would have the blessing? That son was Jacob. But Isaac did not want it that way. He liked Esau and wanted **him** to have the blessing. He could have talked it over with his wife Rebekah but he did not tell anyone about his plan. Quietly he called Esau to his tent and told him to hunt a wild animal, maybe a deer, cook the meat the delicious way he liked it, and he would give Esau the blessing. It was all very wrong of Isaac. It was wrong of Esau, too, for he should have told his father that he had sold his birthright to Jacob for a bowl of soup. It was Jacob's birthright now.

Rebekah must have been watching her husband Isaac. She knew how much he loved Esau, and she must have thought he might try to disobey God's words and try to bless Esau instead of Jacob. She must have been watching for something sneaky and when she listened near the tent, she heard Isaac's plans. Quickly, Rebekah got busy. She told Jacob that his father made plans to bless Esau, and she said, "Fetch me two good kids of the goats, and I will make them savoury meat for thy father, such as he loveth; and thou shalt bring it to thy father, that he may bless thee before his death."

Jacob said it wouldn't work, for he was smooth and Esau was hairy; and if his father felt his skin, he would know Jacob was lying. Rebekah said, "Only obey my voice, and go fetch me them." So Jacob hurried to get the goats and Rebekah made the meat ready.

Then came her plan to trick blind old Isaac. She took some of Esau's good clothes from his tent and put them on Jacob and laid the hairy skin of the goats on his hands and on the back of his neck. Now he would **feel** like Esau. He would even **smell** like Esau. With the plate of bread and meat and a glass of wine, Jacob was ready to go to his father.

Before he gets there, let us look into father Isaac's tent. He was lying on his bed, alone, in the darkness of his blindness. He was not comfortable, because he knew he was trying not to do the will of God. He felt guilty inside. Suddenly

a voice saying, "My father," came through the quietness and he must have jumped a little in surprise, for he said, "Who art thou, my son?"

Jacob lied, "I am Esau, thy firstborn. I have done according as thou badest me. Sit and eat of my venison, that thy soul may bless me."

Isaac was mixed up. He wondered, "How is it that thou hast found it so quickly, my son?"

Jacob lied again, "Because the Lord thy God brought it to me."

Poor, blind Isaac did not know what to think. He said, "Come near, that I may feel thee, my son, whether thou be my very son Esau or not."

Sure enough, his hands were hairy like Esau's, but Isaac still was not sure, for he said, "The voice is Jacob's voice, but the hands are the hands of Esau." Once more he asked, "Art thou my very son Esau?"

Jacob lied again: "I am."

Then Isaac ate the food and drank the wine and asked Jacob to kiss him. That kiss was a lie, too. And Isaac blessed Jacob. He said Jacob would have the blessings of the earth — plenty to eat — and that he would be the ruler over many nations, and his brother would serve him. Then Jacob left.

Almost right away Esau came into his father's tent. He had killed an animal and cooked the meat. Esau did not know that anything was wrong until he said, "Let my father arise, and eat."

Isaac said, "Who art thou?"

That must have seemed like a foolish question to Esau. He answered, "I am thy son, thy firstborn Esau."

Then Isaac trembled and shook greatly. Do you know why? Suddenly he knew what he had done. He had almost blessed the wrong son. He had tried to go against God. What an awful sin! But God had stopped him.

When Isaac told Esau that Jacob had gotten the blessing by a trick, Esau cried for a blessing. But there was none for him. He would serve his brother, just as God had said. Esau was so angry that he said he would kill Jacob after his father died. Rebekah heard him say it, and knew she would have to send

Jacob away to keep him safe.

What an unhappy family! Isaac felt guilty before God, Esau was angry, Jacob was afraid, and Rebekah was sad, especially because she had to send Jacob away. Sinning, cheating, and lying brought much trouble to that family. Sin always brings trouble and unhappiness.

REMEMBER:

We cannot tell just one little lie. Jacob found that out, and he had to keep on lying. We have to keep on telling lies to cover up our first lie, too. Think of that when we want to tell "just one quick little lie."

God Comes to Jacob at Bethel

When Rebekah and Jacob tricked old father Isaac, they both had tried to help God along, to hurry Him, because they had wanted the blessing for Jacob so badly. They got the blessing the way **they** wanted to, by a trick, instead of waiting for God to give it at the right time. Now the family was troubled and unhappy; and soon the family was going to break up. For Jacob was going to run away from Esau.

It was time for Rebekah to tell father Isaac that Jacob was going away, but she did not tell him the real reason — that he was running away because Esau wanted to kill him. No, she told him another reason. Jacob needed a wife who loved the Lord. Esau had already married two wicked, heathen wives, which made Isaac and Rebekah sad; and Rebekah told Isaac that Jacob must never do that. It would be better for him to go far away to her brother Laban's home and find a wife there.

Isaac believed Rebekah's reason and before Jacob left, he blessed him once more, and told him to go to the home that Rebekah had come from to find a wife. But the troubles because of sin were still there. Jacob did not find Esau and say he was sorry and try to make up with Esau, and Esau was filled with hate toward Jacob.

Quickly and quietly, before Esau could kill him, Rebekah sent Jacob away, without an animal to ride on. He would have to walk all the way. All alone Jacob set out for his Uncle Laban's house. It was a long, long way off, and he had to walk many days to get there. While he walked, all alone, Jacob did not have a very happy face. He was leaving his home and his friends and going to strangers he did not know. Soon it would be dark and he was in the open fields, with no place to stay. Remember, there were no motels in those days. The thing that made Jacob feel the most unhappy and lonely was that his God seemed so far away. He had sinned very badly, and he was troubled in his heart by the wicked tricks he had done and the wicked lies he had told. He hardly dared to raise his eyes to look toward his Father in heaven.

Then darkness came, and there was no place to go. Jacob was tired, for he had walked all day; so he lay on the ground with the sky for a roof, the stars for lights, and the stones for pillows.

He slept and dreamed. In his dream he saw a ladder stretching from the earth to heaven. Angels were walking up and down the ladder. What a wonderful sight that was! It was like a little peek into heaven! God stood above the ladder and talked from heaven to Jacob. This is what God said, "I am the Lord God of Abraham thy father, and the God of Isaac: the land whereon thou liest, to thee will I give it, and to thy seed." **Seed** means children and grandchildren, and God promised him as many children as the dust of the earth. God knew, too, how lonely and unhappy Jacob was, and He made Jacob feel happier by saying, "I am with thee and will keep thee in all places whither thou goest, and will bring thee again into this land."

Jacob awoke, and knew that his beautiful dream was real. God was in this place! It was wonderful, but it made Jacob afraid, too, for he was standing at the gate of heaven. He set up his pillow-stone and poured an offering of oil on it and called the name of that place **Bethel**, which means "house of God." Here he made a promise to God: if God will be with me and keep me in the way, so that I come back to my father's house in peace, then the Lord shall be my God. And Jacob promised that he would give a tenth part of all his riches to God. With a happier heart he was ready to travel to his Uncle Laban.

REMEMBER:

The ladder in Jacob's dream stretched from the earth to heaven. It was not a real ladder, of course. It was a picture of Jesus, who makes the way for us to go up to our Father in heaven. We cannot climb to heaven by ourselves because we are always carrying such a heavy load of sin. Jesus took that load of sin away on the cross, so He could bring us to heaven on the ladder of Himself.

Jacob Stays With His Uncle Laban

After God talked with him at Bethel, Jacob must have walked his long, long way with a happier heart. He had a lot of time to think as he walked, and he must have wondered what Laban's country looked like, and how he would like to live there. Remember, Laban was Rebekah's brother, and he was grown up and married now, just as Rebekah was. Shall we find out whether the Lord gave Laban any children?

Watch Jacob! He came to a well, probably the same one the servant Eliezer came to when he found Jacob's own mother Rebekah. At the well Jacob saw shepherds with their flocks of sheep, and he asked them whether they knew Laban.

They said, "We know him; and behold, Rachel his daughter cometh with the sheep."

Jacob was so happy to hear this news that he ran to roll away the big stone that covered the opening of the well, and he gave Rachel's sheep water. Then he

kissed her and told her that he was Rebekah's son, and that Laban was his uncle. Don't you think that Rachel was excited as she ran back home to her father Laban to tell him the news? **Now** it was Laban's turn to run, to meet the son of his very own sister. He kissed Jacob — in those days they kissed one another, instead of shaking hands, as we do now — and took Jacob into his home.

There Jacob stayed for one month with his Uncle Laban and his family. In that month, Laban watched Jacob and he found out that Jacob knew all about farm animals and was a very good shepherd. He saw, too, that Jacob loved Rachel very much but did not love her older sister Leah. Did Laban find out about all the troubles in Jacob's family that made him run away? The Bible does not tell us; but Laban probably asked Jacob why he came, and Jacob could not hide all his troubles from Laban.

What kind of man was Jacob's Uncle Laban? He was not a rich man, but he wanted to be a rich man, and he began to make plans to get rich. This is how he did it: he explained to Jacob that just because they were relatives, he did not have to work for nothing. Then he asked, "Tell me, what shall thy wages be?" These words were a little trap for Jacob, because Uncle Laban knew Jacob wanted to marry Rachel. He would not have to pay Jacob any money. Jacob would work to marry Rachel.

Jacob walked right into the trap that Laban made with his words, and said, "I will serve thee seven years for Rachel thy younger daughter."

Laban was glad, for he was thinking only of himself. He sold his own girl for seven years of work, so that he would get richer. Do you like Laban?

Jacob loved Rachel, who was beautiful and lively and who had sparkly eyes. He did not love her sister Leah, who had soft, tender eyes, and who was gentle and loving. Jacob loved Rachel who was spoiled and loved herself. He did not love Leah who was soft-hearted and who loved the Lord. Whom would you love?

Those seven years that Jacob worked for Rachel seemed only a few days to him, because he loved Rachel so much; and at last the day came when they could get married. Laban made a big party and invited friends to the wedding, just as we do. There was one difference. In those days, the bride wore a heavy veil over her and no one could see what she looked like through it; and Laban gave Jacob the wrong girl. He put the veil over Leah.

The next morning, when an unhappy and angry Jacob found out he had married the wrong girl, he came to Laban and said, "Did not I serve with thee for Rachel? Wherefore hast thou beguiled me?" Beguiled means **tricked.** Do you think that Jacob was remembering the trick he had played on his own father?

Listen to Laban's answer: "It must not be so done in our country, to give the younger before the firstborn." He said that Jacob must serve seven more years for Rachel.

After seven days, Laban let Jacob marry Rachel, too. Now he had two wives. Jacob loved Rachel, but she did not love him. Leah loved Jacob, but he did not love her. Does that sound like a very happy family?

Let us see what the Lord said about it. When He saw that Jacob did not love Leah, He gave her children, four boys, named Reuben, Simeon, Levi, and Judah. But He gave Rachel no children. Rachel was jealous, and asked Jacob to marry her maid, Bilhah, so that Bilhah could have children for her. Bilhah had two baby boys. Then Leah, to pay Rachel back, asked Jacob to marry **her** maid, Zilpah; and God gave Zilpah two baby boys. Then Leah had two more baby boys.

At last Rachel asked the Lord for a baby, and He gave her a baby, whom she named **Joseph.** If we add up all the baby boys, we will know that Jacob had eleven boys in his family now.

REMEMBER:

Rachel was a mother who was beautiful on the outside. She had a pretty face and sparkling eyes. Leah was a mother who was beautiful on the inside. She loved the Lord so much that her heart was beautiful with kindness and goodness that comes from God. Is your mother beautiful on the **inside?**

91

Jacob Leaves His Uncle Laban

For seven years Jacob had worked for Rachel, and he got Leah; and for seven more years he worked for Rachel again. That made fourteen years in all that he had worked for Laban, and Jacob thought it was time to go back to Canaan. But Laban was not happy about **that**! God had been blessing Jacob all the years that he took care of Laban's animals and Laban had many, many more animals now. Laban wanted Jacob to stay; and he said to Jacob, "I have learned that the Lord hath blessed me for thy sake. Appoint me thy wages, and I will give it." Wages is the **money** Laban would pay.

Jacob said he would not work for money. He would stay and work only if he might have some of the animals. Jacob's family was getting big, and he wanted to be a rich man, too, to take care of his family. So Laban and Jacob made an agreement: all the spotted and the speckled cows and goats and all the brown sheep would be Jacob's. The rest would be Laban's.

Do you know what happened? God made the animals have speckled and spotted babies, because God was blessing Jacob with many animals. But Jacob was not quite satisfied with that. He wanted to help God along again, and he tried to get all the strongest baby animals for himself, and leave the weaker baby animals for Laban.

Laban watched, with an angry face, as Jacob was getting more animals and stronger animals than he was. He decided that, if Jacob could cheat a little bit, he could, too. So he changed the kinds of animals that Jacob would get. No more speckled and spotted ones! This time it was only the striped ones. Can you guess what happened? All the animals had striped babies. **Ten times** Laban changed the kinds of animals that Jacob would get, and each time God made those kinds have baby animals for Jacob.

What an unhappy way to live! Jacob was one of God's own dear children, but he did not always act like one. Laban did not care about God's laws. Both of them were busy tricking each other, each one trying to get the most for himself. Then God came in a dream to Jacob. This is what God said: "I am the God of Bethel, where thou anointedst the pillar. I have seen all that Laban doeth unto thee. Now arise, get thee out from this land, and return unto the land of thy kindred." Kindred is **family**.

That was good news for Jacob. Eagerly he went to talk with his wives. They had never been to Canaan, and it would be a strange land for them. What would they answer to God's words in the dream? They said they were ready to go; for they said their father had sold them — for seven years' work — and he treated them like strangers. Besides, the riches that God took from their father were **theirs**.

So Jacob and his family and his servants got ready to leave. But Jacob did not dare to face Laban and say, "God told me to go home." He was afraid Laban would try to keep them there; or maybe he would not let Rachel and Leah go; and maybe Jacob was ashamed because he had tried to cheat Laban and get the best animals for himself. He decided that they would have to sneak quietly away, and he found a good time.

It was the time of the year when all the farmers got together to cut the wool off their sheep. It is called **shearing**. Each farmer would help every other farmer, until all the sheep were sheared. Laban had to go away to shear his sheep, and that was the time Jacob was waiting for.

Now everyone was busy packing the furniture and clothes and blankets and dishes; and the servants were getting the animals in lines, ready for a long, long march. Rachel was busy, too. She stole some small gods, idols that her father worshipped. Then they started out.

Three days later someone told Laban that Jacob and his family had run away. Right away he began to chase Jacob. It was easy for Laban to catch up with Jacob's family, for Laban could ride a camel or a donkey and travel fast. Jacob had many, many animals, baby ones, too; and little children, who had to travel slowly.

Can't you see how angry Laban was, how he said to himself, "Just wait! They won't get away with this!" — until God came to him and told him not to speak bad words to Jacob. Laban did not dare to disobey God, but he still had a little scolding for Jacob. He asked, "Wherefore didst thou flee away secretly? I might have sent thee away with mirth and with songs." Do you think Laban would have done that? Listen to what Laban is saying now: "Wherefore hast thou stolen my gods?"

Jacob answered, "With whomsoever thou findest thy gods, let him not live." He did not know that Rachel had stolen them.

Laban looked in the tents of Rachel and Leah and the servants, but he could not find them. He never did find them. Do you know where they were? In the bags of furniture on the camel's back, and Rachel was sitting on them.

Jacob and Laban talked together then, and gathered stones on a big pile, and they made a promise. They would never pass those stones to do harm to one another; and Laban said "Mizpah," which means "The Lord watch between me and thee when we are absent one from another."

Then they ate and drank together, and early the next morning Laban kissed them good-bye, and went back home. Jacob and his family traveled toward the land of Canaan.

REMEMBER:

Laban said "Mizpah." We could say that word when we go away, too. "Mizpah" asks God to watch over us and our daddies and mothers when we are away from one another. Try to remember to say "Mizpah" the next time you go away.

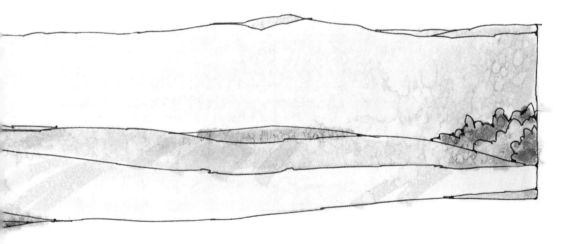

Jacob Goes Back to Canaan

As Jacob and his family came closer to the land of Canaan, angels of God met him. Those angels were a picture of God taking care of Jacob. They did not even talk with him, but they made Jacob think of his dream of angels on a ladder at Bethel, and of God's promise, "I am with thee, and will keep thee."

Jacob needed God's promise, for soon he would have to meet his brother Esau. Did Esau still hate him? Was he still angry? Jacob sent some servants to run on ahead to meet Esau and find out. When they came back, they were afraid! Esau was coming to meet them with four hundred men. Four hundred men was an army that could easily kill them all.

Jacob was afraid, too, and divided his people into two groups, so that if Esau fought one group, the other group could run away. And he prayed. He told God that when he ran away from Esau many years ago, all he had in his hand was a walking stick. Now he was a rich man with a big family, and he thanked God for all His kindness. He asked God to remember His promise to give him many children, and to make a great nation of him.

Jacob thought, too. He thought how a nice present might put Esau in a good mood so that he would not be angry anymore. It was not a present in a box, tied with a ribbon. No, it was a present of animals. Jacob separated some goats, sheep, camels, cows, and donkeys, five hundred fifty of them for Esau. What a lot of animals! What a big present!

Then it was night, and they were near a little stream of water. Jacob sent everyone in his family over the stream and he stayed on the other side alone. As he sat there in the dark night, a man came to wrestle with him, and Jacob wrestled with the man with all his strength. All night they wrestled. Near morning the wrestler touched the hollow place at the top of his hip, and it was hurt and out of joint, and Jacob could not walk straight anymore. He limped badly. Suddenly Jacob knew that he was wrestling with the Angel of God, the Son of God Who would some day be born as Jesus. Jacob was wrestling with God!

Why did God come down to wrestle all night with Jacob? To teach Jacob a lesson. Jacob liked to do everything **his own** way, to help God along. It was easy for him to cheat and to play tricks. He had tricked his father and his Uncle Laban. That night, God made Jacob see that his tricks would not work. God made Jacob see that he was not strong at all. God just **touched** Jacob, and now he could hardly walk. From now on he must let **God** fight for him. That was Jacob's lesson.

Then the Angel said, "Let me go."

Jacob answered, "I will not let thee go, except thou bless me."

The Angel asked, "What is thy name?"

Jacob answered, "Jacob."

The Angel told him, "Thy name shall be called no more Jacob, but **Israel**." Israel means **prince of God**.

Then it was Jacob's turn to ask a question: "Tell me Thy name."

But the Angel would not tell him, for His name is too holy.

Jacob named that place **Peniel**, for, he said, "I have seen God face to face, and my life is preserved." As Jacob limped over the stream of water, the morning sun came up and shone on him, a picture of God's friendly face shining down on him.

Now Jacob was ready to meet Esau. He was not so afraid anymore, for he would meet Esau in God's strength. When he saw Esau coming, he sent the maids and their children to meet him first, then Leah and her children, and last of all Rachel and her son Joseph. Jacob bowed down to the ground seven times before Esau. It was the way people met in those days.

When Esau saw Jacob's family and the big present of animals Jacob had sent him, and when he saw that Jacob had come in peace, his heart became softer and he hugged and kissed his brother. At first he did not want to take such a big present, but Jacob urged him, and he took it.

Esau had an idea: his family and Jacob's family could all live together now. Jacob did not like the idea at all. Esau and his family were wicked. Jacob brought up his family in the love of God. They could never live together. So Jacob told Esau no, but he did not tell him the real reason. Maybe he was afraid to. Instead he said that his children and the young animals traveled too slowly. So Esau left, and Jacob and his family settled down.

He **should** have gone to Bethel, because he promised God he would sacrifice a lamb to Him there. Instead, he stayed and stayed where he was. After ten years, God had to come to him and tell him to keep his promise. What a shame! Do you know what the trouble was? Jacob was not a very strict father, and he had let his family have some idols. Before Jacob could go to Bethel, he had to make his family give him all the idol-gods they were worshipping, and they buried them under an oak tree.

After they came to Bethel, Rachel had another baby boy. But a sad thing happened when he was born. Rachel died. The poor little baby never had a mother to take care of him. Jacob called him **Benjamin**, and he loved his little boy dearly. Now Jacob had twelve sons.

REMEMBER:

It was a shame that God had to remind Jacob to keep his promise to go to Bethel. Sometimes He has to remind **us** to keep our promises, too — to love one another and to obey our parents — doesn't He?

Joseph is Sold

For many years, Jacob lived quietly with his family in the land of Canaan; and as his boys grew up, they helped take care of the hundreds of animals that Jacob had. Joseph was seventeen years old already, almost grown up, and he went to the fields with his older brothers to help with the animals.

Often Joseph came home from the fields with an unhappy face and he would tell his father Jacob that his brothers were very wicked — he heard their bad language and saw the sinful things they did. Jacob listened to Joseph, and he knew it was true, for Jacob was not a very strict father to his boys; besides, he made his older boys angry because he loved Joseph the most. He loved Joseph so much because he was a son of Rachel and because he feared the Lord. The brothers could see that Jacob loved Joseph the most, for he made a special coat for Joseph, a coat of many colors, such as a king's son would wear. That was not right for Jacob to do, for Joseph's brothers wore the rough, old coats that shepherds usually wore.

Do you think Joseph's brothers liked it that their father Jacob loved him the most? Oh, no, they hated Joseph for it. They hated him, too, because he scolded them for their sins, because he was the only one who had a beautiful coat, and because he had dreams.

Would you like to hear about those dreams? In his first dream, Joseph saw shocks of corn tied up and standing in the field. His brothers' shocks of corn bowed down to his shock. When Joseph told them his dream, they understood what it meant — that Joseph would be a king over them — and they said, "Shalt thou reign over us?"

In his second dream, the sun, the moon, and eleven stars bowed down to him. His whole family understood what that dream meant, too. His father, his mother, and his eleven brothers would bow down to him. Even his father Jacob scolded him a little, and said, "Shall I and thy mother and thy brethren come to bow down ourselves to thee?"

Did Joseph dream those dreams because he thought so much of himself? Or did God send him those dreams? God sent them. Deep down in their hearts the brothers knew it, too, but they were jealous of Joseph, and did not want him to be greater than they were.

It was not always easy to find enough grass for their animals to eat, and often the brothers had to wander a long way from home to find enough grass. One time the brothers had been gone from home many days. This time Joseph was not with them. When they stayed away too long, their father Jacob became worried, and he asked Joseph to go out and try to find them.

Joseph looked around a place called Shechem, but they were not there. When he asked a man whether he had seen his brothers, the man said, "I heard them say, 'Let us go to Dothan.' "

There Joseph found them, and he must have come running with a glad face. At last he had found them! He didn't have to wander alone anymore! Then he saw their faces, their wicked, scowling faces. They had seen him coming, all alone, a long way off, and they said to one another, "Behold this dreamer cometh." Oh, how they hated Joseph! What are they saying now? "Let us slay him, and cast him into some pit, and we will say, some evil beast hath devoured him: and we shall see what will become of his dreams." It was his **dreams** that bothered the brothers so much. They hated those dreams.

Reuben said, "Let us not kill him." He suggested throwing Joseph into a deep pit; and he thought that later he would come and pull him out and save him. The brothers listened to Reuben, and took off Joseph's beautiful coat and threw him into the deep pit. Now Joseph was their prisoner. As the brothers sat down to eat, they heard Joseph begging and crying from the deep, dark hole, and they did not feel sorry for him at all. Their hearts were hard.

They didn't pay attention to him until some storekeepers came past. In those days, storekeepers traveled from place to place, selling and trading things. It was Judah who suggested selling their brother to the storekeepers for twenty pieces of silver. At first Joseph must have been happy as they lifted him from the pit, until he saw that he had been sold as a slave, and had to go along with these strange men, to a faraway country. Poor Joseph! Don't you think he cried and cried and begged to go back home? None of his brothers listened.

Then Reuben came back. He looked into the pit, and Joseph was gone! He was the only brother who felt bad about it. The other brothers took Joseph's beautiful coat and dipped it in goat's blood and showed it to their father when they got home. Jacob said, "An evil beast hath devoured him," and he cried and cried for many days. The wicked brothers tried to comfort their father, but they did not tell him the truth. They had to live with that lie hidden in their hearts.

REMEMBER:

When his brothers wanted to kill Joseph, they really did kill him in their hearts. When we hate someone, we kill him in our hearts, too.

Joseph is a Slave in Potiphar's House

Do you remember that Joseph's brothers threw him into a deep, dark pit? When Joseph was afraid in the pit, and cried and begged them to take him out, they would not listen. Joseph cried to God from the pit, too, and begged Him to help him. God listened to Joseph's crying, and answered him — not **Joseph's** way, but **God's** way. **Joseph** thought he would go home in happiness with his brothers. **God** led him while he cried big tears to the land of Egypt, far, far away. **God's** way was best.

Poor Joseph could not see why God let those wicked storekeepers buy him. What had he done to deserve it? Would he never see his father again? Let us follow him to Egypt. There the storekeepers took him to the market place, where people bought and sold things; and they put Joseph up for sale as a slave. Someone could buy him and make him work hard! Joseph must have stood there, afraid and unhappy, and he must have thought about his beautiful dreams. He had dreamed about being a **king,** and now he was being sold as a **slave.**

Someone bought Joseph. His name was Potiphar and he was the captain of some of the soldiers of the king. Joseph had to go with Potiphar, whether he wanted to or not, and become a slave. He was a good slave. Some slaves stole things from their masters. Others were lazy or complained. Joseph worked hard and Potiphar his master trusted him. Potiphar could see that God was with Joseph, for he worked hard, right where God had put him, without complaining; and God blessed Potiphar's house and his farms for Joseph's sake. Soon Joseph became ruler over all Potiphar's house, then over all his fields, with all the slaves who worked in them, and finally over all his money and all his business. Potiphar trusted Joseph to manage all that, and Potiphar did not even bother himself to run his own house anymore.

Joseph was growing up to be a man in Potiphar's house, and he was such a good looking young man! Remember, the beautiful Rachel was his mother. Do you think that Joseph looked like his mother? Potiphar's wife watched Joseph. She liked him and she wished she could be his wife. So she asked Joseph if he would love her. Joseph must have been shocked! He gave her the right answer: you are married to Potiphar already, and he trusts me not to do anything wrong; besides, it would be a great sin against God.

Was Potiphar's wife satisfied with Joseph's answer? Oh, no! Every day she bothered him. One day when Joseph was alone in the house, taking care of his business, she reached out her hand to catch him. She caught the coat he was wearing, and Joseph quickly slipped out of his coat and ran away from that wicked woman.

Then what did she do? She kept Joseph's coat in her hand and shouted and screamed for help until some servants came running to see what the trouble was. She screamed that Joseph was trying to hurt her. When Potiphar came home, she told him that Joseph was a very wicked slave who tried to hurt her. Did Potiphar

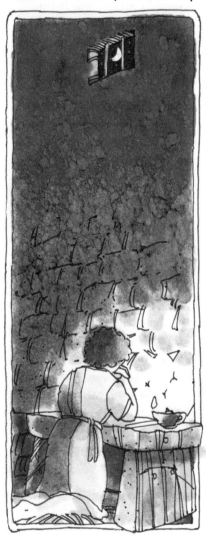

believe her? We do not know. But Joseph was only his slave, and all he could do was get rid of him and throw him into prison.

Prisons were awful places in those days. Often they were built under the ground, and were dark and cold and wet. In the prison they tied Joseph with chains and put his feet in heavy iron chains, so that he could not move. There he lay, sad and all alone, cold and hurting and helpless. And he had not done anything wrong! Why was God doing this to him? He prayed to God and God showed mercy to him and made the keeper of the prison like him. Soon Joseph was not chained up anymore and the keeper let him take care of all the other prisoners. He liked and trusted Joseph, too. The Lord was with Joseph and was making all things well, not **Joseph's** way, but **God's** way.

REMEMBER:

Joseph must have asked God many, many times why He was giving him so many troubles. When God sends **our** families troubles, we can think about Joseph. For God makes everything well for us, not **our** way, but **God's** way.

Joseph Tells the Dreams of the Butler and Baker

Joseph lived in prison many years. Slowly, the keeper of the prison gave Joseph more and more power, until Joseph was running the prison. But he could never see outside the prison walls and he could never go where he wanted to go, for he was still a prisoner. Don't you think he was sad sometimes? Don't you think he wondered why he was all alone in this strange land? And don't you think he wondered why God kept him in prison so long? Then he would pray, and God would answer him and make him forget his troubles and be happy again; and Joseph could listen to the troubles of the other men in prison and try to help them.

One day two new prisoners came. One was the chief baker, the man who was over all the other bakers in the king's palace, who made the delicious breads and cakes for the king. The other was the chief butler. A butler serves wine to the king. We do not know why they were thrown into prison. Maybe the king thought they were trying to poison him. The Bible does not tell us. The butler and the baker stayed in prison for a while, and Joseph was used to seeing them. Maybe he often served their meals to them.

One morning both their faces were sad, and Joseph asked, "Wherefore look ye so sadly today?"

They answered, "We have dreamed a dream, and there is no interpreter of it." An interpreter tells **the meaning** of the dream.

In those days, in heathen countries like Egypt, people thought that dreams were very important. **These two dreams** were very important, for God had sent these special dreams. In Egypt, wise men — not really wise men, but wicked wise men — said they could tell what dreams meant. They really couldn't. The butler and baker said they wished they could talk to one of those wise men and find out the meanings of their dreams. Joseph almost scolded them when he said, "Do not interpretations belong to **God**? Tell me them, I pray you."

The butler told first. He dreamed about a grape vine that had three branches. The branches had little buds, it had flowers, and it had ripe grapes, all on the same branches. In his dream, the butler had a cup in his hand. He picked the ripe grapes, squeezed out the juice, and made wine, ready to put into the king's hand.

103

God told Joseph what the dream meant. The three branches of the grape vine were a picture of three days. In three days the king would let the butler out of prison, and he would work for the king again. Then Joseph said to the butler, "Think about me when it shall be well with thee and make mention of me unto Pharaoh, and bring me out of this house. For I was stolen out of the land of the Hebrews: and here I have done nothing that they should put me into the dungeon." Poor Joseph!

But the baker was eager to tell his dream. The butler's dream had a happy meaning. Maybe his would, too. In his dream, he had three white baskets on top of his head. In that country people often carried things on their heads. In the top basket were all kinds of baked goods for the king, and the birds were eating the good things out of the top basket.

The baker could hardly wait to hear the meaning. Would it be happy? This is what Joseph told him. The three baskets were pictures of three days. In three days the king would cut off the baker's head and hang his body on a tree, and the birds would peck at him. What a sad meaning to **that** dream.

Three days went by. The third day was the king's birthday, and he made a big party. The king called the butler and the baker out of prison, and at that party the butler served the king wine as he had always done. The baker was killed and hanged on a tree.

But the butler forgot his promise to remember Joseph to the king. How could he forget that fine young man, who feared the Lord and who told the meaning of his dream? Didn't he think about it every day when he served the king's wine? I think he did. But it was quite a bit of trouble to talk to the king about a lonely boy from another land. The butler did not really want to bother with it. He was a selfish and thoughtless man. He did not **want** to remember his promise to Joseph. So Joseph stayed in prison.

REMEMBER:

While Joseph was in prison, the Lord was teaching him to wait quietly for God to help him. He was learning that **all his help** came from Jehovah, his God. When the minister says in church, "**Our help** is in the name of Jehovah," shall we think about Joseph and about ourselves?

Pharaoh Dreams
Two Dreams

For two years the butler had been out of prison and back at work serving the king his wine. For two years he had not bothered to think about poor Joseph in the dark, horrid prison. Two whole years!

At the end of those two years something happened. The king had a dream. In the land of Egypt, all the kings were called **Pharaohs.** In his dream, this King Pharaoh was standing near the big river that ran through the land of Egypt. The name of that river was the **Nile.**

As King Pharaoh stood at the edge of the river in his dream, he saw seven fat, well-fed cows come out of the river and begin to eat grass in a pasture by the riverside. Can you make a picture of his dream in your mind? Then out of the river came seven thin, starving cows, who ate up the seven fat, good cows; and after they ate them, they were no fatter.

What a strange dream! It was so strange that he woke up. When he went to sleep again, he had another dream. This time he saw seven fat and good ears of corn growing on one stalk. Seven thin, dried-up ears grew up next; and the seven thin ears ate up the seven good ears of corn.

When King Pharaoh awoke, he was surprised that they were dreams, because they had seemed so real; and he could not sleep after that. He was restless and troubled. God had sent those dreams to King Pharaoh, and somehow God made him know that they were special dreams. Pharaoh did not know that God had sent them. Do you know what he did? He called for his wise men and his magicians. A magician says he can do **magic,** that he has lucky charms and that by his magic he can tell the meanings of dreams. But Pharaoh's wise men and magicians were workers of the devil, and they could not tell King Pharaoh what his dreams meant. Of course not!

Pharaoh **still** did not know what they meant, and it bothered him so much! Then his butler saw the king's troubled face, and he thought of Joseph. He told King Pharaoh about his own dream and the baker's dream when they were in prison together, and how this young man from the land of Canaan had told what their dreams meant. And it had happened just as Joseph had said: the baker was hanged and the butler came back to work.

Very quickly, the king sent a servant to the prison to get Joseph and the servant told him to hurry. What an excitement in the prison! Joseph had to wash himself and change his old prison clothes and shave so fast that his helpers made him run. That is how quickly God brought him out of prison and made him stand in the palace before the king.

Pharaoh started by telling Joseph, "I have heard that thou canst understand a dream to interpret it."

And this is what Joseph answered: "It is not in **me**. **God** shall give Pharaoh an answer of peace." The **first** time he met Pharaoh, the **first** thing he said was that God was his God.

Pharaoh was eager to tell his dreams. He said, "In my dream, I stood on the bank of the river: and there came up out of the river seven kine (kine are **cows**), fatfleshed and well favoured. And seven other kine came up after them, poor and very ill favoured, such as I never saw in all the land of Egypt for badness. And the lean kine did eat up the first seven fat kine: and when they had eaten them up, they were still ill favoured, as at the beginning. So I awoke.

"And I saw in my dream, and, behold, seven ears came up in one stalk, full and good: and, behold seven ears, withered, thin, and blasted with the east wind, sprung up; and the thin ears devoured the seven good ears; and I told the magicians, but there was none that could declare it to me."

Joseph said, "God hath showed Pharaoh what he is about to do." Then Joseph told the meaning. Both the dreams meant the same thing. God had sent **two** dreams to show Pharaoh that it would **surely** happen. The seven good cows and the seven good ears of corn were pictures of seven years when much food would grow, far too much food for the people to eat. The seven thin cows and the seven thin ears of corn were pictures of seven years of famine, when God would not send sunshine and rain to make things grow. Nothing would grow!

Would the seven years of famine be so bad that everyone would die? Oh, no, for God was telling them ahead of time. They could get ready for the famine. Joseph had a plan: in the seven years when too much food grew, everyone should give a fifth part of his food to the king. That means when a man had five bushels of corn he would give one to the king to save for the time of famine; and he would not even miss that one bushel. If everyone would do that, the land of Egypt would have plenty of food for the bad years. Joseph told Pharaoh to find a man to gather all that extra food and build big barns to store it in.

Do you know what man Pharaoh chose? Joseph. He put a linen robe on Joseph, his own ring on Joseph's finger, and a golden chain around his neck, and made him the ruler over Egypt. Only Pharaoh was greater than Joseph in Egypt. Pharaoh gave Joseph a wife, and God gave them two baby boys. He named the first one Manasseh, which means "God has made me forget my troubles," and the second one Ephraim, which means "God gave me work to do in this land." Joseph always thought about God first.

REMEMBER:

When Joseph suddenly became the ruler in the great land of Egypt, he did not become proud and forget God. In everything he did, God was **first** in all his thoughts. Is God always first in **our** thoughts?

Joseph's Brothers Visit Egypt

For seven years God made the sun to shine and the rain to fall and the earth to grow so many crops that the people picked them by handfuls. In Egypt, everyone brought to Joseph one bushel out of every five bushels of food he gathered. Joseph and his helpers had to build big cities filled with barns of wheat and corn and other food, and they gathered so much that they could not count how much they had.

Then the seven years began when nothing would grow, not in any country on the earth. In Egypt when the people cried to King Pharaoh, "We are hungry! We are starving!" he told them to go to Joseph for food; and Joseph opened stores in his food cities and sold the people all they wanted. Soon the news that there was plenty of food in Egypt traveled to all the lands of the earth, and the people from these lands came to Egypt to buy food.

Joseph's father, Jacob, in the land of Canaan, heard about it, too; and he said to Joseph's brothers, "Why do ye look one upon another?" He was telling them to get busy and go to Egypt and buy corn for their animals. Ten of Joseph's brothers got ready to go, but not Benjamin, the youngest. Father Jacob would not let **him** go. Once he had let Joseph go away and Joseph had never come back! No, Benjamin must stay home. Do you think Joseph's brothers **liked** to go to Egypt to buy corn and wheat? I don't think so, for Egypt was the land where their brother Joseph was sold as a slave. Where was he now? They did not know. Going to Egypt made them think of the terrible thing they had done to Joseph long ago. But they obeyed their father and went.

When they came to Egypt and went to one of the food cities, they saw the great ruler of Egypt, dressed in the clothes of Egypt and talking the kind of language they talked in Egypt. They never guessed that this great ruler was their own brother Joseph. But Joseph knew his brothers. They still looked about the same, and wore the same kind of shepherd coats they did when they sold him, many years ago. All his brothers bowed down to him, and Joseph thought of his dreams. They had just come true!

What do you think Joseph did next? He **could** have been very angry and put them all in prison for their terrible wickedness. Or he **could** have said, "I am Joseph," and hugged and kissed them and forgotten all about their wickedness because he was so glad to see them. Or he **could** test them to see whether they were sorry and whether their hearts had God's love in them now. Do you know which one Joseph chose? He chose the test.

He did not tell them who he was, and he pretended that he could not understand the language of Canaan which they talked. He even asked a man to explain to him what his brothers were saying. Then he spoke hard words to his brothers. He said, "Ye are spies." Spies sneak around in other countries to see what the land looks like.

Joseph's brothers were shocked. They said, "We are true men, thy servants are no spies."

Joseph kept saying, "Ye are spies," until his brothers told him they were the sons of one father in Canaan, with one brother (Joseph) who was gone, and one brother (Benjamin) who was at home with his father. **That** was what Joseph wanted to hear: that his father and brother Benjamin were well.

Next he told his brothers they would have to prove that they were telling the truth, and he put them all in prison for three days. While his brothers were in prison, Joseph heard them talking about the awful day when Joseph was crying to them from the dark pit and they would not listen to him; and now, they said, God was punishing them. Poor Joseph cried when he heard them talking. It made him feel so bad, and he wanted to tell them who he was, but he wasn't finished testing them yet.

Before he sent them home, he took Simeon and put him in prison, and told the brothers that Simeon would stay in prison until they came the next time **with their youngest brother, Benjamin.**

Very sadly the brothers started back to Canaan without Simeon. Joseph had loaded food into their sacks and put their money back on top. Along the way, when one of the brothers opened his sack to give his animals some food, he found his money, and all the brothers were afraid. Would the great ruler think they had stolen it? They said, "What is this that God hath done unto us?"

Oh, how they hated to tell father Jacob the bad news! When they came home and told him that the ruler had talked roughly to them, that Simeon was in prison, and that Benjamin must come along the next time, Jacob complained that they had taken his children away. He said, "Joseph is not, and Simeon is not, and ye will take Benjamin away: all these things are against me." Jacob did not look up to God in faith when he said that, for God was holding all Jacob's children safely in His hand: ten in Canaan, Joseph and Simeon in Egypt.

REMEMBER:

When Jacob said, "All these things are against me," he looked only around him, and forgot to use his eyes of faith and look up to God. We can learn a lesson from Jacob, and remember to look up to God and say, "Everything is all right because God is holding us in His hands."

The Brothers Visit Egypt Again

Do we remember that Joseph's brothers did not come back from their trip to Egypt with smiling faces and happy words, even though they had plenty of corn and grain now? There was sadness in their family. One reason was that the ruler in Egypt said that Benjamin must go along next time. The other reason was that every one of the brothers found his money in the top of his sack. They were all afraid!

None of them wanted to go back to Egypt; but, no matter how often they looked at the sky, God sent no rain, and no crops grew. There was nothing to do but go back to Egypt to buy more food. Father Jacob said to his boys, "Go again, buy us a little food." Jacob knew, and his boys knew that they could not go without Benjamin; and Jacob did not want **that**!

Judah answered his father: "The man said to us, Ye shall not see my face except your brother be with you." If Jacob would send their brother with them, they would go down and buy food: but if he would not send him, they would not go down.

Poor Jacob **knew** all that already, but he did not **want** it that way. He was so upset he started to argue. He said, "Wherefore dealt ye so ill with me, as to tell the man whether ye had yet a brother?"

Then all the brothers had to answer their father Jacob. They told him the story all over again, and said, "The man asked us, Is your father yet alive? have ye another brother? And we told him: could we certainly know that he would say, Bring your brother down?"

Finally Judah had an idea which made his father Jacob feel a little better. Judah said, "I will be surety for him: if I bring him not unto thee, then let me bear the blame forever."

And old Jacob bowed his gray head and gave in and said, "If it must be so now. . . ."

The brothers gathered a little present for the ruler of Egypt from a few of the fruits and nuts that would still grow in the famine, they took double money with them, and left for Egypt.

111

When they came to Egypt and stood before Joseph, the great ruler, to buy food, he saw that Benjamin was with them. He told his servant to make ready a noon meal and invite all the brothers to the dinner. The brothers were afraid when the ruler separated them from the crowd and asked them to come to his house; and they **thought** they knew why the ruler was asking them. It was because of the money they found in the tops of their sacks! He must have thought they had stolen it!

Before they went into the house, the brothers explained to the servant that there must have been some mistake, for their money was in their sacks, and that they brought more money this time. The servant only answered, "Peace be to you. I had your money." Maybe the servant was having a little joke all by himself, for he **had** their money, and **then** he put it back in their sacks, as Joseph had told him to do.

The brothers were more and more puzzled by all the strange things that were happening to them; but they came in to the ruler's house, and met Simeon, who had been let out of prison.

Then Joseph came home, and all eleven brothers bowed down to him — again — and gave him the present they had brought. They didn't know he was Joseph, of course, and they didn't know what Joseph was thinking. Was he thinking of his dreams again?

First he asked some questions: "Is your father well, the old man of whom ye spake? Is he yet alive? Is this your younger brother?"

The brothers answered politely, but they were too scared and too nervous to notice how **very** interested in their family the ruler was. And Joseph was so glad that Benjamin was safe with his brothers and was so eager to tell them who he was that he left the room and cried. It was not time to tell yet.

Then they ate. Joseph sat at a separate table, for the Egyptians might not eat with people from the land of Canaan. As the brothers sat down, something very surprising happened. They were seated according to their age, from the oldest to the youngest. They could not figure out how the ruler knew how old each one was.

As they ate, the servants brought five times as much food to Benjamin. Joseph wanted to see whether his brothers were jealous of Benjamin. But they weren't; and as they ate and drank together, they were happy.

REMEMBER:

It must have been hard for Joseph to keep from telling his brothers who he was. But he was not finished testing them to see if God's love was in their hearts. Sometimes God tests us, too, to make us show more love in our hearts to **Him.**

"I Am Joseph"

The next morning the eleven brothers were ready to start for their home in Canaan. As the servant was filling their sacks with grain, Joseph told him to put their money on top, just as he had done the first time. Joseph also told the servant to put his silver cup, with the corn money, on top of Benjamin's sack.

Why would Joseph tell his servant to do a thing like that? It was part of the test of his brothers — the biggest test and the last test. Joseph **had** to know whether his brothers had changed. They had not loved Joseph. Were they sorry now? And did they truly love Benjamin?

As soon as it was light, the brothers set out with happy hearts. The ruler had been nice to them, and Benjamin was with them. They still had questions. Why was the ruler so interested in their father? Why did Benjamin get five times as much food?

Suddenly their talking stopped. The ruler's servant was running after them shouting for them to stop. What was he saying to them? "Wherefore have ye rewarded evil for good?" Then he asked them why they had taken the cup the ruler drinks out of.

They could not believe their ears. They **knew** they had not stolen it, and they tried to show the servant that they were honest men. If they were thieves, they would not have brought back the money they found on top of their sacks. They were so sure that no one had taken the silver cup that they said the thief should die.

Quickly each brother lifted his sacks to the ground and the servant started looking in them, beginning with the oldest brother, even though he knew the cup was in the sack of the youngest brother, because he himself had put it there! The cup was not in Reuben's sack. It was not in Simeon's, not in Levi's . . . nor Judah's . . . nor Dan's — all the way down the line — and the brothers were ready to say, "We **knew** it!" when the servant picked up the silver cup from Benjamin's sack.

All the brothers tore their clothes, a picture of how very bad they felt;

113

and with heavy footsteps they walked back to face the stern ruler once more. There they bowed to him — again.

Judah did the talking. He said, "What shall we say unto my lord? How shall we clear ourselves? God hath found out the iniquity of thy servants: behold, we are my lord's servants."

Joseph answered, "No, but the man in whose hand the cup is found."

Then, very politely, very sadly, and very beautifully, Judah told the ruler the whole story. He told how the ruler had asked, "Have ye a father, or a brother?" He told how the ruler had said, "Bring your brother down to me, that I may set mine eyes upon him."

He told that they thought their father would **die** if Benjamin left him, but they needed food, so their father let them go. He told how their father said one of his boys was torn up by wild animals, and how their father would die if Benjamin could not come back. Judah ended by saying that he would take Benjamin's place and be a servant in Egypt forever, so that Benjamin could go home.

Did Judah's talk make you feel sad? It made Joseph feel sad, too. Now he knew his brothers were sorry. He ordered all the Egyptians out of the room and he cried loudly. His heart was almost bursting as he said, "I am Joseph. Is my father still alive?"

Joseph was so eager for this time to come that he forget how shocked his brothers would be. It seemed as if they were struck by lightning. They could not move. They could not think. They could not talk. It all happened too quickly. So Joseph talked to them. He said, "Be not grieved, nor angry with yourselves, that ye sold me hither: for God did send me before you to preserve life." Preserve means **save**. And he told them one more thing: "It was not **you** that sent me hither, but **God**."

Since there would be five more years of famine, Joseph wanted his brothers to bring their father Jacob to Egypt. He told them to rush home to get their father. He could hardly wait!

Then the great ruler, who was their brother Joseph, hugged Benjamin and cried, and he hugged and kissed all his brothers. After that they all talked together.

REMEMBER:

When Judah told the ruler of Egypt that he would take Benjamin's punishment, he was making a picture. It was a picture of Jesus, Who would be born from Judah's family. Jesus came to our earth to take **our** place and to take **our** punishment and die for **us** so that He could take us home to heaven with Him.

Jacob's Family Moves to Egypt

There was so much excitement in Joseph's house after he told his brothers, "I am Joseph," that the news soon spread to Pharaoh's house. People were saying, "Joseph's brothers have come!" Pharaoh was glad. Now he knew that Joseph was not a poor slave, but the son of Jacob, a great and rich man in the land of Canaan.

King Pharaoh gave some orders to the brothers: go to Canaan and load up your belongings and your animals; get your families and your father and bring them here to live; I have saved the best part of the land of Egypt where you may settle down. Joseph hurried to obey King Pharaoh. He gave his brothers wagons for all their goods and twenty animals loaded with food for the way. To each one he gave a set of new clothes, and to Benjamin he gave five sets and three hundred pieces of silver. He told them not to get into trouble on the way and sent them to Canaan.

All alone in Canaan, their father Jacob was waiting and waiting for his boys to come home. Don't you think he went outside and looked as far as he could down the road toward Egypt? Would Simeon be with them? Would Benjamin? Would all eleven boys come back to him? And when, finally, he saw the little specks of camels in the distance, don't you think he tried to count them to see if all his boys were coming safely home?

Yes, there were his eleven sons! Then they were all talking at once, but they were so happy and so excited Jacob could not make out what the good news was. What was this he was hearing? "Joseph is yet alive, and he is governor over all the land of Egypt." Jacob could not believe that! He was old, and the news was too much for him. He felt faint.

Then his boys told him the story slowly and clearly. At last they had to tell their father that they had lied to him and had sold Joseph into Egypt. The Bible does not tell us that they told their father how sorry they were for their terrible sin, but they must have asked him to forgive them. When Jacob saw their new clothes and the food and the wagons, he believed them. He said, "I will go and see Joseph before I die."

Jacob's boys had their own families and servants by this time, so a great many people had to pack to get ready to move to Egypt — seventy in all. At last they were loaded, and started the long, slow trip.

As he was traveling, Jacob was thinking. Was it right for him to move away from the land of Canaan, which was a picture of heaven? Would God be pleased with that? At a place called Beersheba he stopped and offered a sacrifice to God and God came to him and told him not to fear but to go to Egypt. God promised to make a great nation from Jacob's family in the land of Egypt and to bring them back to Canaan again.

When they came close to the land of Egypt, Judah went on ahead to tell Joseph that they were very near; and Joseph rushed to meet his old father, whom he had not seen for twenty-two years. What a happy time they had then!

King Pharaoh gave Jacob and his family a part of Egypt called the land of Goshen to live in. There they could live separately from the people of Egypt, who served idols; and there they could find pastures for their sheep.

For five more years the famine was over the whole earth. As the years went by, the famine became worse and worse. The farmers did not even try to plant seed anymore; and Joseph gathered all the people of Egypt into cities, so that he could pass out food easily, and nothing would be wasted. During all these years, Joseph took good care of his father and brothers. At the end of the famine, Joseph gave the people seeds to plant, and God made crops grow again.

Jacob lived seventeen years in Egypt, but at last he was so old and weak that he had to stay in bed. Then he called all his sons to him and blessed them before he died. When he died, all his sons mourned for him, and Joseph cried, for he loved his father deeply, mostly because he and his father both loved the Lord so much. After Jacob died, his sons kept a promise they had made to him, to bury him in the land of Canaan, with Abraham and Isaac.

REMEMBER:

Nowadays it does not matter where we are buried after we die. But in the days of the Bible, when God taught His people by pictures, they wanted to be buried in Canaan, which was a picture of heaven.

117

Three Hundred
Dark Years

After their old father Jacob had died, Joseph's brothers came to him because they were worried. They were afraid now that their father was dead, Joseph would hate them and pay them back because of all the evil they had done to him.

They said to Joseph, "Thy father did command before he died, saying, Forgive the trespass of thy brethren, and their sin; for they did unto thee evil; and now we pray thee, forgive the trespass of thy servants."

Joseph cried, because he had told them often that he **had** forgiven them; and he spoke very kindly to them. He said, "Fear not: for am I in the place of God? Ye thought evil against me, but God meant it unto good, to save much people alive."

For many years Joseph and his brothers lived in the land of Egypt until they became old men. Joseph lived to be one hundred ten years old. Before he died, he told his family that God would some day bring them back to Canaan, and he asked them to take his bones along with them and bury them in the land of Canaan.

Gradually all the sons of Jacob died in Egypt. Then only their children and grandchildren were living. So many children were born and so many families grew up that soon they became a great and strong nation of people. They were called **the people of Israel.** Do you remember that after God wrestled with Jacob He gave him the new name of **Israel**? Now all the thousands of people who were born from him were called the people of Israel, or **the Israelites.** Can you remember that?

The people of Israel still lived in the part of Egypt called the land of Goshen, but they were not all shepherds anymore. Some became farmers and others lived in cities. They still built altars and sacrificed lambs on them, and they knew they were making pictures of the sacrifice of Jesus on the cross. They still kept the sabbath day holy and used it to worship God in a special way. But they could not

read the Bible because there wasn't one yet. God did not come to talk with them as He did to Abraham, either. He did not send them dreams, as He did to Joseph. God was silent. . . quiet. . . for three hundred years. Three hundred dark, sad years! All God's people could do was sacrifice and remember.

King Pharaoh, the man who had been so kind to Joseph and his family, died, too. Another man became king; and though the people called all their kings by the name of Pharaoh, **this** Pharaoh was not kind and friendly to the people of Israel. He was afraid of them, for they were more and stronger than the people of Egypt; and he was afraid, if there was a war, the Israelites would join with the enemy and fight the Egyptians and run away from the land of Egypt. It seemed as if King Pharaoh was a very strange man: he was afraid of the people of Israel and yet he did not want them to leave. Why not? Because he wanted to use the Israelites to make him and his country rich.

Pharaoh thought he had a good plan to make the people of Israel stop growing so strong. It was not a good plan. It was a wicked plan. He made the people of Israel his slaves. Whether they wanted to or not, he told them they must make bricks out of straw and mortar and bake them in big ovens out in the open fields under the hot sun. With these bricks he ordered them to build big cities where he stored his weapons for war.

119

Other Israelites had to carry water from the Nile River and pour it over the fields to water them. If they could not carry the loads or if they complained about how heavy the loads were, Pharaoh ordered his men to whip them.

Pharaoh hoped that many of the Israelites would die because of the hard work. But the more mean and cruel he was, the more the people of Israel grew, and the stronger they became. Do you know why? God made them grow. It was a great wonder that He did for His people.

King Pharaoh was disappointed. The slave work was terrible for the Israelites, but it could not kill them. He needed another plan. This plan was even more wicked than his first one. He ordered the nurses who took care of the mothers when they had new babies to save the baby girls alive, but to kill all the baby boys, so that they could not grow up to be soldiers. But the nurses loved God and would not kill His children. They obeyed God and disobeyed the king. And God blessed them.

King Pharaoh was angry. That plan did not work either. He needed a third plan, which was the worst of all. He ordered that every boy that was born to the Israelites must be thrown into the Nile River and drowned, but every girl might be saved. That meant that daddies and mothers would have to take their own — and God's own — boy children and kill them with their own hands in the river, or have the Egyptians grab them and kill them. They **could** not obey Pharaoh.

Why did Pharaoh try so hard to kill the Israelites? Because Satan was in Pharaoh's heart, and Satan always wants to kill God's people.

Why did God send all these troubles to His people? So that they would cry and pray to Him, and beg Him to take them out of the evil land of Egypt and bring them back to Canaan.

REMEMBER:

The Bible says, "We ought to obey God rather than men." The nurses in Israel said it. All God's people say it. We do, too. In all of our lives, **God's** law comes first.

Moses is Born

What an unhappy time it was for God's people in Egypt! Do you remember that wicked King Pharaoh made a law that all the new baby boys who were born to the Israelites must be drowned in the river? Pharaoh sent his soldiers to stand guard and watch the people of Israel and snatch away the baby boys and drown them. No wonder God's people cried hard to Him and begged Him to let them leave the wicked land of Egypt and go back to the land of Canaan.

But it was not quite time yet. The people of Israel were in such a big hurry, and it seemed that God was working so slowly! But He knows everything and does everything at exactly the right time.

Right at this very dark, unhappy time, God gave a special, beautiful baby boy to an Israelite mother and father. This mother and father had a big girl, whose name was Miriam, and a little boy of three years old, whose name was Aaron. Do you think the mother and father were sad and afraid when their new baby boy was born? What if a soldier would find the baby and throw him into the river? No, this mother and father loved the Lord and trusted Him to take care of their baby.

For three months they hid him where no soldiers could find him, probably in a room in their house. But when his lungs became stronger and he cried loudly, they could not hide him anymore. They had a plan: they would obey the king in a special kind of way. The king had said to put the babies in the Nile River, and that is just what they would do. But they would not drown the baby!

Maybe the mother and father smiled to themselves as they made a basket-boat called an **ark** from weeds that grew along the edge of the river and then put something gummy like tar all over it to keep the water out of the little boat. Then the baby's mother laid him in the basket-boat near the weeds that grew at the edge of the water. Now he was in the river! That mother had so much faith and love for God that she trusted God to take care of her baby in this time of terrible danger. The baby's sister Miriam watched him from her place in the river's weeds.

Every day in this warm country of Egypt the princess, the daughter of
Pharaoh, came to take a bath and a swim in the river; and her maids came with
her to take care of her. As she walked along the riverside, she saw something
different in the water. A little basket! Quickly, she sent a maid to get it. When
she opened it, the baby cried. Was he hungry? Was he afraid? The princess'
heart melted. What a special, beautiful baby! She knew it was an Israelite baby,
and she knew that her wicked father ordered them all to be drowned. But she
liked this baby boy and wanted him for her own little boy. The princess was
probably spoiled and selfish and usually got what she wanted.

Just then Miriam, the baby's sister, ran up. Miriam was a girl who could
think very fast. When she heard that the princess wanted to keep the baby,
Miriam offered to find a lady from the Israelites to take care of the baby while
he was still small. When the princess said, "Go," do you know what lady Miriam
ran to find? The baby's own mother. I think his mother must have smiled to
herself as she met the princess and the princess said, "Take this child away and
nurse it for me, and I will give thee thy wages." The baby's mother would get
paid for taking care of her own baby. But the princess was the one who gave the
baby his name. She called him **Moses**, and that means "because I drew him out
of the water."

Some day Moses would be the great leader to take the Israelites out of Egypt, back to Canaan, and God was getting him ready for that. When he was small, he needed a mother who feared the Lord to teach him all about loving and trusting the Lord and keeping His laws. When he was older he would go to live with the princess, and she would take care of him so that he would always be safe from the wicked king's soldiers. God always works everything just right.

REMEMBER:

Moses' mother was so glad she could teach him about God when he was little. Our daddies and mothers are glad, too, that we stay little for quite a long time. Then they can teach us all the beautiful stories God has given us in the Bible.

Moses Runs Away
to the Desert

When he was old enough, Moses went to live in the king's palace, because the princess wanted him to be her son. He went to the very best schools in the land of Egypt and learned so well that when he grew up people called him a wise man. Moses had to learn many things before he could be the leader of the Israelites and take them back to Canaan. People watched when Moses, dressed like an Egyptian, rode through the streets on one of the king's horses. They would probably say, "There goes the son of the princess."

Moses was not happy about that. He was grown up now, forty years old already, and he would not be called the son of Pharaoh's daughter any longer. He was **not** an Egyptian. He was an **Israelite**. They were God's children, and so was he. He was a brother of the Israelites. Moses knew he had to leave the house of Pharaoh and go back to his own people.

When Moses visited the Israelites, he saw that one of his own people was being treated badly by a man from Egypt. The Egyptian was hitting him, beating him! This was the chance Moses was waiting for. After he looked both ways to make sure no one was watching him, he killed the Egyptian and buried him in the sand. Moses did not kill the Egyptian because he was very angry with him. No, Moses had a different reason for killing him. He knew that the Israelites would soon hear that Moses had killed one of their enemies, and then he was sure they would understand that he had come to save them from the cruel Pharaoh who made their lives so sad. Moses was sure his own people would understand that he chose **for** Israel and **against** Pharaoh. He was sure that now they would make him their leader, and he would save them and take them out of this wicked land. Do you think the people of Israel understood? Do you think they all gathered around him the next day with happy faces, ready to follow him?

Let us watch as he goes back to the Israelites the next day. There he saw two of his own people fighting one another. When Moses scolded them for fighting, one of them said, "Who made thee a prince and a judge over us? intendest thou to kill me, as thou killedst the Egyptian?"

Oh, how disappointed Moses was! Now he knew that his people did not understand at all. They were not ready to leave Egypt and go to Canaan. They were not ready to follow Moses, for God had not made their hearts ready. Do you know why this sadness and disappointment happened to Moses? Because he was trying to run ahead of God and lead the Israelites all by himself. He forgot to wait for God, Who does everything at exactly the right time.

Now what would poor Moses do? He could not go back to live with the king. When the king heard that Moses had killed an Egyptian, he would kill Moses. He could not go back to his own people, the Israelites, because they did not want him. The only place left to go was to the desert, a hot, dry, sandy land.

A sad, lonely Moses walked away from his people and walked all alone across the hot, dry desert until he came to a well of water. Seven girls, daughters of a priest who loved the Lord, came to the well to get water for their sheep. As they were getting water, some rough, impolite shepherds drove the girls away from the well. Moses did not like that! He stood up and drove away the cruel shepherds and helped the girls give water to their animals.

That night the girls came home earlier than usual. When Jethro, their father, asked them why they were finished so quickly, they told him about the man in the Egyptian clothes who helped them. And Jethro scolded them. He said, "And where is he? why is it that ye have left the man? call him that he may eat bread."

Moses was glad to go to Jethro's house and he lived there. God had led Moses to the God-fearing Jethro and made him happy there. He married one of Jethro's daughters and for many, many years Moses lived in the desert, taking care of Jethro's sheep. There in the desert Moses learned how to be humble and patient — to wait for God.

REMEMBER:

In school we learn many things, like reading and math and spelling. Moses learned those things in Egypt, too. But we learn many more things. We learn important things like loving God and obeying our parents. Moses had to learn important things, too. Do you know where he learned them? In his desert school, with God for his Teacher.

God Visits Moses in the Burning Bush

King Pharaoh in Egypt died, and another King Pharaoh sat on his throne. But the troubles of the Israelites did not get any better. They became worse. Sometimes the Israelites thought they could not stand the hard work and all the whippings they got. Then they cried to God and asked Him to take them back home to Canaan. God heard them and He remembered His promises to Abraham, to Isaac, and to Jacob, and to all their children, who were the Israelites. He was almost ready to save them out of Egypt.

Where was Moses all this time? He was still in the desert, watching the sheep of Jethro. He had lived in the desert for forty years, and now he was quite an old man of eighty years old, older than most of our grandfathers.

One day he was leading his sheep near a mountain, called Mt. Horeb, and as he was watching his sheep, he saw something very strange. A bush in the desert was burning, and flames of fire were coming from it, but the bush did not burn up. The fire could not burn it. Moses talked to himself, and said, "I will turn aside, and see this great sight, why the bush is not burnt."

Suddenly he heard a voice call, "Moses, Moses." He knew it was God's voice, and he answered, "Here am I."

The Lord told him not to come near to the bush and to take off his shoes, for the place where he was standing was holy. The holy God was there. When God told him that He was the God of Abraham and Isaac and Jacob, Moses

hid his face. He was afraid to look at God with his sinful eyes.

God was making a picture with the bush that would not burn. The bush was a picture of God's people in Egypt. The fire was a picture of the hard work and the sore backs and the cruel beatings they got because they were slaves. It hurt them just as fire hurts us! But, look! The fire could not burn up the bush, because God was in the middle of it. And God was right in the middle of His people, too. The wicked king could not hurt them much longer, for God was coming to save them.

God talked to Moses from the bush and told him to go to Egypt to King Pharaoh and tell him to let the people of Israel go.

Do you know what Moses answered? "Who am I that I should go?"

Many, many years ago, Moses had been ready to lead the people out of Egypt. But he had so much time to think when he was in the desert that now he knew that he could not be the leader of the Israelites. He was not strong enough. No man was. Only God was.

God knew how Moses felt, so He said, "Certainly I will be with thee." He gave Moses a sign, too. He said that on the way back to Canaan, all the people would come past this very mountain and stop to worship Him there.

Don't you think that Moses still felt all trembly inside because he was afraid to go to that wicked Pharaoh and afraid to take up the big work of leading the Israelites out of Egypt? He had questions in his mind. What if he told the Israelites that the God of their fathers sent him and they asked, "What is His name?" What should he tell them?

God made a beautiful answer for Moses. He said, "I Am That I Am." Do you know what that name means? That God never changes. He never needed to be born, and He will never die; and He always has all the power, and He will never stop loving His children.

Then God told Moses exactly what he must do when he went to Egypt. First he must go to his own people, the people of Israel, and tell them that I Am That I Am heard their cries and that He is ready now to save them and bring them back to Canaan.

Next Moses must go to Pharaoh and ask him to let the people go into the desert to sacrifice animals to God. But, God told Moses, Pharaoh would be stubborn and would not let them go. God would have to punish Pharaoh very hard before he would let them go.

REMEMBER:

Everything in our lives is changing. The days change to night, the weather changes from warm to cold, we change from little to big, and our daddies and mothers are changing from young to old. But our God never changes. He never gets old. He always stays the same. He will always love us.

Moses Talks Back to God

Moses was still standing by the burning bush in the desert. God had just finished telling him that it was time now to go to tell Pharaoh to let the people of Israel go. Moses would be their leader. He would take them back to Canaan.

Moses was standing there before the holy God, and he was afraid — afraid of the holy God and afraid of leading the Israelites. He **could** not be the leader of all those Israelites! It was too hard a work for him to do. He **could** not stand before King Pharaoh! What would he say to him? No, Moses did not want to do what God told him to do. But he did not dare to say no to the great God, either.

What did poor Moses do? He made excuses. That means he talked back to God and told him why he couldn't go to Egypt. Would you like to hear how Moses talked back to God? First he said, "They will not believe me, for they will say, The Lord hath not appeared unto thee." Moses was alone in the desert with the Lord. How could he prove that the Lord talked to him if the Israelites said, "Prove that God talked to you."

So God gave Moses three signs to prove it. Here is the first one. He asked Moses, "What is that in thine hand?"

Moses said, "A rod."

Every shepherd in those days carried a rod that he used to keep the sheep together. God said, "Cast it on the ground."

When Moses threw it on the ground, it became a serpent, a poisonous snake. Moses started to run away from it, but God told him to take it by the tail. When he caught it, the snake became a rod again, but not a shepherd's rod anymore. This time it was the rod of God's power, a wonder-rod.

God was making a picture when He told Moses to throw down the rod he used for his sheep. God was telling Moses, "Throw away your work as a shepherd; you're all finished with it." Do you know what that poisonous snake was a picture of? The devil. Now Moses had to go to the land of Egypt where the devil was working, where the devil made all kinds of trouble. But God told Moses he did not have to be afraid of the devil. This is why: Moses could pick up that snake by the tail and it would become God's powerful rod. **God** was going with Moses, and **He** would do all kinds of wonderful things, and **God** would lead the Israelites out of Egypt. Moses did not have to be afraid anymore.

God gave Moses another picture-sign. He said, "Put thine hand into thy bosom." That meant inside Moses' coat. When he pulled his hand out of his coat, it was full of the terrible sickness of leprosy, full of awful sores. That was another of God's pictures. Leprosy was a picture of sin — and that is where the Israelites were — in the sinful land of Egypt. But wait! God told Moses to put his hand back into his coat and pull it out again. This time his hand was all better. That was a picture of God making His people clean and holy and saving them from the sin of Egypt.

God gave one more picture-sign. When Moses came to Egypt, he must take water from the Nile River and pour it out on the land, and it would become blood. Blood is a picture of death. If you bleed and bleed, and lose all your blood, you will die, won't you? That blood meant that there would be death over all the land of Egypt. The whole land would die, for God would send many great punishments to the Egyptians.

What a lot of signs God gave to Moses! Do you think he felt better now? Would he trust God and say, "All right, Lord, I'll go?" No, he wouldn't. He talked back again. He said, "I am slow of speech, and of a slow tongue." Maybe Moses did have a little problem with his talking, but it was only an excuse. Listen to what God said: "**Who** hath made man's mouth? or who maketh the dumb, or deaf, or the seeing, or the blind?" God was scolding Moses. But our God is a very kind God and He promised Moses, "I will be with thy mouth, and teach thee what thou shalt say."

Now did Moses say, "All right, Lord?" No. He said, "Send by the hand of him whom Thou wilt send." That meant, "Don't send me." It was very wrong of Moses to say that to God, and God was angry with him. But God knew that Moses was a sinful man and that he was afraid; so He promised to send Moses' older brother, Aaron, to him. Aaron would do the talking.

Then Moses went home to Jethro and asked whether he might go back to Egypt, and Jethro answered, "Go in peace." Jethro was a wise old man and he must have understood that God had told Moses to go. Moses set out for Egypt with his wife and his two boys, with donkeys to ride on. But after they were on the way, Moses must have decided to send his family back home. It would be such a hard life for them in Egypt, and so dangerous. And Moses would be so busy. So Moses' wife and two boys went back to father Jethro until Moses would come back to them, leading the people of Israel on their way to Canaan.

REMEMBER:
The Lord said to Moses, "I will be with thy mouth, and teach thee what thou shalt say." That was a lesson for Moses. It is a lesson for us, too. Moses did not want to talk for the Lord. Sometimes we don't, either. Quite often we let our mouths talk silly talk or dirty talk, and we forget to ask God to be with **our** mouths, and to use them to talk about Him, to sing to Him, and to pray to Him.

131

Moses and Aaron
Come Before Pharaoh

After Moses had let his family go back to their father Jethro in the desert, God sent Aaron, his brother, to meet him. They had not seen one another for forty years. What happiness they had now as Aaron kissed Moses and they could talk together. Moses told Aaron all the words that God had said, and he showed Aaron the wonder-signs; and together they went back to the Israelites.

Moses had not seen his own people for forty years either. Would they listen to him this time? Would they believe? When the people of Israel came together, Aaron was the speaker. When he told them all the words of the Lord and showed them the signs God had given them, the people believed and bowed their heads and worshipped.

Now it was time to go to Pharaoh. Moses and Aaron asked a little favor of him, one he could easily give them. They asked whether the Israelites might travel for three days into the desert and sacrifice to the Lord and worship Him there. They had worked so hard as slaves, without a vacation, for years and years. Pharaoh could easily have said yes.

He **did** say, "Who is the Lord, that I should obey His voice? I know not the Lord." This does not mean that Pharaoh never heard of the Lord God of Israel. It means that he did not **want to** know Him. He wanted to say that there is no God.

Pharaoh was not a nice man at all. Don't you think he had a wicked smile on his face when he said that Moses and Aaron were keeping the people from their work? Maybe they did not have enough to do. He would take care of that. The Israelites were busy making bricks out of clay and straw mixed, and the cruel Pharaoh told the bosses over the Israelite workers not to bring them straw for the bricks anymore. They would have to hunt and hunt to find their own straw — in the corners of the fields or in the corners of the barns — but they still had to make the same number of bricks each day. Do you think they could do that? Oh, no — no matter how much they hurried!

That was not fair of the king. But that Word of God, "Let My people go," had made Pharaoh's heart hard.

Even though the people scrambled over the whole land to find straw, they could not make enough bricks; and the bosses of Egypt whipped the Israelites for something they could not help. The rulers of Israel went to Pharaoh and complained that it was not fair at all.

All Pharaoh said was, "Ye are idle." That means, "You are lazy. You do not have enough to do." He would not listen.

On their way out of the king's palace, the rulers of Israel met Moses and Aaron, and complained with sadness and anger about the trouble they had made. The rulers even said they hoped God would punish Moses and Aaron for making this trouble come upon the Israelites. Poor Moses was down in the dumps. It seemed to him that God was doing everything wrong. He asked God, "Why is it that Thou hast sent me? Thou hast not delivered thy people at all." Moses and the rulers of Israel could not see that God **first** had to make things worse, before He saved them.

God answered Moses with kind words. He told Moses He was his friend, and He was keeping His promises. But first God would send many punishments to the wicked Pharaoh.

Moses felt better then, but when he went to tell the Israelites, they would not listen, for they had so much hard work, so much suffering, and such hard beatings.

Then it was time for Moses and Aaron to stand before Pharaoh again. Before they went, God told them He would make Pharaoh's heart hard so that he would not listen and would not believe. God wanted to show His wonders and signs to that hard-hearted king so that all the people in Egypt would know that He is the Almighty God.

Pharaoh asked Moses and Aaron to show him a miracle. A miracle is a wonder. Aaron threw down the shepherd's rod, and it became a snake. Pharaoh called his wise men and they threw their rods down, too. Their rods became snakes, too! God let them do it, probably by the power of the devil. Just when they were ready to say, "See! We can do it, too!" Aaron's rod swallowed up all the other rods. Only the rod of the Almighty God's power was left in Aaron's hand. Pharaoh would not believe the Almighty God. He **knew** better, but he would not be humble before God.

REMEMBER:

God's Word made Pharaoh's heart hard, for he was not one of God's children. God's Word makes the hearts of His people soft, and ready to listen. You are listening to one of God's stories right now. Will you say thank-you to Him for making your heart soft?

God Sends the First Three Plagues

The people of Egypt had many gods. They worshipped the sun, the land, the animals, and the river. The Nile River was the most important thing in the life of the people of Egypt. They could water their crops from it, eat the fish they caught out of it, and travel on it in boats. It was their most important god.

Often King Pharaoh went out early in the morning to worship his god, the river. There he stood on the bank of the river, in his beautiful kingly clothes, a smart man who could rule over Egypt very well, but a foolish man because he would not listen to the Lord.

There, at the river, Moses and Aaron found him and met him with these words, "The Lord God of the Hebrews hath sent me unto thee, saying, Let my people go, that they may serve me in the wilderness."

Moses and Aaron told Pharaoh that if he would not let them go, the Lord would turn the water of the river into blood. When Pharaoh did not listen, God told Aaron to take the rod of God's power in his hand and stretch his hand over all the waters of Egypt: the rivers, streams, ponds, and pools. All that water turned into blood.

The king's wise men imitated Aaron and they, too, turned water into blood with their rods. We don't know just how, but God let them do it. But they could not take the blood away! No one in all the land had any water. People had to dig wells to get a little water to drink. All the fish in the river died, and the river stank. For seven days God kept blood instead of water in all the land of Egypt. We call this terrible punishment a **plague**.

Pharaoh went home and did not pay much attention to the plague, for his heart was hard against God. Pharaoh's god, the river that had drowned the baby boys of God's people, was full of blood. God showed Pharaoh that his god was dead.

God came to Moses again and told him to say to Pharaoh, "Thus saith the Lord, Let my people go, that they may serve me. And if thou refuse, I will smite all thy borders with frogs."

Again Aaron stretched out the rod of God's power over all the waters of Egypt and frogs came up out of the waters of the river and streams and ponds. The frogs went over the whole land: in their houses, in their beds, in their dishes and ovens, and on all the people, from the king down to the slaves. It was a horrible plague. No one could get away from the millions of frogs, jumping all over.

135

Once again, God let the king's wise men bring frogs from the river. The people of Egypt worshipped frogs, too. Now they had **too many** frog-gods, and they couldn't live with them! For a moment it seemed as if Pharaoh would give in and obey the Lord. He said if Moses would ask God to take the frogs away, he would let the people of Israel go.

Moses said, "When shall I intreat for thee and for thy servants and for thy people, to destroy the frogs?"

Pharaoh answered, "Tomorrow."

Moses said, "Be it according to thy word: that thou mayest know that there is none like unto the Lord."

Then Moses and Aaron asked the Lord to take away the plague of the frogs, and the Lord heard them. The next day He made all the frogs die. The people gathered them into piles, and once again the land stank. Do you think that Pharaoh kept his promise to let the people of Israel go? No! He made his heart hard.

Suddenly there was another plague over the land of Egypt. God did not tell Pharaoh that this one was coming. He just told Aaron to stretch his rod over the dust of the land and it became tiny bugs, called lice, that crawled over all the people and the animals. Everything was crawling with lice.

This time the king's wise men could not make lice out of the dust of the land. Their tricks did not work, for God did not let them work. He was saying to them: that's enough. These wise men knew that the Almighty God was sending these plagues, for they said, "This is the finger of God." But Pharaoh made his heart hard, as God had said he would.

REMEMBER:

We cannot explain how all these wonders happened. We do not know how water can change into blood and back to water again. We do not know where all the frogs and lice came from. But we **believe** that our great God did all these wonders.

God Sends Plagues Four, Five, and Six

After God had sent three terrible plagues on the people of Egypt, Pharaoh and his wise men knew that God had sent them, and they had to say, "This is the finger of **God**." Now God had to teach the people of Egypt another lesson: that He is **Israel's** God, the God of **His people.** Do you know how He did that? This story will tell you.

Early in the morning Pharaoh went down to the river to worship it. He thought he needed his river-god to take care of him when Moses came to him with the Word of the Almighty God. Wasn't Pharaoh a foolish man?

Moses came to Pharaoh with the same words from the Lord: "Let my people go, that they may serve me." If Pharaoh would not listen, God would send swarms of flies over all the land of Egypt. Pharaoh would not listen, of course, and God sent the flies. Moses did not even have to use the rod of God's power; for it was time for Pharaoh to know that the plague came, not by some kind of magic stick, but by the power of Israel's God. All kinds of flies filled the land of Egypt. They were on every thing the people touched, and clouds of them flew up with every step the people took. The land was filthy with them; and the Egyptians had to stop what they were doing because of the flies. But there was not one fly in the land of Goshen, where the people of Israel lived. From now on, God was going to show Pharaoh and his people that He is **Israel's** God, and Israel would not have any more of the plagues.

Pharaoh could not stand those flies! He called for Moses and Aaron and said he would let the people of Israel make sacrifices to God right in the land of Goshen if God would take away the flies. Moses and Aaron answered, "We will go three days' journey into the wilderness and sacrifice to the Lord our God."

At last Pharaoh gave in and said he would let the people of Israel go, but he asked Moses not to let them go very far away. Moses promised Pharaoh he would ask God to take away the flies **tomorrow**; only Pharaoh must not lie to him anymore.

Moses asked God to take away the flies, and He did. The next day God took **every one** of the flies away. Not one fly was left in Egypt. Did Pharaoh keep his promise to let the people go? No. He made his heart hard.

Once again Moses came to Pharaoh with the same command from the Lord: "Let my people go, that they may serve me." Moses came without his rod again, to show to Pharaoh that the next plague, too, was coming straight from God. In this plague, God put His hand on the animals of Egypt: the horses, donkeys, camels, cows, and sheep; and they became very sick. Many of them died. These

137

animals were the gods of the people of Egypt, and made them rich. Now God was taking away their gods and their riches.

King Pharaoh wondered about the animals of the Israelites. Were they sick and dying, too? So he sent a servant to Goshen, and the servant told Pharaoh that **not one** of the animals of the Israelites was dead; and Pharaoh's heart was hard.

The next plague just came. God sent it without any warning to Pharaoh. God told Moses to take handfuls of ashes in his hands. Do you know where these ashes came from? From the furnaces where the Israelites worked as slaves, making bricks. God told Moses to sprinkle those ashes up to heaven. Those ashes were a picture of the cries and the tears of the Israelites for all the beatings and sufferings that Pharaoh's servants had given them. The ashes sprinkled up to heaven were pictures of the people's cries going up to the Lord in heaven. The Lord answered those cries and sent the ashes back down on the Egyptians. They came down as terrible boils, deep sores all over their bodies. The sores were so awful that Pharaoh's wise men could not even stay standing before Moses and Aaron. All the people of Egypt and their animals had these big, painful sores. Pharaoh knew what the picture of the ashes meant. Do you think he was sorry and let the people of Israel go? Oh, no! God made his heart hard, and he would not listen to God. He did not let the people of Israel go.

REMEMBER:

Pharaoh knew that God is the God of His people Israel. He knew that Israel's God is **King**. But he did not love God. We know that God is King, too. And we love Him. We call Him by another name, too — a beautiful name. We call Him **Father**.

God Sends Plagues Seven, Eight, and Nine

King Pharaoh and his people had one more lesson from God to learn. This was the lesson: that He is the **only God**. Pharaoh and his people had many wicked idol-gods, but Moses' God and our God is the only God! Moses went to Pharaoh with these words from God: "I will send all my plagues upon thine heart and upon thy people; that thou mayest know that there is none like me in all the earth." But Pharaoh would not listen to the only God.

Then God told Moses to raise his rod toward heaven, and the Lord sent a terrible storm. Thunder and lightning and hail rained down on Egypt. Fire mixed with the hail crept wildly along the ground and burned down the plants and the trees and the barley crops that were growing in the fields. No one in Egypt had ever seen such a fierce storm before.

God had warned the people before the storm came that He would send the storm; and He told the people to come in out of the fields and to take their animals in with them. Those who listened to God's words came in. The rest of the animals and people died in the storm. But the land of Goshen, where the Israelites lived, had no storm at all.

This storm was too much for Pharaoh! He called for Moses and said, "I have sinned this time: the Lord is righteous and I and my people are wicked. Intreat the Lord that there be no more mighty thunderings and hail; and I will let you go."

Moses gave Pharaoh this sign: as soon as he was outside the city, he would ask God to stop the terrible storm. And God did. Do you think Pharaoh was really sorry that he sinned? Do you think he kept his promise? No.

Before God sent the next plague, He sent Moses and Aaron to talk to Pharaoh and his servants. These were the words God told them to say: "How long wilt thou refuse to humble thyself before me? let my people go, that they may serve me."

Then God let Moses tell how awful the next plague would be. God would

send grasshoppers that would eat everything that grew in the land of Egypt that was still left after the terrible storm. Those grasshoppers would fill the houses of all the people. It would be a plague that they could not stand!

But wicked Pharaoh did not seem to pay any attention to the words of Moses and Aaron. After Moses and Aaron left, his servants were so worried that they begged Pharaoh to let Israel go, so they would not get the next plague. To please his servants, Pharaoh called Moses and Aaron back, and told them to go and serve the Lord. Then he said **but** who will go? When Moses said that **everyone** of God's people — all the women and children, too — must go, Pharaoh said no. He would let only the men go; and the angry Pharaoh chased Moses and Aaron out of his palace.

All that day and all that night God sent a strong east wind, and the next morning the wind brought the grasshoppers, clouds of grasshoppers, so many that the land was dark with them. They ate everything in their paths, the grass and leaves and crops from the fields and every crumb of food from the houses. As the waves of millions of grasshoppers went over the land, they left it brown and bare, without any food, and the people of Egypt knew that many of them would starve to death.

Then Pharaoh was afraid. In a big hurry he called for Moses and Aaron and said, "I have sinned against the Lord your God. Intreat the Lord your God that he may take away from me this death."

God sent a very strong west wind, and it blew all the grasshoppers out of the land of Egypt and into the Red Sea. Not one grasshopper stayed in Egypt. But God made Pharaoh's heart hard, and he would not let Israel go.

Without telling Pharaoh about the next plague, God told Moses to stretch out his rod toward heaven, and God sent a thick, black darkness over all the land of Egypt. This special kind of darkness was the kind of darkness that was on the earth before God made the light on the first day. The people of Egypt could not turn on any lights, because no light would come through this kind of darkness. The Egyptians could hardly live in that darkness, because people need **light** in order to live. That darkness was God's picture of the terrible darkness of hell. For three days and nights that awful darkness was over the land of Egypt. Don't you think all the people, especially the little children, were crying and afraid? And no one could help anyone else.

But in the houses of the people of Israel God put a special light. It shone out of their houses into the black darkness outside. The light that God shone only on His people was a great wonder.

REMEMBER:

The light that God shone inside the homes of the Israelites is a picture of the light He shines in our hearts. **Jesus** is our Light. He saves us from our sins and leads us to heaven, where there will never be any more darkness.

God Sends the Last Plague

After the plague of darkness, Pharaoh called Moses once more and told him to go out to the desert with the people of Israel to serve the Lord. But their animals must stay home. When Moses said, "Our cattle also shall go with us," Pharaoh became very angry and said, "Take heed to thyself, see my face no more; for in that day thou seest my face thou shalt die."

Moses answered, "I will see thy face again no more."

But Moses was not quite finished talking to Pharaoh. He told about the last plague that God would send over Egypt — the worst one. One night, at midnight, someone would die in every family in Egypt. It would be the firstborn, the oldest child in every family, from Pharaoh's oldest child to the oldest child of his poorest servant. And the firstborn of all the animals would die, too. Every family would have to dig a grave for their oldest child. But no one in Israel would die. The Lord would not let even a dog move his tongue against them. That would be the difference between Egypt and Israel in that night. Moses said that after the firstborn died, Pharaoh would **tell** the Israelites to leave. He would almost **chase** them out of the land!

After Moses told Pharaoh all these things, he left him in great anger and never saw Pharaoh again.

Now it was time to teach the people of Israel how to get ready to leave Egypt. First, each family had to find a lamb, a perfect lamb, one without any spots or any sickness, and separate it from the rest of the lambs. Moses taught the people that the lamb was a picture of the Perfect Lamb of God, Who is **Jesus.**

After four days, each family had to kill its lamb and catch the blood in a basin. Then they must find a branch with some leaves on it and dip the branch into the blood and smear the blood on the two sides of their door and on top of their door. Why do you think each family had to do that? It was a picture that the blood of Jesus that spilled on His cross was covering them and would save them.

Next, they must roast the lamb whole over a fire. If the lamb was too big for one family to eat, they might share it with their neighbor's family. When they ate the roasted lamb, they must eat a bitter-tasting sauce with it. That bitter-tasting sauce was a picture of all the sadness and suffering they had tasted when they were slaves in Egypt.

There would not be time to sit down to eat. They must eat standing up and must be all packed, ready to move out of Egypt; for at midnight God would send

His angel of death over the land of Egypt to kill the firstborn child in every family.

That night, at midnight, everyone in Egypt got up, with a great cry; for they said, "We are all dead men!" There was not a house where someone was not dead.

But in Goshen, where Israel was, the angel of death passed over the houses with blood over their doors. No one was killed in those houses. Do you know what the Israelites called that night? The **passover**, because the angel of death **passed over** them.

Then the Egyptians made the people of Israel hurry. They were so sad and afraid they wanted the Israelites to leave right away. As they almost **pushed** them out of their land, the Lord made them want to give the Israelites all their expensive, beautiful jewelry, their silver, and their gold, until the Egyptians had none left.

In rows of five, the Israelites made a long, long parade as they left the land of Egypt. God told them it was a night they must always remember. It was a night of a great wonder. Such a night would never happen again. As they marched out, five by five by five, the Israelites were making a picture again. They were leaving Egypt, which was a picture of the house of sin, which God hated, and they were going back to Canaan, which was a picture of the house of His love.

REMEMBER:

We are on our way to Canaan, too. Another name for Canaan is heaven. In heaven we will live with God in love forever.

Israel Goes Through the Red Sea

Even though all the people of Israel were in a great hurry to get out of Egypt, they did not forget to keep a promise they had made long ago. They took the bones of Joseph, who had died many, many years before, and carried them along to the land of Canaan, so that they could bury them there.

None of the people of Israel had ever been to the land of Canaan before. How could they find the way? **God** showed them the way. **He** was their leader. During the day He led them by a pillar of cloud, and during the night, when it was too dark for them to see a cloud, He led them by a bright pillar of fire, which they could easily see.

God chose the way He wanted His people to go. He wanted to lead them through the hot, dry desert on their way to Canaan. Why did God choose the desert way? It was very lonely and quiet in the desert, and God wanted His people to learn all about His rules — we call them His laws — there. God would be their teacher in the desert. There was another reason, too. Do you remember that, quite a long time ago, God had promised Moses that He would lead His people past the mountain of the burning bush? Now God was ready to keep His promise, for the mountain was in this desert.

The path on the way out of Egypt was not a very easy one. The people of Israel were carrying heavy loads and all their animals were traveling with them. On each side of them were mountains of rocks. And God was leading them straight toward a big sea of water, called the Red Sea. Just when the people of Israel were ready to complain to God that they could **never** cross over all that deep water, something even worse happened.

Shall we go back to Egypt to see what it was? Back in Egypt, all the funerals for the oldest child of every family were over, and King Pharaoh was feeling sorry that he had let the Israelites go. Now he would not have any more slaves to work for him. He said to his servants, "Why have we done this, that we have let Israel go from serving us?"

Maybe he could still get them back! Quickly he made ready his soldiers and his special carts for war, called **chariots**, which his war horses pulled, and he chased the Israelites.

Now the Israelites knew they were trapped. On each side of them were mountains they could not climb. In front of them was a deep sea they could not cross. Behind them they heard the noise of Pharaoh and his soldiers and chariots and war horses coming to take them back to Egypt. They could not win a fight with Pharaoh, either. Oh, whatever would they do?

They did the wrong thing. They looked **around** them instead of **up**. They looked at the mountains and the sea and the soldiers instead of looking to the great God of the wonders of all those plagues in Egypt. And they grumbled to Moses. Some of the Israelites trusted in the Lord, and they knew that He would save them. They were right, for God came to Moses and said, "Fear ye not, stand still, and see the salvation of the Lord, which he will show to you today." Then He told the people to keep marching forward, for they would never see Pharaoh again.

The Lord moved the pillar of cloud and put it between the Israelites and the Egyptians. The side toward Egypt was a cloud of pitch black darkness so they could not see through it to find the Israelites. The side toward Israel gave the bright light of God's fire.

Then night came. God told Moses to stretch his rod over the waters of the Red Sea, and God made a strong east wind to blow all that night. That wind was a wonder from God which made the water separate and make a high wall of water on each side, and a dry path of sand right in the middle of the Red Sea. God's great wonder made those walls of water stand straight, so that the people of Israel could go through the sea on the dry path. They had faith in God that He would not let the walls of water tumble down on them. All that night they marched through the Red Sea on dry ground.

Toward morning Pharaoh and his army saw what was happening and he decided to follow the Israelites on the dry path. Foolish, wicked Pharaoh walked right into the middle of the sea. When all the Israelites were on the other side, God began to bother the wheels of Pharaoh's chariots, so that they came off. Pharaoh and his soldiers could not go any farther! When they tried to turn around and run back to Egypt, it was too late. Moses stretched his hand over the sea, and the walls of water fell down and drowned Pharaoh and his soldiers, every one of them. All the people of Israel saw that great wonder, and they feared the Lord and believed Him.

REMEMBER:

The Lord led the people of Israel with a pillar of cloud and a pillar of fire. Do you know how He leads us? With the Bible. He tells us that the Bible is the light on our path.

Israel Travels Through the Desert

What a happy morning it was for the people of Israel! At last they were free from all the wicked Egyptians, and safe on the other side of the Red Sea. Moses taught the people a song about the wonder of crossing the Red Sea. It was a song of praise to God. Would you like to hear some of the words of the song? They sang: "The Lord is my strength and song. Pharaoh's chariots and his host hath he cast into the sea; they sank to the bottom as a stone. The Lord shall reign for ever and ever."

Miriam, the sister of Moses, and some of the other women of Israel played music on timbrels and all the people sang to the music of the timbrels. What a glad day of praise to God it was!

But they could not stay at the shore of the Red Sea. It was time to start their long walk through the desert to get to the land of Canaan. The desert they were in was called **The Wilderness of the Wall.** It was called The Wilderness of the Wall because on one side of them was the Red Sea and on the other side was a rough, high wall of rocky mountains. The ground underneath their feet was not smooth sand, but it was stony and uneven. They had to watch out for holes and for poisonous snakes which lived in the desert. All day long the hot sun beat down on them. It was quiet and lonely and dangerous in this wild, rocky desert, making the people tired and afraid. But they did not have to be afraid, for God was with them.

After they had traveled for three days in the heat, all the water they had taken from Egypt was gone. Where would they find water in this dry desert? Not very much farther they found a place with water. But their happiness changed to grumbling after the first few people tasted it. They had to spit it out. They could not drink it, it tasted so bad. And they called the place **Marah,** which means **bitter.**

Now all their songs of happiness were gone, and the people grumbled to Moses and said, "What shall we drink?" Moses cried to the Lord, and He showed him a tree, which Moses threw into the waters; and they became sweet and good to drink.

The Bible says that God was **testing** His people at Marah. How was God testing them? They had just seen all God's wonders in the plagues on Egypt and in the crossing of the Red Sea. **Then** they could sing happy songs of praise. **Now**, when they were hungry or thirsty or scared, the Lord was teaching His people not to grumble but to run to Him for help. They saw a picture right in front of their eyes. Those bitter waters of Marah were a picture of the troubles they would have in the desert. When the tree made the waters sweet, they saw a picture of God making all their troubles better. God was teaching them always to trust Him — with happiness in their hearts.

After they had passed Marah, the people came to Elim, where they found twelve wells of water and seventy palm trees. What a beautiful spot to stop to rest awhile. The Israelites stayed at Elim for about a month — about thirty days. Then they traveled on again.

Soon all the food they had taken from Egypt was gone, and they forgot all about the lesson God had taught them at Marah. Instead, they complained to

Moses with angry words. This is what they said: "Would to God we had died by the hand of the Lord in the land of Egypt, when we sat by the flesh pots, and when we did eat bread to the full; for ye have brought us forth into this wilderness to kill us with hunger."

We should remember that not everyone of the Israelites was one of God's true children. God's true children in Israel did not grumble. They trusted Him and prayed.

The Lord took care of all the people, even those who complained to Moses; and He gave them bread and meat. In the evening He sent birds — smaller than chickens — called quails, which they could catch and cook and eat. In the morning He rained bread from heaven and He scattered it on the ground for all the people. When the people woke up in the morning and saw the bread that looked like small white seeds all over the ground, they said, "Manna!" That means, "What is this?" And it tasted so good, like wafers or crackers made with honey. They could pick it up from the ground and eat it, or they could boil it and bake it into little cakes.

God gave the rules for the manna. Every morning God would rain it from heaven, and the people might gather enough for only one day. If they picked up too much, it would spoil and get worms in it. On the sixth day they had to gather twice as much manna — enough for the seventh day, too, for that was God's holy day. On that day God would send no manna.

Wasn't God good to His people? When they could not get food in that terrible desert, He rained it down every morning. He taught His people to trust Him for their food each day. He teaches us that, too.

REMEMBER:

Quite often we are hungry and thirsty, aren't we? Then we need food, just as the people of Israel did. The Bible tells us that our souls — inside of us — are hungry and thirsty, too — for Jesus' goodness and salvation. The Bible calls Jesus the Bread of Life.

God Gives Water From the Rock

After the people of Israel walked three more days, they came to Rephidim. Rephidim was not a beautiful resting place as Elim had been. All they saw there was a big, bare rock, standing high and alone. There was no grass. There were no trees. There were no wells. It was hot. And they were so thirsty.

God knew that there was no water near this hot desert rock, but He led the people there anyway. Do you know why? So that they would trust **Him** to give them water. Did the people trust Him? Listen to what they said to Moses: "Give us water." They did not pray, they would not wait for God, even though He had just given them the wonderful gift of manna. Do you know what else the people said? "Is the Lord among us, or not?"

Moses answered, "Why chide ye with me? Wherefore do ye tempt the Lord?"

As the people became more thirsty, they became more angry with Moses. They **did** blame him. They asked him why he brought them out of Egypt to kill them and their animals with thirst. And they looked around for stones to throw at Moses.

Oh, how could those people forget to trust in God? How could they forget all the wonders that He poured down on them? Not **all** the people of Israel forgot to trust in God. Some of them quietly prayed to God for help.

Moses prayed, too, and asked God what he should do with the people, who were ready to throw stones at him; and God answered him. God stood on that high, flat rock. Probably He stood in the pillar of cloud on the rock; and He told Moses to hit the rock with the rod of God's power. When Moses hit the rock, water — streams of it — flowed from that hot, dry rock. Everyone could see that **Moses** did not give them water, but **God** did. It was a great wonder. And it was a picture. The rock was a picture of our Lord Jesus Christ, Who is **The Rock**, and Who gives us living water. Do you know what living water is? It is not the water we usually drink, but it is Jesus' promise to save us from our sins and bring us to heaven to live with Him forever. Never forget to trust Jesus for that living water.

When streams of water flowed from that hot, dry rock, the people rushed forward to get water for themselves and for their animals. Not everyone could get to the water at once. They had to take turns; and some of the old people, and the sick people, and those who were tired were the last ones to get to the stream of water.

When those people finally came to the water, they ran into a terrible danger. Wicked enemies came running out of the desert to fight them. These wicked enemies were soldiers from the country of Amalek. They had run all the way from their own country, through the desert, to bother the Israelites. Why would they do that? Because they hated God and they hated God's people. They wanted to kill God's people. And these wicked soldiers purposely waited until the old and the sick and the tired people were getting water. Then they sneaked up from behind to fight them. They were not brave enough to fight the strong soldiers in Israel. We call people like that **cowards.**

Now God called the people of Israel to fight back. Moses chose a young man named Joshua to lead the soldiers of Israel to fight the soldiers of Amalek. What did Moses do? He went to the top of a hill with the rod of God's power in his hand. It showed all the people that they were fighting, not by Moses' power, not by Joshua's power, but by **God's** power; for when Moses held the rod high, Israel won, and when he put it down, Israel lost the fight, and Amalek won.

Did you ever try to hold a rod up high over your head with both your hands? For a long, long time? Your arms just won't stay up. Poor Moses' arms were too tired to hold up that rod. But he **had** to hold it up. Do you know how he did it? His brother Aaron and a man named Hur were on the hill with Moses. They set Moses on a stone and each man stood on one side of Moses and held up one of his arms for him. They stayed that way until the sun went down and it was too dark to fight. Israel won the fight with Amalek, by God's power.

Then Moses wrote the story of Amalek in a book, so that everyone would remember it; for the Lord wanted the people of Amalek killed, because they were a picture of the devil and his wickedness. Moses did one more thing. He built an altar and called it **Jehovah-nissi,** which means, "Jehovah is my flag!"

151

REMEMBER:

A flag tells what country we live in. In our country of America we have a red, white, and blue flag. But we have a much more important flag — the same one Moses had. He said, "Jehovah is my flag." Jehovah is a beautiful name for God. Jehovah is **our** flag, too. He rules us, and we live all our lives to please Him; and when we die, we will go to His country. It is called heaven.

Israel Comes to Mount Sinai

Day after day the Israelites traveled on in the hot, lonely desert until they came to a mountain called the mountain of God. It is also called Mount Sinai. This was the mountain where God had talked with Moses out of the burning bush. Do you remember that? God had promised Moses that His people would come back to the mountain on their way to Canaan. And here they were!

They set up their tents around the mountain and stayed a long time — more than a whole year — for God was going to teach them many things while they were here at Mt. Sinai. The Israelites had just come out of the land of Egypt, the land of sin and idol-gods. Some of the Israelites worshipped idol-gods and did some of the same sins the Egyptians did. Now it was time for God to teach all the people of Israel how to worship **Him**, how to obey **Him**, how to love **Him**, and how to serve **Him** only. For He is the only God, the great and holy God.

First God called Moses to the top of the mountain and told him what to say to the people. Because God is so pure and holy, and because His people were covered inside and outside with all their sins, He could not let the people come close to His holy mountain. God told Moses to make a fence between God and the people. Moses told the people to scrub themselves and wash their clothes clean, for in three days the Lord Jehovah would come down to talk to them. Making themselves clean on the **outside** was a picture of being sorry for their sins and being clean on the **inside**.

Then God came down to the top of the mountain in a thick cloud. On the morning of the third day, God made thunder and lightning on the mountain, and a thick cloud covered the top of the mountain. The mountain smoked so much that it looked like the smoke of a great furnace was going up, and the people heard the loud voice of a trumpet. As the trumpet-sound became louder and louder, the whole mountain shook with a great earthquake. The people were so frightened when they saw the wonders of their great and holy God that they trembled and shook. All those wonders were almost too much for them to see.

God called Moses up into the mountain again, but soon He sent him back down to tell the people to stay back, behind the fence; for they might not get close to see God's pure holiness. They would die if they did. So Moses went down again, and then God talked to His people. What did He say to them? He

told them the rules they must follow to serve Him. He told them the things they **must** do and the things they **must not** do. We call those rules God's **law,** or the **Ten Commandments.** God gave those commandments to us, too. They are the rules for our lives. Would you like to know what they tell us?

God told the Israelites — and us — to worship Him only. We may not have any other kinds of gods to trust in or to pray to; and we may not make any pictures of God, for He is too high and holy. We cannot see Him with our sinful eyes, and we cannot make pictures of His holiness.

God told the Israelites — and us — to keep His great name very holy, to talk about Him very seriously and very reverently, and never to use His precious name in a wicked way, by swearing.

God told the Israelites — and us — to keep His special day holy. **Sunday** is His special day: to go to church, to pray to Him, to sing His praises, to hear His Words from the Bible, to love Him, and to be happy that He is our Father.

God told the Israelites — and us — to love and obey our fathers and mothers because **God** put them over us to teach us how God wants us to live. God will not let us do what **we** want. That is not good for us. We must do what **God** wants; and our daddies and mothers know how God wants us to live.

God told the Israelites — and us — never to kill anybody, not even to hate anyone in our hearts. He told us to keep our bodies pure and our minds clean from all dirty thoughts and our mouths clean from all dirty words. He told us not to steal — that means to take things that do not belong to us — not even to sneak a penny from mother's purse or a cookie from the cookie jar.

God told the Israelites — and us — that we must always tell the truth. God hates lies. He hates it, too, when we say bad things about other people. And God ended His law by telling the Israelites — and us — not to wish for all kinds of things that we do not have, not to want all the nice things that we see in this world, but God told us to wish for the very best things. What are the very best things? They are God's love and His kindness and His saving us from our sins. Do you know what happens when we have the best things from God? We are happy. We are happy with the sunshine and the rain, with the snow and with the hot summer days, we are happy to sing to God, and we are happy that Jesus took our sins away. Are you happy?

REMEMBER:

It is not easy at all for us to keep all these commandments of God, and we cannot do it by ourselves. Every day we must ask God to help us to do what He wants us to do. When we ask Him, He answers, and He helps us.

Israel Worships the Golden Calf

The people of Israel heard the voice of Jehovah their God when He talked from the top of Mt. Sinai and when He told them all the words of His law; but the people were afraid when they saw God's great glory and when they heard His great voice sounding like a trumpet. They were afraid to listen. They asked Moses to go up to the top of the mountain alone and listen to all God's rules and tell them after he came down again. Moses went up the mountain to God and stayed there for forty days and forty nights.

While Moses was at the top of the mountain, God wrote the ten commandments for the Israelites with His own finger on two big stones. He taught Moses many, many more things, too. He told how the people of Israel must worship Him; what their church must look like, and what they must do when they went to church; and He gave the rules for building it.

The people of Israel stayed at the bottom of the mountain all the days that Moses was with God in the cloud at the top of the mountain; and the days seemed so long for the Israelites. They just waited and waited.

When they were too tired of waiting, many of the people came to Aaron and said, "Make us gods, which shall go before us." They wanted Aaron to make an idol, like the ones they worshipped in Egypt. They said they did not know what had happened to Moses. Do you think they **really** did not know? All they had to do was look up, and they would see the cloud where God and Moses were.

Aaron was not a strong leader as Moses was. He should have scolded the people for even **asking** for an idol. He did not scold. He asked them for their beautiful golden jewelry to use to make the idol. Maybe he thought they would not give it away. But they did. Those wicked Israelites were ready to give it all away so that they could sin.

Did Aaron tell them **now** how wicked they were? No. He melted all that gold and made the shape of a calf — a baby cow — from the gold, and told the people, "These be thy gods, O Israel, which brought thee up out of the land of Egypt."

Aaron and the people said **no** to God and **yes** to an idol made of gold. They said that even when they could see the wonders of God all around them: they were getting God's manna every morning; the mountain was still shaking with God's holiness; and God's thick cloud was above them. They knew better, but they did not **believe**. They did not **want** God. They took off their clothes and danced sinful dances to the golden calf; and they ate and drank and played. Not everyone of the Israelites worshipped that idol-calf. Don't you think those who truly loved God with all their hearts went home and cried about all that wickedness?

The people of Israel knew that God could see them, but they did not care. **God** cared. He told Moses what the people were doing and told him to hurry down the mountainside. This is what God called them: a stiff-necked people. Their necks were so stiff with sin that they would not turn to the Lord. God was

so angry with them that He said He would burn them all up, and start over to make a new people from Moses' family.

Was Moses happy about that? Oh, no! He begged the Lord to turn away from His anger; and he reminded the Lord of His promise to Abraham and Isaac and Jacob to make this great nation from **their** children. Then the Lord turned His anger away from the people and did not burn them up.

Moses went down the mountainside, carrying the two big stones that had the law of God written on both sides, the law that God had written with His own finger. Part way down, Moses met Joshua, who was there, waiting for him. Joshua heard the noise in the camp of the people of Israel and thought it sounded like the noise and shouting of war; but Moses told him it was the sound of a party, a party to an idol god.

Can you think how sad and angry Moses felt as he and Joshua hurried down the mountain? What would they see when they came to the Israelites? There it was! The golden calf, and the people dancing around it! Moses' anger was so hot when he saw the terrible sin that he threw down the stones of the law and broke them, a picture of the people of Israel who were breaking God's law by serving an idol. Next he burned the golden calf, ground it up to powder, put it into the people's water, and made them drink it. Then he scolded Aaron.

As Moses looked over the Israelites, he saw many people, still naked and dancing; and he called out, "Who is on the Lord's side? let him come unto me."

Some of the people of the family of Levi came, and Moses told them to take their swords and punish those wicked sinners by killing them. About three thousand people died that day.

Now poor Moses was so sad. He felt so bad that the people had sinned such a great sin. There was only one thing to do: pray to God to forgive their sins. Moses asked whether he might take the punishment instead of the people of Israel, whether he might go to hell instead of them — so much he loved them. But God said no.

REMEMBER:

When Moses wanted to take the punishment instead of the Israelites, he was a beautiful picture of Jesus. **Moses** could not save the people from their sins. He was only a man. God sent His own Son, **Jesus,** to take the punishment of sin for all His people. He took that punishment on the cross where He died to save us.

The Israelites Build the Tabernacle

After the people of Israel sinned by worshipping the golden calf, many of them were very sorry. They were sad and they cried. Moses asked God to forgive their sins; and God, Who is full of love and mercy to His people, forgave them and took their sins away.

Then the people had to get busy. It was time to build the place where they would worship God: their church. God had given all the rules about it to Moses in the forty days when he was at the top of the mountain. The church of the Israelites in the desert would not look one bit like the churches we go to. It was called a **tabernacle.** Do you know what a tabernacle looks like? A tent. They **had** to worship God in a tent, because they were traveling to the land of Canaan and every time they started walking, they had to pick up the tent and carry it with them.

Before they started building it, Moses chose two men who were very good workers to take charge of the work of building the tabernacle. Next, Moses asked the people to give some of their most precious things to use for the tabernacle: golden bracelets and rings and earrings, beautiful stones, sweet-smelling perfumes, fine wood and cloth. And, with willing hearts, the people of Israel brought more than Moses needed to build the tabernacle.

Shall we watch the people of Israel as they got busy building the tabernacle? They made a big yard, called a courtyard — about as big as the yards of four houses. The men made high fence posts out of fine wood for this big courtyard, and the women used fine white thread to make tall white curtains all around it. When the men set up the fence posts and tied the pure white curtains between them, they made a high wall. No one could see over it into the courtyard.

There was a door, of course; and that was a white curtain, too. On the door curtain the women sewed beautiful patterns of blue, purple, and red thread. If they pushed the door curtain aside and went into the courtyard, they would have no roof over them. The sky was their roof. The floor was the sand of the desert.

Inside the courtyard was a very big square altar. The people built it from wood and covered it with shiny brass. On top of the altar they made a grill something like we have on our barbecue grills, and on this grill the priests would offer lambs to be burned to God. Who were the priests? They were God's

ministers who worked in His tabernacle. When the tabernacle was finished, the priests would offer a lamb to God, a picture of Jesus dying for their sins. But when the priests killed the lamb and burned it, their hands would be dirty, and they would need a place to wash them. God told them to make a very big bowl to hold water for washing themselves and the animals. The bowl was beautiful. Do you know what it was made of? Shiny, silvery metal that the women used for mirrors. They gave their mirrors for God's house.

The most important part of the tabernacle is still coming. Inside the courtyard the workers had to build a tent with two rooms in it. They made a roof over this tent of beautiful cloth covered with the skins of animals, to keep the inside of the tent dry and clean. The women made a beautiful curtain for the doorway of this tent, too, with designs of blue, purple, and red sewed on it.

In the first room of the tent were three small pieces of furniture. The workers built a small golden table with a tiny golden railing around it. On that table they would keep twelve loaves of bread. That table of bread was a picture of Jesus, for Jesus is the Bread of Life. Then they made an altar from wood, much smaller than the one in the courtyard, and covered it with gold. They made incense from the sweet-smelling spices and perfumes the people brought to them. They could burn this incense to God; and it was a picture of the prayers of God's people going up to heaven and smelling very sweet to Him. The third piece of furniture they made in this room was a golden lampstand with seven little bowls of oil burning brightly to God. The lampstand was a picture of God's people, who are the light of the world, and who let it shine out in the world. This first room was called the Holy Place, and after it was finished, only the priests might go into it.

In the other room of the tent the workers built a small wooden box and covered it with gold. On the top they made two golden angels with their wings spread out. It must have been beautiful! This box was called the ark. Inside that ark Moses would put the stones with the ten commandments written on them. This room was called the Most Holy Place, and only **one** priest might go into it only **once** a year. Then he would sprinkle that ark with blood, a picture of the blood of Jesus, which He shed to wash our sins away.

The women made white robes with blue, purple, red, and gold designs for the priests to wear when they worked in the tabernacle. On their heads the priests wore hats with these words on them: "Holiness to the Lord." The priests taught the people to worship in holiness to the Lord.

All these beautiful things that the people of Israel made for the tabernacle were pictures, pictures of God's church in heaven, and pictures of Jesus, Who saved His people to take them to that church in heaven.

REMEMBER:

Our churches are different from the tabernacle. We do not need those pictures anymore. But we have the same Jesus that the Israelites had. We are all saved by His blood.

Two Sins at Sinai

After half a year of hard work with willing hands and hearts, the Israelites finished the tabernacle. Now they had a special place to worship God. God showed the people how very special the tabernacle was, for His cloud came down and rested on the tabernacle, and His glory filled it. His glory was so bright and holy that Moses could not even go into the tabernacle.

The people of Israel must have been so happy! They had such a beautiful house where they might worship their God. But their happiness did not last very long.

Not everyone in Israel loved all those pictures of heaven in the tabernacle. Not everyone wanted to listen to God and do what He told them to do. Two very bad sins crept into the hearts of some of the Israelites just before they were ready to leave Mt. Sinai and go on to Canaan.

You remember, don't you, that only the priests, who were God's ministers, could offer sacrifices to God and work in His tabernacle. God chose **Aaron and his sons** to be priests. Two of Aaron's sons were called Nadab and Abihu. They were priests with Aaron. But they were priests who did not love God. They were the men who sinned.

The awful sin happened probably on the very first day that they offered sacrifices in the beautiful new tabernacle that they had just finished building. It should have been a happy day — a celebration! It wasn't.

Nadab and Abihu did not obey God's rules. God told them, in His rules, that when they lit the sweet-smelling incense in the Holy Place, they must use some of the fire from the altar where the lambs were burned. The **blood** of the

lambs was in that fire, and that blood was a picture of Jesus' blood. They **had** to go into God's Holy Place with a picture of Jesus' blood.

Nadab and Abihu did not do that. They used fire, just ordinary fire, from somewhere else, to light the incense. By doing that, they said they would serve God **their own** way, not God's way. They did not want God's altar-fire, and they did not want to come to God with Jesus' blood.

In a flash, the fire of God came down and burned them, and they died. It was God's quick punishment for a dreadful sin.

One more sin happened about the same time. There was a boy in Israel who had two different kinds of parents. His father was an Egyptian. His mother was an Israelite. This boy's father did not stay in Egypt when the Israelites went out of his country. No, he came along to Mt. Sinai with the Israelites; but in his heart this father loved the idol-gods of Egypt. He did not love the Lord. And this boy probably had to live in a home where his mother said, "Serve the Lord with all your heart," and where his father said, "It's all right to serve Egypt's idol-gods a little bit, too." That was a very sad way to live.

Listen to what this boy did. He started a quarrel. A quarrel is a fight. We do not know what the quarrel was about. Maybe he wanted to have a place in the tents of the Israelites even though his father was from the land of Egypt. But he lost the fight.

Do you know what he did then? He said terrible things about God. He called God wicked names. And God heard him. Moses told the people who heard his wicked words to put their hands on his head, and the rest of the people threw big stones at him until he died. That was a hard punishment for a very bad sin.

REMEMBER:

The boy's hard punishment teaches us to remember how great and holy our God's name is. It teaches us to hold His name very carefully in our hearts and to say very beautiful words about it with our lips.

The Israelites Complain in the Desert

It was time for the Israelites to leave Mt. Sinai and go on to Canaan, and God gave the rules for marching. The tabernacle would be taken apart and put on wagons; and it would travel in the middle, with the family of Levi all around it to take care of it. All the other families in Israel would travel in a square around the tabernacle. Canaan was not so very far from Mt. Sinai, and it would take the Israelites only about eleven days of marching to get there.

God gave a sign so that the people would know when to go and when to stop. We remember that God's cloud rested on top of the tabernacle. When the cloud lifted, the people knew it was time to move on. When the cloud rested on the tabernacle, they stopped.

They had traveled for only three days when they started to grumble and complain to Moses. We do not know why, but we can guess that they were tired of the hard life in the hot, dry desert. When they complained, God sent His fire from heaven and burned the people along the outside edges of the camp. They knew that God's fire meant that He was angry with them. Do you think they stopped their complaining? No, they did not pay any attention to this sign from God.

They came to Moses with more grumbling and complaining. This time they wanted better food. They said, "We remember the fish which we did eat in Egypt; the cucumbers, and the melons, and the leeks, and the onions." They wanted something that **tasted** good. They **hated** the manna, and they said it made them dry away. They said they wanted **meat** to eat. Then the people — most of the people — stood in their tent doors and cried.

That crying was a very wicked crying. They were crying because God was giving them manna, the wonderful bread from heaven. That bread from heaven was a picture of Jesus, Who is God's Bread from heaven, Who feeds His people with His Words of life, and Who saved them. Those wicked Israelites did not want a picture of Jesus. What did they want? They wanted food from Egypt, the land of sin. They wanted the food that was a picture of all the sins in the world that they wanted to do: to sing wicked songs, to dance, and to worship idols. They did not want **Jesus**. They wanted **sin**.

Poor Moses felt so bad. In his sadness he told God that he could not take care of all those Israelites anymore. It was too hard for him. He was sure he would slowly get weaker and weaker, and then die; and he told God it would be better to let him die right away. Moses was feeling sorry for himself.

God felt sorry for Moses, too. It was so hard for him to lead all those Israelites! God **helped** Moses, too. He told Moses to choose seventy men who were rulers of the people and God put His spirit into their hearts, to make them wise, so that they could help Moses take care of all the people.

Moses really wanted God to give the people meat to eat, and God promised to send the people meat, not for one day, or two days, or five or ten or twenty days, but for thirty days — a whole page of the calendar. How would the Lord give so many people so much meat out there in the desert? By a wonder. He made the wind blow and quails came up from the sea. Remember, quails are birds a little smaller than chickens. God sent so many quails that they were lying for ten miles around the camp of the Israelites. They could not see the end of the quails.

The people thought that all they had to do was pick up as many as they wanted and cook and eat them. They were wrong. First they had to be sorry for their sins and have clean hearts and thank their great God for His wonder. Most of them forgot God because they were so greedy for that quail meat.

As soon as they bit into the meat without thinking about God, God was very angry; and He sent a terrible sickness as a punishment. Many of the people of Israel died.

REMEMBER:

Did you ever wonder why we pray before our meals, and after them? We tell God that we get our food from **His** hand, and we ask Him to make us holy, by praying in Jesus' name. That is the way God wants us to take the food He gives to us.

Miriam Sins

Miriam was Moses' older sister. Do you remember that quite a long time ago we had a story about her? Then she was a girl who was watching the baby Moses in the basket in the river. She was a girl who could think fast. She called the baby Moses' mother to take care of him when the princess found him.

We had another story about Miriam. She was the leader in the singing when the Israelites sang a glad song to the Lord when He drowned Pharaoh in the Red Sea. Miriam loved to sing to the Lord, and she liked to teach the people and help to lead them. She was good at it! But, because she was so smart and so quick and such a good leader, she thought too much of herself. We call that being proud.

Aaron, Moses' brother, was not such a good leader. Once he listened to the people and made a golden calf for them to worship. Now he listened to Miriam and did what she told him to do.

What was Miriam saying? She was scolding Moses. Why was she scolding? This is what had happened. Moses' wife must have died, and now he married another wife; but she was not a lady from Israel. She came from a country called Ethiopia. **God** did not scold Moses for marrying this lady. **Miriam** did. She did not think the lady was good enough for Moses.

Miriam scolded Moses for another reason, too; and this was why she was **really** unhappy with Moses. She said that God did not speak **only** to Moses. He spoke to Aaron and Miriam, too. They could be leaders of Israel with Moses.

Miriam's scolding was a very wicked scolding. She wanted three leaders of Israel: Moses, Aaron, and Miriam. God wanted one leader: Moses. She wanted to have all the people look up to **her.** God wanted all the people to look up to **Him.** Miriam did not want Moses to rule over her, and she did not want to obey Moses. God wanted all the Israelites, Miriam too, to obey Moses.

Do you think Moses was very angry with Miriam? Do you think he scolded her back? Oh, no. He did not say anything to her, but very humbly he waited for the Lord to speak and settle the trouble.

Suddenly, God called to Moses and Aaron and Miriam and told them to come to His tabernacle. When they got there, God called Miriam and Aaron to the door of the tabernacle and talked to them. He told them that Moses was a very special prophet. He had even talked with the holy God on Mt. Sinai.

God told Miriam and Aaron more. He made a picture with His words, a picture of a house. He told Miriam and Aaron that Moses was building a house, God's house. He was teaching the people all God's laws, and the people had to walk just the way God's laws told them to. Those laws were the **floor** of God's house. They walked in God's laws like they walked on the floor of a house. Moses was building the floor of God's house. Some day Jesus would come and finish building God's house. The perfect house that Jesus built is in heaven.

When God told Miriam and Aaron that picture-story, they could see that it was a great sin for them to think that **they** could build God's house, too. Moses was a picture of Jesus. Miriam and Aaron were not. They might not think so much of themselves.

Miriam and Aaron had sinned, but Miriam's sin was greater; and God punished her with the terrible sickness of leprosy, a sickness of big, deep sores like Job had.

Moses ran to God and cried to Him to make Miriam better. God heard Moses' prayer and after seven days He made her better. All the people stayed there for those seven days, waiting for Miriam to be made better. That horrible sickness made her heart sorry and humble again, and she could obey Moses without thinking of herself first.

REMEMBER:

We are just like Miriam. We like to be first; we like to have the biggest piece of cake; and we like to boss other people around. That is because we think too much of ourselves, and we forget God. Pray to Him to make us sorry and humble again.

167

Moses Sends Out Twelve Spies

What a lot of excitement there was in the camp of the Israelites! They had traveled a few more days, and now they were at the doorway to the land of Canaan. At last they were right at the edge of the land God had promised!

Before they made plans to go into the land, Moses chose twelve men, one man from each family in Israel, to look over the land of Canaan to see what it was like. We call these men **spies**. Moses told the twelve spies what to look for: to see whether the cities they had to fight had big walls around them; and to see how many people lived in the land.

The spies stayed in the land of Canaan for forty days, looking around. How eager the people were to hear what they would say when they came back! When the people crowded around them, the spies **showed** what kind of land it was. They brought something back with them. In Canaan they had cut such a big, heavy bunch of grapes that they had to hang it from a strong stick and two men, one on each end, carried that stick. All the spies told what a rich land it was, a land to grow everything they needed. What happy news!

Then the faces of ten of the spies changed. They put on long, sad faces as they told that the cities in Canaan were very big and very strong and had high walls around them. And all over the land they saw many people, strong people, giants! The ten spies said they could not ever win a war with those strong cities and with those people who were giants.

But two of the spies, Joshua and Caleb, did not agree with the other spies. Caleb said, "Let us go up at once, for we are well able to overcome it." Overcome means to **win**. Joshua and Caleb trusted in God and knew He would be with them.

The ten spies argued back: "We be not able to go up against the people; for they are stronger than we." And the ten spies told all the people of Israel that when they were in Canaan they felt like grasshoppers under the feet of those big giants. The trouble with those ten spies was that they wanted to fight all by themselves. They did not trust in God to help them, the God Who worked great wonders.

Whom do you think the people listened to? Most of them listened to the ten spies. They did not go to their tents to sleep that night but stayed up and cried loudly all night to make sure Moses and Aaron heard how bad they felt. That was very wicked crying, for they said they wished they had died in Egypt or in the desert. They cried that they would choose another leader who would take them back to Egypt. They would rather go to Egypt, which was a picture of hell, than to Canaan, which was a picture of heaven. They were really crying because they did not **want** God and His laws, and they did not **want** to worship Him in Canaan.

Moses and Aaron fell on their faces to show how very sad they were. Joshua and Caleb, the two good spies, said beautiful words to the people of Israel. They said, "Fear ye not the people of the land; the Lord is with us: fear them not."

But the people were so wicked they wanted to throw stones at Joshua and Caleb. Then God came in His glory and brightness to the tabernacle and told Moses He would kill the people with a sickness and make a new people from Moses' family. Moses prayed for the people and begged God to show His mercy to Israel and forgive this great sin; and God forgave the sins of those who were His own children, who were truly sorry.

But because of the great sin, they would have a great punishment. First, the Lord killed the ten spies. Then He said that all of the people would go away from Canaan back to the desert again, for forty years, one year for each day the spies were in Canaan. They would get their wish to die in the desert, for everyone older than twenty years except Joshua and Caleb would die in the desert and would never go into Canaan. Only their children would go into Canaan.

REMEMBER:

If we are children who love the Lord, we are going to Canaan, too. Our Canaan is heaven. On our way we can say the words of Joshua and Caleb, "The Lord is with us."

Korah, Dathan, and Abiram Rebel

After they listened to the ten spies, the people of Israel said they did not want to go into Canaan. They were so wicked that they said it would be better to die in the desert. God told them that is exactly what would happen. Everyone older than twenty years, except Joshua and Caleb, would die.

Now were the people happy? No, they changed their minds again and acted like naughty little children. Some of the people took their swords and said that now they were ready to go to fight the people in Canaan. Moses told them not to go, for the Lord would not be with them, but they went anyway; and the people from Canaan chased them back. They could not win without the Lord.

They knew that because they did not trust in the Lord, they **had** to go back into that wild, rough desert for forty years. Oh, how they hated to start marching again! Probably they were still in the same place, at the doorway to Canaan, when three men of Israel, named Korah, Dathan, and Abiram, started more trouble. They got two hundred fifty leaders of Israel on their side and many of the people followed them.

All together they went to Moses and Aaron and said that the trouble was all Moses and Aaron's fault. They blamed Moses and Aaron for all the punishments God had sent. They said that the Lord was with the people of Israel, that the people were **holy. They** wanted to go into Canaan, but Moses and Aaron were stubborn and would not let them. Was that true? They said that Moses took them out of the wonderful land of Egypt to kill them in the desert, and Moses was doing wrong by not leading them into Canaan. These men said those words because they did not believe God nor love Him.

Moses fell on his face and asked God not to listen to those wicked men. Then he told Korah, Dathan, Abiram, and the two hundred fifty leaders of the people to go to the tabernacle the next day with their censers. Censers were long-handled pans that the priests used to take fire from the altar and bring it to the altar of incense. Korah wanted to be the priest instead of Aaron, and he had made his own firepans.

The next morning Korah and his men stood at the door of the tabernacle. Dathan and Abiram would not come. When God saw all those wicked men holding firepans that belonged only to Aaron and his family, God shone in His bright glory. Suddenly the Lord told Moses and Aaron to go away, so He could burn up the people in a moment. Moses prayed for the people, and God told all the people to move away from Korah, Dathan, and Abiram and their followers.

The people moved away and there stood Korah, Dathan, and Abiram at the doors of their tents, with their families. Then Moses talked to all of the people. He told them that the evil words of Korah, Dathan, and Abiram were not true. He said, "Hereby ye shall know that the Lord hath sent me to do all these works; for I have not done them of my own mind."

Moses said that if these men died the ordinary way that people died, then they would know that God had not sent him to be their leader. But if a great wonder happened, and the earth opened up its mouth and swallowed them down into a grave before they died, then the people would know that God was angry with these men.

As soon as Moses finished talking, the earth opened up and swallowed Korah, Dathan, and Abiram, their families, their tents, and all that they owned; and God's fire burned the two hundred fifty leaders who were on Korah, Dathan, and Abiram's side. When the people heard the screams of the wicked men and their families, they were afraid and ran away.

The Lord told Aaron's son to take the firepans that were still lying there and melt them in a fire and shape the shiny brass of which they were made into a cover for the altar. Whenever the people saw that cover on the altar, they would remember that only Aaron and his sons could offer sacrifices on the altar to God.

Do you think the rest of the people went quietly to their tents in humble fear before their great and holy God? No, they did not — not all of them. The very next day some of the people, with very hard hearts, came to Moses and Aaron and said, "**Ye** have killed the people of **the Lord**." They blamed Moses and Aaron for the punishment God had sent, and they called Korah, Dathan, and Abiram people who loved the Lord. How could they speak such awful words? They **knew** better, but their hearts were evil.

Once more God came in anger and sent a plague, a sickness that made people die very quickly. Aaron ran for fire in his firepan to put on the altar of incense, a picture of prayer to God; and he stood between the living and the dead, for thousands of people died in the plague.

REMEMBER:

People who don't believe in God always tell the **opposite** of the truth, not because they do not **know** any better, but because they do not **want** God's truth. We, who are God's people, want to say the truth about Him and about everything else.

173

Moses
Sins

With heavy hearts and sad faces, the people of Israel turned around and started to wander through the desert, back and forth, around and around, without going anywhere, waiting for the forty years to end. There was nowhere to go for the forty long years. During those years, all the older people — the mothers and fathers — would die. Maybe we would want to ask: why didn't the Lord let all the older people die right away and then the younger ones could go right into Canaan? The answer is that God needed the older people to take care of the little children until they were old enough to take care of themselves. Slowly God would let them die when they were not needed anymore.

The Bible does not tell us much at all about those forty years. We know that God sent the manna every day, that the people's clothes never wore out, and their feet did not get swollen in the hot desert sand. At last those forty terrible years were ending. Almost all the older people were dead and the children who had grown up in the desert were fathers and mothers now.

These new fathers and mothers knew all about the hard life, the sad and dark times in the desert; and they knew why the Lord sent these awful years: because of the sins of their parents. Would **these** fathers and mothers be different? Would **they** trust the Lord and obey Him with all their hearts?

Let's visit them as the forty years were ending. They were near to Canaan again, and they had no water. They knew that God often gave them water from a rock, by a wonder. Did they ask Him for a wonder?

Listen to them complain to Moses: "Would God that we had died when our brethren died before the Lord! And wherefore have ye made us to come up out of Egypt, to bring us into this evil place?" They were using the same words their parents had used!

174

175

Moses and Aaron went to the door of the tabernacle and God told Moses to take his rod, to speak to a rock there, and it would give water for the people and their animals. Poor Moses always had to listen to so much complaining and so much wickedness. This time he was angry and impatient with the people, and he shouted at them, "Hear now, ye rebels, must we fetch you water out of this rock?" Rebels are **people who fight** — who fight against God.

Then Moses disobeyed God and instead of speaking to the rock, he hit it twice; and water flowed out of it. God saw Moses' sin, and talked to him. God said, "Because ye believed me not, ye shall not bring this congregation into the land which I have given them."

Didn't Moses believe God? Oh, he believed that God **could** give water from the rock, but he thought that God **would not** give water to **rebels** — to those who fight against God. That is why Moses hit the rock twice — not to get water, but to show that the dry old rock would not give water to **rebels**! Moses was wrong. He forgot to see that God's true, loving people were there, too. Worse yet, Moses did not **want** to bring out water for the people. He was ready to tell God to let the people die of thirst. But God brought out water for the people anyway.

Because Moses would not obey the Lord, the Lord could not let him lead the people into Canaan. That was a hard punishment for a bad sin, wasn't it? Do you know that Moses was a picture of Jesus? Moses was not a perfect picture, though. He led the people **up to** Canaan, the picture of heaven, but he sinned, and he could not take them **into** Canaan, the picture of heaven. Jesus is the perfect Savior, Who never sinned and Who leads us through our desert in this world right into heaven when we die.

REMEMBER:

We are very often just like Moses. We are angry, and shout and disobey, instead of trusting God and doing His will. When we pray, shall we ask God to take away our sins through the blood of Jesus on the cross and make us praise Him?

God Sends Fiery Serpents

To get into the land of Canaan, the Israelites had to walk through a country which belonged to other people. The people who lived in this country were called the people of Edom. How did they come to live in this land? Maybe you remember that quite long ago we listened to the story of the brothers Jacob and Esau. Jacob was the father of the Israelites, and Esau was the father of the people of Edom. It was Esau's children who lived in this country.

The Israelites said to the people of Edom, "Thus saith thy brother Israel, Let us pass through thy country." The Israelites promised to walk only on Edom's roads and promised not to step on anything growing on their farms; and if they needed water, they would buy it from the people of Edom.

Edom said no. To show the Israelites that they meant it, the people of Edom gathered their strong men into an army to fight the Israelites. They hated the people of Israel. Do you know why? The people of Israel loved the Lord, just as their father Jacob had loved the Lord. The people of Edom hated God and God's people, just as their father Esau hated God, because they were children of Satan.

The Israelites did not try to fight the people of Edom, but turned around and took the long, long way of getting into Canaan by walking all around the big country of Edom. That made the people of Israel very unhappy.

177

Before they marched very far, they stopped a while at a mountain called Mt. Hor. While they were there, God told Moses and Aaron and Eleazar, Aaron's son, to walk up the side of the mountain. This is where Aaron would die. God could not let Aaron go into Canaan, for he had sinned with Moses when Moses hit the rock instead of talking to it.

When Moses and Aaron and Eleazar were high enough on the mountain so that all the people could see them, Moses took the priest's robe that Aaron was wearing from his shoulders and put it on the shoulders of his son Eleazar. This was the sign that Aaron's son would be priest after Aaron died.

We do not know how Aaron died or how he was buried on the mountain. Moses and Eleazar came down from the mountain alone, and the people stayed and cried and felt sad for thirty days.

Then they marched on again toward Canaan. When they came around the far side of Edom, they had to walk through the worst desert they had come through so far. It was dangerous! This place was full of poisonous snakes.

The people were so tired and sad. They were so sick of the desert. Just when they thought they were going straight into the land of Canaan, they had to go the long way around. God was not taking them the easiest way into Canaan, but the hard way of trouble; and the Israelites forgot that God was sending them the hard way because He loved them and wanted them to trust Him.

They were thirsty, too, and were so tired of eating manna every day. They started to complain to Moses about all their troubles. That was wrong of the Israelites. It was as if they were saying they did not **like** the way God was leading them. They thought they knew better than God.

God punished their disobedience by sending fiery serpents. Serpents are snakes. They were called **fiery** serpents because their poisonous bites burned in the people's skins like fire. Those snakes were pictures of the poison of sin burning in the people's hearts.

The people knew they did wrong; they were sorry and repented, and said, "We have sinned." Do you think God took away the serpents then? No, He did something else. He made the people better. This is what God told Moses to do: to make a serpent out of shiny brass and put it up on a pole. Everyone who had been bitten and who looked up at that brass snake on the pole would get better. Some of the Israelites were made better only in their bodies. Some were made better in their hearts from the snakebite of sin.

That brass serpent was a picture. When Moses lifted the serpent on the pole, he was making a picture of Jesus being lifted up on the cross, where He died to take away the snakebite of sin from His people.

REMEMBER:

The people of Israel could not get better from their snakebites and they could not get better from the poison of sin all by themselves. Neither can we. Sometimes we are so wicked that we **like** to sin. But when God puts His grace in our hearts, He makes us look up to the cross of Jesus, Who died there to save us.

The Story of Balaam (1)

The Israelites finally walked around the country of Edom. Next in line was the country of Moab, another country that hated God and worshipped idols. When they asked the rulers of Moab whether they might walk through their land, Moab said no. Once again, the Israelites walked the long way around. When they were almost up to the place where they would go into Canaan, they came to one more country — the country of a very strong people, called the Amorites. Two strong kings, Sihon and Og, ruled over these people, who lived in cities with big walls around them and who had many weapons for fighting wars.

The Israelites used words of peace when they asked the Amorites whether they might walk through their country. They would not walk into their farms, nor drink water from their wells; and if they needed food, they would buy it.

God made King Sihon's heart hard, and he said no. He came out against the Israelites with a big, powerful army. But the Lord fought for Israel, and they won. They killed many of the Amorites and chased them from their cities so that there was nothing left of the armies of the Amorites. All the other countries heard how Israel had won that great war, and they shook with fear. That is just what God wanted them to do. Now all the countries would know that God was fighting for Israel.

The king of Moab was afraid. His name was Balak. He was the one who **would not** let them walk through his country, and he did not dare to fight the Israelites. He thought that King Sihon with his strong army would easily win over the Israelites. And now Israel had destroyed Sihon's strong people. King Balak was worried. What would the Israelites do now? Would they fight and kill his people, too?

Then King Balak had an idea. He would get someone to curse Israel. To curse is to say wicked words of punishment. Balak knew just the man who could say words of cursing about Israel. He had heard that those curses came true, too. In those lands, where people did not believe in God, they trusted in magic charms, they believed in witches, and they thought that words of cursing would really happen.

The man whom King Balak wanted was Balaam. Balaam was a man who had heard of Jehovah God, and who knew how he was supposed to worship God. He could even say very nice words about God, but in his heart he did not mean a word he said, for he was a very wicked man who wanted everyone to believe that he had a great power — the power of magic spells.

King Balak of Moab needed Balaam to put a magic spell over the Israelites. He thought that Balaam could pray to God to let him curse Israel, and then God would change His mind and curse His people. Do you think that God would ever curse His own people? No, that would never happen.

King Balak sent some very important men from his country with a big present to Balaam to ask him to come to Moab and curse Israel. Balaam felt quite proud and he invited the men to stay overnight, so that he could ask the Lord during the night whether he might go along with them. He probably was not **really** going to ask God because he knew God would not let him go, but he wanted to think of a way to go, for he wanted that present very much.

That night God came to Balaam and said, "Thou shalt not go with them; thou shalt not curse the people: for they are blessed."

Balaam must have had an unhappy face the next morning. He still wanted to go, but he had to tell the important men, "The Lord refuseth to give me leave to go with you."

When the men came back to King Balak and told that Balaam would not come, King Balak thought he knew why. The present was not big enough. He knew what to do: send more important men with a much finer present. That would make Balaam come!

Oh, how Balaam wanted that great present! Oh, how he wanted King Balak to honor him! He told the very important men that he had to obey the word of the Lord. In his heart, Balaam did not want to obey. He did not care about God or His people.

Once more, he told the men to stay overnight, and once more God came to him and said, "Rise up and go with them; but yet the word which I shall say to thee, that shalt thou do."

With a happy face the next morning, Balaam made his donkey ready and rode back with the men to the country of Moab.

REMEMBER:

Balaam loved the nice things of **this** world. He did not love the things of **God's** world. Do we like games or fun or television more than going to church or to Sunday School? God wants us to love the things of **His** world.

The Story of
Balaam (2)

Early in the morning Balaam started out riding on his donkey with two of his servants for the land of Moab. Do you know where else Balaam was riding? Right into God's hot anger! Balaam had said to himself that probably God would let him curse Israel. Would God let Balaam curse His own people so Balaam could get that great present and become a rich man? Balaam **really** knew better. He knew that God would **bless** His people. But Balaam's eyes toward God were blind. He was blinder than his donkey.

Along the road God's angel came down from heaven and stood, blocking the road, with a sharp sword in his hand. The donkey saw the angel. Balaam did not. The donkey turned off the road into the field and Balaam used his whip to turn her back onto the road.

A little farther up the road Balaam was riding on a small path through a vineyard. A vineyard is a field of grapevines. On each side of the path was a wall; and there stood God's angel again. The donkey saw the angel. Balaam did not. The poor donkey was afraid of the angel and did not know how to get out of the way, so she pressed herself against the wall and crushed Balaam's foot. Balaam used his whip on the donkey again.

At last, in a very narrow place where there was nowhere to turn away, the angel stood in front of them once more. The donkey saw the angel. Balaam did not. The frightened donkey slid to the ground under Balaam. Then Balaam was very angry, and whipped her a third time.

Suddenly a wonder happened. The donkey began to talk. Our great Lord of all the earth can make an animal talk if He wants to. Listen to what the donkey said: "What have I done unto thee, that thou hast smitten me these three times?"

Balaam answered, "Because thou hast mocked me! I would there were a sword in mine hand, for now would I kill thee."

The donkey talked again: "Was I ever wont to do so unto thee?"

Balaam said, "Nay." Nay is another word for **no.**

Balaam did not seem to be very surprised at all by the wonder of the donkey

who talked. He seemed to have only one thing in his mind — to get a lot of riches — until God opened his eyes, and he saw the angel of Jehovah with his sharp sword in his hand. Then it was Balaam's turn to be afraid. He fell on his face to the ground while the angel scolded him. Balaam told the angel he had sinned and would go back home again if the Lord wanted him to. But God told him to go on to Moab, for He was going to use wicked Balaam to bless Israel.

When Balaam came to the land of Moab, he did not tell King Balak what had happened on the way. He let King Balak promise him many fine riches; and then he made himself ready to say words of cursing about God's people. Balaam and King Balak went up to a high hill where they could see all the people of Israel, and Balaam asked King Balak to build seven altars so that he could sacrifice seven bulls and seven rams on them. He did that to try to please the Lord so that the Lord would let him curse Israel. Balaam sacrificed those animals with his **hands**, not with his **heart**, for he did not love the Lord at all. Then he went away by himself to try to work a magic spell to curse Israel.

God came to him and put words into his mouth, and Balaam's words were that God would always take care of His people and make them great. That does not sound like cursing, does it?

King Balak did not like those words. He said, "I took thee to curse mine enemies, and thou hast blessed them altogether."

Balaam had another idea. He would stand so he could see only a small part of the Israelites. If they looked small, maybe his magic spell would work. He offered seven sacrifices on seven altars again, and went a little way off to work his magic.

God came to him and put beautiful words into his mouth. Balaam said that God's people would be strong like a lion, and God would always be with them. Does **that** sound like cursing?

King Balak was angry. He told Balaam to keep still. But Balaam wanted to try to go against God once more. After he offered seven more sacrifices on seven altars, God put many words of blessing into his mouth. Balaam could not stop blessing God's people. He told that God's people would be like a garden by a river, and like tall, strong trees. He told that they would win over their enemies. And the last thing he told was the best of all. He told that some day a Star would come out of the people of Israel. That Star would be Jesus. He would come to save them and take them to heaven.

When King Balak heard those words, he clapped his hands together because he was so angry. Then, with unhappy faces, King Balak went back to Moab and Balaam went home.

REMEMBER:

The Star that was born from the people of Israel is the Star of all of God's people. We are God's children, aren't we? That Star is **our** Jesus, Who always blesses us.

Two Spies Go to Jericho

At last the people of Israel had marched right up to the edge of the land of Canaan. Moses felt so sad that he could not be the one to lead them into the promised land; but he had sinned when he hit the rock, and he might not go in. He wanted to. He had led the people for so many years in the wild, hot desert, and he had had so many troubles with the people. Now if only he could go into the land of Canaan, he would have happiness at the end of all his troubles. So he prayed to God and begged God to let him go; but God said, "Speak no more unto me of this matter."

God led Moses to the top of a mountain, and by a wonder He let Moses see the whole land of Canaan from that mountain. Now Moses knew that he would **see** the land and would never **go into** the land of Canaan; but Moses was old, and God had a better land, the Canaan up in heaven, waiting for him. He took Moses there, and buried his body in the mountain. No one knows where.

Joshua was the man God chose to lead the people into Canaan; and after Moses died, God came to talk with Joshua. God promised to make Joshua **brave** to fight the enemies and to make him **strong** to lead the people. God made one more promise: He would be with His people wherever they went and make them win over their enemies by His great power.

Before the Israelites went into Canaan, Joshua sent two spies into the land and told them to go into the city of Jericho, a big city with high walls around it. Jericho would be the first city Israel would fight. It was a very wicked city. Joshua did not send those two spies because he was afraid, for God had already told him that the Israelites would surely win. But **God** wanted those spies to go to Jericho so that they would meet Rahab. Would you like to meet her, too?

Rahab lived on the wall of the city. Just think! The wall was so thick that a house would fit on top of it! Rahab was called a **harlot**, which means she was a bad woman. She was a heathen idol-worshipper. But Rahab seemed to be changing. She had heard that God had led His people through the Red Sea on dry ground, that He fed them in the hot, dry desert, and just lately she heard how God had helped them win over those two strong kings, Sihon and Og. God put His grace into her heart, and she believed in Him.

Everyone in the city of Jericho was talking about the Israelites, whose great God was with them; and Rahab heard the news that now they were ready to come into Canaan. Maybe she was watching for them. With her house on the high wall, she could easily see a long, long way.

Then the two spies came to Jericho, and Rahab met them in the city and took them to her house on the wall. The Bible does not tell us that the two spies looked the city of Jericho all over. They did not have to. All they had to do was listen to Rahab. What was Rahab saying? This is what she said: "We have

heard how the Lord dried up the water of the Red Sea for you; and what ye did to the two kings of the Amorites, Sihon and Og, whom ye utterly destroyed. And as soon as we had heard these things, our hearts did melt. I know that the Lord hath given you the land." She was telling the spies that the people were so afraid that their hearts melted. They knew that their battle was lost already.

By this time the king of the city of Jericho heard that the spies were in Rahab's house, and he sent some servants to get the men and bring them to him. Quickly Rahab took the spies to the flat roof of her house and hid them under some flax (something like straw) which was drying in the sun.

Then she went to the door and talked to the king's servants. She told them that two men had come to her house, but she did not know who they were. She said the men went away again, but she did not know where; and she told the servants that they had better go quickly and chase them.

Was that true? No, Rahab told a lie, and that lie was wrong; but she told that lie to save the lives of the two spies. Then she went to the roof where the spies were hiding and let them down the wall of the city by a rope from her window, and told them to run and hide in the mountains for three days until it was safe for them to go back to Joshua.

Before the spies left, Rahab asked them to save her and her family alive when the Israelites came to win the battle with Jericho. The spies promised and made a sign with Rahab. If she had a red rope hanging from her window on the wall, they would see it and come to save her.

Then the spies left, and after they had hid in the mountains, they ran back to Joshua and with great happiness they said, "The Lord hath delivered into our hands all the land."

REMEMBER:

Sometimes we are afraid, too. But we are never so afraid as the people of Jericho were; for we trust in our God, Who is always with us, and Who always takes care of us.

Israel Crosses the Jordan

Before the people of Israel could get into Canaan, they had to cross the Jordan River. Joshua led the people up to the river, and told them that they had three days to get ready to cross. They had to get food ready and their clothes packed; but, much more important, they had to get their **hearts** ready before God, for in three days they were going to walk right in the path of a wonder! They had never done that before.

What did the Jordan River look like? It was the time of the year that God sent much rain, and the river had so much water in it that the water ran over the river's banks and flooded the land all around. The waters rushed very, very fast down the river; and where the Israelites were, it was as deep as two people standing on top of one another. How would they ever get across?

The Lord knew how. He told the priests to take the ark, that beautiful, golden box that had the commandments of God written on the stones in it, and walk ahead of the people. When the feet of the priests stepped into the waters of the Jordan River, they had to stop, for then God was ready to show them His wonder. The waters suddenly stopped their rushing and piled up in a high wall near the city of Adam, about fifteen miles up the river. Now there was dry land where the river had been.

God told the priests holding the ark to stand near the edge of the river, between the people and the high wall of water. Then the people started to cross over, passing right in front of the ark. Why did God's ark have to be between the people and the high wall of water? It was a picture that God made for the

189

people. We remember that on the golden covering of the ark the priest had to sprinkle the blood of a lamb once every year. That blood was a picture of the blood of Jesus that covered their sins and kept them safe. The ark standing in the river was a picture of **Jesus**, Who covered His people and kept them safe from the rushing water of the Jordan River. As the people hurried across the river, they knew they were seeing a great wonder. They knew that God's great glory broke through from heaven for all His people to see.

While the people were crossing the river, Joshua chose twelve men, one from each family in Israel, to pick up a big stone from the sand at the bottom of the river and carry it to the other side. There the twelve men had to set the stones, one on top of the other, to make a high pillar. Joshua told them to make another pile of twelve stones at the side where the people stepped into the river. A pile of twelve stones would be on each side of the river. Those stones were pictures, too — pictures that God saved His people out of Egypt and brought them safely through the desert **and the Jordan River** to the land He promised them.

Why did God want those high pillars of stones to be at the edges of the river? So that their children would ask, "Why are those stones piled up that way?" and then the fathers and mothers would say, "The Lord dried up the waters of the Jordan River so that we could pass over." Then the little children would have to ask, "Didn't we always live in the land of Canaan?" And the fathers and mothers would say, "No." Then they could tell them the beautiful story of how God saved them out of the land of Egypt, the picture of the land of death, and how God took them through the awful desert, the picture of trouble and sin, and brought them safely through the Jordan River to Canaan, the picture of heaven. Don't you think their children loved that story?

Five days after they were in the land of Canaan, God stopped sending the manna. The people did not need it anymore. They could eat the food that grew in the land of Canaan now.

REMEMBER:

The Jordan River is a picture for us, too. It is a picture of all the sins that we do and think and say every day. Just as God dried up the flood of the river, He dries up the flood of our sins. And when we die, He will take us through the Jordan River to our Canaan up in heaven.

191

The Walls of Jericho Fall Down

What happy hearts the people of Israel must have had! They were in Canaan, their own land, at last! But they could not build houses and settle down and live in peace — not yet — for strong enemies were all around them. The land was full of people who worshipped idols, and Israel had to fight for a long time to get the land for themselves.

The first city they must fight was the strong city of Jericho, with walls thick enough to have houses built on top of them. You remember, don't you, that Rahab lived in this city? How would they fight this great city? Joshua must have been thinking hard about how he must lead the people of Israel to fight Jericho. Oh, he knew that God would give Israel the victory. God had promised that. But how did God want the Israelites to get those high walls down? Burn them? Knock them down?

As Joshua was thinking, all by himself, he saw a man who looked like a soldier with a sword in his hand. But the soldier was not a man. He was the Son of God, Who would some day be born as the Baby Jesus. The Son of God came down to help Joshua, and He looked like a soldier with a sword in His hand. He told Joshua how to lead the Israelites against the city of Jericho, and He promised once more that Israel would win.

The Lord did not tell Joshua to burn down the walls of Jericho, nor to knock them down. No, that is the way people of **this** world fight. **God's** people would not have to fight, because God would fight for them. He would take down the walls of Jericho by a wonder.

The Lord told the Israelites they were to get up early in the morning, leave their tents, and march around the city of Jericho once. He gave very strict rules about the march. The soldiers would go first. Behind them would march seven priests blowing trumpets made of the horns of rams. Next the priests who carried God's ark would come. At the end of the march came the rest of the Israelites. They might not shout nor make any noise nor even say a word.

Joshua and the Israelites obeyed the Lord and the first morning they all marched quietly around the city of Jericho once and then went back to their tents. What did the people inside the city think about all the marching? Don't you think they were watching from the windows, wondering what would happen? They were so afraid! Their hearts were melting with fear! And they had locked all the gates of the city tightly.

When the Israelites finished marching around the city and nothing happened, the people inside Jericho did not know what to think. Would they march again the next morning? Yes, very early the next morning the Israelites were all marching around the city again, in the same order. For six days the Israelites marched around the city just once, quietly, without saying a word. Probably the people inside the city of Jericho were smiling on day number six because nothing happened. Probably they said, "It's silly to march around our city without fighting. That marching can't hurt us!"

Then came day number seven. On this day God told the people of Israel to march around the city seven times, and after the seventh time they must shout loudly, for the Lord would give them the city of Jericho. Oh, how afraid the people of Jericho must have been when the Israelites kept on marching around their city one, two, three, four, five, six, seven times.

After the seventh time, the priests blew their trumpets and all the Israelites shouted loud shouts; and God made those great walls fall down flat, every part of them, except the part where Rahab's house was built. There in her window was the red cord. The spies went to her home and saved her and all her family.

God won the victory over Jericho. **He** fought for His people. God told them to kill all the people of Jericho except Rahab and her family and to kill all the animals; and if they found any beautiful things made of silver or gold, they must give it to God for His tabernacle. That would be their thank you to God for giving them the city of Jericho.

REMEMBER:

God gave the Israelites rules for marching around Jericho. **We** are marching, too. Do you know where we are marching? To heaven. God gives us rules, too. He tells us to love Him, to pray to Him, and to obey Him.

Achan
Sins

The next city the Israelites had to fight was only a little one. When Joshua sent some men on ahead to look it over, they came back with the news that Joshua would not need **all** his soldiers to fight. About three thousand soldiers would easily be enough to take this small city, called Ai. So Joshua sent his soldiers to fight.

Of course the Israelites expected that God would fight for them; and when the soldiers of Ai came out and killed thirty-six Israelite soldiers, the rest of the soldiers could hardly believe their eyes. They were so afraid that their hearts melted like water, and they ran to tell Joshua the terrible news.

When Joshua heard it, he tore his clothes — a sign that he felt **very** sad — and he lay down on his face in front of God's ark. Then he prayed. But it was not a happy prayer to God. He said, "O Lord, what shall I say, when Israel turneth their backs before their enemies?"

God answered Joshua with sharp words. He said, "Get thee up; wherefore liest thou thus on thy face? Israel hath sinned."

The Lord did not mean that every person in Israel had sinned. But **someone** in Israel had sinned, and his sin was so bad that all the people of Israel were troubled because of that sin. God told Joshua what the sin was: someone had taken of the riches of Jericho for himself. Remember, when God had fought for them at Jericho, He had told them to bring the riches of silver and gold as a sacrifice to His tabernacle. Someone did not obey God. Someone wanted those riches of silver and gold instead of wanting God's blessing. And someone brought that silver and gold from the wicked city that God had cursed right into the tents of Israel. No wonder God could not let Israel win that battle against Ai. The silver and gold of the devil was in the way!

Who was the man who did not obey the Lord? Joshua did not know. God knew. And the man who stole from Jericho knew it the minute he stole it. Did he tell? Oh, no. The man who stole knew why the thirty-six men were killed. It was **his** fault. Did he tell? Oh, no. The next morning Joshua asked the twelve families — we call them **tribes** — of Israel to come forward by turns to find out who did it. Joshua cast lots to find out. We do not know exactly how he cast lots. Maybe he put the names of all the tribes of Israel into a box and pulled out one name. Whatever way he cast lots, it was God Who chose. God chose the tribe of **Judah**. Did the man tell now? Oh, no. When the whole tribe of Judah stood before Joshua and he cast lots again, and God chose one of the families from Judah, did the man tell now? Oh, no. Finally, out of that one family from the tribe of Judah, the man **Achan** was chosen. Did he come right up to Joshua and tell his sin? No, Joshua had to make him tell.

Then Achan told what he had stolen: a beautiful robe, two hundred pieces of silver, and a piece of gold. He told where he had hidden them: in the dirt under his tent. Joshua sent men to his tent, and there they found the stolen riches. How little those riches seemed! What a **tiny** handful Achan traded for the love and mercy of God that never ends. It was an awful trade that Achan made, wasn't it?

Achan's family must have helped him with his stealing, for the Israelites had to punish his whole family. The saddest part of this story is that Achan was not sorry and did not ask God to forgive him and his family. The people of Israel threw stones at them until they died; and then they burned them with fire. At last the sin was taken out of the way; and the Israelites learned that God would let them win only when they were obeying Him.

REMEMBER:

Achan made an awful trade, a wicked trade. He traded God's love for silver and gold. Shall we ask God never to let **us** trade His precious love for anything on this earth?

Israel Wins the Victory at Ai

Now that the terrible sin of Achan was put out of the way, the Israelites could go on to fight against the city of Ai once more. Before they started out, the Lord spoke kind words to them. He said, "Fear not: I have given into thy hand the king of Ai and his people." The Lord told them, too, that after they had killed the people, they might take the animals and any beautiful things they wanted for themselves.

Then God Himself gave the plan for the battle. This is what they did. Some of the soldiers marched very quietly in the darkness of the night and hid along the side of the city until the morning light came. Early the next morning Joshua led the rest of the soldiers from another direction right toward the gates of the city of Ai. The people of Ai could easily see Joshua and his soldiers marching toward them. But they did not see the other part of the army that was hiding quietly alongside their city. Joshua stood where both his armies could see him.

When the people of Ai saw Joshua's army coming, the soldiers rushed out to fight them. Do you know what Joshua's soldiers did then? They acted as if they could not fight, and they turned around and ran away. The soldiers of Ai chased them, and soon all the people — the women and the children, too — ran out of the city to chase Joshua's soldiers.

As soon as the city was empty, Joshua gave a sign to the soldiers who were quietly hiding. The sign was that he stretched out his spear toward Ai. The sign meant that the soldiers who were hiding would run quickly into the city and set it on fire. When some of the people of Ai who were chasing Joshua's army looked back, they were shocked! Their city was burning! The first thing they thought of doing was to run back. Maybe they thought they could save some of their things. As soon as they turned back, they saw Israel's soldiers coming out of the city to fight them. What should they do now? Turn around? Look! The other part of the army had turned around and all the people of Ai were trapped between the two parts of the army of Israel.

God told them to kill all the people of Ai, and not to let any of them get away. All the time the Israelites were fighting, Joshua kept his spear stretched out toward the city of Ai, until the fight was over. That stretched-out spear was a picture of the Lord's hand stretched out to help His people until all their enemies were destroyed.

By this time the people of Israel were almost in the middle of the land of Canaan already. There, in the middle of the land were two mountains, called Mt. Ebal and Mt. Gerizim. God told half of the Israelites to stand on Mt. Ebal and the other half to stand on Mt. Gerizim. The priests had to stand in the valley below with God's ark.

Then Joshua began to read God's law to them. The people of Israel had to learn that God's law does two things: it blesses those who obey it and it punishes — we may call it **curses** — those who do not obey it. Mt. Ebal was the mountain of the curse; and when Joshua read in the law "Cursed are those who do not obey the law," all the people on Mt. Ebal answered "Amen." When Joshua read in the law "Blessed are those who love the Lord and obey His law," the people on Mt. Gerizim answered "Amen." God's people had to learn that God's blessing would come to them only if they obeyed God's law.

REMEMBER:

We do not have to stand on Mt. Ebal anymore to hear all about God's punishments because Jesus came to die for us and take the punishment of our sins away. Shall we thank Him every day for taking away our punishment?

The Gibeonites Trick the Israelites

The people who lived in the land of Canaan were so surprised that the Israelites had already marched to the mountains of Ebal and Gerizim, right in the middle of the land. No armies had been able to stop them. They knew in their hearts that the Israelites had won all their battles because the Lord helped them; and they could see how, with the Lord's help, the Israelites would win the war with every city in the land of Canaan.

What could they do to help themselves? They could see that it was no use to fight. They would lose the battle just as all the other kings lost to the Israelites. But they must do something! They could not give up without a fight! They decided that if their armies were big enough and strong enough, they might be able to win the battle with the Israelites. Many kings of strong cities with their soldiers got together with a huge army to make war with Israel. God made their hearts hard, so that they were ready to fight with big armies against God and His people.

The city of Gibeon did not agree with the other kings. Gibeon was a large city in the middle of the land of Canaan; and Gibeon could see that it did not matter to God whether armies were big or small, strong or weak: for God did not fight the way people of this world fight. God helped Israel with His wonders.

The people of Gibeon decided not to fight. They tried a trick instead; and they figured that, even if the trick didn't work, nothing would be lost. They would be killed if they fought anyway. And their trick just **might** work!

Watch them get ready for their trick. They chose some men who put on old, dirty, dusty clothes and broken, patched shoes. In those days people drank a kind of sour wine, which they kept in bottles made of skins of animals. The men from Gibeon put their wine in old, ripped animal skins. When the wine leaked out, they patched the skins, and ended up with a sticky mess. Some of the bread they took was dry and hard. The rest was moldy.

Now they were ready to leave their city and travel a short way to the place where Israel had set up their tents. This is what the Gibeonites said: "We be come from a far country because of the name of the Lord thy God, for we have heard the fame of him."

Then the Gibeonites told that in their far, far country they had heard how God had saved His people out of Egypt, how He had taken care of them in the desert, and how He was fighting for them in Canaan. They said they wanted to be friends with the Israelites.

Joshua and the rulers of Israel answered them that maybe they lived right among them. They did not trust the men from Gibeon.

The men from Gibeon said they would **prove** they were from a faraway country. They showed Joshua and the rulers of Israel their bread — dry and hard, or moldy; and they told how it was taken hot from their ovens on the day they left their country. They showed their sticky, dripping wineskins and told that they were new when they left their country. Their clothes and shoes were new, they said, and wore out on their long trip.

Joshua and the rulers of Israel did not ask them questions. They did not say, "Where is your country? What is the name of your country? Who is your king?" No, they **liked** the idea that men from a faraway country wanted to be friends with them, and they believed the lie of the Gibeonites and made an agreement to be friends with them.

201

What should Joshua and the rulers have done? They should have asked God what to do about these men. Instead, they were careless and quickly made friends.

Three days later they found out that the Gibeonites were their neighbors. When the people of Israel found out, they were angry with Joshua and the rulers. They **should** have been angry, too, for God had told Israel to destroy all the cities in Canaan. Now what could Joshua do? He **had** to obey God's command to destroy all the cities — Gibeon, too — but he **could not** go back on his promise to save the people of Gibeon alive. Of course, he could not do both those things. He could not kill them and save them alive. So he and the rulers scolded the Gibeonites, but kept their promise and made them to be slaves for the Israelites — woodcutters and water carriers — all their lives.

REMEMBER:

Joshua and the rulers were in a lot of trouble because they were careless. We are often careless, too; and we must learn to stop to think, and act carefully. Remember, God gave us wonderful minds to use.

The Sun
Stands Still

In our last story we heard that some of the kings of the strong cities in the land of Canaan decided to get together all the soldiers they had to fight against Israel. Maybe if they had enough soldiers, they would win a great battle with the Israelites. Five kings of five strong cities joined together with their armies to fight.

While they were getting their soldiers ready, they heard the shocking news that the city of Gibeon had made peace with the Israelites by playing a trick on them. They heard that Joshua was going to keep his promise to keep them alive. The people of Gibeon had not dared to fight, and yet they were saved alive. Those five kings were so angry with Gibeon! They started marching to fight — not Joshua — but the city of Gibeon. They were going to punish Gibeon for making peace with Joshua, and they wanted to get the city of Gibeon for themselves. That would stop Joshua and the Israelites, they thought. Maybe they could win over Israel yet! Do you think they could?

When the people of Gibeon heard that five huge armies with five strong kings were coming to fight them, they sent men running as fast as they could to Joshua with these words, "Come up to us quickly, and save us, and help us: for all the kings of the Amorites that dwell in the mountains are gathered together against us."

Joshua answered their cry for help by taking his soldiers and starting out right away. All night Joshua and his soldiers ran, through the darkness, to get to Gibeon; and in the morning the five strong kings had a big surprise they didn't like: the army of Israel was waiting for them and started fighting them before the five kings were ready. The Israelites already knew how the battle would turn out because the Lord had promised Joshua before they set out that they would surely win.

What a strange battle that was! Do you know what happened? God fought for the Israelites! He threw big hailstones down from heaven and those hailstones hit only the soldiers of the five kings. None of those hailstones hit a soldier from Israel. That was a great wonder! And those hailstones killed many more people than the swords of the Israelites did. Don't you think the soldiers of the five kings were terribly afraid of those awful hailstones coming down from the sky, and falling on them? They started to run away, and the Israelite soldiers chased them. The five kings were not very brave either. They left their armies alone and hid in a big cave. Joshua told his men to roll big stones in front of the cave so the kings could not get away.

There was so much fighting to do that day. Soon the sun would go down and then the battle would have to end, because no one can fight a war in the darkness. How they wished the day would be longer, so they would have more time to kill God's enemies. And then the wonder happened! Joshua talked to the sun and the moon and commanded them to stand still. The Lord listened to Joshua and gave him power over those great lights in heaven. For a whole day the sun did not go down. The day stretched out twice as long as usual.

Can we understand such a great wonder? No, we can't. But we **believe** it, and we know that our great God can stop His world for a day much more easily than we can stop a clock in our house.

Can we understand **why** God made such a great wonder? Yes, we can. The soldiers of the five kings were **God's** enemies, and the Israelites were doing **God's** work. They had to fight **God's** wars because those enemies were in the land that belonged to Israel, and they needed more time for **God's** work that day.

When God listened to Joshua and gave him power to stop the sun from going down, He was giving us a picture again. Joshua was a picture of Jesus. Jesus is the Lord of all things — of the sun and moon, too — and for a little while God let Joshua be a little picture of his great Lord.

Now the Israelites had plenty of time to chase their enemies. They killed almost all of them, but not one Israelite died in that battle. After the battle was over, Joshua brought out the five kings and put his feet on their necks and killed them. He did not do this to be mean but to show to all the Israelites that they were the rulers over their enemies. That made the Israelites feel more brave, for they still had many, many enemies to fight before the land of Canaan would be ready for them to live in.

REMEMBER:

We fight battles every day, too. But we do not fight with swords and spears because we fight a battle against our sins — all the naughty things we say and do. We fight by praying that God will keep us from doing all those sins.

The Last Days of Joshua

The Israelites kept on fighting their enemies in the land of Canaan for a long, long time. Up and down the land they went, making war with God's enemies. At last God told them it was time to stop and to settle down and live in Canaan. Not all of their enemies were killed yet, but God said they could keep on making war with their enemies after they were settled. God did not want His people just to sit back and do nothing. All their lives they had to fight **God's** battles with **His** enemies.

Do we remember that there were twelve families in Israel and that we call these families **tribes?** The tribes might not settle down anywhere they pleased. God had a place chosen for each of the tribes, and as Joshua cast lots — maybe by matching the name of the tribe with a part of the land — God's hand guided the choosing, and every tribe got just the right piece of land. In the middle of the land God chose a place for His tabernacle. It was called Shiloh, which means **peace** and **rest.** Jesus is called Shiloh, too. He is **our** peace and rest.

Slowly the wars stopped, and the people began to build their houses and dig their wells in the parts of Canaan that belonged to them. Don't you think they were happy to be settled in peace in their own land? Many years passed, and Joshua and the rulers of Israel were getting to be old men. They knew they would soon die.

Before he died, Joshua called all the people of Israel together. He wanted to talk to them once more. Shall we listen, too, while he talked to the Israelites? Joshua had happy words for them. He told the people to remember how God had saved them out of Egypt and brought them through the desert to the land He had promised them. Joshua told the people to remember how the Lord fought for them and destroyed all their enemies and gave them this beautiful land.

Then Joshua gave them God's promise: God would keep on fighting for His people whenever they fought their enemies. He said, "The Lord your God, he it is that fighteth for you, as he hath promised you."

But God knew, and Joshua knew, that His people were sinners; and Joshua gave them a warning: they must always love their God and obey Him. Joshua told the people never to worship idol gods and never to marry the wicked people who still lived in the land, for they would bring the Israelites much trouble. That trouble would **hurt** the Israelites! They would feel as if they were caught in a trap — a trap of sin — and couldn't get out. And those wicked people that they would marry would feel like sharp thorns or prickers in their sides. Prickers hurt, don't they? That's the way the wicked people would hurt Israel if they made friends and married one another.

Then Joshua made a promise to the people. He said, "As for me and my house, we will serve the Lord." The people answered him, "We will also serve the Lord; for he is our God." After Joshua told them to obey all God's commandments, he sent the people home, and soon after that he died.

Now the Israelites did not have a leader anymore. Would they still keep their promise to serve the Lord? For a while they did. But slowly the fathers and the mothers became older and died one by one. Soon all the soldiers who fought with Joshua were dead, and their children grew up to be the fathers and mothers.

These children could not remember any of the great wonders the Lord had done because they had not been born then. Oh, they had **heard** their fathers and mothers tell all the stories about them, but they were not very interested in those stories of God's greatness. They said they were tired of fighting wars against God's enemies. They wanted to live quietly and farm their land.

These new fathers and mothers watched the wicked people who still lived in the land, and they saw what fun they had when they worshipped their idols. They danced and sang and had parties and were not sorry for their sins. And many of the Israelites **liked** those idols and started to worship them, too. Not all the Israelites worshipped idols, but many of them did. They did not keep their promise to serve the Lord their God.

What did God do about His people who were sinning? He sent them a punishment, a strong king and his army who came right into the land of Canaan and ran over their fields and lived in their cities. Now the Israelites were in trouble and they cried to God to save them. God heard them and called a leader, or a **judge**, to help them. His name was Othniel. Othniel led them in the fight against the strong king and his army, and God gave Israel the victory. Then Othniel taught them to leave their idols, to be sorry, and to worship the Lord again.

REMEMBER:

God teaches us the same thing He taught the Israelites. He teaches us to say **no** to sin and **yes** to Him.

Ehud,
the Left-handed Judge

The time that this story happened was a very mixed-up time for the people of Israel. Ever since Joshua died, they did not have a strong leader who could keep all the people together and teach them to fear the Lord. Of course, they did not **really** need a great king and leader, for **God** was their king; and they should have obeyed and trusted Him and worshipped Him in the tabernacle at Shiloh. But God was in heaven, and they could not see Him, so they forgot Him and did not obey His laws. They did what **they** wanted to do — and the thing they liked to do most of all was to worship all kinds of idols.

God looked down from heaven at His people. They were still His people, but they were His people who were sinning very badly. We all know what happens when our daddies and mothers see us doing very wrong things. They **must** stop us, and they **do** stop us, by spanking us. That is what the people of Israel needed — a spanking. But our great God in heaven did not spank them as our daddies and mothers spank us! No, He punished them a different way. He sent an enemy with a strong army who came running right into their own land of Canaan. That was God's way of spanking them.

The enemy was the army of the country of Moab. Do you remember that once the king of Moab was so afraid of the Israelites that he sent for the wicked Balaam to curse them? **Now** the Lord made the army of Moab very strong, and they were not afraid to fight Israel. This time it was Israel's turn to be afraid, for God had stopped helping them because of their sins. The Lord let the army of Moab be so strong that they ran all the way to the city of Jericho. Once God had made the strong, thick walls of Jericho fall down flat for His people. **Now** God let the wicked king of Moab come and build his palace in Jericho and live there with his soldiers. That wicked king of Moab, whose name was Eglon, did even more. He said that this city was his and he was their king. Then he made a rule that all the people of Israel had to pay him money every year. He made them pay so much money that the people of Israel became very poor.

Don't feel too sorry for the Israelites, will you? They knew they were doing wrong, but they were stubborn, and would not turn to the Lord and say, "Please forgive us, Lord." Do you know how long that wicked King Eglon stayed in Jericho and made them pay money? Eighteen years. That is a long time. You will be finished with high school by the time you are eighteen years old.

God was ruling from heaven for all that time. It was almost as if He had to spank His people for eighteen years! At last they turned and cried to Him and asked Him to help them. God answered them and sent them a ruler called a **judge** whose name was Ehud. Ehud was a very strong and brave man. He was brave because God put His spirit inside Ehud. He was one of God's true worshippers who had not served idols. He told the people to turn to the Lord.

This year it was Ehud's turn to go, with some other men, to take the money to the king. After they gave the money to the king, they left. But Ehud went only a little way back with the rest of the men, and then turned around and went back alone to King Eglon's palace. The king was sitting in his summer parlor, a room with windows to catch the summer breeze, when Ehud came back to him and said, "I have a secret errand unto thee, O king."

Many servants were standing around the king, and they probably looked

Ehud all over, wondering whether he had a sharp sword under his long, loose coat. They were looking on the wrong side of his coat, for Ehud was left-handed, and carried his sword on the opposite side of his body from other soldiers. There, underneath his coat, hanging from his belt, was a thin sword with two sharp edges. And the servants never saw it!

As soon as Ehud said, "I have a secret errand," the king asked all his servants to leave. When Ehud and King Eglon were alone, Ehud said, "I have a message from God unto thee." And King Eglon stood up. He was a very fat man. As he stood up, Ehud reached with his left hand for his sword, and pushed it hard into the fat king's belly, so that he fell down dead upon the floor.

Then Ehud locked the doors of the summer parlor and ran back home. When the king's servants came back to their king, they found the doors locked. They waited and waited for the king to come out of his parlor. At last they took a key and opened the doors, and found their king dead on the floor.

The soldiers of Moab were all mixed up now that their king was dead, and they started to run back home to Moab. But Ehud was quicker than they were. He gathered many soldiers of Israel and chased the soldiers of Moab and killed ten thousand of them. The Lord gave them a great victory that day.

REMEMBER:

Ehud was brave only in the Lord. That is the only way to be brave. Do we pray that God will make us brave to do His will, too?

Deborah and Barak
Judge Israel

After God used Ehud to save His people from the king of Moab, Ehud was the judge over Israel for many years; and he taught them to worship the Lord again.   But after Ehud died, everyone forgot God and did what was right in **his own** eyes again. They worshipped idols and did all the wicked things the heathen people of the land did.

God saw all their wickedness and sent Jabin, the king of Canaan, with his soldiers and with nine hundred chariots — remember, chariots are wagons for fighting — and they ran all over the land of Israel. This king and his soldiers made the people pay them money, too. They ran over Israel's farms and helped themselves to anything they wanted, and they pushed the Israelites right out of their houses and lived in them. The roads were not safe to travel on because the soldiers of King Jabin would hide and then jump out and steal whatever the Israelites had. The only place they were safe was in a big city with a strong wall around it; and even if they lived in a big city, they were afraid, because their wells were outside the walls, where it was dangerous; and they fought among themselves about who would be the first to get water and run back inside the walls where it was safe. If any of the people saw one of Jabin's soldiers, he would run because not one of the people had a sword or a spear to fight with. No one wanted to fight. What a wicked, unhappy time it was! For twenty years the Lord let King Jabin and his soldiers run over their land. It was one of the saddest times in the lives of the people of Israel.

At last they turned and cried to the Lord and once more He sent them a leader, called a judge. But the judge was not a man. Usually God chooses men to be the leaders. They are often stronger and braver than women are. Besides, God made women to be mothers to take care of their children, just as your mother takes care of you; and that is the nicest kind of work. But this time God chose a **woman** for a judge. He could not find even one man who had enough trust in Him to lead an army and fight for God's people.

So God used a woman and filled her with His Spirit. Her name was Deborah, and she sat under a palm tree and taught the people all about God's commandments.

God told Deborah to send for a man whose name was Barak, and tell him to take ten thousand Israelite soldiers and go to Mt. Tabor. But Barak was afraid to go to war without Deborah. Deborah said, "I will surely go with thee," and together they took their ten thousand soldiers up the mountain. When Sisera, the captain of King Jabin's army, heard that the Israelite soldiers were on Mt. Tabor, he rushed to the mountain with his huge army of soldiers and his nine hundred iron chariots.

It **looked** as if Deborah and Barak and their little army were caught in a trap on the mountain. But they weren't! Deborah said to Barak, "This is the day in which the Lord hath delivered Sisera into thine hand: is not the Lord gone out before thee?"

Barak and his army ran fast down the mountainside, and the Lord fought for them. He bothered the wheels of Sisera's chariots, just as He had bothered Pharaoh's chariots in the Red Sea, so they would not go. Then the Lord called His stars in the sky to help fight Sisera and his army. We do not know just how the stars fought that wicked army, but probably pieces of stars fell on them so that they died. A river that flowed near there fought for Israel, too. The Lord made it too full of water, so that it flooded over its banks and rushed very fast. Many of Sisera's soldiers drowned in the rushing river. God was using parts of His world which He created to help His people Israel.

The battle went so badly for the army of the Canaanites that Captain Sisera left his army and ran away by himself. He knew where to go: to the land of the Kenites. It would take him three days of running to get there, but the Kenites were friendly to him, and there he would be safe. At last he arrived, hot and

213

tired and thirsty. Jael, one of the women of the Kenites, saw him coming and invited him to come into her tent to rest. She told him not to be afraid. But Sisera **should** have been afraid, for Jael's heart was with **God's** people, not with Sisera.

When he asked for a drink of water, she brought him milk and butter, and when he lay down to sleep, she covered him. Sisera told her to tell a lie — to say no — if anyone came and asked, "Is there any man here?" Then he fell asleep, and Jael got busy. She took a nail, probably a tent nail, and pounded it through his temples, the bones near his eyes, right into the ground, so that he died. Was that wrong for Jael to do? No, for Sisera was **God's** enemy, and God wanted him killed, so that His people would win the victory. **God** led Sisera's steps to Jael's tent so that he would be killed, and **God** blessed Jael. After the Lord helped Israel win this great victory, Deborah and Barak sang a beautiful song to the people about all of God's wonders.

REMEMBER:
Our God is the same God Who saved Deborah and Barak. He saves us and takes care of us, too. Ask your daddy and mother to sing a song about God's great wonders with you.

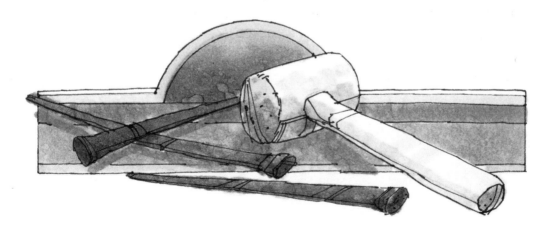

God Calls Gideon

For forty years the Israelites had peace in their land. For forty years Deborah and Barak taught Israel the fear of the Lord and called the people to serve Him. Then Deborah and Barak died and Israel turned again, with all their hearts, to worship idols. They lived in wickedness. They needed a spanking again. The way that God spanked them this time was by sending the Midianites, a wild, rough kind of people who liked to live in other people's lands.

The Midianites wandered over the land of Israel for seven years. That was not a **long** time, but it was a **terrible** time. This is what the Midianites did: they acted like robbers. When the corn and the wheat in the fields were ripe and the Israelites were ready to cut it and put it into their barns, the Midianites would swarm over their farms, taking away everything they could grab, even the farm animals. What they couldn't take, they burned. The Israelites had nothing left. To the Israelites, these Midianites seemed like grasshoppers swarming over their farms, taking everything they saw. It wasn't any use for the Israelites to plant their farms and their gardens, for the Midianites would steal their crops before they could eat them.

Oh, how afraid the people of Israel were! Many of them left their houses and lived in caves in the mountains. They couldn't find enough to eat. Some of them were starving. After seven terrible years, they finally turned to the Lord and asked Him to help them.

First God sent them a prophet who scolded them for not obeying Him. Then God sent His Angel, Who was His special Angel, His own Son, Who would someday be born on earth as Jesus. The Angel of God came to a man named Gideon. Where did the Angel find him? He was hiding in a hole in a rock, so that the Midianites would not see him gathering in some of his wheat. This is what the Angel said to Gideon: "The Lord is with thee, thou mighty man of valour." Valour is **bravery**.

Gideon did not feel like a strong, brave man. He said, "Oh my Lord, if the Lord be with us, why then is all this befallen us? Where be all His miracles which our fathers told us of?"

But the Angel just told him to go and save Israel, for **God** had called him. Poor Gideon still could not understand why the Lord wanted **him**. He did not think much of himself. He said, "My family is poor, and I am the least in my father's house."

Once more the Angel of the Lord promised, "Surely I will be with thee."

Still Gideon did not feel very brave. If only he could have a special sign from God! So he asked the Angel for one. Quickly he ran to get some bread and meat, and laid it out on a rock. It was an offering to God. The Angel touched the food of Gideon's offering with His rod and a fire came from the rock and burned the offering. And then the Angel was gone! Gideon knew that God had sent fire for his offering and all was well. He built an altar to God there and gave it just the right name: Jehovah-Peace.

Now it was time for Gideon to get to work. Everywhere in the land of Israel were altars to the idol-god Baal. There was even one in his father's yard. God told Gideon to break it down and build an altar to God instead and sacrifice one of his father's animals on it. God was showing Gideon that he had to say "Down with Baal" before he could say "God with us."

Gideon wanted to obey God, but he was afraid; so he worked at night. In the morning, when all his family and friends saw that their idol-god Baal was smashed, they wanted to kill Gideon, but Gideon's father said, "If Baal be a god, let him plead for himself."

By this time Gideon knew that the people of Israel were looking to him to lead them to fight the Midianites. Gideon tried so hard to trust in God alone as he called his soldiers together, but he knew that he was still a weak man. He needed one more sign, a picture that God would surely go with him; and he asked God to give him the sign he needed.

Gideon took a fleece. That is a nice, thick, woolly piece of the skin of a sheep. He put the fleece outside at night, and asked God if in the morning the fleece could be wet with dew and all the ground around it dry. Early the next morning Gideon went out to look. Sure enough: he could wring a bowlful of water out of the sheepskin; but all the ground was dry. Then he asked God to change the sign around so that the next morning the fleece would be dry and the ground would be wet. Sure enough: that happened, too.

Gideon's sign was a picture. The sheepskin was a picture of Israel. The wetness of God's dew was a picture of God's blessings. Would God bless His people? God answered, "Yes." Would God bless His people even though many of them had been worshipping idols, and the sheepskin was dry? God's answer was "Yes." Now Gideon was ready to go out to fight.

REMEMBER:

When we see the wet, sparkling dew on the grass in the morning, think that it is a picture of God's blessings on us.

217

Gideon Wins the Victory by Faith

Very early in the morning, Gideon was awake. He had no sleepiness in his eyes anymore, for today he had to fight the battle of the Lord against Midian. Many soldiers had come running to him and they were ready to fight, too. This time the Lord was not ready yet. Why not?

God came to Gideon that morning and said he could not go to fight the Midianites yet. Gideon had too many soldiers. Too many? Did you ever hear of a leader of an army having **too many** soldiers? Oh, no! He always wants more soldiers so that he can win. Besides, Gideon had only thirty-two thousand soldiers. That is not a very big army. The Midianites had so many soldiers in their army that they looked like grasshoppers over the ground; and no one could count how many camels they had.

Why did God want Gideon to have a **small** army of soldiers? So that the Israelites could not say, "Our own hands have saved us." **God** was going to fight for Israel. He told Gideon to tell all the soldiers who were shaking because they were afraid that they might go home. God didn't need them. Twenty-two thousand soldiers went home, and Gideon had only a tiny army of ten thousand soldiers left.

The Lord was not satisfied. Do you think that Gideon was surprised when God told him he **still** had too many men? Gideon had to take his men to a stream of water for a drink, to test them. Some of the soldiers got down on their knees or lay down flat to get their drinks. Gideon put these men in one group. Some of the soldiers stooped over and used their hands as helpers as they lapped up water with their tongues, as dogs lap up water. These men went into another group.

When the soldiers took their drinks, they showed how they felt. Those who got down on their knees were thinking about themselves. They wanted to be comfortable when they took their drinks. Gideon sent these men home. The soldiers who stooped down and put their tongues into the water were thinking about being careful and watching for the Midianites while they drank. Those were the fighters God wanted! But there were only three hundred of them! Everyone else had gone home.

By this time it was not early in the morning anymore. The day was over. Night had come. God came to Gideon again and promised to save Israel from the Midianites with only three hundred soldiers. But God looked into Gideon's heart and knew that he was afraid. He told Gideon to take his servant and run close to the army of the Midianites. He would hear words which would make his heart strong and brave.

Gideon and his servant ran to the Midianite army and listened in the darkness while one soldier told another soldier about his dream. He dreamed that a little loaf of bread fell into the army of the Midianites, went into a tent, turned the tent over, and smashed it. The other soldier said he knew what that strange dream meant. The loaf of bread was a picture of Gideon's tiny army smashing down the huge army of the Midianites. Gideon knew that God had sent that dream to the soldier.

Then Gideon was ready to go back to his soldiers and say, "Arise; for the Lord hath delivered into your hand the host of Midian." He divided his soldiers into three groups and gave each man a trumpet in his right hand and a lighted torch — something like a candle — in a jar in his left hand. What funny things to fight with! Don't you think people would say, "That's not the way to fight a war!" But we must remember that Gideon's soldiers carried these things **by faith** in God.

Now it was the middle of the night as the soldiers went down to the Midianites. Gideon told his soldiers to do just what he did. Suddenly, in the quiet of the night, when all the Midianites were sleeping, Gideon and his soldiers blew on their trumpets, broke their jars with a crashing noise, and held their torches up, shouting all the time, "The sword of the Lord and of Gideon!"

Those awful noises and the strange lights must have scared the Midianites out of a sound sleep. But did it scare them so much that they killed one another? No, the Lord mixed them all up so that they fought and killed their own soldiers. Then the rest of Israel's army chased them. But **the Lord** won the victory. Gideon and his three hundred men won it only by faith in the Lord.

REMEMBER:

We are not very big yet, and sometimes we are afraid, just as Gideon was. Will we do what Gideon did: ask God to make us trust in Him? He will tell us words that will make us brave, like, "The Lord is **my** Shepherd."

Jephthah Keeps His Promise

Gideon had gotten old and died and could not lead the Israelites in the way of God's laws anymore. Almost right away the people of Israel turned their backs to God and worshipped idol-gods. This time they found more idols than ever. They served the gods of all the heathen people around them: the gods of the Moabites and the Ammonites and the Philistines. They **liked** lots of idols.

The holy God in heaven looked down at Israel and was very angry with them. He sent them a hard punishment again. This time it was the soldiers of the land of Ammon. For eighteen years the soldiers of Ammon fought the Israelites and ran over their land, taking whatever they wanted. They were mean and cruel rulers over the Israelites.

At last the Israelites cried to the Lord and said they were sorry and put away their idols. God heard them and was merciful to them and promised to send them another judge to save them from the cruel soldiers of Ammon. The Lord chose Jephthah, a strong, brave man. This does not mean that he had big, strong muscles, but that he was a strong, brave man in his heart because he trusted in his God.

Jephthah was not a very happy man. There was trouble in his family. Jephthah had the same father as his brothers had, but not the same mother; and after his father died, his brothers threw him out of the house and made him run away to another city. There he lived for many years, sad and alone.

After he went away, many troubles came to the city where Jephthah had lived. The troubles with the wicked soldiers of Ammon were getting so bad and the people were crying to God so hard! They needed someone who was strong in the Lord to save them! They needed Jephthah! The rulers of the city went to Jephthah and asked him to come back and help them fight the soldiers of Ammon. Jephthah did not trust the men from his city. First they threw him out, and now, when they needed him, they begged him to come back. And they never said they were sorry! Jephthah made them promise him that, after the Lord let him win the battle, **he** would be their ruler. **Then** he went back to his own city.

Jephthah did not get his soldiers ready for a big war with Ammon right away. No, first he tried to settle the war by talking with the king of Ammon. He tried to make peace without fighting. Jephthah sent servants to the king of Ammon with this question: "What hast thou to do with me, that thou art come against me to fight in my land?"

The king of Ammon answered, "Because Israel took away my land."

Then Jephthah sent more servants to the king of Ammon and tried to explain to him how God led the Israelites out of Egypt and gave them the land of Canaan as their special land. He tried to explain to the king how silly it was to say that their idol-god Chemosh gave Ammon the land of Canaan, because the Almighty God gave it to His people Israel.

Do you think the king of Ammon listened to Jephthah's words of peace? No. He wanted to fight.

God put His Spirit into Jephthah's heart, and he went out with his soldiers to fight against Ammon. Before he left, he made a promise to God. Another word for a promise is a **vow**. This is what he promised: when he came back in peace from the battle, whatever came to meet him would be the Lord's. Jephthah was quite sure that a person — one of his family or one of his servants — would meet him. That person would be the Lord's. If an animal met him, it would be offered as a sacrifice to the Lord.

Then Jephthah went to fight, and the Lord gave the Israelites a great victory over the army of Ammon. When Jephthah came home his little girl, the only child he had, came to meet him, dancing with timbrels, to celebrate the victory that God had given. Poor Jephthah ripped his clothes because he felt so sad. He knew someone or something would meet him. He didn't know it would be his only child.

Jephthah told her, with sadness in his voice, that he had promised to offer the first thing that met him to the Lord. Jephthah did not burn his little girl on an altar to God. That would be wrong. But he offered her whole life to serve the Lord.

What did Jephthah's daughter say about it? She asked her father to let her go away for a little while to feel sad because she could never get married and be a mother, for she would be too busy working the Lord's work. When she came back, she lived her whole life as an offering to the Lord. That was a wonderful way to live, and the women of Israel remembered Jephthah's daughter every year.

REMEMBER:

Jephthah taught us a lesson when he tried to settle the fighting with peaceful talking. When we have fights with our friends, remember Jephthah, and use soft, peaceful words instead of our fists. Jephthah's way was God's way, for God says, "A soft answer turneth away wrath." Wrath is **anger.**

The Story of Samson (1)

All the stories about the judges start the same way: the Israelites were wicked again and served idols; and God sent an enemy to bother them. This time it was the Philistines, who ruled them for forty years. Forty years is a long time.

This time the Lord was going to use a different way to save Israel from the Philistine soldiers. He was going to save them by **one man.** One day the Angel of the Lord came to a woman who was from the tribe of Dan. She and her husband had no children, but they wished they had children. That was the news of the Angel: they were going to have a baby boy, a special boy who would be called a Nazarite. A Nazarite had to leave the sins of the world alone and live in holiness to God. A Nazarite had to live with three rules all his life: he might not cut his hair, he might not eat grapes or drink the wine from grapes, and he might not touch a dead body. These three rules were pictures of living **separate** and **holy** to the Lord.

Soon the words of the Angel came true, and God gave them a baby boy, whom they named Samson; and as he grew up, the Lord blessed him. But as he grew up, he did not always behave as one of God's children. Samson and his parents lived near the edge of the land of Israel, next-door to the land of the Philistines; and his father and mother let Samson wander over the hills to the land of the Philistines. They let him do what he wanted to do. And as he grew still older, he became a strong-willed boy who did not obey his parents but who saw to it that he got his own way. His parents had spoiled him, and now they did not know what to do with him.

When he grew up to be a man, he still wandered wherever he pleased in the land of the Philistines. There he saw a Philistine girl he wanted to marry. Just think! Samson was called by God to live a holy life, and now he wanted to marry a heathen girl who worshipped idols. He did not ask his parents whether he might marry her. He **told** them to get her for his wife.

His father and mother, who loved the Lord, talked to him about how wrong it was to marry a Philistine girl and told him to find an Israelite girl who loved the Lord. Do you know what Samson answered? "Get her for me; for she pleaseth me well."

His poor parents could not understand Samson. They did not know that the Lord was working in Samson's heart, so that he **wanted** to live in the land of the Philistines. If he lived there, he could make trouble and fight God's enemies. But Samson was not making trouble in the right way. It was not **right** of him to marry a wicked girl.

Samson's father and mother went with him to the land of the Philistines to see the girl he wanted to marry. On the way Samson did what he usually did — he wandered away from his parents, off by himself. Suddenly God put a young, roaring lion in his path. Why did God do that? To show to Samson how strong he was; for God's Spirit came on Samson and he could tear the lion's jaws apart as easily as he could tear apart a baby goat. Don't you think Samson was surprised and filled with wonder by the great strength God gave him?

Some time later he was on the way to the girl's house again — this time he was going to marry her — and he thought about the lion and went to look at its dead body. There, in the dead lion, the bees were making honey. He did not tell his parents nor the Philistine girl about the lion or the honey.

In those days, a wedding party lasted seven days and the man who was married needed friends with him. Samson did not take any friends along, so the Philistines found him thirty friends, not real friends, but wicked friends. At their wedding party, Samson told a riddle, not just for fun, but to make trouble with the Philistines. This was the riddle: Out of the eater came forth meat, and out of the strong came forth sweetness. We know that the riddle was about the lion Samson killed, but the Philistines at the wedding did not know anything about it. There were rules about guessing the riddle, too. If they guessed the answer, Samson had to give them thirty sets of clothes. If they could not guess it, they had to give Samson thirty sets of clothes.

Those Philistines didn't play fair. They went to Samson's wife and told her to make Samson tell the answer. Then she could tell them. For all the seven days of the party, Samson's wife begged and teased and cried to get him to tell her the answer. On the seventh day he finally told her the answer, and she told it to the Philistines. They came to Samson with the answer: What is sweeter than honey? And what is stronger than a lion?

The Spirit of the Lord came on Samson, and with great strength he killed thirty Philistines and gave their clothes to his friends who weren't **really** his friends. Then he went home angry, and Samson's wife was given to another husband.

REMEMBER:

Samson was one of God's children who fought by faith. But he was not an obedient boy. Because he did not obey his parents, he did not live in a happy home. Is **our** home a happy one? Do **we** obey our parents?

The Story of Samson (2)

Samson and his parents lived very close to the land of the Philistines and Samson must have heard that his wife was married to someone else now; but he said, so that everyone could hear, "I will go to my wife." Why did Samson say that? It was Samson's way of telling his own people, the Israelites, that he was going to make trouble, that he was going to fight the Philistines again.

The father of Samson's wife must have been surprised and scared to see Samson at his door. He never expected to see **him** again. To make peace, he offered to let Samson marry his wife's younger sister. Samson would not hear of that! He did not come to make peace. He came to make trouble.

Samson made plans to fight God's enemies all by himself. None of the Israelites was interested in helping him, so he turned to animals of the forest to help him. He caught three hundred young foxes, and tied them, two by two, by their tails. Between the tails of the two foxes he put a torch, which would burn as soon as he lit it. How could one man take care of three hundred wild foxes, make them stand still to get their tails tied together, and not have them all run away? He couldn't, not without God's help. God made the forest animals help Samson. It was a wonder.

At the same time, it was cruel of Samson to tie those tails together and then light the torch so that the foxes' tails started to burn. Samson was a strange man. It is hard to understand him. Those poor foxes went wild when they were set on fire. They ran as fast as they could, right through all the farms and fields of the Philistines, just where the Lord led them, so that they burned up the fields of the Philistines.

When the Philistines found out that Samson had sent those foxes, they tried to make peace with him by burning his wife and her father. They thought if they did that Samson would stop being angry. They did not understand that Samson was angry with **all** the Philistines because they were God's enemies and were making God's people serve idols. He killed many of the Philistines and then ran back to Israel and lived in a cave on the top of a rock called Etam.

The Philistines followed him. They were afraid of him, but they were angry, too, and came to kill him. When the people of Israel saw the Philistine soldiers in their land, they were afraid, too, and asked, "Why are ye come up against us?"

The Philistines answered, "To bind Samson."

That made the men of Israel feel better. Now they knew the Philistines would not fight **them**. They said that they would even help the Philistines tie up Samson. Can you imagine that? That the Israelites would tie up their leader and give him to their enemies? Listen to what Samson's own people said to him: "Knowest thou not that the Philistines are rulers over us?"

The people of Israel had walked so far away from God that they did not even mind that the Philistines ruled them. They liked the idols of the Philistines and they liked the way the Philistines lived. They did not care about worshipping God anymore. They did not act like God's people at all. They knew God had sent Samson to save them. They knew that was why God made him strong. But they did not want him to be their leader. How sad that must have made Samson feel!

The men of Israel promised not to kill him. They would only tie him up.
With three thousand men — just think, three thousand against one — the Israelites
came to the top of the rock and tied him with new ropes, and carried him down
from the rock. When the Philistines saw that their enemy was all tied up and
helpless, they shouted; and the Spirit of the Lord came on Samson and he broke
the thick, strong ropes as easily as you could break a thread that was burned.
A burned thread would fall apart. So did the ropes. Samson picked up the
nearest thing he could find. It was the jawbone of a donkey. With it, all alone, he
killed one thousand Philistines. No, he did not do it all alone. God was with
him. It was a wonder from God.

Samson had fought hard under the hot sun in a warm country, and he was
very thirsty when the battle was over. If he did not get water, he would die.
But there was no water in that place. Samson told God how badly he needed
water, and God opened a hollow place in the jawbone and made water come out
of it so that Samson could drink. After that, Samson judged Israel twenty years.

REMEMBER:

In this story some of the people of Israel sided with the wicked Philistines
rather than with God. That was wrong. We may never side with wickedness and
be friends with wicked people, not even a little bit. We are **God's** friends.

The Story of Samson (3)

Samson judged Israel for twenty years. He taught the Israelites to walk in God's ways; and the Israelites listened to him and started to worship the Lord again, and they agreed with Samson that the Philistines were God's enemies.

Near the end of those twenty years, Samson went back to his old sin: he liked to visit the heathen Philistine girls; he liked their pretty faces. This time he found a girl in the city of Gaza. He visited her house and stayed there until after dark, when the big gates of the city were closed and locked. The Philistines were watching him. They said they would wait for him all night and in the morning they would kill him. Do you think they **really** dared? They didn't even have to try because at midnight, when Samson wanted to go home and he found that the gates were locked, he picked up those huge, heavy gates, with their posts, and carried them up to the top of a hill. Probably he was laughing to himself at the trick he played on the Philistines. But it was not so funny for the Philistines, for any enemy could come into their city now.

One day, a little later, as Samson went through the country of the Philistines, he walked into the same kind of sin once more: he saw a pretty Philistine girl, named Delilah, and went to live with her. Samson liked Delilah, even though he knew all the time it was wrong to love a heathen girl. Delilah did not love Samson. She only pretended to. She acted kind and loving so she could help the Philistines capture him. Delilah loved her idol-gods and her wicked Philistine friends. They promised her very much money if she would find out for them what made Samson strong. If they knew **that** secret, they could capture him.

Delilah promised to help her friends and she asked Samson what made him so much stronger than other men. Samson **should** have been scared. He **should** have known that he could not trust Delilah. He **should** have told her that he was a special young man, a Nazarite, holy to the Lord. And then he should have run away from her.

Instead of doing that, Samson lied. He told her if he was tied with seven green branches, strong branches that could not break, he would be weak like other men. Delilah tied him with seven green branches. Maybe Samson even let her tie him up. In another room, her Philistine friends were hiding, and when she called out "The Philistines be upon thee, Samson," they could not get him because he broke the ropes as if they were threads.

Delilah acted as if her feelings were hurt. She scolded him because he mocked her and lied to her. She made Samson feel uncomfortable, but he knew he could not tell her his secret. So he told another lie: "If they bind me fast with new ropes, then shall I be weak, and be as another man." Once again Delilah tied him up, and called, "The Philistines be upon thee, Samson," and he broke the ropes as if they were threads.

Delilah knew that Samson was telling her lies, but she thought if she bothered him long enough, he would finally break down and tell the truth. Samson's next lie was nearer to the truth. It had something to do with his hair. He said if Delilah divided his hair into seven parts and wove those parts together, he would be weak. So while he slept, Delilah wove the seven parts of his hair and called, "The Philistines be upon thee, Samson." He awoke out of his sleep, and walked away, too strong for the Philistines.

Then Delilah worked harder than ever on Samson. She wouldn't give him any peace. Day after day she pestered him until he was sick to death of it all. He **knew** he could not trust her. He **knew** he should run far away from this wicked woman. But he wanted to live with Delilah a little while yet. He wanted to enjoy his sin a little bit longer. So he told her his secret. He told how he was a Nazarite, holy to God, ever since he was born. He told that he might never cut his hair because his long hair was a picture of being holy to the Lord. He told that if his hair were cut, he would be as weak as other men.

Delilah knew that this time Samson told her the truth. While he slept on her knees, she had a barber cut his hair, and this time she told the Philistines to come with the money in their hands. Then she called, "The Philistines be upon thee, Samson;" and Samson did not know that God had gone away from him.

231

Now he was weak, and the Philistines could easily capture him. They put out his eyes, tied him up, and made him grind corn and grain in prison. Poor Samson! And Delilah did not care!

In prison, Samson had a lot of time to talk with God. His hair began to grow again, too. Then one day the Philistines had a big party for Dagon, their idol-god; and someone said, "Call for Samson." They wanted to make fun of him. When Samson came to the party, he asked the boy who was leading him to let him lean against the big pillars that held the building up. Then he asked God to make him strong just once more. Leaning with all his might on the pillars, he pulled the whole building down. Samson died with the Philistines, and he killed more Philistines at his death than he did in his whole life.

REMEMBER:

When Delilah asked Samson why he was **different,** he told her lies. When someone asks us why we are different, we will tell the right answer, won't we? We will say that we are God's special children, holy to the Lord.

Naomi and Ruth

Near the end of the time that the judges ruled, after they had taught the people of Israel God's law over and over again, the Israelites **still** were worshipping idols instead of Jehovah, their God. They **still** did what was right in **their** eyes, not what was right in **God's** eyes; and they needed one of God's spankings again. This time, instead of sending an enemy with a big army, God kept back His rain and dried up His earth with dry winds and a hot sun so that the food in the fields and gardens would not grow. We call that a famine. Many people starve to death in a famine. God's people should have asked, "Why is God doing this?" They would have known the answer, too: "Because we are serving idols and will not be sorry and turn to God."

Most of God's people did not ask the right question. Let us visit the house of Elimelech and Naomi, who lived in Bethlehem. Elimelech was the father, Naomi was the mother, and they had two boys. This is the question they must have asked: "Where shall we go to get away from the famine?" They were supposed to stay in the land of Canaan because it was a picture of heaven, but they went to the heathen country of Moab, which was a picture of sin and death.

Elimelech and Naomi were God's children who were doing the wrong thing. God watched them go to wicked Moab, and soon after they came to that strange land, He made Elimelech die. Naomi should have heard what God was saying by making Elimelech die: "You are living in the wrong land;" but Naomi liked it in Moab, and stayed there for ten years. The famine was over, but Naomi stayed in Moab. Her two boys grew up without knowing God's people and without worshipping in His tabernacle; and when they were older, they married girls from Moab.

Then God had to talk harder to Naomi. He did not talk to her with a voice. He talked to her by making both her boys die while they were still young men. This time Naomi listened to what God was saying by taking her two boys. She knew she must go back to the land of Israel.

Ruth and Orpah, the two Moabite girls her boys had married, walked a little way with Naomi as she started her trip back to the land of Israel. Pretty soon, Naomi told them to go back home to their own people. She didn't have any more boys for them to marry. Ruth and Orpah loved Naomi and didn't want to leave her and go back. They said, "Surely we will return with thee unto thy people."

Finally Orpah decided she should go back to Moab. She cried and kissed Naomi because she felt so sad; and then she turned around and went back. Ruth would not turn around and go back, not even when Naomi told her to go back to her own people and her own gods. She said, "Intreat me not to leave thee. . . for where thou goest I will go. . .thy people shall be my people, and thy God my God."

When Naomi saw that Ruth wanted to go with her and would not change her mind, she did not talk about it anymore. Together Naomi and Ruth came back to Bethlehem, the city that Naomi had left ten years ago. She must have looked older and paler and sadder, for everyone was saying, "Is this Naomi?"

She asked them not to call her Naomi, which means "happy," but to call her Mara, which means "bitter" or "sad;" for she went away with a full family, and came back empty. Naomi did not blame the Lord for her troubles. She knew the Lord gave her trouble because of her own sins.

Then she and Ruth settled down in a house in Bethlehem. But they were poor. How would they get enough food to eat? God took care of them. In His law He told His people how to take care of His poor people who did not have enough to eat. This is what they must do: when they harvested the corn or the wheat or the barley or the grapes in their fields, they might not take every bit of it for themselves. If they dropped some, or if they left some at the edges of their fields, they might not pick it up. They must leave it for the poor. Then the poor people could pick it up. This was called **gleaning.**

Naomi knew a man who was a kind of cousin to her and who feared the Lord, too. His name was Boaz, and he was a rich man with many fields. Naomi sent Ruth to glean in the fields of Boaz. When he saw this strange young girl gleaning in his fields, he asked, "Whose damsel is this?"

His servants told him, "It is the Moabitish damsel that came back with Naomi."

Then Boaz remembered! He had heard of Ruth! He talked to her and was kind to her. He told her to stay to pick up barley and wheat in his fields and to help herself to food and drink on his farm. And he told his workers to drop some handfuls on purpose for her. Ruth had found a man who feared God to take care of her.

REMEMBER:

God's people love one another and take care of one another. When some of God's people are sick or poor, we help them and bring them food, because we love them. We love them so much because we both love the same Lord.

Ruth and Boaz

Every day Ruth had something to do. Every day, when she gleaned in the fields of Boaz, she saw how kind he was and how much he loved the Lord. And every day Boaz saw that Ruth had left her idol-gods and was learning to love Jehovah God. Boaz liked Ruth and Ruth liked Boaz.

Suddenly all the work in the field was finished. All the wheat and barley was cut, and Ruth had no more gleaning. Poor Ruth! What would she do now? Naomi knew. She was an Israelite who knew God's laws. She knew that if someone's husband died, her husband's brother or some other close relative should marry her. Ruth's husband had died, and Naomi knew that Boaz was a close relative to them. Maybe **he** could marry Ruth. Then Ruth would not be sad and lonely anymore. And God might even give her some children to make her happy.

Naomi told Ruth what to do: she must change her clothes. She had been wearing special clothes to show how sad she was that her husband had died. Now she would wear other clothes that meant she was ready to marry someone else. Then she must go to see Boaz that very night.

Where was Boaz that night? He was on his threshing floor. It was the big stone floor where they took all the wheat and barley and loosened the outside kernels and let them blow away. They saved the insides and piled them into sacks. That work took a long time and sometimes the workers stayed there all night and slept on the big stone threshing floor.

Boaz stayed at his threshing floor with the workers; and after they ate a good supper, he stayed right there to sleep, to be ready for work early the next morning. When it was very dark and quiet, Ruth walked onto the threshing floor of Boaz, and saw where Boaz was sleeping. She lay down at his feet and pulled a corner of his cover over her. She was making a picture when she did that. The picture said: cover me and take care of me.

At midnight Boaz woke up with a scare because he saw someone lying at his feet. He said, "Who art thou?"

She answered, "I am Ruth," and she asked him to spread his covering over her because he was a near relative.

Boaz knew all about God's laws, too. He promised to take care of her the very next day. She stayed there with Boaz until it was almost light and Boaz filled her apron with barley and told her to go home to Naomi.

That day Boaz went to the gate of his city, where the rulers sat, and he took with him a man who was even closer relation to Naomi and Ruth than he was. In front of the rulers, Boaz asked the other man whether he wanted to marry Ruth. That man had the first chance. The man said he was not ready to marry Ruth. Maybe he was married already. Maybe he did not want to marry a girl from the heathen country of Moab. We do not know why.

Do you think Boaz was happy? If the other man could not marry Ruth, then it was Boaz' turn. Now he could marry Ruth. That is what he wanted to do. In those days, this is what they did: the other man took off his shoe and gave it to Boaz. It was a sign that he gave up Ruth to let Boaz marry her. All the rulers watched as he gave Boaz his shoe.

Then Boaz and Ruth were married. What a happy day that was! Boaz was one of God's children who loved God with all his heart; and Ruth was God's dear child whom He had brought out of wicked Moab so that she could serve Him in Israel. Soon God gave Boaz and Ruth a baby boy. That boy, when he grew up, was the grandpa of King David. And King David was one of the grandfathers of Jesus. **Now** do you see what God did? He brought Ruth out of Moab so that she could be one of the grandmothers of Jesus!

REMEMBER:

We do not know what kind of face Ruth had, but we know that she had a beautiful heart that loved the Lord. It doesn't matter what kinds of faces we have, either. God looks at our hearts. Is **your** heart beautiful with love for God?

Samuel is Born

After Samson had died with the Philistines, the Lord called another man to judge Israel. His name was Eli, and he came from the family of Aaron. In Shiloh near the middle of Israel, where God's tabernacle was, Eli sat on a seat at the gate of the tabernacle; and there he taught God's people when they came to worship Him.

God's people could not go to His tabernacle every Sunday as we go to church each Sunday. It was too far away; and many people who lived **very** far away from the tabernacle at Shiloh went only once a year to sacrifice a lamb to God and to take presents to the tabernacle.

Elkanah and his family lived very far away and went to the tabernacle only once a year. Elkanah had married two wives. His first wife, Hannah, did not have any children, and Elkanah was disappointed. He wanted to have children, so he married another wife. That was very wrong of Elkanah. He could not be patient and wait for God to give him children, and he was not obeying God's law that said he might marry only one wife.

Elkanah's two wives gave him trouble. He loved Hannah the most; and Peninnah, his second wife, was jealous. The Lord gave Peninnah many children, but He still did not give Hannah any babies. Peninnah teased Hannah and talked hard to her. She kept telling Hannah that children were pictures of God's blessings — and Hannah didn't have **any** children. Then poor Hannah would cry and ask the Lord for a baby.

Once every year the whole family — Elkanah, Hannah, Peninnah, and her children — went to the tabernacle at Shiloh with a lamb to sacrifice to God and with an offering of thanks. As they ate their meal at God's house, Elkanah gave some of the meat to Peninnah and her children; but he gave twice as much to Hannah because he loved her so much. That made Peninnah angry, and she teased and mocked Hannah with words of hate. She kept telling Hannah that God did not love her because He didn't give her any children. Hannah did not answer her back. She just cried and could not eat. Year after year her enemy, Peninnah, said mean words to her, and Hannah became more sad every year as they went to God's tabernacle.

One year, after the meal, Hannah could not stand Peninnah's mocking words any longer. She left the table and went into the tabernacle to talk with God. Oh, she must have told God her troubles many times before, but never **right here in His house**. She asked God to **show** that He was blessing her by giving her a baby boy; and she promised that her boy would serve God all his life. Hannah was whispering her prayer to God, and no sounds came out of her lips.

Old Eli, the judge, who was sitting at the gate, watched Hannah. He thought she was acting so strangely. She must have drunk too much wine. Suddenly poor Hannah heard him say to her, "How long wilt thou be drunken? put away thy wine from thee."

Don't you think Hannah must have looked up, terribly surprised? Through her tears she told old Eli that she was not drunk. She told how she had been praying for a baby and promising the baby to the Lord. Then Eli blessed Hannah and asked that God would give her a son. Now Hannah's face was not sad anymore as she went home.

After they were home, God remembered Elkanah and Hannah and gave them a baby boy, whom they named **Samuel**, for she said, "I have asked him of the Lord."

For a few years, when Samuel was small, Hannah did not go to the tabernacle at Shiloh. She stayed at home to take care of her baby. When he was old enough to dress himself and feed himself, so that he did not need his mother so much anymore, Hannah took him along to the tabernacle.

There she showed him to Eli and told him how God had answered her prayer, and then she kept her promise to God: she left Samuel with Eli at the tabernacle to live there and to serve the Lord there. Do you think Hannah was sad to leave her little boy and go home without Samuel? Do you think little Samuel was lonesome for his mother? Maybe, at first. But he remembered his name: Samuel — asked of the Lord. It was time for Samuel to do God's work.

REMEMBER:

We, too, belong to the Lord. For a little while we are given to our mothers and fathers; but we **belong** to God, and we must serve Him all our lives.

The Philistines
Take Away God's Ark

Every day the boy Samuel helped old Eli with the work of the tabernacle. People came every day to sacrifice lambs to the Lord. Old Eli had two grown-up boys who helped, too; but they were wicked helpers. They did not care about God's house, and tried to do as much wickedness as they could. Eli was not strict with his two sons. He should have made them stop their terrible wickedness, but he only said, "Why do ye such things?" and his sons did not even listen to him.

God saw all the wickedness of Eli's two sons, and He sent a prophet to tell Eli that God would punish his family by having him and his two sons die in one day. Do you think Eli talked with his boys and **made** them stop their wickedness? Do you think his boys were sorry and obeyed the Lord? They didn't. Their wickedness only became worse.

The days and the years went by. Every year Samuel's mother came to the tabernacle to worship the Lord, to see Samuel, and to bring him a new coat. He kept on growing and needed a bigger one each year. Samuel probably saw his mother only once a year. That must have been a happy time for them both!

One day as Samuel was growing up, the Lord came to him. The Lord had been quiet for a long time as He watched all the evil that His people were doing. Samuel did not know yet what God's voice sounded like; and then one night God came to him in a quiet voice, so that Samuel would not be afraid.

God called, "Samuel," and Samuel answered, "Here am I." He thought old Eli was calling and he ran to him and said again, "Here am I."

But Eli said, "I called not, lie down again."

After he lay down, God called again, "Samuel." Again Samuel got up and went to Eli and said, "Here am I."

And again Eli said, "I called not, my son; lie down again."

For the third time God called Samuel, and for the third time Samuel ran to Eli and said, "Here am I."

Then Eli knew that it was **the Lord's** voice calling Samuel. He told Samuel how to answer the Lord the next time: "Speak, Lord; for thy servant heareth."

When God came to Samuel again, He told him the sad news about Eli and his family: Eli and his two sons would die on the same day. **Now** Eli would have to listen because **God's** voice was speaking. Samuel did not go straight to Eli. He was afraid to tell. In the morning he told Eli all of God's sad words.

Not very long after that, the people of Israel went to fight the Philistines. God did not tell them to. They just did what was right in **their own** eyes. In that battle God let the Philistines kill forty thousand Israelites.

The Israelite soldiers seemed surprised and asked, "Wherefore hath the Lord smitten us today before the Philistines?" They really knew the answer. God was not blessing them when they were living in such great sin. But they thought they knew the answer to their problem: they would take God with them to the next battle with the Philistines. Do you know what they took? God's holy ark, the one that the high priest might sprinkle with blood only once a year. They

243

went into God's Most Holy Place and took His ark out onto the dirty, bloody field where they would fight the Philistines. They took that ark without making their hearts clean before God. They said that the **ark** would save them. Would the ark out there in the mud and dirt save them? No, it wouldn't because God had left the ark and was not there to help them. Hophni and Phinehas, Eli's two boys, took the ark. And Eli did not stop them!

When the Israelite soldiers saw the ark coming, they shouted so loudly that the earth rang. Soon the Philistines heard about the ark, and they were dreadfully afraid; but they decided to fight like brave men anyway. That day the Philistines won a great victory over Israel and killed thirty thousand Israelite soldiers. Hophni and Phinehas were both killed, too; and the Philistines took the ark to their own land.

Poor Eli sat by the tabernacle, shaking with fear. He knew that God's ark was gone, and he could hear the noise of the fighting. At last a man came running to him with news. He told Eli these four things: the Israelites are running away from the Philistines; many Israelite soldiers are killed; Hophni and Phinehas are dead; and the ark of God is taken to the land of the Philistines.

When Eli heard the news about God's ark, he could not stand it anymore. He was such an old man — almost one hundred years old — and he fell backward and broke his neck and died. That is how the sad day ended — the day that God's glory left Israel.

REMEMBER:

Israel did not think much of their holy God or His holy ark. They dragged it to the battlefield. We must never forget how holy our God is; and when we read the Bible or go to church, we will always remember to bow before His holiness.

God's Ark Makes Trouble for the Philistines

With wicked hands the Philistines took God's ark from the field where they had won the war with the Israelites. Then they ran back to the city of Shiloh in Israel and killed God's priests and set fire to the city. They were trying to **destroy** the worship of God. That means to take the worship of God right off the earth.

Those wicked Philistines were trying to fight God. Now that they had His ark, they thought they had captured the God of the whole earth. We know better. God had left His ark when Eli's wicked sons stole it from the tabernacle. What did the Philistines do with His ark? They took it to Ashdod, one of their great cities, and put it into the temple of their idol-god Dagon. The top half of Dagon looked like a man, and the bottom half looked like a fish. What an ugly god they had! This is the god they **thanked** for helping them destroy the worship of Jehovah-God.

Deep down in their hearts, the Philistines knew they could never capture the God of the whole earth; and deep down in their hearts the Lord was bothering the Philistines. They were afraid of God. That is probably why some of the Philistines got up early in the morning to see if everything was all right in the temple of Dagon. Everything was not all right. Dagon, that ugly idol, had fallen on his face to the ground. It looked as if he were worshipping the ark. **God** made it look that way, as if Dagon were saying, "Jehovah is God. Dagon is nothing." The Philistines knew what God was telling them, but they would not pay attention. Quietly, they picked up their great god — who was not great at all — and set him in his place again.

The next morning some of the Philistines hurried to the temple of Dagon again, and they saw their idol lying flat before the ark, with his hands and his head cut off. God did that, and He was making that broken idol to be a picture for the Philistines. Hands are pictures of **doing something**. A head **thinks**. Without hands and a head, Dagon was not worth **anything**. He was just the stump of a fish.

That was just the beginning of the trouble in the land of the Philistines. First, the Lord sent sickness to the city of Ashdod where His ark was. The people of Ashdod had sores and boils which made them very sick. Many, many of them died. Besides that, the Lord sent thousands of mice, which ran wild over the land and destroyed their crops in the fields and bit the people, carrying the sickness from one person to other people.

Now the people in the city of Ashdod were not so happy that they had the ark. All their people seemed to be dropping dead! They asked, "What shall we do with the ark?" They did not want to take it back to the land of the Israelites and say that they had lost the battle with the Lord; but they did not want all the Philistines to die either. What did they do? They made their hearts hard and said that **God** did not send the sickness to Ashdod. The sickness just happened.

So they sent the ark to Gath, another great city of the Philistines, to see what would happen; and God followed the ark with trouble and sickness and death. The people in Gath had the same kinds of boils and sores as the people of Ashdod. **They** were all dying, too. **They** did not want the ark in their city.

Next they sent the ark to Ekron, another city of the Philistines; but the people of Ekron would not take the ark. They begged the rulers of the city of Gath to take it away because they did not want to be dead people.

There was nothing to do but take the ark back to the land of Israel, and the rulers of the cities got the ark ready to go. Though they were not truly sorry for sinning against God, they sent along an offering for their sin. They wanted

to stop God's anger against them by sending five golden mice and five golden boils, pictures of the terrible sicknesses they had had.

Those wicked Philistines still did not want to believe that the God of Israel, the God of the ark, sent the sickness. They made one more test. They took two cows who had just had baby calves, harnessed them to a wagon with the ark and the golden presents on it, and let the cows and the wagon go.

If the cows followed **their own** wills, they would have gone straight to their babies, who were crying for their mothers. If they were led **by God**, they would walk on the road that led back to Israel without paying attention to their babies. While the rulers of the Philistines watched them, the cows walked the Lord's way, back to the land of Israel.

REMEMBER:

The Philistines tried to get their hands on God and kill Him. The wicked men of this world always try to get their hands on God. When God sent His Son Jesus to earth, they tried to kill Him, too. That was the time that God **let** them nail Jesus to the cross, so that He would die — to save us from our sins.

247

Bethshemesh
and Mizpeh

The five rulers of the five great cities of the Philistines went along with the ark of God, which the mother cows were pulling on the wagon. Straight to the land of Israel they went and came to Bethshemesh, the nearest city of Israel. The Israelite farmers, busy working in their fields, gathering in their wheat, looked up at the strange parade coming down the road: two cows pulling a wagon with a box and golden presents on it; and five rulers of the Philistines coming on behind.

Suddenly they knew what it was! The ark! Oh, they were happy! They stopped their work and started to run toward a very big stone in a field, where God was leading the wagon. The Israelites knew that only the men from the tribe of Levi might work with God's holy things, and they called some of the Levites to take the ark of Jehovah-God and the golden mice and golden boils and put them on the large stone. Then the men of Bethshemesh broke the wood of the wagon, built an altar to God, burned the wood on the altar, and offered the cows as a thank-you sacrifice to God. After that, the five Philistine rulers went back home.

All the people of Bethshemesh were so happy and so interested in God's ark. They had never seen it before; and everyone was crowding around to get a good look. They were nosy!

Before they knew what was happening, many people dropped dead. The Lord killed them. Now they were not laughing and singing! They were screaming and crying.

Why did the Lord come so quickly to kill those people who wanted to get a good look at His ark? The answer is that it was very wrong to look at God's holy things with wicked eyes, and the Israelites knew it. God's law told them not to look at His holy things, or they would die.

But the Israelites at Bethshemesh had forgotten all about God's law. They did not want to remember the rules for worshipping God. It was much more fun to worship Baal; and, without any change in their hearts, with all their sins still in them, they rushed to look at the holy ark with nosy faces and wicked eyes. The Lord, Who is so holy, could not let that sin go. He had to teach them to obey Him. That is why they died.

The men of Bethshemesh asked, "Who is able to stand before this holy Lord God?"

Instead of making their hearts clean, they decided to get rid of the ark, and they sent it away to another city. There they put the ark into the house of a man named Abinadab. They **should** have been sorry for their sins and they **should** have taken the ark to God's tabernacle where it belonged, and where He could live with them again. But they left God's house empty and hid God's ark away in the house of Abinadab for twenty years. Think of that! God's ark was hiding away in prison for twenty years, and the people did not care.

God cared. He let the Philistines keep bothering the Israelites for those twenty years. After those twenty years the Israelites cried to Him to help them in their trouble. The Lord heard them and sent Samuel, who told them what to do: put away all your idols, and turn with all your hearts to serve the only God. Israel listened and put away their idols and served the Lord only.

Samuel told the Israelites to come together at Mizpeh, and he would pray to the Lord for them. When they came to Mizpeh, the people did not eat that day but prayed with Samuel and said, "We have sinned against the Lord."

All this time the Philistines were watching the Israelites, and they saw that **this** was the time to fight Israel. The Israelites had come without their swords and spears and could not fight back. The Philistines would march like a wall around them and kill them all.

When the Israelites saw the great danger they were in, they asked Samuel not to stop praying to God for them. Samuel kept on praying for them and offered a sacrifice to the Lord, and the Lord answered. He thundered with a great thunder and made the Philistines run away in great fear. The Israelites chased them and killed many of them.

Then Samuel set up a stone and called it Ebenezer. Ebenezer means, "Hitherto hath the Lord helped us."

REMEMBER:

Often we are like the men of Bethshemesh. We forget how holy and pure our God is; and when we pray to Him, we do not get our hearts ready. Remember to think about how great and good our God is **every time** we pray.

Israel Asks for a King

When Samuel grew up, he traveled back and forth through the land of Israel, teaching the people and offering sacrifices. One day, in one of the cities, the rulers of all the tribes of Israel came to him and asked him a question that made him so surprised and sad. They said, "Give us a king to judge us."

Samuel was surprised and sad because the rulers of Israel wanted a king so that they could be just like the wicked people around them — the Moabites, the Philistines, the Ammonites. He was surprised and sad because the Israelites already **had** a king. God was their King. Many of the Israelites were tired of having God for a King and were tired of listening to a judge who told them God's words.

At first Samuel did not answer the people. He went to God and prayed about it. How surprised he must have been once more when God answered, "Hearken unto the voice of the people in all that they say unto thee." God explained to him that they didn't want **Samuel** because they didn't want **God.** God and Samuel spoke the same words.

When Samuel told the rulers of the people that a king would not always be kind to them but would take their money and some of their animals and their wheat and corn for himself, the rulers answered, "Nay, but we will have a king over us." They would not listen to Samuel. Not all of the Israelites asked God with wicked hearts for a king. Those who loved the Lord with pure hearts wanted **God** to be their King.

Samuel sent the rulers of Israel home, saying, "Go ye every man unto his city." God would not give them a king right away. Samuel kept going through the land of Israel, judging the people and sacrificing lambs on their altars. One day, when he was in one of the cities, the Lord told him in his ear that tomorrow he would send him the man who would be the king of Israel. The Lord told Samuel, too, that the king would save the people from the Philistines. Poor Samuel could not understand why the Lord would give the wicked people in Israel a king, but he obeyed the Lord and waited to meet the man God would send to him.

251

Would you like to meet the man who would be the first king of Israel, too? Then come with me to the tribe of Benjamin. One of the men of the family of Benjamin was called Kish. He was a rich man, with much land and many animals. But he was having trouble. His donkeys — probably many of them — had gotten away, and now they were lost. Someone would have to go to find them.

Kish had a son, a grown-up son, who was a very nice-looking man, brave and strong, and very tall: about a head taller than most people. His name was Saul. Father Kish said to Saul, "Take one of the servants with thee, and arise, go seek the asses." Asses is another word for **donkeys.**

Saul and his servant looked and looked for the donkeys, but they could not find them. After they had been gone for three days, Saul started to think about his father. By now his father would not care about the donkeys anymore but was probably worried about Saul and his servant. Maybe they should go home.

His servant had a better idea. He had heard that the man of God was in the city near by. Perhaps **he** could show them where to look. That man of God was Samuel. Saul thought it was a good idea to go to Samuel, too. Up the hill to the city they went, where they found some young girls who told them to go up one more hill, and there they would find the man of God ready to sacrifice a lamb on an altar in front of all the people. If they hurried, they would still be in time for the sacrifice.

Saul had **heard** of the man of God, who was Samuel, but he had never **seen** him; and he didn't know that Samuel was **waiting** for him. As Saul and his servant hurried up the hill, they met Samuel, and Saul asked where he could find the man of God. Don't you think Saul was surprised when Samuel said, "**I am** the man of God"?

Many more words came tumbling out of Samuel's mouth, so fast that Saul could hardly believe them. Samuel said, "Ye shall eat with me today; and I will tell thee all that is in thine heart. And as for thine asses that were lost three days ago, set not thy mind on them, for they are found. And on whom is all the desire of Israel?"

The desire? The **best**? The best was to be the **king**.

Saul did not think very much of himself. Wasn't he from just a little tribe in Israel, and wasn't his family just a little one in his tribe? But Samuel took Saul and his servant home with him after the sacrifice. They had the best places at the dinner table, and Saul had the best food at the meal. Afterwards, Samuel and Saul talked together a long time.

REMEMBER:

It seemed as if Samuel and Saul just happened to be in the same city on the same day. But **the Lord** had led them both there that day. The Lord leads us, too, when we meet our friends, and wherever we go. He guides every step we take.

God Gives Israel a King

When the prophet Samuel invited Saul to eat dinner with him, he did not tell anyone else that God had chosen **Saul** to be the king. Even the next morning, when Samuel and Saul got up early, they did not tell anyone their secret. Saul sent his servant on ahead while he talked on the roof of the house with Samuel. Roofs of houses in those days were flat, with railings around them, with steps leading up to the roof; and people used their roofs as we use porches.

Before Samuel let Saul go home, he took a bottle of sweet-smelling oil and poured it over Saul's head. We call it **anointing**. The anointing with oil was God's way of telling Saul he would be king.

Then Samuel gave Saul three signs that would surely happen. When they happened, Saul would know that Samuel was **truly** God's prophet and that all his words would come true. The first sign was that Saul would meet two men, and they would tell him his father was worried about him. The second sign was that he would meet three men carrying three goats and three loaves of bread. They would give Saul two loaves of bread. The third sign was that he would meet some of God's prophets, singing and playing instruments.

Saul left Samuel then and went on his way. Would all these things happen to him? Yes, all three signs happened, just as Samuel had said! Saul was happy! He had a secret! He was going to be the greatest man in the land! And when he heard the prophets talking and singing, the Lord gave Saul a new heart, a heart that was strong and brave, a heart that could rule over the people.

Saul stayed with the prophets of God for a while, and talked and sang with them; and all the prophets were surprised. They looked at one another and said, "What is this that is come unto Saul the son of Kish? Is Saul also among the prophets?"

Why were those prophets so surprised at Saul? Before that day Saul had never wanted to talk about God and sing His praises. He never wanted anyone to tell him to obey God's law. He didn't like to hear Bible stories or offer sacrifices or talk about Jesus. What **did** Saul like to talk about? His farm, his family, his work, and having a good time. Saul was not one of God's own children. In his heart he did not love God.

When Saul came home to his father's house, he did not tell anyone his secret. For a little time he worked on his father's farm again, until the day that Samuel called all Israel together to Mizpeh to show them the man God chose to be king.

Many, many people came to Mizpeh, and some of them had to come from very
far away. They had to take pots and pans and food and clothes and even tents to
sleep in along the way. When they all came to Mizpeh, they piled all their stuff —
we call it baggage — in one place, in a huge pile. What a big pile of baggage that
must have been!

After they had tied up all their animals, the people sat down to listen to
Samuel. He still scolded the Israelites because they wanted a **man** to be their
king instead of **God.** Then, in front of all the people, he chose the man who
would be their king.

First, all the tribes walked in front of Samuel, and God chose the tribe of
Benjamin. When all the families in the tribe of Benjamin walked in front of
Samuel, God chose the family of Matri. When the family of Matri walked in front
of Samuel, God chose Saul, the son of Kish. But where was he? He was gone!
People started to look for him, but they could not find him. He was hiding.

Why was Saul hiding? He was afraid. He had no God to trust in or to help
him. He could only trust in himself, and he was too afraid to be the king. The
people asked the Lord where he was and the Lord told them: "He hath hid himself among the stuff." There he was, hiding behind the huge pile of baggage.
When they found him and set him in front of all the Israelites, all the people saw
what a strong and handsome man he was, and that he stood higher than all the
people from his shoulders upward. Then all those excited people shouted, "God
save the king!"

REMEMBER:

People like Saul, who do not love God, have to live all their lives alone,
without God. They can never go to Him for help. But we who love God call Him
our Father, and He always listens to us and helps us.

Saul Helps
Jabesh-Gilead

Some of the people of Israel were not happy with their new king. They had been so eager to go to Mizpeh to see who it would be. They could hardly wait! But when Samuel had called his name, Saul was too scared to be there. He was hiding! After they found Saul, and the Israelites shouted, "God save the king," they all went home, and Saul went back to his farm. What kind of king was that? Some of the men of Israel said, "How shall this man save us?" Only a few men, whose hearts God had touched, went home with Saul.

Then one of the cities of Israel, called Jabesh-Gilead, was having trouble. Nahash, the king of the wicked Ammonites, was bothering the people of Jabesh-Gilead. He came with his armies to fight them. Why didn't the people of Jabesh-Gilead get their soldiers and fight back? Because they had stopped serving Jehovah-God and were worshipping idols. Now that they had trouble with the Ammonites, they had no God to help them. Their idol-gods could not help them, and they did not **want** to trust in the Lord.

What could the people of Jabesh-Gilead do? They could promise to do what Nahash the king of the Ammonites wanted them to do: they would make friends with him and be his slaves and work for him. What a terrible thing that was! God had told His people **never** to be friends with the heathen people who served idols. Now the people of Jabesh-Gilead were going to be the **slaves** of the heathen people, too.

That isn't all. The wicked king Nahash said he needed a **sign** that the people of Jabesh-Gilead would serve him as his slaves: he would take out everyone's right eye. How awful! And if Nahash could do it to the men of Jabesh-Gilead, he could go through the whole land of Israel, putting out the people's right eyes. It would be a sign that Nahash and the Ammonites were the rulers over Israel.

The people of Jabesh-Gilead could not let the cruel Nahash do **that**. They asked for seven days to try to get help from the rest of the people of Israel, and Nahash gave them the seven days. He was sure they would not get help from the rest of Israel anyway. At first, it seemed as though Nahash was right. When the people of Israel heard the sad story, they were sorry and they cried, but they did not offer any help to the people of Jabesh-Gilead.

Then one day as Saul was coming out of his field, he heard all the people crying. He asked, "What aileth the people that they weep?" and then they told him the bad news.

Saul did not cry. He was angry, furiously angry. The Spirit of God to make him strong and brave came upon Saul, and he cut up his oxen that were pulling his farm wagon into pieces. Then he sent men through all the land of Israel with the pieces of the dead oxen in their hands. They had to say, "Whosoever cometh not forth after Saul and after Samuel, so shall it be done unto his oxen."

The people did not want their animals cut up. The fear of God fell upon them, and all the soldiers started to run to Saul to help him. So many soldiers came that soon Saul had an army of three hundred thirty thousand men; and he sent the news to Jabesh-Gilead that tomorrow by the time the sun was hot they would have help.

How happy the people of Jabesh-Gilead must have been! They were tricky, too. They did not tell the wicked Nahash that they were getting help. All they said was, "Tomorrow we will come out unto you, and ye shall do with us what seemeth good unto you."

King Nahash was sure that the people of Jabesh-Gilead were getting no help. Tomorrow he would put out their right eyes. He was not ready at all for Saul's big army that was waiting for them in the morning. Saul and his army fought the Ammonites so hard that the Ammonites ran in every direction. No two Ammonite soldiers could stay together. Saul and his army won a great victory.

Now the Israelites were happy with King Saul, and they wanted to kill the Israelites who did not like Saul; but Saul would not let them do that. He said, "Today the Lord hath wrought salvation in Israel."

REMEMBER:

King Saul knew that the Lord is God. He knew that God made his army win over their wicked enemies. But Saul did not love the Lord. God's own dear children are different from Saul. We say that He is God with **love** and **thanks** in our hearts.

The Lord Saves Israel Through Jonathan

Saul had been king of Israel two years and he was trying to get an army together. So far he had three thousand young soldiers. **Saul** taught some of the soldiers how to fight and his son **Jonathan** taught the rest of them. What a hard time they had! They did not have any sharp swords and spears to fight with, but only tools like axes and plows and forks that they took from their farms. Do you know why? The Philistines were ruling over them, and they had taken away all of Israel's swords and spears and would not let them make anymore weapons for fighting. Only Saul and Jonathan had a sword and spear.

Besides that, the Philistines had put their soldiers all over the land of Israel to keep watch. Jonathan, Saul's son, was brave and he fought some of the Philistine soldiers and won the battle. When the Philistines heard about it, they were angry and made their big armies ready for war with Israel.

Saul called all the men of Israel to fight the Philistines, but when they came to him, he did not lead them to the battle. He was afraid. So were the soldiers. They started to run away, and many of them hid in caves and in big rocks and in the woods. Soon only six hundred frightened soldiers were left with Saul.

Where was Jonathan? He was near to the army of the Philistines, with his armor-bearer. His armor-bearer was a man who carried Jonathan's armor. What was armor? It was pieces of strong iron that a soldier wore over his chest and his legs, and a strong iron helmet for his head. If someone tried to kill him with a spear, that strong iron would stop the spear, and the soldier would not get hurt. But a soldier did not wear his armor **all the time** — only when he fought. When he did not wear it, his armor-bearer carried it.

The army of the Israelites was standing near a high rock. The army of the Philistines was standing across from them near another rock. Between them was a valley. Jonathan and his armor-bearer could not sit still. They left the army of the Israelites without telling anyone and climbed the rock up to the

259

army of the Philistines and let the guards of the army see them. Jonathan was not afraid. He trusted in God and loved Him with all his heart; and he believed that the Lord could save Israel by a big army or by only two men. Maybe God would save them by two men: Jonathan and his armor-bearer.

But Jonathan did not know for sure if it was the Lord's will to save Israel by two men. He needed a sign: if the Philistine guards saw them and said, "Stand still," it would be a sign that they must not fight; but if the guards said, "Come up unto us," it would be God's sign that they must climb all the way up and fight.

Suddenly the Philistine guards saw Jonathan and his armor-bearer. Those wicked Philistines boasted, "Come up to us, and we will show you a thing."

Jonathan and his armor-bearer climbed up with their hands and their feet, for now they knew that the Lord would let them win over the Philistines.

What a surprise for the Philistines. They were scared! In a moment, Jonathan and his armor-bearer had killed twenty Philistine soldiers. Why didn't those Philistines fight back? The Lord made their hearts melt with fear and at the same time He sent a terrible earthquake. The ground under them was shaking! The Philistines were so mixed up and so afraid that they began to beat one another down.

Across the valley on the other high rock, Saul and his six hundred soldiers watched as the Philistines started killing one another. Then the Philistines ran, and it looked to Saul as though their army was just melting away. Saul said, "Number now and see who is gone from us;" and they discovered that Jonathan and his armor-bearer were missing. Now that the Philistines were running away, all the Israelite soldiers who were hiding in caves suddenly became brave again and chased the Philistine army.

Before they left, King Saul commanded that no one was to eat any food that day. It would take too much time, and Saul wanted to have all the honor of winning over his enemies. That was a very foolish command. Fighting in that warm country was hard work, and a little food and drink would have made the soldiers feel so much better.

Jonathan did not hear his father Saul's command. He was far ahead, fighting; and when he came to a woods and found honey dropping from a tree, he ate some of it and felt better. He did not know he was doing anything wrong.

That night, when the people asked God whether they should go on chasing the Philistines, He did not answer. Something was wrong. Saul decided someone had sinned, and he cast lots. Saul and Jonathan were on one side, and all the people were on the other side. Saul and Jonathan were chosen, and then Jonathan explained that he disobeyed a command that he did not even hear.

Saul said he must be punished anyway. Jonathan must die. The people would not hear of it. They said, "Shall Jonathan die, who hath wrought this great salvation in Israel? God forbid." And they rescued Jonathan from his foolish father.

REMEMBER:

Saul loved himself and fought the Philistines for **his own** honor. Jonathan loved the Lord and fought for **God's glory.** Shall we try to be like Jonathan in all the things we do, and do **everything** to God's glory?

261

Saul
Disobeys

Samuel came to Saul one day with a message from God: Saul must go out to fight the Amalekites, whom the Lord hated. Samuel told Saul to kill **everyone** of the Amalekites — the fathers and mothers, the grandfathers and grandmothers, and even all the children — and **all** their animals, and to destroy everything that they had; for they were a very wicked people, and God wanted them wiped off the earth.

Saul gathered a large army of two hundred thousand soldiers and went to fight the Amalekites; and the Lord gave the Israelite soldiers a great victory. Saul and the Israelites destroyed all the people **except** the king, and they killed all the animals **except** the best of some of the sheep and oxen. Do you think that was good enough obedience?

No, it was not. This is what God said to Samuel: "It repenteth me that I have set up Saul to be king: for he is turned back from following me, and hath not performed my commandments." Now Samuel knew that Saul had not obeyed the Lord.

Poor Samuel could not sleep all that night. He cried and prayed to God all night, because he felt so sad and sorry about King Saul's disobedience. The next morning Samuel got up early to be ready to meet King Saul and his soldiers as they came back from the war, but he did not find them. Someone told him that Saul went another way, to Gilgal, to set up a big pillar to celebrate the victory in the war. Why did Saul go another way? Because he knew he did wrong and did not want to meet Samuel?

Samuel had to follow Saul to Gilgal. He would not let Saul get away! Saul could see Samuel coming, and in his heart he was not happy to see him; but he put on a friendly face and went out to meet Samuel. Samuel did not even have to ask him whether he obeyed God's command. Saul talked first. The first thing he said was, "I have performed the commandment of the Lord."

Samuel asked, "What meaneth then this bleating of the sheep in mine ears, and the lowing of the oxen which I hear?"

Saul had an answer ready. He was ready to blame someone else. He said, "The **people** spared the best of the sheep and of the oxen to sacrifice unto the Lord." He was telling Samuel that keeping them to sacrifice to the Lord was **good**. Was it?

Then Samuel had to scold Saul. He said something like this: when you were afraid and did not think so much of yourself, the Lord made you king; now that you are king, you think so much of yourself that you think you know better than the Lord. Samuel had more words for Saul. He said, "To obey is better than sacrifice, and to hearken than the fat of rams." Saul and the people did just the opposite. They would **not** obey but brought a sacrifice — a wicked, disobedient sacrifice — instead.

The last words of Samuel were the worst. He told Saul the bad news that the Lord would take away the kingdom from his family and make someone from another family to be king.

Then Saul was afraid and said, "I have sinned;" and he begged Samuel to turn and worship the Lord with him, as if nothing had happened.

Samuel could not do that! He could not change God's words! He could not worship the Lord with the man from whom God had just taken the kingdom!

Samuel had nothing more to say to Saul and he turned to leave him. As Samuel turned to leave, Saul pulled on his coat to keep him from going, and Samuel's coat ripped. When Saul did that, he was making a picture of what would happen. Samuel told him about it: the kingdom would be ripped from him and would be given to one of his neighbors, who was better than Saul.

263

Even after those words, Saul begged Samuel to change his mind and worship the Lord with him in front of all the people, so that Saul would still be honored in front of all the people. Samuel gave in and worshipped the Lord there with Saul. But first he commanded that Agag, the Amalekite king, had to be killed, as God had said. After that, Samuel went home and did not ever see Saul again.

REMEMBER:

We can learn much from Samuel's words to Saul: "to obey is better than sacrifice." When our daddies and mothers tell us to do something, God wants us to **obey** them, and not to do **anything else,** not even bring them a present.

Samuel
Anoints David

Samuel was sad. Saul seemed to be doing everything wrong, all because he did not love the Lord and do what He said. Samuel was sad that Saul might not be king anymore.

God came to him one day and said, "How long wilt thou mourn for Saul?" God had work for Samuel to do. He must go to the city of Bethlehem and pour some sweet-smelling oil over one of the sons of a man named Jesse. That boy would be the next king of Israel, a king who would love the Lord.

But Samuel had a problem. He asked the Lord, "How can I go? if Saul hear it, he will kill me." Samuel knew that Saul would do everything he could to keep **himself** on the throne, as the king of Israel. He did not want anyone else to be king instead of himself.

The Lord had an answer to Samuel's problem. He told Samuel to take an animal with him and tell the people that he was going to Bethlehem to sacrifice the animal to God. Samuel had been going through the land for so many years, sacrificing to the Lord. No one would think it strange, not even Saul. The Lord told Samuel one thing more: to invite Jesse to the sacrifice.

When the people of Bethlehem saw Samuel coming, they were afraid. Had they done something wrong? They asked Samuel, "Comest thou peaceably?"

He answered, "Peaceably."

Then he told the rulers of the city and Jesse and his sons to wash themselves and their clothes before he made the sacrifice. That was a picture of making themselves clean on the inside before God.

Samuel was so eager to see Jesse's sons! One of them would be the next king! Jesse's sons must have been eager to meet Samuel, too. He was the great prophet in Israel and important company. But they did not know why Samuel looked at them all so closely. He was waiting for God's voice to tell him, "This is the one."

First the oldest boy, Eliab, came up to Samuel. He was such a tall, fine-looking young man that Samuel thought that Eliab surely was the one God would choose. He wasn't; for God told Samuel he was looking at Eliab the wrong way: **Samuel** was seeing how nice he looked on the outside, but **God** was looking at Eliab's heart. Eliab's heart was not the loving heart God wanted.

Abinadab come next, and then Shammah, but God told Samuel He did not choose them, either. Seven of Jesse's boys came up to Samuel, and the Lord did not choose any of them.

Now what? Samuel asked Jesse, "Are here all thy children?"

Jesse answered, "There remaineth yet the youngest, and he keepeth the sheep."

Samuel said, "Send and fetch him."

He could hardly wait for the young shepherd boy! And Samuel was so happy when he saw him! The shepherd boy had reddish hair, beautiful eyes, and a lovely face; and his name was David.

The Lord said, "Arise, anoint him: for this is he." When he poured the sweet-smelling oil over David's head, probably only Jesse and David and Samuel knew the secret.

Then Samuel went home, and David went back to his sheep in the grassy pastures. He took his harp with him, and while he watched the sheep on the quiet hills around Bethlehem, he played tunes on his harp and made up songs: songs about the way God made the sky, with its fluffy clouds, songs about the sunshine and the rain that God sent, and songs about trusting in God. Maybe the

one he liked best was "The Lord is my Shepherd." David had many quiet, happy days with his sheep and with his Shepherd, Who was God. David was not ready to be king yet.

Now we must leave this quiet, happy shepherd boy and peek at King Saul. Most of the time these days, he had an unhappy, ugly face; for he could not forget Samuel's words, "The Lord hath rent the kingdom of Israel from thee this day, and hath given it to a neighbour of thine." Saul thought about it. Who would his neighbor be? If only he could lay his hands on him!

Then Saul would be angry and quiet, or he would be impatient and shout; and when the Lord sent an evil spirit inside him to trouble him, he sometimes behaved like a crazy man.

His poor servants did not know what to do with King Saul sometimes. They wondered whether quiet music would make him feel better; and when they looked for someone to make quiet music for Saul, they found David, the shepherd boy. When David came to Saul with his harp, he took with him a little present. He played his harp when the evil spirit came over Saul, and Saul loved David.

REMEMBER:

The difference between David and Saul was that David lived in peace and love with God and Saul would not listen to God nor love Him. Aren't you glad you can live like David, in love and peace with God?

David Kills Goliath

All the time that Saul was king, he fought wars with the Philistines. Now Saul's army and the Philistine army were getting ready for another battle. Each army was on a high hill, with a valley between them.

The battle is not ready to start yet, for see who is walking out of the Philistine army down into the valley there. A giant! His name is Goliath, and he comes from a family of giants in the land of the Philistines. Look what he is wearing: heavy rings of iron armor around his body and a heavy iron helmet on his head. In his hand is a huge, sharp spear, too heavy for us to lift. Goliath is so tall that he would touch the ceiling of a room, and so wide that he would not fit through a doorway. Listen to what he is saying: "I defy the armies of Israel this day." He is **against** the Israelites and **against** Israel's God.

Then he asked the Israelites to choose a man to fight him. If the Israelite soldier won, the Philistines would be the servants of the Israelites; and if Goliath won, the Israelites would be the servants of the Philistines. Of course, Goliath expected to win; but no Israelite soldier came out to fight Goliath. No one dared. For forty days Goliath came out and dared someone to fight him. But no one dared.

Then David came running to the army of the Israelites. He was not staying at Saul's house anymore. When Saul left for the war, David took his harp and went back home to his father Jesse in Bethlehem. There he was, back on the quiet hillsides, watching his sheep. His three oldest brothers were soldiers in Saul's army, and his father Jesse was worried. **Everyone** in Israel had heard about the awful giant, and they were all greatly afraid.

Jesse chose David to run to the army to find out what was happening and how his brothers were. David was young, but his father trusted him. He took with him a present of corn, bread, and cheese, and set out early in the morning. Just as he came to Israel's army, they were shouting the war-cry, and the Philistine army and Israel's army stood facing one another.

David only had time to find his brothers and ask them how they were before the proud, mocking giant strutted up and down before Israel's army, cursing Israel and Israel's God. Don't you think that shivers went up and down David's back as he heard the giant's wicked words about God? For David was brought up, as we are, to **love** and **fear** God's holy name. David could not stand to hear Goliath's boasting words, and he asked why no one would fight him.

Eliab, David's oldest brother, answered David with cruel words. He said, "Why camest thou down hither? and with whom hast thou left those few sheep? I know thy pride, and the naughtiness of thine heart; for thou art come down that thou mightest see the battle."

David did not talk back to his brother but kept asking why no one fought Goliath. Finally, someone told King Saul about David; and Saul sent for him.

When David came to Saul, he said, "Thy servant will go and fight with this Philistine."

Saul answered, "Thou art not able to go against this Philistine to fight with him."

Then David told Saul a story: how a lion sneaked out of the woods one day, and how a bear came running at the sheep another day; how they each stole a lamb, and how David rushed out to save the lambs from their sharp teeth; and how he killed the lion and the bear. He told Saul that if the Lord saved him from the lion and the bear, He could save him from the giant, too.

Saul said, "Go, and the Lord be with thee."

When Saul gave David his heavy brass armor, and David put the clumsy armor on his body and the helmet on his head, he could not move. No, he could not fight in **that!** He took it off and ran in his shepherd's coat, with his slingshot in his hand. As he went to meet the Philistine, he chose five smooth stones from a brook and put them in his shepherd's bag and met the giant.

What a sight that was! A strong, huge giant, a good fighter, with heavy armor and a great spear; and a young boy in a shepherd's coat, with a slingshot.

Again Goliath cursed; and he said, "Am I a dog? Come to me, and I will give thy flesh unto the fowls of the air." Fowls are **birds**.

David gave him a beautiful answer: "Thou comest to me with a sword, and with a spear, and with a shield, but I come to thee in the name of the Lord of hosts."

Then a wonder happened. As David ran toward the giant, he put a stone in his slingshot and let it go. God guided that stone, and it hit Goliath in his forehead. There must have been a terrible stillness in both the armies as the giant toppled over and fell on his face, dead. David ran to the giant, took his sword, and cut off his head with it. Then the Philistines ran, and the Israelites won a great victory.

REMEMBER:

David's only help when he fought Goliath was the name of the Lord. David always trusted in that name. We do, too.

David and Jonathan

After David killed the giant Goliath and after Israel had won the big battle with the Philistines, David went back to Saul and told the whole story: how the wicked Goliath cursed God; how David told him, "I come to thee in the name of the Lord of hosts;" and how the Lord of hosts guided the stone from his slingshot to kill the giant.

What an exciting story it must have been! Don't you wish you could have been there to listen? Someone listened. His name was Jonathan, and he was Saul's son. Oh, how he liked David's story, especially the part about David's help being in the name of the Lord; for Jonathan loved the Lord with all his heart, too.

That day David and Jonathan became friends, friends who liked to talk about the same things, and friends who loved one another with their whole hearts. It was the most beautiful friendship the Bible tells us about. Do you know why it was so beautiful? Because David and Jonathan both loved the Lord so much, and they rested their friendship in Him.

They talked with one another as often as they could; and when they talked, Jonathan could see that David would be the next king. Jonathan knew that he would never be king, because his father Saul had sinned, and the kingdom had been taken from him. But Jonathan wasn't sad. He was glad that David would be king.

He even took off his coat and his sword and put them on David. It was a picture of David being king instead of Jonathan.

Saul was not glad that David and Jonathan were friends, and he was not glad when he started to think that maybe it was David who would be the next king. From that day on he watched David, and David behaved himself very well.

Then one day there was war with the Philistines again. By this time the Philistines were afraid of the Israelites, and they ran away from the Israelite soldiers. Saul and David went out with the soldiers to fight and won many battles with the Philistines. When the wars were over, they came marching back to Israel with the soldiers; and the ladies — the grandmothers and the mothers and the daughters and the wives and the sisters — lined up along the streets to watch the parade of soldiers. They were so happy to see the soldiers back again that they took their tambourines and sang songs. This is what they sang:

Saul hath slain his thousands,
And David his ten thousands.

Now Saul was really angry. When he listened to the women singing their songs, over and over, he knew that they thought more of David than of him. He was jealous of David and wanted to kill him. He knew it was wrong of him to hate David, and he knew that it was God's punishment for him, but he made his heart hard and would not listen to the Lord.

The next day the Lord bothered Saul with an evil spirit inside of him again. David took his harp and played sweet, peaceful music to make Saul quiet, but Saul did not become quiet. He became more and more angry, and he threw his sharp spear at David. But David was quick and jumped out of the way without being hurt.

Now David knew how much Saul hated him, and we might think that David was very much afraid of Saul. He wasn't. It was just the other way around. Saul was afraid of David; for Saul was a wicked man, and David was a righteous man, with God on his side.

Saul kept thinking about killing David. Now he had another idea. **He** would not kill David. He would let the **Philistines** kill him. And he would be sneaky about it so that David would never know. This is what Saul did: he promised David that if he went out and fought the Philistines very bravely, he would give David his daughter Merab to be his wife. Saul thought David would surely be killed by the Philistines.

David went out and fought the Philistines bravely, and God took care of him. When he came back, Saul did not keep his promise. He let Merab marry someone else.

Then Saul had one more plan. He told David that if he and his soldiers killed one hundred Philistines, David might marry his other daughter, Michal. Once again, Saul hoped that David would be killed, but the Lord was with him and he killed **two hundred** Philistines. This time David married Michal.

REMEMBER:

God had promised that Jesus would be born from the children of **David's** family. When Saul tried to kill David, he was really trying to kill Jesus.

Saul Tries to Kill David

Saul kept thinking about killing David. He did not even care what people thought about him so long as he could get rid of David. His son Jonathan knew and his servants in the palace knew that Saul would keep on trying to kill David. It was the most important thing in his life!

How sad that made poor Jonathan feel! His father wanted to kill David, his best friend, whom he loved with all his heart. But Jonathan knew what to do. He went to talk quietly with Saul, his father, and he said just the right things. This is what he told his father: David did not do anything wrong; he has been very good to you; he killed the giant and saved our land; and do you want to kill him without **any reason**?

Don't you think Jonathan made his father feel ashamed? Jonathan was right, and Saul knew it. Saul promised not to try to kill David anymore, and he called David back to his palace to live.

Soon there was war with the Philistines again; and David went out as a captain of Saul's army to fight. The Lord gave him and his soldiers a great victory. Do you think Saul was happy about that? Oh, no! He was jealous of David, and angry, and more afraid of him than ever. As all those wicked thoughts about David went through his heart, the Lord sent the evil spirit into his heart, and Saul was very upset.

He needed David's quiet music again. But as David played on his harp, Saul did not become quiet. He threw his sharp spear at David. David jumped out of the way, the spear hit the wall, and he ran out of the room.

He ran home. We remember, don't we, that he had married Michal, Saul's daughter; and Michal was not like her father Saul. She **loved** David and tried to help him. When David came home to her, she knew David was in danger, and she urged him to hurry and climb out a window and run away into the darkness of the night.

Michal was right. David **was** in danger. Saul had sent men to watch David's house through the night and to kill him the next morning. While David was running away into the darkness, Michal was busy. She took an idol, a big idol that she liked to worship, and laid it in the bed. Then she put goat's hair around the idol's head, and made it look like a man sleeping in the bed.

When Saul's servants knocked on the door the next morning to get David, she said, "He is sick."

The servants ran back to Saul with the news. Saul said, "Bring him up to me in the bed, that I may slay him."

When the servants came back and looked at the bed with the idol in it, they had a surprise. Now they knew that Michal had played a trick on them. Michal's trick had worked, too! David had enough time to get away.

Where did David go? To Samuel the prophet, his old friend. He could tell Samuel all his troubles and be safe with him. Samuel lived with a school of young men who were prophets and who learned about God's Word.

Saul heard that David was with Samuel and the prophets, and he sent his servants there to capture David. But the Lord made them listen to the prophets; and the servants were so busy talking about God's Word that they did not get David. Three times Saul sent some servants and three times they talked about the Lord and forgot about David. Then Saul himself went to get David, but the Lord made him talk about the Lord, too, all night. And David had time to run away again.

REMEMBER:

When Saul and his servants talked about God and forgot to capture David, it was a **wonder.** Remember that God always keeps His people safe, and He holds the hearts of men, even of kings, in **His** hands.

David and Jonathan Meet

David felt bad. He left his friend Samuel and went back to find Jonathan. He had so many questions to ask Jonathan: "What have I done? and what is my sin before thy father, that he seeketh my life?"

Jonathan **could not** believe that his father Saul would kill David, for David had done only good to Saul. Jonathan tried to cheer up David, but David felt blacker than ever when he said, "There is but a step between me and death." That was not a very good thing for David to say. He was not trusting God, for God had promised that he would be king, and God would not let him die!

Still, David had to know whether Saul was **really** trying to kill him, whether he could stay near Jonathan or whether he had to run away again. So he and Jonathan made a plan together. Tomorrow would be a special day, a day of offering sacrifices and having a feast, for it was the first day of a new month and God had told them to celebrate with sacrifices and feasts.

This was the plan: David was supposed to go to the dinner feast at Saul's house, but he would purposely stay away; Jonathan would go, and if Saul asked where he was, Jonathan would tell a lie — that David went home to his father in Bethlehem; and if Saul did not get angry about it, David would be safe; if Saul was angry, he would know that Saul wanted to kill him.

David and Jonathan made some more plans. This is how Jonathan would let David know how Saul felt. David would be hiding in the field near a big stone all the days of the feast, and Jonathan would come out with his bows and arrows. He would take an arrow, aim, and shoot it. If he did not shoot the arrow very far, it would mean that David was safe. If he shot the arrow far away, with all his strength, it would mean that David would have to run for his life.

They followed their plan, and David did not go to the feast the first day. His seat was empty, and Saul noticed the empty seat, but he thought that something must have happened, that he was not ready for the feast. When David's seat was empty the second day of the feast, Saul asked Jonathan why David was not at the feast.

Jonathan answered, "David earnestly asked leave of me to go to Bethlehem."

Then Saul became very angry. Do you know why? At the feast, David would have been close enough so that Saul could have killed him. Now he couldn't. Besides that, he told Jonathan that so long as David was alive, Jonathan could not become king. And Saul wanted Jonathan to be the next king, even though God had told him his son would never be king.

Jonathan knew why his father Saul was so angry. He knew, too, that he never would be king, and he was happy about it. When Saul said, "Send and fetch him unto me, for he shall surely die," Jonathan answered, "Wherefore shall he be slain? What hath he done?"

The angry Saul picked up his spear and threw it at Jonathan. He threw it at his own son! The spear did not hit Jonathan, and he got up from the dinner table in hot anger. Do you know why he was so angry? Not because his father threw the spear at **him**, but because of the shameful way he treated **David.**

Oh, what a sad heart Jonathan must have had. It was time to tell the bad news to David. With a little boy to carry his bow and arrows, Jonathan set out for the field where David was hiding. He took his bow, and with all his strength shot one of his arrows far past the servant-boy. As the boy ran to get the arrow, he called out, loudly enough for David to hear, "Is not the arrow beyond thee? Make speed, haste!" The little boy ran but did not know that those words were

a secret sign to David. After he brought the arrow back, Jonathan sent his servant-boy back home.

As soon as the boy was gone, David came from his hiding place. His poor face was so sad! He had had three days to be alone and to think about all his troubles. He could not go home now to Michal, his wife, because Saul had let her marry another man; and now he must run away again and leave his very best friend. But he had done nothing wrong to deserve all this.

David and Jonathan cried when they saw one another. They were strong, brave soldiers, but they loved one another so much that they cried in their time of trouble. They promised always to be kind to one another's families. Jonathan went back to the palace then, and David went away, sad and alone. But he was forgetting something. He forgot to look up to God for all his help. He forgot that God was taking care of him, and he forgot to ask God **why** He was sending all this trouble to him.

REMEMBER:

David and Jonathan were beautiful friends. But they were only pictures of even more beautiful friends. **We** are beautiful friends of Jesus. He is the most beautiful friend we ever could have. He told us, "Ye are my friends."

Saul Chases David

David was running away from Saul. Where would he go? Most of the time he was hiding in the desert, far away from people, where it was hot and wild and lonely. He did not have to hide all alone, for his friends knew where he was and came to stay with him. Soon many men came to live with David, and he trained them to be his soldiers.

Saul should have stayed at home and ruled over Israel and fought the Philistines, but he didn't. The only thing he wanted to do was to chase David so that he could kill him. He left his work of taking care of his people and took soldiers with him to chase David in the desert.

When he heard that David and his soldiers were hiding in the desert of Ziph, Saul took his soldiers and hunted for David all through the desert. He could not find him, because God was taking care of David all the time and would not let Saul get near him. Saul could not find David, but **Jonathan** could. Friends always seem to find one another. In a woods in that desert they met for a sad-happy little time. Jonathan made David feel stronger in God. He told David, "Fear not: for the hand of Saul my father shall not find thee; and thou shalt be king over Israel." They made their promises to be kind to one another's children again, and Jonathan went home. It was the last time they saw one another on the earth.

Then some of the people who lived in the desert of Ziph came to Saul and told him they knew where David was hiding and they would help capture him. Saul and his soldiers hurried to find David, and with the people of Ziph helping them, they found David near a mountain. Saul and his soldiers made a circle around the whole mountain and David and his men were trapped. They did not know how to get away. It was the most dangerous time of David's life.

What would they do? They did not have to do anything, for the Lord was busy saving them. He sent the Philistines to bother the Israelites, and a man of Israel came running to Saul to tell him to come quickly and save them. Saul and his soldiers ran back to chase the Philistines out of the land, and David and his men were safe once more.

Did Saul stay at home where he belonged and rule over Israel after his battle with the Philistines? No, the first thing he thought about was chasing David again. He **knew** he was fighting against the Lord's will, but he did it anyway. Now he heard that David was in a rocky part of the desert, called Engedi. It was a rough land, with many holes and caves.

Saul took three thousand soldiers to Engedi to try to capture David. When he came to a cave, he felt tired, and lay down at the front of the cave to rest and sleep a while. What he did not know was that David and his soldiers were deep inside the cave. They had made it their home for a little time.

When David's soldiers saw that Saul and his soldiers were sleeping near the opening of the cave, they tempted David to do something wrong — to go out and kill the sleeping king. Then all David's troubles would be over. He wouldn't have to run away anymore.

Do you think David listened to his soldiers? Oh, no, he couldn't do that! He was learning to trust the Lord and he was learning to wait until it was **God's** time for Saul to die. He scolded his men and said he would not touch the man who was anointed king by the Lord.

David **did** do something, though. He tiptoed very quietly to the sleeping Saul and cut off a piece of Saul's robe. After he had done it, he was not sure it was the right thing to do.

Then he watched until Saul awoke and got up to leave the cave. From inside the cave he called, "My lord the king." What do you think Saul's face looked like when he saw David holding a piece of his robe? Oh, he must have had a surprised look on his face!

Then David talked to Saul. He told how his soldiers wanted him to kill Saul. He told that he would **never** kill the Lord's anointed king. And then he **proved** that he would not hurt Saul: he could easily have killed him, but he only cut off a little piece of cloth.

Would you like to have been Saul? What could he answer David? He said, "Thou art more righteous than I." He said that he knew David would be the next king of Israel. For a little moment, Saul was sad and sorry. He knew he was wicked, but his heart did not change. He was not truly sorry. Then he went home, and David ran off to hide again. He knew he could not trust Saul.

REMEMBER:

David and Jonathan would never see one another on earth again. That made them sad. But they were happy, too, because they would be together again in heaven. When someone we love dies, we are sad. . .and happy because all God's children see one another again in heaven. Aren't you happy about that?

283

David and Nabal

David and his men ran out to the desert again and hid near the farm of a very rich man named Nabal. Nabal had thousands of sheep and goats; and while his shepherds were out in the fields taking care of all the animals, David and his men never bothered the shepherds nor took any of their sheep or goats. Instead, they kept them safe from wild animals and from robbers.

Then, one day, it was time for Nabal to start shearing his sheep. **Shearing** was cutting the wool off the sheep. It did not hurt the sheep any more than a haircut hurts us. The farmers and their helpers all got together to help one another with the shearing and to have a happy time while they worked. When the work was finished, they all celebrated and had big feasts.

David and his men were not having big feasts. They were hungry and were having trouble finding enough food. So David sent ten of his young men to greet Nabal with peace and to ask a little favor. He told his ten young men to say that David and his men had been very good to Nabal and they kept all of his sheep safe — they were just like a safe wall that kept all dangers away. Now would Nabal give them a little food?

Nabal knew what he should say to David. He should have said, "Yes, I will give you all you need, with a happy heart." Nabal knew that God's law said that the rich people must help the poor people who were hungry. Nabal knew that he was so rich and he had so much food he would never even miss it. Do you hope that Nabal was kind to David and his men?

He wasn't. Nabal was a mean, wicked man, and he said to David's ten young men, "Who is David?" He said he would not help David because David was running away from Saul. Nabal was **for** Saul and **against** David. He was **for** wickedness and **against** holiness. He was **for** the devil and **against** Jesus. His answer to the ten young men was **no**.

Oh, David was angry when his men told him Nabal's answer. Can you think how David felt? He was always being chased by King Saul and had to live in the hot, wild desert. Now he had been so nice to Nabal, and when he was hungry, Nabal gave him only wicked words. That was too much for David! David was angry. He took four hundred men and set out to kill Nabal and his family. David was angry, but it was not a good kind of anger. He might not kill Nabal.

While David and his soldiers were running to get Nabal, some of the servants of Nabal told his wife, Abigail, what had happened. Abigail was just the opposite of Nabal. She was beautiful and good, and she loved the Lord. Abigail hurried to get ready a present of food — meat and corn and raisins and figs and wine. She put the food on donkeys and ran to meet David. She did not tell Nabal what she was going to do.

Soon she and her servants saw David coming down a hillside. How could she meet such an angry man, who was in such a bad mood? What should she say to him? Quickly she got down from her donkey and fell on her face and bowed to David and asked him to let the blame be on her.

She told David that she knew what a foolish, wicked, cruel man Nabal was; and she begged David **not** to be as wicked as Nabal was. She begged him not to be so angry that he would kill Nabal; for some day David would be the king, and he would not like to remember such a bad sin.

David listened to Abigail and he was not angry anymore. He thanked her for the present of food and turned around and went back.

Abigail went home to Nabal, but she could not talk with him because he had drunk too much wine at his feast and was very drunk. The next morning, when he was not drunk anymore, she told him how she had stopped David from killing him. When Nabal heard her words, his heart died and became as a stone inside him. Ten days later the Lord made Nabal die.

When David heard that Nabal was dead, he sent his servants to get Abigail so he could ask her to be his wife. She came, and David married her. Do you think he was happier now that he had such a pretty, God-fearing wife?

REMEMBER:

When God gave Nabal a heart of stone, He made it to be a picture of Nabal's hard, stubborn heart that would not listen to God. God gives us, His children, soft hearts that listen to Him and try to do His will.

David Saves
Saul's Life

More than a year went past. David was still hiding in the desert with his small army of men. And Saul was still chasing David, trying to kill him. Saul **knew** he did not have to be afraid of David, for David would never hurt him. He found that out when David could have killed him, but only cut off a piece of his robe instead. In this story, David showed Saul once more that he would never hurt his king.

He was hiding in the desert of Ziph again, near a mountain. The people from the desert of Ziph told Saul where David was, and Saul took three thousand soldiers to come to capture David. Wasn't that foolish of Saul? Three thousand soldiers to capture a David who would never hurt him? By this time Saul was not afraid of David anymore. His heart was so filled with wicked hate that he would not stop trying to kill him.

While David and his men were hiding in a cave of the mountain, Saul and his army made their camp on the other side of the mountain. David sent out spies to find out just where their camp was. There they were — David and Saul — close together again.

When night came, David wanted to go to visit Saul's army. Why did he want to go? He wanted to show Saul once more that he would not harm him. Abishai, one of David's men, offered to go with David; and together they crept softly into the army of their enemies. Oh, that was a dangerous trip! What if a soldier awoke and saw them? But, no, even the men who were supposed to be guarding the soldiers were asleep.

There, in the middle of the camp, lay Saul sleeping, with his spear stuck into the ground near his head, and his water bottle close by. Abishai whispered to David, "God hath delivered thine enemy into thine hand; now therefore let me smite him, I pray thee."

David had to whisper a scolding to Abishai. He said he would trust **the Lord** with Saul's life. Maybe the Lord would take Saul's life away from him, or maybe Saul would die in a battle, but David would not even **think** of killing him.

In the quiet darkness of the night, David and Abishai took Saul's spear and his water jug and tiptoed back to their own side of the mountain, a long way off. On their way out of the camp no one awoke and stopped them, not even the guards, who were supposed to be wide awake, keeping watch over the army. They couldn't stay awake, for God had sent a deep sleep on them. It was a **wonder** that God had sent, so that David would be safe in Saul's army camp.

From the top of the mountain on the other side, David shouted loudly to Abner, the captain of Saul's army, "Answerest thou not, Abner?" He probably had to wake Abner up.

Abner, probably sleepy and angry, shouted back, "Who art thou that criest to the king?"

Then it was David's turn to shout. He poked a little fun of Abner when he said something like this: "Aren't you a brave man? Why didn't you take care of your king? Someone wanted to kill the king. You could die, Abner, for not taking care of the king!" And he showed him Saul's spear and water jug.

By this time Saul was awake and was listening to the words that were shouted from the other side of the mountain. He knew whose voice that was! It was David's! How ashamed he must have felt when he called, "Is this thy voice, my son David?"

David answered, "It is my voice, my lord, O king." Then, sadly, he asked Saul, "What have I done?"

He told Saul how sad he was that he had to run away from his own land of Canaan, the land God promised to His people. And he told Saul that he must not run after him anymore, for he was no more dangerous than a tiny flea.

Saul said, "I have sinned: return, my son David: for I will no more do thee harm." Saul was ashamed, but he was not sorry before God.

David asked one of Saul's men to come to get the spear and water bottle, and Saul called once more to David, "Blessed be thou, my son David: thou shalt both do great things, and also shalt still prevail." Prevail means **win**.

Those were Saul's last words to David. Saul and David never saw one another again.

REMEMBER:

Saul said to David, "I have sinned," but he was not really sorry for his sin. We say, "I have sinned," too, but God makes us sorry for our sins and promises to wash us clean from our sins with the blood of our Lord Jesus.

Saul Goes to the Witch of Endor

Many things were happening in the land of Israel these days. Saul was back at home, ruling the people. Samuel, God's prophet, had become very old and died. Where was David? He had run, for a little while, to the land of the Philistines to get away from Saul. God had led David to go to the land of the Philistines so that Saul would be the only leader of the army of Israel. God wanted Saul to be the only leader in the next battle against the Philistines, for that would be Saul's last battle.

The Philistines gathered their soldiers together into a big army to fight the Israelites. From a hill in Gilboa, Saul looked down on the huge army of the Philistines. What a big army they had! He needed **all** the soldiers of Israel to fight such a big army; but when he had his army all ready, Saul did not go out to fight. He was trembling and afraid. Why? When he was younger, he had fought the Philistines so bravely and had won so many battles. That was when God had put a brave Spirit into his heart. Now God had taken that Spirit away and had given it to David.

Instead of the Spirit from the Lord, Saul had an evil spirit in his heart; and he went farther and farther away from God. By this time, he was so filled with all his wicked thoughts and actions he could not think of God anymore. Now he was in trouble. Now he was scared. He wanted to ask God what would happen in this big battle. But God was far away from him and did not answer.

What could he do? If God would not answer him, he would ask God's prophet, Samuel, to tell him God's answer. But Samuel was already dead, and a dead man can't talk. Still Saul did not give up. He wanted to talk to Samuel so badly, he decided to try to talk with dead Samuel's spirit from the grave. Samuel's spirit was in the **living** Samuel, and was really in heaven with God, and would not come down to Saul. We know that, don't we?

Watch what Saul is doing. He is getting ready to visit a witch, someone who can work magic through the power of the devil. Not very long ago Saul had destroyed all the witches or chased them out of the land of Israel. But he had not found all of them. One was still living at Endor, about twenty miles away. Now Saul disguised himself — that means that he put on other clothes so that he looked different from the way he usually looked — and he took two servants with him, and together they went out and visited the witch at night.

The witch was afraid when she saw her visitors that King Saul might find out about her, but Saul promised that she would not be punished.

So the witch asked, "Whom shall I bring up unto thee?"

Saul answered, "Bring me up Samuel."

The witch could not **really** bring dead Samuel back from the grave to talk with Saul. She only pretended to, by using her tricks and her magic that wasn't really magic. Suddenly she screamed, for her tricks did not work this time. The Lord stopped her, and made her see an old man. That was a wonder from the Lord and the witch knew it. She knew, too, that her visitor was really King Saul. She said, "Why hast thou deceived me? For thou art Saul."

God did not let King Saul see the old man whom the witch saw. He said, "Be not afraid: for what sawest thou?"

The witch said, "An old man cometh up; and he is covered with a mantle." A mantle is a **coat**.

We do not know just how God made the witch see an old man. Maybe God **did** send Samuel back. Maybe He made it **seem** like an old man. We **do** know that it was a special wonder. Samuel's voice asked why Saul bothered him after he had died. Saul told him that the Lord had left him and would not answer him, and he **must** know what was going to happen in the battle with the Philistines.

Then Samuel told him. In the battle the Israelites would be beaten by the Philistines, and Saul and his sons would be killed. When Saul heard the terrible news, he fell down flat on his face, for he had eaten no food all that day.

The witch was scared and troubled by all these things that were happening in her house, and she ran to get food for Saul. She was trying to be kind to Saul in his time of deep trouble. She offered him food for his body: bread and meat. She should have offered him food for his heart: she should have told him to be sorry and turn to the Lord and live.

At first Saul would not eat, but the witch and his servants begged him to take a little food. After they ate, Saul and his servants went out into the dark night, feeling sad and hopeless. It was Saul's last night on earth. Tomorrow would be the battle.

REMEMBER:

When people have no God to trust in, they turn to the devil and the world of magic and charms and witches. This is one of the worst kinds of wickedness, and we must always hate it with all our hearts.

Saul Dies in Battle

Morning came — the last morning of Saul's life. He probably hardly slept, after that terrible night at the witch's house. As a bright new day dawned, he should have been acting like the king of God's people, bravely leading his army against the wicked Philistines.

But Saul was not thinking about winning the battle for God's glory. He was not thinking about leading the Israelites to win the victory. He was selfishly thinking about saving his own life. Maybe, if he was careful, he could **still** go against God's will, and not be killed in this battle; so, instead of leading his army, he stayed near the back with some of his soldiers to protect him.

Israel's army was on the hillsides of Mt. Gilboa. The Philistines' army was on the flat country below them. Israel should have run down the hillsides and started the battle, but they had no leader; so the Philistines started the battle by rushing into the hillsides of Mt. Gilboa.

Right away, the battle went badly for the Israelites. Many were killed. Oh, if Saul would only come and bravely lead his soldiers to fight! But he didn't. He still stayed behind. Maybe, if he was careful, he would live. But, see, the Philistine soldiers were coming closer to Saul. Already his three sons — Jonathan was one of them — had been killed, and his soldiers were running away from the Philistine soldiers.

Saul started to run, too. He could not run fast enough, and the Philistine soldiers came closer and closer to him and found him and hurt him. Oh, he was afraid! Now Saul knew that he must die, but he did not want a Philistine to kill him. He asked his armor-bearer — remember, he was the servant who carried Saul's armor — to take his spear and kill him, but his armor-bearer would not kill his king. He, too, was so terribly afraid.

What could Saul do now? He did the very worst thing he could have done. The last thing he did in his life was the most wicked. He set his sword up straight in the ground, with the sharp point up. Then he fell on it and killed himself. He took away the life that God had given him. When his armor-bearer saw what Saul had done, he set up his sword and killed himself, too. Now Saul and his three sons and his armor-bearer were all lying dead on the battlefield.

The rest of the soldiers kept running away from the Philistines. Many of the Israelites, when they saw that Israel was losing the battle, ran out of their cities and hid. And the Philistines moved into their cities and lived in them.

Then the battle day was over, and night came. The Israelites were sad and tired and afraid. Many, many of them were lying dead on the battlefield. The Philistines were happy and wished that morning would come so that they could go to take the swords and spears that the Israelite soldiers had left behind. There, the next morning, when they came to the battlefield, they found the dead Saul and his three sons.

Those wicked Philistines cut off Saul's head and put it into the temple of their idol-god Dagon. They put his armor into the temple of another idol-god and hanged his body on the wall of one of their cities, for the rain to fall on, for the sun to burn, for the wind to blow on, and for the wicked Philistines to mock. Then they did the same things to the bodies of Saul's three sons. What cruel wickedness those Philistines did to the king of God's people!

The men of the city of Jabesh-Gilead heard of the horrible thing the Philistines had done. The men of Jabesh-Gilead liked Saul and felt kindness for him in their hearts; for once, many years ago, Saul had run all night to fight a battle for them and save them from the Ammonites who were going to put out their right eyes. The men of Jabesh-Gilead had never forgotten how Saul had helped them. Do you remember that story, too? Now the men of Jabesh-Gilead traveled all night to the city where the dead bodies were hanging, and they took them down and burned them and buried them, with love and kindness in their hearts. For seven days they did not eat, as a last act of kindness to Saul and his family.

REMEMBER:

God tells us that our bodies are **His** houses, and we may not do bad things to our bodies. We may not take away the life that God puts into our bodies, as Saul did, and we may not do wicked things to our bodies as the Philistines did. God wants us to put our bodies into the grave when we die; and when we go to heaven, He will give us new bodies.

295

David Hears News of the Battle

Do you remember that David was living in the land of the Philistines for a while? He was not nearby when Israel lost the terrible battle with the Philistines and when Saul and his sons were killed. Three days passed and David still had heard no news of the battle.

At last a man came running to David and his men, but he looked so strange. His clothes were ripped and he had dust on his head. Ripping his clothes and putting dust on his head were pictures of feeling very, very sad. The man bowed to David before he said anything.

David asked, "From whence comest thou?"

The man answered, "Out of the camp of Israel am I escaped."

Oh, David was eager to know what had happened! He could hardly wait to ask, "How went the matter? I pray thee, tell me."

Then came the man's sad news: "The people are fled from the battle, and many of the people also are fallen and dead; and Saul and Jonathan his son are dead also."

Could David believe the story of this strange man? He **had** to know whether his story was really true. So he asked, "How knowest thou that Saul and Jonathan his son be dead?"

This is the story the man told: I was in Mt. Gilboa, where the battle was, and I saw Saul leaning on his spear; when he called to me and asked me to kill him because he was hurt, I went and killed him because I was sure he could not live anyway; and I took the crown that was on his head and the bracelet from his arm, and here they are."

Was the man's story true? Did he really kill Saul? No, we know that Saul killed himself. But David and the men that were with him believed his story. They ripped their clothes, too, and cried, and did not eat anything all day. They cried because Saul and Jonathan and the Lord's people were dead.

Do you wonder who this strange man was? David did, too. He asked, "Who art thou?"

The man said, "I am an Amalekite."

This man, the Amalekite, was from the family of the wicked Esau, from the family that God hated. What was that Amalekite doing on the battlefield of the Philistines and the Israelites? We do not know. Probably he was wandering around, looking for things to steal from the dead soldiers. He had probably stolen King Saul's crown and bracelet, and then made up his lie. This was the kind of man who came to David.

Why do you think he told the lie that he killed King Saul? He must have thought that David would be happy that Saul was dead, for now David would be king. The wicked Amalekite expected David to thank him and praise him and give him a present.

He was not ready for David's next question: "How wast thou not afraid to destroy the Lord's anointed?"

Remember that twice before David had been able to kill Saul, but he saved his life instead. David would not kill God's anointed king. Now when the Amalekite lied and said that he killed King Saul, he got no praise and no present. He got the worst of punishments. David told one of his young men to kill him. The young man struck him and he died. The Amalekite **had** to die because of his lie.

Afterward, David made a beautiful, sad song. He sang that the beauty of Israel was gone. Do you know why? Because Saul and Jonathan were dead.

In his song, David asked that the mountains of Gilboa would get no dew or rain, and would dry up as the desert, so that nothing would grow on them. Do you know why? Because the heathen Philistines fought and killed Saul and Jonathan and God's people there.

He sang, "How are the mighty fallen!" The **mighty** were God's people and Saul and Jonathan.

David ended his song by singing about how much he loved Jonathan. It was such a great love because he and Jonathan loved one another with the love of Jesus.

REMEMBER:

When the Amalekite told his lie, he listened to the devil, and because he told the lie, he was killed. It is always wrong to tell a lie, even though we aren't killed for it. God says to tell the truth in love.

David Brings Back the Ark

Now that King Saul was dead, David did not have to stay in the land of the Philistines any longer. He asked the Lord whether he should go back to one of the cities of his own tribe of Judah, and the Lord told him, "Go up." He even told David which city to live in — in Hebron.

The men of Hebron were glad to see David and they anointed him with oil and made him king over the tribe of Judah. David was not king over all Israel. Not yet! One of Saul's sons was still living and he was ruling over the rest of Israel; but after seven years, when Saul's son was dead, the people from all the tribes of Israel came to David and asked him to be king over them. Once more David was anointed with oil to be king, and this time he was king over all God's people.

One of the first things he did was to fight against the city of Jerusalem. Heathen people by the name of Jebusites were living there. With God's help, David and his army easily captured the city of Jerusalem, and David gave it a new name: the City of David. It was a beautiful city, built on high hills. On one of those hills he built a great palace for himself.

But David was interested in something much more important: he wanted to bring God's holy ark to the city of Jerusalem. Do you remember long ago, in the days of Eli, when his wicked sons had taken the ark to the battlefield, the Philistines had stolen it and taken it to their cities? Later the Philistines brought it back to Bethshemesh in the land of Israel. And that story had a sad ending, too, for the men of Bethshemesh looked at the ark with sinful eyes, and God killed them. Ever after that time, for about seventy years, the ark had been hiding away in the house of Abinadab.

Now David called the leaders of the people of Israel and told them to go through the land of Israel and ask the people to go along to get the ark back. David told them why. They had not talked with God, nor asked Him what they should do in all the days of King Saul. The ark was a picture of God living with His people, and David wanted to teach the people to live with God, for He was the most important One in their lives. They needed God's ark!

299

David was very busy getting ready to bring back the ark. He gathered all sorts of musical instruments — harps, and trumpets, and tambourines, and cymbals — so that the people could praise God as they walked along the way, with music and with singing. He built a new cart, too, and had oxen pull it. Thousands of Israelites came to go along with David. At last they were ready, with joy in their hearts and songs on their lips, to make a parade to get the ark. Two of Abinadab's sons were taking care of the ark. They put the ark on the new cart.

Everyone was happy until the oxen stumbled and the cart shook. When Uzzah, one of Abinadab's sons, saw that the ark might fall, he put out his hand to keep God's ark still and steady. In that very minute, God killed him. There he lay dead, by the ark of God.

Now no one was happy. David was sad and afraid. He would not go any farther. Close by was the house of Obededom, and there they left the ark. Now no one was singing. Everyone went home, and poor David went back to Jersalem without the ark.

What was wrong? Why did God kill Uzzah? Over and over again David must have asked those questions. And then he knew the answer. He and the people had done it all wrong. They had been **too careless** and **too happy**. They had made a big parade with too much music and singing. And they had forgotten to be sorry for their sins first, their sins of serving idols and of leaving God's ark hidden away in a house. They had forgotten to ask God to take those sins away. They did one more thing wrong. They carried the ark the wrong way. The men from the tribe of Levi were supposed to put a stick through the golden rings on the ark and carry it on their shoulders — not on a cart.

After three months, when David heard that God was blessing Obededom's family, he talked with the people of Israel again. This time he taught them the **right** way to get the ark. And this time they went to get God's ark with **reverence** — that means **God's holy fear** — in their hearts. With the singers going first, then the ark, and then David and the people, they walked the right way back to Jerusalem.

When the Lord helped the Levites who were carrying the ark, the people stopped and offered a sacrifice to the Lord, a picture of the washing away of their sins. David was so happy that he danced before the Lord.

Michal, David's wife, looked out of a window and saw David dancing before the Lord. She did not have God's love in her heart, and she scolded David with cruel words because he danced in front of all the people. David answered her with kind words: "It was before the **Lord**, which chose me ruler over Israel: therefore will I play before the Lord." God blessed David, but he gave Michal a punishment. She never had any children.

REMEMBER:

David and the people of Israel learned that they could not praise the Lord until they were sorry for their sins. We learn that, too. First we must tell God how sorry we are and ask Him to take away all our sins, and then we can sing happy songs of praise to Him.

David Wants to Build God's House

Oh, David was happy to have God's beautiful ark in the city of Jerusalem, which he called the City of David. He took the ark to one of the mountains, called Mt. Zion, and built a little tent for it. David knew that God's precious ark did not belong in a **tent**. It belonged in the **tabernacle**, which Moses and the people of Israel built while they were in the desert. But where was the tabernacle? Far away in Gibeon, another city in Israel.

Maybe David should go to Gibeon and get the tabernacle and take it with him to Jerusalem. Then the tabernacle and the ark could be together again, as the Lord wanted them to be. David didn't go to get the tabernacle. He had another idea, a much better idea! What was it?

We will have to wait a little while to find out, for first David had so many wars to fight for the Lord. God told him to kill the heathen people that lived in the land, and it took David and his army many years to finish all the battles. At last David rested from his fighting and went to live in his palace in Jerusalem.

Now was the time for his idea! He called the prophet Nathan and told him about it. He said he wanted to build God a **new** house, a great and beautiful house, called a temple, and put God's ark in the temple instead of in the tabernacle. This is what he said to Nathan: "See now, I dwell in an house of cedar, but the ark of God dwelleth within curtains."

Nathan answered, "Go, do all that is in thine heart; for the Lord is with thee."

Nathan said that without talking to God first. He should have; for in the night God came to him and said that **some day** He would live in a beautiful temple in Jerusalem, but it was not time yet for Him to live in a temple. God told Nathan something else: David was not the man whom God chose to build it. Why not? David was a fighting king, a king of war, who had to kill many enemies for the Lord, and who had much blood on his hands from all his battles. God wanted a man who was peaceful and quiet to build His house. Who would that be? God told Nathan it would be one of David's sons. His name would be Solomon.

Do you think David grumbled and complained to the Lord when Nathan told him he might not build God's great house? Oh, no! He prayed a very humble prayer of thanks. He said, "Who am I, O Lord God?" And he thanked God for raising him up from being a shepherd boy to being the king over all God's people. David knew that God knows best and always plans everything right; and he said, "Wherefore thou art great, O Lord God: for there is none like thee." And he didn't ask the Lord about building a temple again.

David must have thought quite often of his dear friend Jonathan who had been killed in the terrible battle with the Philistines. He remembered his promise, which he had made in love, to be kind to Jonathan's family.

David asked his servants, "Is there yet any that is left of the house of Saul, that I may show him kindness for Jonathan's sake?"

There **was** someone. Jonathan had a son named Mephibosheth. On the day of the awful battle long ago, he was only five years old, and he had stayed at home with his nursemaid. Then the sad news of the battle had come: his father Jonathan and his grandfather Saul had both been killed, and the Philistines were running over the land. The poor nursemaid was so afraid! She knew they must run away from those heathen Philistines, and in her hurry she picked up the young boy, Mephibosheth — and dropped him. He hurt his legs and feet, and could never walk again.

Now Mephibosheth was not five years old any more. He was grown up already. But he still could not walk. David called Mephibosheth to his palace, and Mephibosheth bowed with his face to the ground to King David.

David said, "Fear not: for I will surely show thee kindness for Jonathan thy father's sake." David gave Mephibosheth all the land that had belonged to King Saul and Jonathan, and asked him to eat at the king's table, with all of David's sons, for the rest of his life. So Mephibosheth lived in Jerusalem and always ate at King David's palace.

REMEMBER:

Sometimes when we ask the Lord for something, He says no. He said no to David when David wanted to build Him a temple. David thanked and praised the Lord when He said no. Can we do that, too?

David
Sins

King David was a great king. He fought the enemies of the Lord, and the Lord gave him the victories. The people of Israel were becoming a great and strong nation. When David saw how great he had become and how great Israel had become, he forgot to be humble before the Lord, and say, "Who am I, O Lord God?" Instead, he fell into a great sin: he became **proud** of himself.

He knew that God's law told him not to marry many wives, but he did not listen to the law of God. Many heathen kings had a lot of wives, to show how great they were, and David wanted to show that he was just as great as they were.

And King David was getting lazy. When the enemies came, David should have led his army against them. But he was proud and thought he was too big a king now, so he sent the captain of his army to lead the soldiers to the battle. While the soldiers were fighting hard in the Lord's battles, David was at home, taking it easy.

One evening, probably after he had taken a nap, David walked on the flat roof of his palace. Remember, his palace was on a high hill in the city of Jerusalem, and David could look down on the rest of the city. As he was walking, he saw a very beautiful woman washing herself; and he asked who she was. Someone told David: "Bathsheba, the wife of Uriah the Hittite."

Then David fell into a second great sin, the sin of **stealing**. He told his servants to get her and bring her to him. David already had many wives, and Bathsheba was already married to someone else. Yet he wanted to **steal** her from her husband, and he wanted **her** to be his wife, too. Bathsheba came and stayed with King David that night, just as if they were already married.

David **wanted** her for his wife, but she **could not be** his wife because Uriah was her husband. Where was Uriah all this time? He was a soldier in the army and was away, working hard, fighting wars against God's enemies. Now David fell into his third great sin, maybe the worst sin of all. He wrote a letter to Joab, the captain of his soldiers, and asked him to put Uriah in the most dangerous part of the fighting and then leave him there alone, so he would surely be killed.

Captain Joab did what King David asked him to do, and put Uriah in a very dangerous place where he would certainly be killed. Do you know what happened? Uriah was killed. And King David and Captain Joab were to blame. When the messenger came running to tell David the news that Uriah was killed, David blamed the **enemies** for killing him. He did not blame himself.

Bathsheba mourned and felt sad for seven days because her husband was dead and then she became David's wife. It looked as if David had covered up all his sins. He didn't. God was watching all he had done; and the Bible tells us, "But the thing that David had done displeased the Lord."

Almost a year went past. That must have been a hard year for King David. He knew he had sinned, but he told himself he had done no wrong; and he would not tell the Lord he was sorry. His heart felt so troubled, it felt like the waves of the ocean pounding through him.

In that year, a baby boy was born to David and Bathsheba. Then, after almost a whole year, God sent a prophet to David. His name was Nathan. Nathan did not scold David. He told him a story. Would you like to hear it? Nathan told David that there were two men in a city. One was rich and the other was poor. The rich man had many flocks and herds of animals on his farm, but the poor man had only one little lamb, which he loved so much that he treated it like one of his children. It lived right in his house. One day the rich man had company from a faraway place. He could easily have killed one of his farm animals and he would never have missed it, but he didn't do that. He went to the poor man and took away the only lamb he had, the one who seemed like one of his own children, and killed it for food for his company.

Oh, David was angry with that rich man when he heard the prophet Nathan's story. He said the rich man would surely die, and he must give the poor man **four** lambs. David did not know that Nathan's story was not a true story, but only a picture story.

How shocked and afraid David must have been when Nathan said, "**Thou art the man.**" That rich man was a picture story of David! David was rich and had all the wives he wanted. Uriah was like the poor man, with only one wife — and David took his only wife and then killed Uriah. David was worse than the man in the picture story. Nathan had one more word from God: because of his sin David would always have trouble in his family and the little baby boy that was born to David and Bathsheba would die.

Poor David! **Now** he was sorry. What could he say? He could only say, "I have sinned against the Lord." And Nathan answered, "The Lord also hath put away thy sin." David's sins were washed away by the blood of Jesus. And after a while God gave David and Bathsheba another baby, whose name was Solomon.

REMEMBER:

David was such a miserable sinner. So are we. When David was so sorry for his sins, he showed that he was one of God's own dear children. So do we. God washed David clean in Jesus' blood. He washes us, too, if we are His children.

Absalom Rebels

For many years there was peace and happiness in the land of Israel. David had fought God's enemies and chased them out of the land. His kingdom had become great and rich; and he taught the people to obey God's holy laws and to serve Him with all their hearts. It was the best time ever for Israel.

Then trouble came. The trouble-maker was one of David's own sons, whose name was Absalom. He was grown up already and was a very handsome young man with long, heavy hair and a face everyone talked about because it was so beautiful. Absalom knew what a good-looking young man he was, and it made him very proud of himself. He thought so much of himself that he decided he should be king. But his father David was king! That did not matter to Absalom. He did not care about his father David and he did not care about David's God. He cared only about himself.

How could Absalom become king while his father was still sitting on the king's throne? Absalom thought he knew how. He had a plan, a **sneaky** plan, a **very wicked** plan. Every day he took fifty men to run ahead of him as he rode in the streets in his chariot, pulled by horses. That made the people think he was a very important son of King David, and they listened to him when he talked to them. What did Absalom say to them? He said he wished they would tell him their troubles.

When they told him their troubles, he would say something like this: "If I were king, I would surely help you and do the right thing for you." Then he would say unkind words — lies — about his father David. He would tell them that David was not a good king; and he turned the people's hearts **against** King David and **for** Absalom. He fooled many of the people by his nice talk. They thought he really cared for them.

For about three years Absalom kept up his sneaky plan of telling lies about his God-fearing father, and David never knew it. Who would think that his very own son would try to steal the kingdom from him? Poor David did not know that anything was wrong.

Then one day Absalom asked his father David whether he might keep a promise to the Lord to serve Him in the city of Hebron; and David answered, "Go in peace."

As soon as Absalom left, he sent spies running through all the land of Israel, blowing trumpets and shouting, "Absalom reigneth in Hebron." Many men ran to Hebron to follow Absalom and make him king. What kind of men were they? They were wicked men, who hated God's law and who hated God's good King David. More and more men joined Absalom.

And then David heard about it. A man came running to tell him that the hearts of the people of Israel were turned to Absalom. Do you think that David went to fight Absalom and his men? No, he didn't. Maybe he thought Absalom's army was too big, or maybe he did not want to have a war, with blood and killing, with his own son.

David didn't fight. He was too sad to fight. He ran away. He left his beautiful palace in the beautiful city he had built and walked away barefoot and crying. Many of his friends walked with him, crying with King David.

Now more trouble came to David. A messenger came running to say that Ahithophel, one of David's wise men, had left him and gone over to Absalom, to be Absalom's wise man. The other wise man, whose name was Hushai, and who loved David, had come to meet David, with his clothes ripped because he felt so sad. But what good could wise man Hushai do to a king who was crying and running away?

King David had an idea about that. He told Hushai to go back to Absalom and **pretend** that he would be Absalom's wise man now; but Hushai would **really** tell Absalom wise things that would be good for King David. So Hushai went to Absalom and said, "God save the king." Absalom thought he meant **King Absalom**, but Hushai really meant **King David**.

Now Absalom had two wise men, one who was for Absalom and one who was for David; but he didn't know it. When he asked, "What shall we do?" the wicked Ahithophel told him not to fight a war with David's men, but to send his soldiers to capture **only** David, while he was sad and tired. David couldn't fight back and they would easily capture him.

Then it was wise Hushai's turn to talk. He **knew** they could capture poor David when he was sad and tired. He **knew** what Ahithophel said was true; but he had to save King David. He had to make his trick work. He probably nodded his wise old head and made believe that he knew much better than Ahithophel did. He told Absalom not to run after David right away, for David was a good fighter and would be like an angry bear. They would not capture **him**! He told Absalom to wait a while and get all Israel together to fight David and his men. Hushai knew that David had to rest before he must fight Absalom.

What happened? God made Absalom and his men listen to wise Hushai, who told what was best for David. And wicked Ahithophel went out and hanged himself.

REMEMBER:

When Absalom told the people how much he cared about their troubles, he really cared only about himself. Wicked people always think of themselves. We, who are God's children, truly love our neighbors because we have God's love in our hearts.

310

The Sad Battle

Poor King David was so tired and hungry and sad. He had been running away all day from his son Absalom; and now, when it was almost dark, he had no place to go. He and his men had to sleep in the fields that night. Many of David's friends came running to him with presents of beds and furniture, of food and pans to cook it in. That would make poor David more comfortable. But it could not take away his sadness, for tomorrow would be a terrible day: a father would have to go to war with his son.

Through the night more and more of David's friends ran out to him. Thousands of his soldiers came to fight for their king, and David knew just what to do, for he had been a soldier all his life. He divided his soldiers into three groups, with three leaders. But when David said that he wanted to go to fight in the war, too, his people would not hear of it. They said, "Thou shalt not go forth: if half of us die, they will not care for us; but thou art worth ten thousand of us."

David listened to his people, and said, "What seemeth you best I will do." And sadly he stood at the side of the gate as his soldiers went to war with his son Absalom, his wicked son, but the son that he still loved. He had to say one thing more to his soldiers as they left. He asked them to be careful with Absalom and not to kill him. It would be so hard for David if Absalom were killed. After all the soldiers had heard King David's command, they left for the war.

Absalom had started all the trouble, but he did not start the fighting. He was not a soldier and did not know how to lead an army. So David's men went out first against Absalom's army and started the fighting. Absalom's soldiers were not trained to fight and they turned around and ran — right into a deep woods. Twenty thousand of Absalom's soldiers were killed that day, but the woods killed more men than the swords of the soldiers. Absalom's soldiers were caught in the vines that hung from the trees, or they ran into low branches, and were killed. The Lord made even the trees of the woods fight for David.

Where was Absalom? He saw many of his soldiers lying dead all around him, and he gave up trying to lead his army. But he was still alive and he was alone. Maybe he could get away! As he rode his tired mule as fast as it would go, they ran under big oak trees. Suddenly Absalom ran full force into the thick branches of a huge oak tree and his head caught between the branches so firmly that he could not get loose. His mule went on, but Absalom hung in mid-air. He could not get up or down. Don't you think he was terribly afraid?

While he was hanging there, one of David's soldiers saw him. He ran and told Joab, the captain of David's army, "I saw Absalom hanged in an oak."

Joab scolded, "Why didst thou not smite him to the ground? I would have given thee ten shekels of silver."

The soldier talked back to Joab: "Though I receive **one thousand** shekels of silver in my hand, yet would I not put forth mine hand against the king's son."

What could Joab say? His soldier would not disobey King David, and Joab knew his soldier was right. But Joab did not have an obedient heart. He took three darts and shot them through Absalom's body as he hung there helplessly. Joab's ten young men shot darts at him, too, so that he died. What a cruel, disobedient way to kill the king's son.

Then Joab blew the trumpet loudly. Absalom was dead. The war was over. He sent two fast runners to take the news to David.

There sat King David, at the gate, waiting for news. Suddenly the watchman on the roof saw a man running, and he called to David that he saw a man running alone. Then he called to David that he saw another man running alone. Now David knew he would get news. He could hardly wait! Did his soldiers win? Was Absalom still alive?

The runner Cushi talked. He told the happy news first. The war was over. David's soldiers had won. But he could hardly finish telling the news before David asked, "Is the young man Absalom safe?" And then Cushi had to tell the sad news that Absalom was killed.

Poor David cried and cried for a long time. He said, "O my son Absalom, would God I had died for thee, O Absalom my son."

But David was forgetting something when he was crying for Absalom. He forgot about all his people who loved him so much and fought so hard for him and won the battle for him. Joab had to scold King David and tell him to go out to talk to his people. King David stopped crying and talked to his people and they took him home to his palace again.

REMEMBER:

King David loved his son Absalom so much. But King David's love was a love that came from a sinful heart. We have a King Who loves His children with a perfect love. His name is Jehovah God. We are His children.

313

David Numbers the People

At last all was peaceful and quiet in the land of Israel. King David was back in his palace and his enemies were not bothering him anymore. The Israelites were having a nice, easy life, with plenty of food and money. It **seemed** as though everything in Israel was just right now, but it wasn't. The people became lazy and did not fight against their sins and did not serve God with all their hearts. The Lord saw it and was angry. He did something to **correct** His people. That means to make his people turn away from their sins and turn to the Lord, to serve Him in holiness again.

This is what happened: the Lord used Satan to tempt King David to count all the soldiers in Israel. Satan put the idea into David's mind, and then David decided to count them. Now, there is nothing wrong with counting soldiers, but it was wrong for King David because he had a sinful reason. He wanted to feel proud about the great army he had, he wanted to brag about what a great king he was, and he wanted to boast that **he** could fight all his enemies. That was very wrong of David. He was forgetting to put all his trust in his God.

He knew he was not leaning on God's arm when he told Joab, the captain of his army, to count all the soldiers. Joab knew it, too, and he argued with King David. He said something like this: "May the Lord give you a hundred times more soldiers, David, but do not do this wicked thing."

Did David listen? No. For almost a year Joab and his men counted all the soldiers in each tribe in the land of Israel. Oh, Joab was tired of counting! Before he had quite finished, he told David about the thousands and thousands of soldiers he had counted. But by this time, David was not very interested. He was feeling sad and guilty before the Lord. All those big numbers had not made him happy, after all; and David went to God and said, "I have sinned."

We know that our pure and holy God will not just let sins go, don't we? When King David asked the Lord to take his sin away, the Lord sent the prophet Gad to him with these words: "Thus saith the Lord, I offer thee three things: choose thee one of them, that I may do it unto thee. Choose thee either three years' famine; or three months to be destroyed before thy foes; or else three days the sword of the Lord, even the pestilence, in the land."

Do you understand what David had to choose? In three years of famine the crops would not grow and many people would starve and die. In three months of being chased by their enemies many people would be killed and much of the land would be destroyed. In three days of a plague, a terrible sickness from the Lord, the Israelites would drop dead by the thousands. What terrible things David had to choose from! And the worst part was that he knew **he** had sinned, and the poor people of Israel had to suffer for it.

David felt so troubled! But he knew which one to choose. He chose the last one — the three days of the plague from the hands of the Lord. Do you know why? He said, "Let me fall now into the hand of the Lord; for very great are his mercies."

Then the sickness began. On the first day, from morning until the time for the evening sacrifice to God, seventy thousand people died. In the evening, when the people looked up, they could see the angel of the Lord, with his sword in his hand, in the air over the city of Jerusalem. He was not killing any more people, for the Lord had told His angel, "It is enough." The Lord in His great mercy had stopped the awful sickness after only one day.

As the angel stayed over the city of Jerusalem, the prophet Gad came to David once more and told him to build an altar and make a sacrifice to Jehovah God on one of the mountain tops. There were two mountain tops in the city of Jerusalem. On one of them David had built his palace. That was Mt. Zion. On the other one, called Mt. Moriah, Abraham had gone, long ago, to sacrifice his son Isaac to God. Do you remember that? Now God told King David to sacrifice to Him on **Mt. Moriah**, on the threshing floor of a man named Ornan.

When King David came to the mountain, Ornan was working with his wheat on his threshing floor. Ornan wanted to **give** his threshing floor to King David, but David answered, "No, but I will **buy** it for the full price."

315

Then David built an altar to the Lord and offered the oxen from Ornan's farm on it. When the sacrifice was all ready, God sent fire from heaven to burn the sacrifice; and He commanded His angel to put away his sword of death.

When King David saw the wonder of the fire from the Lord, and when he saw how He forgave the sins of His people, and how He showed kindness in stopping the sickness, David called this place **the house of God**. Right away King David started to carry beautiful stones and wood and gold and brass to the mountain. They would soon be used to build a new house to God. That house would be called God's **temple**.

REMEMBER:

The angel of the Lord went back to heaven without killing all the people. But their sins still had to be paid. David's sacrifice was a picture of the Lord Jesus, Who really paid for all their sins by dying on the cross. We believe He paid for our sins, too.

Solomon is Made King

So many things had happened to King David during his lifetime. When he was younger, very often he had to run away from King Saul and live outside in dark caves in all kinds of weather. Later he had to lead the army of Israel to fight God's enemies, and he had to stay out on the battlefield with his soldiers. David had a hard life. Now he was seventy years old — as old as a grandfather — and his poor body was tired and worn out and sick.

God had promised King David that his son Solomon would be king after he died. God had promised, too, that King Solomon would build Him His beautiful house, called His temple, where all God's people could worship Him. David was so happy about that! For many years he had been getting things ready for God's temple: beautiful kinds of wood, gold, silver, precious stones, iron, and special kinds of cloth.

King David's other children knew that God had chosen Solomon to be the next king; but Adonijah, one of David's older boys, did not want it that way. He wanted to be the next king. Even though he knew that God had promised the kingdom to Solomon, he went ahead with his own plans. He invited many men who were not on David's side to a big feast near a lovely spring of water in the king's garden. At this big party, Adonijah's friends would put a crown on his head and make him king. What a wicked plan! They were not afraid of King David, either, for they knew that he was old and sick; and they thought he couldn't do anything about it.

When Nathan the prophet heard what Adonijah was doing, he hurried to Bathsheba, Solomon's mother, and told her to go quickly to the room where King David was lying sick and tell him how Adonijah was making plans to be king instead of Solomon. The prophet Nathan promised to come, too, and tell David that the story was really true.

Bathsheba rushed to King David's room, and after she bowed to the king, she told David how he had promised that **Solomon** would rule; but now **Adonijah** was calling himself king at a big party, and King David did not even know about it. What shocking news for old, sick David! Just then the prophet Nathan came into the king's room, and told the same story. He said that they were even shouting "God save king Adonijah."

When David heard all their words, the Lord gave him enough strength to get up and take care of his people Israel. First, he **promised** Bathsheba that Solomon would surely be king. Then he made plans to make Solomon king right away. He started to give orders just as he used to do when he was a younger king.

This is what King David ordered: the king's mule for Solomon to ride on must be decorated with the king's decorations; the king's soldiers must march alongside; Nathan the prophet and Benaiah, the captain of the soldiers, must go along, too; and Zadok, God's high priest, would anoint Solomon to be king with

a horn of oil. As the king's parade started, they blew their trumpets and shouted, "God save king Solomon." The people of the city of Jerusalem heard it, of course, and they came streaming from their houses and joined the grand parade for their new king, playing on their musical instruments and shouting, "God save king Solomon." They were so happy and they shouted so loudly it seemed as if the earth would break from all the noise.

Adonijah and his friends at their party could easily hear the noise, and some of them were asking, "Wherefore is this noise of the city being in an uproar?"

Just as they finished eating, a messenger came running to them, saying, "Verily our lord king David hath made Solomon king."

When he told all about the parade and the happiness and shouting of the people, everyone at Adonijah's party was afraid and went away. What was Adonijah to do? He ran to a place where he knew no one might kill him — to the altar of burnt offering — where he stooped down, begging that the new King Solomon would not kill him. Solomon sent a servant to get his brother Adonijah. He told his brother that if he behaved himself well, he would not die; and then he said, "Go to thine house."

Afterward King David called all the people of Israel together and God gave him strength to leave his bed once more to talk to them. He told how God had chosen **Solomon** to sit on his throne. He told how he had been getting precious things ready for God's temple that Solomon would soon build, and he asked the people to help and to give gifts for God's house with willing hearts. He told Solomon and all the people to keep God's commandments and to serve Him with gladness. Then, once more, this time in front of all the people, Solomon was anointed to be king.

Soon good King David died, and King Solomon ruled over Israel.

REMEMBER:

David asked the people of Israel to give gifts for God's house with willing hearts. We are just like the Israelites, for we like to bring our gifts to God's house, too. God's house is our church. Our gifts are our songs and our prayers and our money.

King Solomon Dreams a Dream

Solomon was a very young man when he became king over the people of Israel. One of the first things he did was to call all the people together to the city of Gibeon for a great celebration. Do you know why they all went to Gibeon? God's tabernacle was there, and what better place could Solomon choose to celebrate than God's house?

His old father David had told Solomon that his work would be to teach the people the right way to serve the Lord; and the first thing the new King Solomon did was to lead the people in the worship of Jehovah God. In front of all the people he sacrificed **one thousand animals** on the altar of burnt offering.

His old father David had told Solomon, too, that he must get busy and build the beautiful, rich, new house for God, called His temple. His temple must be built **just right**, exactly as God wanted it; and Solomon knew he must work on it for many, many years.

When the new King Solomon stood before all his people, and when he thought how young he was and how much work God wanted him to do, don't you think he must have wondered whether he could do it well enough? God knew what King Solomon was thinking and He knew what hard work Solomon would have to do. That night God came to him in a dream and asked him a short question. He said, "Ask what I shall give thee."

Solomon knew what he needed most of all. He said, "Give thy servant wisdom and an understanding heart." **Wisdom** means to know how to say the very best thing and do the very best thing for God's people. God liked Solomon's answer. He promised King Solomon that no one who lived before him or after him would have such a wise heart as he would have. And because Solomon asked God for just the right thing, God promised him two more blessings: great riches and honor; and, if he kept the commandments of the Lord, he would live a long life.

After Solomon awoke from his dream, he went back home to Jerusalem. He was so thankful and happy for all the goodness that God promised him that he offered more sacrifices to God in Jerusalem.

Soon two women came to him with a bad problem. One of the women did the talking. She told King Solomon how she and the other woman lived together in the same house, and that they each had a tiny baby. These babies were so small that they slept in the same beds with their mothers. Then the mother told that one night, in her sleep, the other mother rolled over on her baby, and it

died. She told how the other mother must have gotten up quietly, at midnight, and traded babies. The other mother took her live baby, and put the dead one in her arms.

She told King Solomon how she was going to feed her baby in the morning. . .and it was dead. But, no, she told the king, it couldn't be. This wasn't her baby. She knew her own baby!

Then the other mother talked. She said, "Nay, but the living is my son, and the dead is thy son."

The first mother argued back: "No, but the dead is thy son, and the living is my son."

After King Solomon listened to their story, he said, "The one saith, This is my son that liveth, and thy son is the dead: and the other saith, Nay; but thy son is dead, and my son is the living. Bring me a sword."

When a servant brought the king a sword, he said, "Divide the living child in two, and give half to the one, and half to the other."

Do you think King Solomon would really have let his servant cut that baby in half? No, but he was giving both mothers a test. King Solomon knew how the real mother of that live little baby would feel. He knew she would not let her baby be killed. She would rather give it away. And that is just what happened. The real mother cried out, "O my lord, give her the living child, and in no wise slay it."

Now Solomon knew that the mother who had told the story was the real mother of the living baby, and he said, "Give her the living child, and in no wise slay it: she is the mother."

King Solomon's wise test had worked; and this story of Solomon's wisdom and many more stories spread over the whole land. All the people knew that his wisdom came from God.

REMEMBER:

The Bible tells us that Solomon was one of God's children. He asked for an understanding heart. But he wasn't the only one of God's children who asked for an understanding heart. We do, too. We ask God for a heart that understands how great He is, how much He loves us, and how He saves us from our sins.

King Solomon
Builds the Temple

If we could go back and visit King Solomon when he ruled over the people of Israel, what would we find? We would **not** find any Philistines or Moabites or any other enemies running over the land. We would **not** see any wars or fighting; for King Solomon's time was a time of peace. We **would** see a rich and happy land with a very wise and a very busy king.

Why was King Solomon so very busy? He was getting ready to build the temple, and he needed ever so many helpers. Some of his helpers he sent to King Hiram's land to cut down big cedar trees. He needed the wood from the trees for God's house. Thousands of his other helpers cut huge stones out of the earth, some of them bigger than a man, and brought them to Jerusalem, where the temple would be built. Still other helpers made beautiful designs in cloth and in wood; and some collected precious stones and gold and silver. Solomon needed so many things for God's house.

After four years of getting everything ready, Solomon and his workers were ready to start building. If you could have stood near Mt. Moriah where they were building the temple, you would not have heard any sounds of building, no pounding of nails or sawing of boards; for everything was cut according to the patterns God showed them, and all the parts fit together without the noisy work of pounding. The people built God's house **quietly** and **reverently**.

Shall we wait for seven years until the temple is finished and then make believe that we are going to the land of Israel to visit it? What would we see? We would come into a big yard with a wall around it, and the first thing we would see in the yard would be the big, high altar of burnt offering, where the people brought their lambs to be killed and sacrificed as a picture of Jesus the Lamb, Who was killed and sacrificed for their sins. Near to the altar was a large bowl which held a lot of water. It was called a **laver**, and the priests used it to wash in after they finished their sacrifices.

If we walked a little farther, we would see a tall building about as long as two big houses next to one another, and it would be made of those very large stones that King Solomon's helpers cut. This building was God's temple. Some steps led up to a porch. Two tall pillars stood on the porch, one on each side of the door. We would see beautiful pictures of fruits carved on these pillars. The tops of the pillars looked like lilies just opening up. Both pillars were covered with shining gold. The door between the two pillars had pictures carved on it, too: pictures of palm trees and angels and lilies; and these were covered with gold, just as the pillars were. Can you imagine how wonderful this must have looked?

We might not open that golden door and go in, for only God's priests might go into His temple. But the Bible gives us a little peek into the beautiful room on the other side of the door. It was called the **Holy Place**. If we could see into it, we would find that the stone walls were covered on the inside with the cedar wood that Solomon's helpers cut down. All the walls had carvings of lovely pictures, and these pictures were covered with gold, so that they looked like golden pictures. The floor and ceiling were covered with gold, too.

324

In this room were ten golden candlesticks, and each candlestick had seven branches for candles. As these candles burned brightly, they were pictures of our holy God Who is **The Light**. In this room were also ten golden tables of bread, and they were pictures of our God Who is the **Bread of Life**. One more thing was in this room: the golden altar of incense. The priests burned sweet-smelling incense on the altar day and night because it was a picture of the prayers of all God's people going up to heaven and smelling sweet to God.

On one wall of the Holy Place was a golden door. Hanging in front of the door was a gorgeous cloth, called a veil, embroidered — that means **sewed** — in colors of blue and purple and red. Behind that door was the **Most Holy Place**, a small, square, golden room. If we could look into it, we would see a golden box. On top were two golden angels with their wings stretched out. The faces of those golden angels looked down at the box. The box was called the **ark** and in it were the two stones with God's law written on them. The top of the ark was called the mercy seat. Once a year the high priest sprinkled the blood of a lamb on the mercy seat. It was a picture of the blood of Jesus which takes away our sins.

What a rich and beautiful house King Solomon had built! And God was pleased with His house. He came down in a cloud and His glory filled the temple.

REMEMBER:

King Solomon's temple was very beautiful and precious, just exactly right for the Lord of heaven and earth. That temple was a picture of God's true house in heaven — God's very precious house — where we will go to live with Him forever.

The Queen of Sheba Visits Solomon

After King Solomon and the people of Israel finished building the temple, they had a big celebration which lasted fourteen days. We call it a **dedication**. That means that they promised that they would use the temple as **God's** house and they would come to His house to thank Him and praise Him and worship Him.

From one end of the land to the other, the people of Israel flocked to the temple for the celebration. They sang songs of praise to God while the priests played on harps and cymbals; and they offered many, many sacrifices to God. Then King Solomon walked to a big brass platform, dropped to his knees, spread his hands out to heaven, and prayed a beautiful prayer. In his prayer he asked God to bless His people when they worshipped Him in His temple, to love His people, and to forgive their sins. The Lord answered King Solomon's prayer by having His cloud of glory fill the temple; and all the people bowed with their faces to the ground.

Then the people went home, and King Solomon was ready to start building his own palace. It took him thirteen years. All the people in Israel and all the people in the lands around Israel heard of the rich and great houses Solomon had built. One lady especially was very interested in King Solomon's work. We do not know her name, but we know that she was the queen of a faraway land. The Bible calls her the Queen of Sheba. She had heard many big stories about King Solomon's richness and wisdom, but she would not believe them all. She thought that no one could be so great and wise as that! Yet, she was very interested in seeing this King Solomon and his people, and she decided to make the long trip to the land of Israel. The Queen of Sheba was a very rich queen, and she loaded her camels with expensive spices, gold, and precious stones. She also had many riddles and hard questions for King Solomon to answer. She wanted to hear for herself how wise he was.

Shall we come along once more and follow the train of camels, with the Queen of Sheba leading them? They were coming to the land of Israel, and the first city they wanted to visit was Jerusalem, the temple city. In our minds we will follow the great queen and see what she saw.

At the top of Mt. Moriah she saw the lovely, golden temple, with its pillars and doors, its embroidered curtains and precious stones and beautiful wood. It was so wonderful it must almost have taken her breath away. Down the mountainside she could see the king's palace. King Solomon's palace was connected to the temple by wooden steps. As she walked down these steps, she could see a yard with many great buildings. In the center was the king's palace. In each corner of the yard was a building: in the first corner, the house of the forest of Lebanon, where King Solomon kept his weapons for war — swords, shields, and spears; in the second corner, the house of judgment, where people might come with their troubles and get help; in the third corner, the house of pillars, where the people could meet people from other lands; in the last corner, the house for King Solomon's wife, the queen.

In King Solomon's palace the Queen of Sheba saw beautiful furniture and rich hangings on the walls and lovely gardens outside. She saw the great feasts, with foods from all over the world served in plates and cups of gold. She saw that King Solomon had so much silver that it was as common as stones on the ground. She saw King Solomon's throne, made of precious ivory covered with gold, with carved lions at the arms and six lions on each side of six steps leading to the throne, all covered with gold. She saw much more: fourteen hundred horses and chariots and twelve hundred men to take care of them; ships that sailed all over the world and brought back gold, silver, precious stones, beautiful wood, horses, monkeys, and peacocks. The Queen of Sheba saw so many riches that her eyes could hardly take them all in.

She **heard** so much, too. She heard King Solomon tell her all about the stars in the sky, about animals and bugs, about plants and flowers. Solomon knew many things about God's world. But Solomon knew much more. The queen listened as Solomon told her all about his great God Jehovah Who made the world, and she listened as Solomon told her how to worship Him. She listened as he answered her hard questions.

No wonder the Queen of Sheba almost fainted! She said, "I believed not their words, until I came, and mine eyes had seen it: and, behold, the one half of the greatness of thy wisdom was not told me."

After that, she and King Solomon exchanged gifts and she went back home to her own land. The Bible does not tell us whether the Lord gave her faith to believe on Him or not, but her words make us think that she, too, believed in the Lord, just as you and I do.

REMEMBER:

Are you wondering **why** the Lord sent the Queen of Sheba to King Solomon? It was so that the whole world would know about Solomon's riches and wisdom and peace. For King Solomon was a picture of **the** great and wise King, our Lord Jesus Christ, the Prince of Peace. Now **we** can see how King Solomon was a picture of Jesus, too.

The Last Part of King Solomon's Life

All over the world people heard about King Solomon. They heard how rich he was and how beautiful he had made his city of Jerusalem. They heard how wise he was and how much he knew about God's world. Many great and rich men from other countries came to see King Solomon and his greatness, and he began to feel proud.

Would you like to know what King Solomon did when he was feeling very strong and proud? He tried to live like the kings of the other countries of the world. In those days great kings collected many beautiful young girls to be their wives. They made palaces for the girls to live in, and the more pretty wives they had, the more important kings they were.

Solomon wanted to be an important king in the world, too. He wanted everyone to honor him. So, as he became older, he collected many, many beautiful girls to be his wives. These girls were from heathen countries, countries that were the enemies of Jehovah God. King Solomon knew he might not marry these girls. He knew that God's law told him not to become very rich in silver and gold and not to have many wives. He knew that he was supposed to read the book of God's law every day, and obey it, and turn to the Lord his God with all his heart. Twice already God had come to King Solomon, telling him that He would bless Solomon and go with him and his children, if he loved the Lord and obeyed His commandments. But, the Lord warned King Solomon, if he walked in wicked ways, the Lord would take the kingdom away from him and his children, and bring evil on his house.

Do you think King Solomon thought about these words of Jehovah God and listened to them? No. His heart was too proud to listen to God. Instead, King Solomon turned to worse and worse wickedness. When his heathen wives from wicked countries took their idol-gods along with them, King Solomon let them worship those idols, right in his own palace. When those wives asked him to make altars so they could sacrifice to their idol-gods, he gave them a hill in Jerusalem for their idol altars, and set up altars for three heathen gods: the sun-god, the moon-god, and the king-god. There, right near God's holy temple, those wicked wives — one thousand in all — could worship their idols in the sight of the people of Israel.

God in heaven was watching all that Solomon was doing, too, and He was angry with Solomon. Now He had to talk to King Solomon again, maybe through the mouth of a prophet. The Lord had bad news for him because he was not keeping all the laws God had commanded him. God told him three things: He would take the kingdom of Israel away from King Solomon and his children; He would break apart the people of Israel into two kingdoms and would give Solomon's family only two tribes to rule over; but God would not do it while Solomon was alive. All this would happen to King Solomon's son. Even this terrible news did not make King Solomon turn to the Lord with all his heart.

The Lord had to send more trouble to King Solomon and the people of Israel. Two army captains from enemy lands began to gather soldiers together and bother the land of Israel. The Lord sent trouble from **inside** the land of Israel, too. This is what happened: King Solomon had many men working on building a strong wall around the city of Jerusalem, and he found a man named Jeroboam, who was a good worker and a good leader, to be their ruler. One day, as Jeroboam was leaving the city of Jerusalem, probably after his day's work, the prophet Ahijah met him in the field. They were alone in the field. No one else was around. Suddenly the prophet caught Jeroboam's new robe, pulled it off him, and tore it into twelve pieces. Then he gave ten of the pieces back to

Jeroboam. What the prophet did was a picture of the twelve tribes of Israel. God was going to give ten tribes to Jeroboam to rule over, and King Solomon and his children would have only two. God was going to break up His people Israel into two parts! Jeroboam was glad. He would soon be king! He must have told everyone about it. When King Solomon heard the news, he tried to kill him, and Jeroboam had to run away to the land of Egypt.

Soon King Solomon died, sad because he had sinned so much in the last part of his life. But Solomon was one of God's own children, and God forgave all those sins and took him to heaven.

REMEMBER:

Do you know why God let Solomon's family keep a little part of Israel? Because He had promised his father David that his children would always be kings until the Great King, Jesus Christ, would be born from his family. God always keeps His promises.

Rehoboam is Made King

The Bible tells us about only one son of King Solomon. His name was Rehoboam. We know that Rehoboam's mother was not an Israelite, but was one of Solomon's heathen wives from the wicked land of Ammon. When Rehoboam was a little boy, he was brought up by a heathen mother who loved idols and by his father Solomon who did not listen to God's commandments. When Rehoboam grew up, he knew all about worshipping idols instead of the living God.

After King Solomon died, all the Israelites **should** have gone to the city of Jerusalem to make Rehoboam the next king, for he was Solomon's son. But they didn't go. Why not? There was trouble in the land of Israel. One of the big and strong tribes in Israel — the tribe of Ephraim — was unhappy. The people of Ephraim were jealous because God had chosen the tribe of Judah to be the tribe of the kings, and because He had chosen Jerusalem to be the king's city. They wanted the city of Shechem, in their own tribe of Ephraim, to be the king's city.

So the people of Ephraim stayed at home, and the rest of the tribes of Israel gathered in the city of Shechem in Ephraim's land. What was Rehoboam to do? How would he become king without the people? He went to the city of Shechem in the tribe of Ephraim and told all the people there to make him king in Shechem.

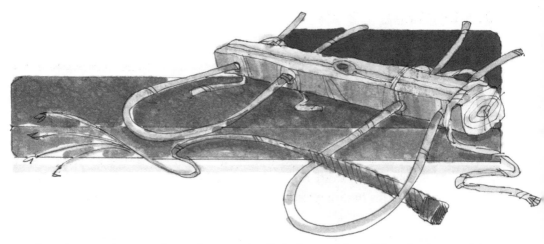

But the people weren't ready to make Rehoboam king. They had something to say to Rehoboam first, and they made pictures with the words they said. They told Rehoboam that his father Solomon had made them carry loads and that he had tied them together like horses with a heavy wooden yoke, so they could pull big loads. Now, you don't think King Solomon really treated the people like horses, do you? No, he didn't. What the people meant by their picture-words was that King Solomon made them pay so much money and he made them work too hard for him. The people asked Rehoboam to be a little bit easier on them, and then they would serve him.

Rehoboam answered, "Come again unto me after three days."

During those three days, Rehoboam asked the wise old men what he should do. They answered, "If thou be kind to this people, and please them, and speak good words to them, they will be thy servants forever."

Next Rehoboam asked the young men, just as old as he was, what he should do. They told Rehoboam to tell the people that he would be much harder on them than his father was and that he would make their loads much heavier. They told Rehoboam to make a picture with his words: to say that if King Solomon hurt the people with whips, he would hurt them with whips with **hooks** at the ends.

Then the three days were over. The people were waiting for Rehoboam's answer. What did he say to them? He talked roughly to them, and said, "My father made your yoke heavy, but I will add thereto: my father chastised you with whips, but I will chastise you with scorpions." Scorpions are whips with hooks in the ends.

Rehoboam **thought** he was being strong and brave by saying these words, but he was wicked and foolish. He did not listen to the wise words of the old men, but followed the foolish words of the young men.

When the tribes of Israel heard Rehoboam's rough words, **ten** of the tribes answered, "Every man to your tents, O Israel," and they all went home without making Rehoboam king. The ten tribes sent for Jeroboam from Egypt and made him king instead.

Only two tribes were left: Judah and Benjamin. They made Rehoboam their king. Now there were two kings in Israel and the people of Israel were broken into two parts. The ten tribes were called **Israel** and the two tribes were called **Judah**.

It was very wrong of Rehoboam to talk so roughly to the people of Israel, but it was far more wrong for the ten tribes of Israel to leave Rehoboam and the tribe of Judah. Do you know why? Because **Jesus** would be born from the tribe of Judah and from the family of Rehoboam. The people of the ten tribes of Israel were running away from **Jesus!**

REMEMBER:

God is very wise and He is very good to His people. Even when He sent Israel trouble and even when he broke apart their country, He was leading His own people to Jesus. He leads us to Jesus, too.

Jeroboam Teaches Israel to Worship Idols

From now on in our Bible stories we must remember that God's people were divided into two parts: Israel and Judah. Israel, the part of the ten tribes, had just made Jeroboam their king. As soon as he became king he made the walls of the city of Shechem very strong, for he was going to be king in Shechem, not in Jerusalem, where God's temple was. Rehoboam, king of the two tribes, lived in Jerusalem.

King Jeroboam knew right away that he had one big problem: the worship of the Lord. The temple was in Jerusalem, where King Rehoboam lived. If the people went to King Rehoboam's city to serve the Lord, they might let King Rehoboam rule over them, too, and kill Jeroboam. And King Jeroboam didn't want that! What was he to do? He called all his rulers together — and they were just as wicked as he was — to tell them his plan. He wanted to set up his own temple and make his own gods. The rulers agreed with him. So King Jeroboam set up two temples, one on each end of his land, and made golden calves for the people to worship. He even told the people of Israel, "Behold thy gods, O Israel, which brought thee up out of the land of Egypt." Instead of getting priests from the family of Levi, as God had said, he made priests for his golden calves of the lowest kinds of people. What a terrible sin of Jeroboam: to lead all of Israel to worship idols.

King Jeroboam sinned much more than that. God had given Moses the rules for the special days when they should have feasts and sacrifices to Him. Jeroboam decided to disobey God and have feasts **when** he wanted them and **how** he wanted them. So he set a time when all Israel was invited to a feast for the golden calves. Do you know what the people saw when they came to the feast? They saw an altar to the golden calves and Jeroboam, not the high priest, standing ready to make a sacrifice on the altar. Everyone knew that **only** a priest might make a sacrifice, but no one stopped King Jeroboam.

While the eyes of all the people were on Jeroboam and the altar, they noticed some movement. Someone was coming through the crowd. A prophet! And he was shouting! He was shouting to the altar. He told the altar that some day, many years later, one of the good kings of Judah would burn the bones of the idol-priests on this very altar. He shouted more words to the altar and they came true right away: "Behold, the altar shall be rent (rent means **broken**), and the ashes that are upon it shall be poured out."

King Jeroboam was angry. He did not want to hear those words. In anger he pointed to the prophet with his arm stretched out and called, "Lay hold on him."

Then a quiet hush must have come over the crowd: for King Jeroboam's arm dried up and he could not pull it back again. The altar broke, too, and the ashes poured out, as the prophet had said. The people were seeing two wonders from the Lord.

Now King Jeroboam was afraid and he begged the prophet to pray that God would make his arm better. The prophet prayed and the Lord healed his arm. Then the prophet turned around and started for home; for the Lord had told him not to stay to eat bread or drink water, but to go directly home.

At the feast were two sons of another prophet, an old man. The two sons ran home to tell their father the story of all the excitement at the feast and of the prophet who shouted to the altar. Oh, that old prophet was interested in their stories! He asked, "What way went he?" His boys saddled his donkey and the old prophet went to find the younger prophet. He was so eager to talk with him. There, under an oak tree, he found him. How happy he was! He said, "Come home with me, and eat bread."

The younger prophet answered, "I may not. For it was said to me by the word of the Lord, Thou shalt eat no bread nor drink water there."

The old prophet was so disappointed that he told a lie. He said, "I am a prophet also as thou art; and an angel spake unto me by the word of the Lord, saying, Bring him back with thee into thine house."

The younger prophet listened to the lie. Maybe he **wanted** to go to the old prophet's home. He disobeyed the Lord and turned around. But God's blessing did not go with him, for while they were eating the Lord told the old prophet that the disobedient prophet would never be buried in a grave with his own family. Would he die on the way home?

He left the old prophet's home then and a lion met him and killed him, but did not tear him in pieces nor eat him up. The lion did not hurt the prophet's donkey either. It was a wonder from God.

People who went past stopped to see the wonder and then went back into the city to tell the old prophet what had happened. Don't you think the old prophet was sad because the disobedient prophet died on account of **his** lie? He ordered his boys to bury the prophet next to his own grave.

And what did King Jeroboam think of all these judgments the Lord brought to his land? Wouldn't you think he would cry out to the Lord to forgive him and his people their awful sins? He didn't. He made his heart hard and turned again to his idols.

REMEMBER:

The next time we are disobedient shall we think of the prophet who died? We deserve to die, too, when we disobey. But our loving Father has sent Jesus to die instead of us, to take the punishment for our sins.

The Prophet Elijah and King Ahab

Many years went by. Wicked King Jeroboam had died and five more kings had ruled Israel after him. Those five kings were wicked, too, each one a little more wicked than the one before him. Then **Ahab** became king of Israel and ruled for many years. While he was king, he led the people into worse and worse sins. First he married Jezebel, the daughter of the heathen king of Zidon, where the people worshipped the idol Baal. When Jezebel came to Ahab's palace to live, she taught the people of Israel how to worship Baal. Now the Israelites were worshipping King Jeroboam's golden calves and Baal. What a black night of sin it was for Israel!

Suddenly, like a flash of bright light in that black night of sin, the Bible tells us about **Elijah**. We do not know where he was born or who his father and mother were, or where he went to school. All we know is that God called him to be His prophet — to speak God's Word to wicked King Ahab and wicked Queen Jezebel. One day there he stood before the rich King Ahab, wearing a coat of camel's skin, the kind of coat poor people wore.

What did the prophet Elijah say to King Ahab? He told King Ahab where he stood: he stood before **Jehovah**. Then he spoke only a few more words: "As Jehovah God of Israel liveth, before whom I stand, there shall not be dew nor rain these years, but according to my word."

Then Elijah was gone. The Bible does not tell us what the wicked Ahab thought when he heard that his land would have no rain **for years**. Maybe he wondered what would happen to the gardens and farms and animals without water or how the people would live without water.

We will not stay with King Ahab but will follow the prophet Elijah. God told him to hide near the brook Cherith and live alone there. A brook is a little river. Why did God send Elijah to the brook? Because there he would be safe from Ahab. God did not need him in Ahab's palace right now. There at the cool, sparkling brook Elijah could get plenty to drink, but how would he get his food? God took care of that. He wouldn't let His Elijah starve. He commanded the ravens, those greedy, big blackbirds, who usually want to grab every bit of food for themselves, to bring bread and meat to Elijah every morning and every evening. That was a wonder; and each day Elijah trusted God and waited for the wonder of the ravens to bring him his food. Do you wonder what Elijah did all alone at that brook every day? Don't you think he prayed? He must have prayed for God's **true** people in the land of Israel whose crops would not grow and whose animals would die because God didn't send rain. He must have asked God to take care of them each day just as God was taking care of Elijah.

Then the brook dried up. The Lord told him, "Arise, get thee to Zarephath." Zarephath was not even in the land of Israel, but in the heathen land of Zidon, where the people worshipped Baal, the land where Queen Jezebel had come from. God asked Elijah to go **outside** the land of Israel. Elijah obeyed.

When he came to the gate of the city of Zarephath he saw a widow — a lady whose husband had died — gathering some sticks to make a fire, and he asked her for a drink of water. As she ran to get him a drink, he called after her, "Bring me a morsel of bread in thine hand."

Then the poor widow had to tell Elijah her sad story: those sticks in her hand were for a fire to cook the last meal for her son and herself. They had flour and cooking oil left for only one meal. After that they would die. What did Elijah say? "Fear not; make me a little cake first, and bring it unto me, and after make for thee and for thy son." For God would never let her flour barrel nor her pot of oil get empty, until the day that God would send rain again. There would always be food. That, too, was a great wonder. And the heathen woman from Zarephath **believed!** She knew that Elijah was God's prophet and she obeyed him because she was one of God's own believing children.

After Elijah had stayed with the widow for a while, her son became sick, so sick that he died. Oh, how sad that poor widow was to lose her only son.

When she told Elijah the sad news, all he said was, "Give me thy son." He carried him upstairs and prayed hard to Jehovah his God. Then he stretched himself three times on top of the boy. He was making a picture by breathing his breath into the boy: it was a picture of God's breath which gives **life**. God heard Elijah's prayer and gave the boy life and breath again. When he brought the living boy to his happy mother, she said, "Now I know that thou art a man of God, and that the word of the Lord in thy mouth is truth."

REMEMBER:

When Elijah made the picture of God breathing life back into the boy, he was making a picture of a wonder. It was a picture of the life that God gives His people in heaven forever. In heaven we will always breathe the breath of life.

Elijah at Mount Carmel

For three and a half years Elijah had been hiding from King Ahab. All this time not one drop of rain had fallen on the land of Israel. The hot sun had beat down and baked the ground as hard as stone. People and animals were starving because they could not get food and water. And all this time King Ahab had hunted for Elijah but could not find him, because God would not let him.

Suddenly one day God said to Elijah, "Go, show thyself unto Ahab; and I will send rain upon the earth."

When Elijah came to King Ahab's house, he wasn't at home. Where was he? He had gone, with Obadiah his servant, to look carefully over every bit of land to see whether there were any little blades of grass for his animals. We would have liked the servant Obadiah. Even though he had to work for the wicked King Ahab, and even though he saw priests of the idol Baal all around him, he loved the Lord. When wicked Queen Jezebel ordered all God's prophets to be killed, Obadiah hid one hundred of them in caves and fed them bread and water every day.

Now King Ahab and Obadiah divided the land between them and each went looking a different way. As the servant Obadiah walked along looking for grass, Elijah stood in front of him and said, "Go, tell thy lord, Behold, Elijah is here."

Obadiah didn't really like to tell King Ahab that. What if the Lord, by a wonder, would snatch Elijah away and hide him again! Then King Ahab might kill Obadiah. But Elijah told him not to worry and said, "As the Lord of hosts liveth, before whom I stand, I will surely show myself unto him today."

Elijah waited as Obadiah went to get King Ahab. And there came King Ahab to meet Elijah. What did his face look like? Don't you think it looked hard and angry? It must have, for the first thing he said to Elijah was, "Art thou he that troubleth Israel?"

341

Elijah answered, "I have not troubled Israel: but thou and thy father's house." The **real** trouble was that Ahab and the people of Israel had disobeyed God's commands and served the Baal-idols.

Elijah kept talking to King Ahab, and as he talked a crowd of people came to listen. What did Elijah say? He said there would be a contest. First, King Ahab must send for the four hundred fifty prophets of the idol Baal and come with them to the top of the beautiful Mt. Carmel. That is where the contest would be held. What **kind** of contest would it be? A contest to choose between Baal and God. Elijah scolded King Ahab and the people and said they might not dance back and forth between two gods, and he ended by saying, "If the Lord be God, follow him: but if Baal, then follow him."

What did the people answer? Not a word.

It did not **seem** to be a fair contest: **four hundred fifty** prophets of Baal to **one** prophet of the Lord. When they all went up to Mt. Carmel they saw an altar to the Lord, but it was broken down because it had not been used for so long. Elijah said he would use the Lord's altar and he told the four hundred fifty prophets of Baal to make an altar to Baal. Next he took two animals — bulls — and laid one on the Lord's altar and gave one to the prophets of Baal for their altar.

Everything was ready for the two sacrifices except the fire, for Elijah had said, "Put no fire under it." Then he said, "Call ye on the name of your gods, and I will call on the name of the Lord: and the God that answereth by fire, let him be God."

That was the contest: and all the people answered, "It is well spoken."

The prophets of Baal did what Elijah told them, even though they did not want to. They began to pray to Baal to send fire. Oh, how they prayed to their idol: from morning to noon, and from noon until at least the middle of the afternoon. Louder and louder they shouted, jumping up and down on their altar, cutting themselves until they bled so that Baal would feel sorry for them. All the while Elijah poked fun of their dead idol and told them to shout louder. That was not wrong of Elijah because he was doing it for **God's** glory. So they shouted louder and kept up their wild praying until there was hardly any breath left in them anymore.

Now it was Elijah's turn. With everyone watching him, he quietly repaired the broken altar to the Lord with twelve stones. Next he did a strange thing: he asked for twelve barrels of water to be poured over the altar and the animal on it. He would show those Baal-priests that God's wonder-fire could lick up the water, too.

Then Elijah prayed a short, quiet prayer. He said, "Hear me, O Lord, that this people may know that thou art the Lord God."

Quickly the fire of the Lord fell and burned the sacrifice and the altar and even licked up the water. When the people saw it, they fell on their faces, saying, "The Lord, he is the God;" and Elijah ordered the four hundred fifty Baal prophets to be killed.

Elijah's work wasn't finished yet. There on top of the mountain he sat, with his face between his knees, and prayed — prayed for rain. Six times he sent his servant to look at the sky for rain, and six times the servant saw nothing. But the seventh time he saw a cloud as big as a man's hand, and Elijah told King Ahab to hurry home before the rain from the Lord came.

Suddenly the sky was black with rain clouds and wind; and the hand of the Lord led Elijah safely into the city before the hard rainstorm came.

REMEMBER:

There is only **one** God. He is the God of the Wonder. Aren't we glad He is **our** God and Father?

343

Elijah Runs to the Desert

How happy Elijah had been on the mountaintop when the people of the ten tribes of Israel had shouted, "The Lord, he is the God!" It seemed to him that all those people were sorry for serving Baal and were ready now to serve Jehovah with all their hearts. He thought that the battle with Baal was over and all Israel would turn to the Lord. Even King Ahab had let Elijah kill the four hundred fifty prophets of Baal. When Elijah had stood on top of Mt. Carmel, he felt on the mountaintop of happiness and on the mountaintop of trust in God.

Then everyone had hurried home and the big rainstorm had come. As soon as King Ahab came home, he told his wicked wife Jezebel about all the things that happened on Mt. Carmel, how Jehovah-God had the victory over Baal. When he told Jezebel that the four hundred fifty Baal-prophets were killed, she was furiously angry and she sent a servant to tell Elijah that tomorrow she would kill him. Why did Jezebel tell him that? Probably to scare Elijah into running away, far out of the country. That is what Queen Jezebel wanted — to have Elijah far away.

Elijah did just what Queen Jezebel wanted him to do. He ran away for his life. He was afraid. Are you surprised that he was afraid of Jezebel? Yesterday on Mt. Carmel Elijah was not afraid of King Ahab. He was not afraid of the Baal-prophets, and he was not afraid of all the people. With the Lord's help, he had stood all alone.

But that was yesterday. Today it seemed to him that everything had gone wrong. Now he knew that when the people of Israel had shouted to the Lord it must have been with their mouths, not with their hearts; and wicked Jezebel was still the queen. She was still ruling over Israel and she could find many more prophets of Baal. Today it seemed as if the big contest on Mt. Carmel had not done any good. Poor Elijah was down in the dumps. He decided to give up, to quit. He wasn't going to be the Lord's prophet anymore.

Sadly he walked out of the country, into the hot, dry desert. After he walked a whole day, he lay down under a juniper tree. He felt so bad he asked the Lord to let him die. He said, "It is enough; now, O Lord, take away my life; for I am not better than my fathers."

He was all worn out, and he fell asleep after he said this. As he slept, the Lord took care of him. Twice He sent an angel to wake him and give him food and water, for Elijah would not have any more food for forty days and forty nights.

When Elijah awoke, he walked farther into the desert until he came to Mt. Horeb. There he found a cave and lived in it; and there God came to him with this question: "What doest thou here, Elijah?"

Elijah did not dare to tell the Lord that he was quitting, that he didn't want to be God's prophet any longer. Instead, he grumbled and complained to the Lord about the people of Israel, how they **would not** serve Jehovah-God, how they had broken down God's altars, and even killed His prophets. He ended by saying, "And I, even I only, am left; and they seek my life, to take it away."

How did God answer Elijah's grumbling? He told Elijah to stand on the mountain and He would pass by him. First the Lord sent a strong wind, such a sharp, fierce tornado-wind that it broke the rocks on the mountain. But God did not come to Elijah in the wind. Next the Lord sent an earthquake, and the ground under him trembled and shook. But God did not come to Elijah in the earthquake. Then the Lord sent a fire, a hot, burning fire. But God did not come to Elijah in the fire. Do you know why the Lord sent the wind, the earthquake, and the fire? They were pictures of God's terrible punishment for the wicked. God did not come to Elijah in these terrible punishments.

345

He came to Elijah in a still, small voice. Maybe it was a quiet wind, whispering Jehovah's voice. God was showing Elijah that He did not need a lot of noise — not a tornado, not an earthquake, not a fire — to save His people. The Lord saves them **quietly,** with a still, small voice in their hearts. The Lord was making Elijah see that He was still the Ruler of heaven and earth. And He made Elijah feel much better by telling him that He still had seven thousand people in Israel who had never bowed to the idol Baal. Elijah wasn't all alone after all!

And the Lord would not let him quit. There was work for him to do. He had to go back to the land of Israel and find the farmer Elisha. Sure enough, he found him plowing his field. Elijah threw his coat over Elisha's shoulders and Elisha knew what that meant. He was called to be God's prophet after Elijah; and he was ready. He gave a goodbye feast for the people of his house and then went with Elijah, to help him as one of God's prophets.

REMEMBER:

There is one thing we may never say to the Lord. That is: "I quit." All our lives, day after day, we must love Him and serve Him and obey Him. Every day we must do His work. He puts His still, small voice into our hearts so that we love to do His work.

Ahab and Naboth

In this story we will go back to Ahab, who was still king of Israel. It was summertime. King Ahab and Queen Jezebel were at their summer palace, where they could enjoy the cool breezes and get away from the summer's heat.

But their summer palace was not nice enough to suit King Ahab. He wanted more land. Near to his palace was a vineyard. A vineyard is a garden of grapes. King Ahab wanted that garden of grapes. If he pulled all the grapes out, it would make a lovely spot for a garden of herbs. Herbs are sweet-smelling, spicy plants.

The trouble was that the vineyard did not belong to King Ahab. A man by the name of Naboth owned it. Naboth's family had gotten it from the Lord when the Israelites had come into the land of Canaan; and the rules of the Lord about the land were strict: every family must keep its own land. Naboth must give the land to **his children**, not to King Ahab. Of course King Ahab knew that when he came to Naboth and said, "Give me thy vineyard, that I may have it for a garden of herbs: and I will give thee a better vineyard than it; or, if it seem good to thee, I will give thee the worth of it in money."

Naboth was one of God's own children, one of the seven thousand who had not worshipped Baal; and he would never disobey God's command. He told King Ahab that the Lord would **not let him** sell his piece of land. His answer was no, and an unhappy Ahab went home.

Watch what King Ahab did after he came home. He had a long, sour face, and he lay on his bed with his face to the wall and would not eat, just like a naughty, spoiled, little boy. His wife Jezebel wanted to know what the trouble was, and after King Ahab told that Naboth would not sell him the land, Queen Jezebel said, "Arise, and eat bread, and let thine heart be merry. I will give thee the vineyard of Naboth."

King Ahab must have known that his wife would do some wickedness to get the vineyard, but he did not stop her. What did that wicked Jezebel do? She wrote letters to the rulers of the city and stamped them with King Ahab's stamp. This is what the letters told the rulers to do: tell everyone in the city to stop eating, because someone had sinned a most terrible sin, and no one must eat until that sin was out of the way. That someone was Naboth. Next she told them to get Naboth and set him where everyone could see him; and then the rulers had to find two wicked men who would say that Naboth had cursed God and the king.

Oh, what terrible lies those were! Do you think the rulers would listen to Queen Jezebel and tell all those lies? If they did, Naboth would have to die. Yes, they listened to wicked Jezebel and told those awful lies about Naboth, for they were very wicked, too. They did not care that he had to die because of their lies about him.

Everything went exactly as Queen Jezebel had planned. Two wicked men said, "Naboth did blaspheme God and the king." Then poor Naboth and his sons were carried away and stoned to death. And wicked Jezebel, who had acted as if there were not a holy God in heaven, told Ahab to take the vineyard, for Naboth was dead.

The holy Lord was watching all this wickedness from His throne in heaven, and as King Ahab was starting out for the vineyard that had belonged to Naboth, God sent the prophet Elijah to meet him. There, in the vineyard of the dead Naboth, Elijah met Ahab; and Elijah spoke the first words. He said, "Thus saith the Lord, Hast thou killed, and also taken possession?" King Ahab did not answer those questions. He **should** have said, "Yes, I let wicked Jezebel do it."

Elijah went on speaking the word of the Lord. He told King Ahab about the punishments God was going to bring on him and his family. He told King Ahab, "In the place where dogs licked the blood of Naboth shall dogs lick thy blood."

Don't you think that Ahab would have been afraid and sorry? He wasn't. All he said to Elijah was, "Hast thou found me, O mine enemy?" Elijah was Ahab's enemy because Ahab was God's enemy.

Then Elijah told King Ahab the rest of the punishments. He told that the dogs would eat Queen Jezebel's body, too. And he told that all of King Ahab's family would be killed. King Ahab knew that the prophet Elijah was speaking **God's** words and that **God** was angry with him.

When he heard all the words of the Lord, he felt bad. He tore his king's robes and put on rough clothes and walked quietly. He was sad about his punishments but not about his sins. And because Ahab was humble before God, the Lord said He would wait with some of His punishments until after King Ahab was dead.

REMEMBER:

When King Ahab sinned, he didn't want God to find him. When God's children sin, we are glad that God finds us, for He tells us to go to Jesus, Who will make us sorry and take away all our sins.

King Ahab Dies

After King Ahab had killed Naboth and taken his vineyard, he was so afraid of the Lord that he stopped worshipping Baal and said he would serve Jehovah. Ahab's heart did not **really** want to serve God, because he **really** loved idols; so he set up the golden calves which King Jeroboam had made and told the people of Israel to worship God **through** the golden calves. He even found four hundred men to be prophets, make-believe prophets of God. Another name for them is false prophets.

You remember, don't you, that God's people were broken up into two parts: the ten tribes of Israel and the two tribes of Judah. Ahab was king over the ten tribes of Israel and King Jehoshaphat ruled the two tribes of Judah. One day King Jehoshaphat left Judah and went to King Ahab's palace in Israel to become friends with Ahab. Wasn't that a strange thing for him to do? King Jehoshaphat feared the Lord, and King Ahab's heart was with his idols. King Jehoshaphat was just like us: he did sinful and foolish things sometimes.

King Ahab made a big feast for King Jehoshaphat and then asked him whether he would help him fight the army of the wicked Syrians. King Jehoshaphat promised he would go along to help and then he began to wish he hadn't promised. What if the Lord didn't want him to go? He should have asked first. So he said to King Ahab, "Inquire, I pray thee, at the word of the Lord today."

King Ahab called his four hundred false prophets, those make-believe prophets of God, and told them to ask the Lord whether he should go to war. The prophets all answered, "Go up, for the Lord shall deliver them into the hand of the king." That means Ahab would win.

But King Jehoshaphat was not satisfied. He knew they were not **true** prophets of the Lord. He asked, "Is there not here a prophet of the Lord, that we might inquire of him?"

Ahab answered, "There is yet one man, Micaiah, but I hate him."

Why did King Ahab hate Micaiah? Because Micaiah never said anything good about him. Micaiah had to come to him so often with God's words and scold him for his wickedness. King Ahab did not like to be scolded, so he had put Micaiah in prison. But King Jehoshaphat wanted a true prophet of the Lord, and King Ahab sent a servant to get Micaiah. While the servant was gone, the leader of the four hundred false prophets made little horns of iron and held them up to his forehead to show how God would push Israel's enemies away from them.

When the prophet Micaiah came to stand before the two kings, Ahab asked him, "Shall we go to battle or shall we forbear?" Forbear means **not to go.**

Micaiah answered, "Go, and prosper: for the Lord shall deliver them into the hand of the king."

King Ahab was surprised at his words and didn't believe them. He said, "How many times shall I adjure thee that thou tell me nothing but that which is true in the name of the Lord?"

Then Micaiah told a story. He told that the Lord had sent him a vision — something like a dream when he was awake. In this vision Micaiah saw Jehovah sitting on His throne in heaven with all His beautiful angels around Him. The Lord told His angels that He wanted King Ahab to go to war and be killed there. Who would persuade Ahab to go? Some of God's angels said one thing and some another. Then one of the angels said he would go and be a lying spirit in the minds of all those four hundred prophets. He would put a lie in their minds! They would believe that King Ahab should go to fight that war. And God would make him be killed there.

Do you know what the leader of the four hundred prophets did then? He slapped Micaiah's cheek. He **knew** Micaiah had the true Spirit of the Lord, and yet he was very angry. Micaiah was not afraid, for the Lord was with him. But King Ahab was angry and put Micaiah back into prison.

At the same time, the words of Micaiah scared King Ahab. He did not dare to go to the battle dressed as a king. Instead, he wore the clothes of an ordinary soldier. He thought if he did that no one would recognize him and maybe he could be smarter than God and not be killed. King Jehoshaphat put on his king's robes and went along to the war, but by now he wished very much he had not promised to go, because he believed the words of the Lord that Micaiah had spoken.

351

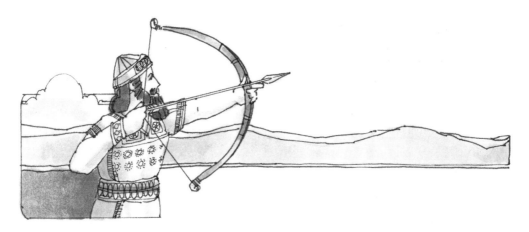

When the enemies, the Syrians, saw a king, they thought it was Ahab and ran after him. But Jehoshaphat cried out, and they knew they were chasing the wrong man; and the Lord helped him get away. Then one of the Syrian soldiers shot an arrow and it hit a man between the two pieces of his iron armor, near his waist. That man was King Ahab, and he was badly hurt. The Lord had guided that arrow to hit King Ahab.

Now King Ahab wanted to go home, but he stayed until the sun went down and then he died in his war chariot. His servants took the chariot home, and as they washed the blood away, the dogs licked King Ahab's blood, as the prophet Elijah had said they would. The wicked king had died and God's words came true.

REMEMBER:

The leader of the four hundred prophets was angry and slapped Micaiah's face. When we are angry we are quick with our hands to slap, too, aren't we? That is very wrong. It is right — but not easy — to say that we are wrong and that we are sorry.

God Sends Fire From Heaven

While Ahab had been the king of Israel, it looked on the outside as if he had ruled quite well. He had worked hard to make the country rich and strong. He had built great cities to keep the people safe. His big army of soldiers had made the heathen nations around Israel afraid to come to fight.

Now King Ahab was dead and his son Ahaziah became the new king. Before the Bible tells us anything about this new king, it tells us that the land of Moab started trouble. They were getting an army ready to fight Israel now that King Ahab was dead. That was the new King Ahaziah's first trouble.

Soon he had much worse trouble. He had a bad fall through a railing on his house. It may have been a railing at the window of his upstairs bedroom or a railing around an upstairs porch in his house. King Ahaziah was hurt badly, but he was not dying. He **wanted** to get better so that he could rule Israel and fight the soldiers of Moab. He **had** to know whether he would get better!

So he told his servants, "Go, inquire of Baalzebub the god of Ekron whether I shall recover of this disease." Recover means get better.

Ekron was a heathen city in the land of the Philistines. The people in Ekron had a special kind of Baal-god called Baalzebub. That name means "lord of the flies," the lord who could bring flies or take them away. King Ahaziah was going to ask the fly-god whether he would get better.

The king's servants never made it to the city of Ekron, for the Lord in heaven was busy getting His servant ready, too. He sent His angel to tell the prophet Elijah, "Arise, go up to meet the messengers of the king."

When Elijah met the messengers from the king, he had sharp words of scolding for them. He asked, "Is it not because there is not a God in Israel, that ye go to inquire of Baalzebub the god of Ekron?" This is what Elijah meant: you are going to Baalzebub because there is no God in Israel, aren't you? Then Elijah said more words from the Lord: Ahaziah will surely die.

King Ahaziah was not going to die of the hurts of his bad fall. He was going to die as a punishment for his terrible sin. What was that sin? He had acted as if there were no God in heaven. He **wouldn't** pay attention to Him. Of course he knew all about Jehovah God Who made the heavens and the earth. He knew all about His wonders and he knew His prophet Elijah. But he turned his back to God and to His prophet and would not listen. He went to an idol prophet, the lord of the flies, instead. For that he was going to die.

Now those surprised servants turned right around and went back to King Ahaziah and told him about the man who came to meet them with the words of scolding and punishment. They had to tell King Ahaziah that he was going to die.

Ahaziah asked, "What manner of man was he which came up to meet you, and told you these words?"

The servants told about the man with a coat of camel's hair, and the king said, "It is Elijah."

Ahaziah knew what he was going to do: kill him. He would not listen to God's words from Elijah's mouth anymore. He sent a captain from his army with fifty soldiers to take Elijah roughly and kill him. As Elijah sat at the top of a hill, the captain called, "Thou man of God, the king hath said, Come down."

Elijah answered, "If I be a man of God, then let fire come down from heaven, and consume thee and thy fifty."

And the fire of the Lord came down and burned those wicked soldiers. When his soldiers didn't come back to Ahaziah, his heart was hard and he sent another captain with fifty soldiers. The second captain came to Elijah and shouted, "O man of God, come down quickly."

Again Elijah answered, "If I be a man of God, let fire come down from heaven, and consume thee and thy fifty."

And again the fire of the Lord burned those wicked soldiers who did not even care that they wanted to kill God's holy prophet.

Now one hundred men and their captains were dead. Did King Ahaziah give up? No, he sent another army captain with fifty soldiers. But the third captain was different. He went up the hill alone and fell on his knees, bowing before Elijah and before Elijah's God. That army captain made a picture by falling on his knees: he was saying, as he bowed, that Jehovah was **his** God, too. He begged Elijah not to ask for fire from heaven but to go with him to King Ahaziah.

The angel of the Lord told Elijah, "Go down with him: be not afraid of him."

Elijah went back with the captain and told King Ahaziah the dreadful words that Ahaziah did not really want to hear: "Thou shalt not come down off that bed on which thou art gone up, but shalt surely die." So wicked King Ahaziah died in his sin.

REMEMBER:

When the third captain bowed before God and Elijah, his body made a picture of praying to his God. Our bodies make pictures when we get on our knees and pray, too. We are saying, "Thou art the great God, and we are Thy little children. Take care of us."

Elijah Goes to Heaven

You and I do not know when we are going to die. We do not know the exact day that we will go to heaven. Elijah did. He knew just when he was going to heaven and he knew he would not die first. God told him he would go to heaven by a great wonder.

What did Elijah do on his last day on earth? He took a long walk, and all along the way he visited some schools, special schools, called schools of the prophets. At these schools young men who loved the Lord and who wanted to be teachers of His Word learned how to be the Lord's prophets.

Visiting those schools was the **best** thing Elijah could do on his last day on earth; for Elijah was a great prophet, God's special prophet. He could talk to those young prophets and tell them always to teach the Words of the Lord and always to preach against Baal and the idol-gods.

There were three schools for prophets in the land of Israel, and Elijah took the prophet Elisha along when he visited them. When they visited the first school, at Gilgal, Elijah told Elisha: "Tarry here; for the Lord hath sent me to Bethel." Tarry means to **stay**.

But Elisha knew that a great wonder would soon happen and he answered, "I will not leave thee."

On they went to Bethel to the second school for prophets. As soon as they came there the prophets asked Elisha, "Knowest thou that the Lord will take away thy master today?"

And he answered, "Yea, I know it."

Once more Elijah said to Elisha, "Tarry here; for the Lord hath sent me to Jericho."

And once more Elisha answered, "I will not leave thee."

The young prophets at Jericho asked Elisha whether he knew that the Lord was going to take his master away today; and once more he answered, "Yea, I know it."

For the last time, Elijah asked Elisha to stay behind, for the Lord had sent him to the Jordan River; and for the last time Elisha said, "I will not leave thee."

Fifty young prophets stood far back from the Jordan River, watching. They saw Elijah and Elisha come to the river and they saw Elijah roll his coat up tight and hit the waters of the river with it. They saw the waters open up and make a path so that Elijah and Elisha could walk over on dry ground.

When they were on the other side, Elijah had one question for Elisha: "Ask what I shall do for thee before I be taken away from thee."

Elisha asked for something beautiful: a special gift of God's spirit to be poured out over him. Elijah said Elisha would have it if he saw him taken away to heaven. As they walked on, God sent a chariot of fire and horses of fire. Those two prophets knew why God sent a chariot and horses: because Elijah had been God's soldier all his life, fighting God's battles. Then a strong whirlwind took Elijah into heaven. As he went up, his coat fell down upon Elisha's shoulders. Then Elijah was gone, and Elisha knew that he was to be God's prophet instead of Elijah.

All alone he walked back to the Jordan River. When he came to the edge of the river he hit the water with Elijah's coat and asked, "Where is the Lord God of Elijah?" By a wonder the Lord made the waters open up, and Elisha walked across.

As soon as he was over the river, three things happened to Elisha: first he talked to the **prophets**. They asked him a very strange question. They wanted fifty young prophets to look for Elijah. Maybe the big storm-wind had carried him to a high mountain or a deep valley. Why did they think that? Because they did not believe that God took Elijah to heaven. They did not believe His wonder. Elisha's answer was no. But the prophets begged to go, and at last Elisha let them go to learn their lesson: to know that God is the great God of the wonder. They looked for three days but did not find him.

Next Elisha came to the **people of Jericho.** They liked their lovely city, but their water was terrible. Elisha asked them to bring him a new bottle filled with salt. The salt was a picture of healing, of making something better. When Elisha poured the salt on the waters of Jericho, the Lord healed them and made them sweet.

The third thing that happened was terrible. Elisha talked to **wicked people.** On his way back some very wicked young men met him and poked fun of him. They shouted, "Go up, thou bald head; go up, thou bald head."

What did they mean when they shouted that? They were asking Elisha to go up **to heaven,** just as Elijah had gone. They did not believe that Elijah had gone to heaven and they would prove it by poking fun of Elisha and calling him a name. Those young men hated God's prophet and mocked God's great wonder. That was a horrible sin! Elisha cursed them and God sent two bears who killed forty-two of those wicked young men.

REMEMBER:

We will not go to heaven as Elijah did. We will have to die first. But we will not be afraid to die, because we are safe in the arms of Jesus, and He carries us to heaven.

Israel Goes to War With Moab

Do you remember that when wicked King Ahaziah became king of the ten tribes of Israel, the king of the land of Moab became very brave and said to Israel, "We will not be your servants any longer"? Soon after that King Ahaziah had his bad fall and died. Now his brother Jehoram was king of the ten tribes of Israel and the king of Moab still felt brave and would not serve Israel anymore.

Let me tell you about the people of Moab and their king. The people of Moab raised sheep, for theirs was a land of grass and of deserts. Mesha, the king of Moab, was called the sheep-king. Every year Mesha and his people paid thousands and thousands of sheep to Israel. Now they said they would not pay any more sheep.

King Jehoram of Israel wouldn't let Moab get away with that! He began getting his army ready to fight Moab. But deep down in his heart he was afraid to go alone with his army to fight, so he sent servants to ask Jehoshaphat, king of the two tribes of Judah, to come with his army and help Jehoram fight Moab. Jehoshaphat **should** have said no, for King Jehoram was just like the other kings of Israel: he worshipped idols.

But Jehoshaphat answered, "I will go up."

The two armies started to march toward the land of Moab. On their way they went through the land of Edom and the king of Edom and his army joined Israel's and Judah's armies. Now **three** armies were marching to Moab; the heathen army of Edom, the wicked army of Israel, and the God-fearing army of Judah.

For seven days these three armies marched through hot, rocky desert lands on their way to Moab. When they were almost at the edge of the land of Moab, they ran out of water. What would they do now? They could not go on and fight without water. The soldiers and their animals needed water — lots of it. They could not turn around and march back home for seven days in the hot, dry desert. They would all die of thirst.

Wicked King Jehoram of Israel blamed the Lord. He said the Lord brought them all to Moab without water so He could kill them. That was a terrible thing to say about the Lord.

King Jehoshaphat of Judah did not listen to Jehoram. He knew what to do. He asked for a prophet of the Lord. One of the servants knew that the prophet Elisha was near — God had seen to that — and King Jehoshaphat was happy.

The three kings went to Elisha's tent, but Elisha did not have nice words for them. He told wicked Jehoram, "Get thee to the prophets of thy father and the prophets of thy mother." Those were **Baal's** prophets.

Elisha was angry that these two wicked kings, the king of Israel and the king of Edom, came to him. But King Jehoshaphat was there, too, and he loved the Lord; and for his sake Elisha would ask the Lord what they should do. That was not easy, for Elisha was angry and upset with the two wicked kings. He wasn't in the right mood to listen to the Lord. So he said, "Now bring me a minstrel." He needed someone called a minstrel to play soft music to make him quiet and ready to listen to the Lord.

Soon God came to him with His word, and His word was good. God's word always is. God said that the soldiers must make the land full of ditches and in the morning, without wind or rain or a storm, God would fill those ditches with water. It would be a wonder. God also promised that they would win the war with Moab.

Sure enough, early the next morning God sent water from the way of the land of Edom, and all the soldiers and animals had plenty to drink. The soldiers of Moab were up early, too, just as the sun was coming up. As they were getting ready to fight, they saw the sun shining on the ditches of water, and it shone red. The water in the ditches looked like blood to them and they thought they knew what had happened: the three kings had fought among themselves and killed one another.

As the soldiers of Moab rushed to find good things to take from the dead soldiers, the **live** soldiers rushed at them and won a great victory over Moab. It was really not the soldiers' victory. It was the Lord's.

REMEMBER:

Sometimes we feel like Elisha: angry or cross or upset. Then we are not ready to listen to the Lord. We may not stay that way. We must make ourselves ready to listen to the Lord. Sometimes quiet music helps us.

Three Wonders

After the Lord had given the great victory over Moab to the Israelites, their enemies went back to their own land and the prophet Elisha went up and down the land preaching to the people and teaching in the schools of the prophets.

Most of God's prophets in Israel were poor. It was hard in those days to serve the Lord and teach His ways and still earn enough money, for the people who served Baal **hated** God's prophets and made life hard for them. One day one of God's prophets died and his wife — we call her a widow — was left alone with their two little boys. She owed a man some money and now she didn't know how she could pay him. If she could not pay him, that man was allowed to take her two sons and make them slaves, to work for him; and that is just what that hard-hearted man was going to do.

In her trouble, the poor widow went to Elisha and begged him for help. Elisha asked, "What hast thou in the house?"

All she had was a pot of oil, sweet-smelling oil that people sold to get a little money. Elisha told the poor widow to borrow as many empty pots and pans from her neighbors as she could. Then she and her sons must go home and close their door, for the Lord would work a great wonder to help them. Elisha told her to pour oil into all those pots and pans she had borrowed. As her boys hurried to bring her empty pans and take away the full ones, she said, "Bring me yet a vessel;" and one of her boys had to answer, "There is not a vessel more." A vessel is a **pan**.

When she told Elisha, he said, "Go, sell the oil and pay thy debt, and live thou and thy children of the rest."

How happy the widow and her boys must have been, and how they must have thanked Jehovah, Who showed them that He was their Help in trouble.

On another day, when the Lord had kept back His rain so that hardly any food grew in the fields, Elisha was with some of the younger prophets, probably teaching them. When it was time to eat, Elisha told his servant to set the pot over the fire and get food ready for them. Where would they find food in those days of famine? Out in the fields and woods, where they gathered wild plants for a kind of vegetable soup.

As they were eating, one of the men called to Elisha, "O thou man of God, there is death in the pot."

Maybe he saw a poison vegetable or maybe he tasted a strong, bitter taste. Would they all die? No, for Elisha said, "Then bring meal." Meal is flour. When he threw it into the soup, the prophets could eat it without any harm. **Elisha** did not work this wonder. **God** did. He showed the prophets that He could change His way of working and make His good wholesome flour take away the poison of the weed. It was God's picture of showing His prophets and us that His good and great salvation saves us from the poison of death and hell.

As Elisha traveled through the land he met a great woman from the city of Shunem. Maybe she was great because she was rich. Maybe she came from a great family. Maybe she was great because she was a leader in the fear of the Lord. We do not know her name. When Elisha passed her house, she urged him to stay with her overnight for a good rest and for quiet talks about the wonders of their Lord.

Elisha must have enjoyed stopping there, for he passed by quite often; and the great woman asked her husband to make a special room for Elisha with steps on the outside of the house so he could go to his room without bothering anyone. In that room they put a bed, a table, a chair, and a light. Now Elisha could use this room as his own home.

He wished he could do something for this kind woman and her husband. Gehazi, Elisha's servant, had an idea. He knew what she wanted: a baby. She and her husband had no children. Elisha told Gehazi to call her and he told her that next year she would be hugging a new baby boy. Elisha could not promise her a baby, but the Lord, through Elisha, promised her the baby. At first it was hard for the Shunamite woman to believe the wonderful news, but the next year she **was** hugging her baby boy.

As he was growing up, the boy often followed his father into the fields as the workers cut down the wheat. It was very hot in that part of the land, and one day he complained to his father, "My head, my head."

His father told a servant, "Carry him to his mother."

But the boy had gotten too much sun and at noon he died.

His sad mother laid him on Elisha's bed and took a donkey to ride to Elisha. The Lord had not told Elisha about her terrible trouble and he was surprised when Gehazi told him the Shunamite woman was coming. When she came, she fell down at his feet, crying, "Did I desire a son of my lord?"

Then Elisha knew that her son had died. He sent Gehazi ahead with his staff to lay on the face of the boy. The woman would not leave him, and Elisha followed her home. He must have been talking with the Lord on the way home, for when they got there he knew what he must do. He went to his room and prayed. Then he stretched himself over the boy, his mouth on the boy's mouth, his eyes and his hands on the boy's eyes and hands; and the boy's body became warm again. Elisha walked through the house and stretched himself on the boy again. This time the boy sneezed seven times and opened his eyes. He was alive! Elisha called his mother and said, "Take up thy son."

REMEMBER:

What a happy wonder God made through Elisha. But it was more than that. It was a picture of God raising all His children from the black death of hell to the most beautiful life of heaven. He gives us that beautiful life through Jesus, our Savior.

Naaman is Healed

The people of the land of Syria were enemies of the people of Israel and every now and then they sent soldiers into the land of Israel to steal everything they could. One time they stole a young girl from Israel and carried her back to the land of Syria. What cruel soldiers those Syrians were to take away that poor young girl, who must have cried and cried when she knew she would never see her father and mother again.

But never forget that our God in heaven was ruling and He was leading this sad young girl to Syria for a special reason; for she became a maid in the house of Naaman, the captain of Syria's army. Naaman was a great man, a captain who could win many battles, but he had a horrible sickness — leprosy. Leprosy made many big sores on people's bodies, sores that hurt and itched and slowly killed parts of their bodies. No one knew how to cure leprosy, but Naaman wanted more than anything else to be cured of his sickness that seemed like a living death.

The little maid to Naaman's wife told about the prophet Elisha and said if Naaman were in Israel the prophet would surely make him better. Naaman hurried to the king of Syria and told him that there was a prophet in Israel who could make him better. So the king of Syria sent Naaman with a letter and a present of gold and silver and ten suits of clothes to the king of Israel. The letter said, "I have sent Naaman my servant to thee, that thou mayest recover him of his leprosy."

He sent the letter to Israel's king, not to Elisha the prophet. Why did the king of Syria do that? Because he was a wicked, heathen man. He thought that Elisha was a man who could do magic tricks, and he thought Elisha lived in the king's palace. He did not understand that it was **God** Who did wonders through Elisha.

Oh, the king of Israel was upset when he got that letter. He tore his clothes because he felt so bad. All kinds of questions went through his mind. How could he make Naaman better, when he was only a man? Did the king of Syria send this letter to him to pick a fight with him?

Soon Elisha heard that the king had ripped his clothes and he sent the king of Israel a scolding: "Wherefore hast thou rent thy clothes? Let him come now to me, and he shall know that there is a prophet in Israel."

So Naaman, the proud, rich man, came with his horses and chariot to Elisha's house. He felt far too important to go into Elisha's poor home, and he stood outside waiting with all his servants for Elisha to come out to him. Elisha didn't come out; for he had to teach Naaman that God's prophet was much more important than the captain of Syria's army. He had to teach Naaman that **the Lord**, not **a man**, would make him better.

That is why Elisha sent a servant to tell Naaman to wash himself seven times in the Jordan River and he would be well. When Naaman heard that, he was so angry! The Jordan River was a shallow, muddy river. The rivers in his country were ever so much nicer. But his servants begged him to obey the Lord and wash in the Jordan. Naaman listened and dipped seven times in the river and his skin and flesh were made healthy again.

Naaman was cured of more than his leprosy; for his sickness was only a picture of the leprosy of sin in his heart. When he washed in the Jordan River, the Lord gave him a healthy body **and** a new heart, washed in the blood of Jesus from all its sin. What a happy and thankful Naaman went back to Syria, carrying some of the earth from Israel so he could build an altar on it to the Lord when he got back home.

Before he left he begged Elisha to take a present, but Elisha would not, for God's wonders cannot be bought with money. Gehazi, Elisha's servant, thought it was a shame that they did not get any of Naaman's riches. He was a selfish, greedy man; and he had a plan. He followed Naaman down the road and told a lie: that two prophets had come to visit Elisha and they needed some clothes and some money. Naaman believed the lie and urged him to take a lot of money and the clothes.

Quietly Gehazi went back home and hid his riches. Elisha asked him, "Whence comest thou, Gehazi?" and he answered, "Thy servant went no whither."

Elisha knew he was lying and he spoke a punishment from God: the leprosy of Naaman would be with Gehazi and his children forever.

REMEMBER:

We have the leprosy of sin in our hearts, too. Only God can make us better from that leprosy by washing our hearts in Jesus' blood. That is why we pray, "Father, make us clean from our sins."

God Makes the Syrians Blind

Some time after Naaman was cured of his leprosy and after wicked Gehazi had left him, Elisha was busy teaching the young prophets again. This time they were living near the Jordan River. The school of the prophets must have been growing, for the house where they lived was too small to hold them all. The prophets asked Elisha whether they might go to the woods near the Jordan River and cut down trees to build a new, bigger house.

Elisha answered, "Go ye."

But these prophets did not want to go without Elisha, for they loved him dearly and felt very close to him. They said, "Be content, and go with thy servants."

And Elisha answered, "I will go."

As one of the young men was chopping down a tree, the heavy iron head of the ax let loose from the handle. Can you imagine that heavy ax head flying full speed into the river and landing deep in the soft mud at the bottom? The young prophet felt so bad about it, for the ax did not belong to him. It was borrowed. He cried to Elisha, "Alas, master! for it was borrowed."

Elisha asked, "Where fell it?"

After the young man showed him the place, Elisha cut down a stick, put it into the water, and the ax head floated. The man could put out his hand and take it. He knew that Elisha, all by himself, could not make his ax head float. He knew that the Lord had heard his cries and saved him out of his trouble by changing His regular rules about iron, making it to float, not to sink.

Now we will leave Elisha for a few minutes and go over to the middle of the land of Israel, where the king lived. There was trouble in Israel. Those wicked Syrians were bothering the people again. This time they were sending groups of soldiers to camp in the land of Israel; and from their camp they would run in all directions, taking what they wanted and killing whom they pleased.

Suddenly things seemed to go all wrong for the king of Syria and his soldiers. When he made secret plans with his soldiers to camp in a certain place, the army of Israel would be there waiting for them, ready to fight. When they decided to sneak quietly to another secret camping place, the army of Israel would be waiting to fight them there, too. Many times the king of Syria and his soldiers were beaten back by Israel's soldiers.

Oh, the king of Syria was mixed up and angry! How could the Israelite soldiers **always** know just where he was going to camp when he was trying to keep it a secret from them? And then he thought he knew the answer: one of his soldiers was not honest — he was telling the king of Israel all about their plans. He asked, "Will ye not show me which of us is **for** the king of Israel?"

They answered, "None, my lord, O king."

Then they told him about the great prophet Elisha who knew every secret word of the king of Syria. God told Elisha, of course; and Elisha told the king of Israel, and the king of Israel had his soldiers ready for the Syrians.

Now the king of Syria knew what he would do. He would get Elisha. He sent spies to find him and when they found out he was in Dothan, the king came in the night with a great army of soldiers and his horses and war chariots. He was going to show Elisha how powerful he was. Early in the morning, when Elisha's servant got up and saw all those soldiers, he was afraid; but Elisha prayed that God would open the servant's eyes and he saw that the hills around the city were covered with God's holy angels, and with horses and chariots of fire. They did not have to be afraid at all.

369

Then Elisha asked the Lord to make all those Syrians blind. Probably they could still see with their eyes, but they were blind in their minds. They were all mixed up. Sometimes God laughs at His enemies. And Elisha must have laughed at God's enemies, too, for he played a little joke on them. He said, "This is not the way, neither is this the city."

He led them right into the middle of the city of Samaria, where the king lived, and then he asked the Lord to open their eyes. How afraid those Syrian soldiers must have been! At first the king of Israel wanted to kill them, but Elisha told him to feed them and let them go home and think about God's power. And the Syrians did not come back to Israel for a long time.

REMEMBER:

When the Syrian soldiers gathered all around Elisha's city at night, he slept peacefully through it all for he knew that his God never sleeps. Elisha's God is our God. We can sleep in peace, too, for He always watches over us.

The Syrians Surround Samaria

For a long time the Syrians did not bother the Israelites; but one day they made their armies ready and marched to the land of Israel all the way to the city of Samaria, where the king lived. There the army of the Syrians stopped and surrounded the city. That means that they stood around it for days and days, letting no one go into the city or come out of it. If they stayed long enough, the people of Samaria would run out of food; and when they were starving, they would give up and be the servants of the king of Syria.

The people of the city of Samaria did not dare to go out to fight the Syrian army for they would not put their trust in the Lord nor ask Him to help them. They would rather serve idols. And so they began to starve. Even the worst kinds of food, like the head of a donkey, cost very much money. As the king of Israel, whose name was Jehoram, walked along the top of the strong wall of Samaria, one of the women of Samaria called out to him, "Help, my lord, O king."

The king answered, "What aileth thee?"

Then she told the king a most awful story: she told that her neighbor woman had not kept her promise. They had agreed that yesterday they would boil and eat the first woman's son and they had done that yesterday; and today they would boil and eat her neighbor woman's son, but her neighbor had hidden her son away.

When the king heard the words of the woman, he tore his clothes. He knew that the Lord had said that these terrible things would happen if they did not serve Him, and he knew that he should tell Israel to be sorry for their sins and that he should lead them back to the Lord. But he didn't. He blamed Elisha, God's prophet, and sent one of his servants to kill him. Then King Jehoram followed his servant to Elisha's house.

These are the words that the wicked Jehoram told his servant to speak to Elisha: "This evil is of the Lord; why should I wait for the Lord any longer?"

Oh, those were wicked words, for Elisha had told the king that they must wait for the Lord. **He** would save the city by a wonder.

When King Jehoram came to Elisha's house, Elisha had words from the Lord ready for him: tomorrow there would be plenty of food in the city; flour and barley would be sold for small pieces of money. Tomorrow the Lord would send His wonder.

The king of Israel was leaning on the arm of a rich man — the Bible calls him a **lord** — and this lord talked back to Elisha. He did not believe the word of the Lord! And he poked fun of it! He said that the words of Elisha couldn't come true even if the Lord made windows in heaven and sent flour and barley falling down as rain. He was making a funny picture with his words and mocking at God's wonder.

Elisha answered him, "Thou shalt see it with thine eyes, but shalt not eat thereof."

That night four lepers sat at the gate outside of Israel. Because of their sickness of leprosy, they might not live with other people. But they, too, were starving. They said to one another that they would surely die if they sat at the gate of the city any longer. They would die if they went into the city, for there was no food there, either. But if they went to find food in the tents of the Syrians that were around the city, they might die and they might live. It was their only chance.

As it began to get dark, they took a long way around and tiptoed to the back part of the camp of the Syrians. Quietly they peeked first into one tent and then into another. What a surprise they had! The tents were empty. No one was in the camp of the Syrians. For the Lord had made the Syrians hear noises of big armies with horses and chariots marching down to fight them; and they thought the Israelites were getting armies from other countries to help them. The Lord put great fear into their hearts and they ran, not stopping to take their things with them.

So the four lepers took food and drink and carried gold and silver out of the tents with them. But they knew that they must not keep the good news to themselves — they must run to tell the king the news.

When King Jehoram heard the news, he must have known that **this** was the wonder Elisha told about. **This** was the way God was saving Israel. But, with a hard heart, the king said it must be a trick. The Syrians were probably hiding in the field. So he sent men on horses to find out. They found no one in the Syrians' camp. The men followed the path that the Syrians took and it was strewn with clothes and pots and pans that they had dropped in their hurry.

The next morning King Jehoram set up a store at the gate of the city where the people could buy flour and barley and all kinds of food for small pieces of silver. The rich man who had mocked Elisha was the storekeeper. He saw the wonder of the Lord but he had none of the good things, for the starving people were in such a hurry for food that they trampled over him and he died. God's words always come true.

REMEMBER:

The wicked Jehoram **knew** that the Lord made the wonder of scaring the army of the Syrians, but he did not want to believe it. Shall we thank God every day that He gives **us** grace in our hearts to believe His wonders?

373

Jehu is Made King

Do you remember that when Ahab was king he did so much evil? Do you remember that when Naboth would not sell King Ahab his field Ahab killed the God-fearing Naboth? And do you remember that God said that because of that wicked sin Ahab and his family would all have to die terrible deaths? In this story we will hear that God's words came true.

King Ahab had already died in the war with the Syrian soldiers and now his son Jehoram was king of Israel. Jehoram had been fighting a war with the Syrian soldiers, too; and in the war he was hurt. He had to go home to his palace to rest and get better.

The captain of Jehoram's army was Jehu. He was still with all the other captains of the army of Israel, having a meeting about the war, when suddenly a prophet ran into the room. This prophet was a servant of the great prophet Elisha. He said, "I have an errand to thee, O captain."

Jehu and the prophet went into another room, where the prophet poured sweet-smelling oil over his head and said, "Thus saith the Lord God of Israel, I have anointed thee king over the people of the Lord."

Then he told the new King Jehu what his work would be: to kill the family of the wicked Ahab. And without another word the prophet ran out of the room, back to Elisha.

When Jehu came back to the other captains, they wanted to know what the prophet had said. They could see that the man was dressed as a prophet and that he carried a bottle of oil; but those captains were evil, unbelieving men, and they mocked God's prophet. They asked, "Wherefore came this mad fellow to thee?" A mad fellow is a crazy man.

Jehu told them that the prophet had anointed him king over Israel. What excitement there was then! The soldiers threw down their coats so Jehu could walk on them and they blew trumpets, shouting, "Jehu is king."

But Jehu was in a hurry. Quickly he climbed into his chariot and his fast horses pulled it to the palace where King Jehoram was resting and getting better. While Jehu was still a long way off, the watchman in the tower near the palace saw him coming, but he didn't know who it was. When the watchman told the king about the chariot and horses he saw, the king sent a man on horseback to meet the chariot, with these words, "Is it peace?"

When the man on horseback met Jehu and asked, "Is it peace?" Jehu said, "What hast thou to do with peace? Turn thee behind me."

After Jehoram sent another servant to meet Jehu and that one did not come back, either, the watchman said he thought that **Jehu** was driving the chariot, for he was driving furiously. That means very fast.

So King Jehoram got up from his bed and went to meet Jehu. They met in Naboth's vineyard, and it was not a happy meeting. Jehu had no words of peace for Jehoram — only death. As Jehoram started to run away, Jehu picked up his bow and arrow and shot his bow with all his strength through Jehoram's heart, and he died. Jehu ordered that Jehoram's dead body must be thrown into Naboth's vineyard, so that the dogs could lick his blood, as the Lord had said.

375

Then Jehu went right on to obey God's commands. To the palace he went to find Queen Jezebel, the wicked queen who had taught Israel the worship of Baal. Jezebel heard that Jehu was coming and she knew she would have to die, so she fixed her hair and put black paint on her eye lashes so she would look nice when she died. She did not think of the holy God and she was not sorry for her sins. She thought only about how she looked on the **outside.**

When Jehu came into the gate of the palace yard, she looked out from a window. She heard Jehu shout, "Who is on my side? Who?" Two or three servants looked out the window and Jehu told them, "Throw her down," and they threw her down and she died.

Jehu went into the palace to eat and drink and then he decided that, because Jezebel was a queen, they should bury her. He told some servants to bury her, but it was too late: the dogs had already eaten her body. The word of the Lord had come true.

REMEMBER:

In his heart, Jehu was no better than wicked Ahab and Jezebel; for Jehu obeyed God's commands only for **his own honor,** so that everyone would see how great he was. God's children obey His commands for **God's honor,** because they love Him so much.

The Last Days of the Kingdom of Israel

After King Jehu had killed wicked Ahab's family, God had more things for him to do: he had to make the people stop worshipping Baal and he had to get rid of all the priests of the idol Baal. Jehu tried to put all the worship of Baal out of Israel. But he kept the golden calves which wicked King Jeroboam had made many years ago, and the people still worshipped those golden calves. While he was king, Jehu made the army of Israel very strong and for a long time the enemies of Israel did not bother them. Remember, though, that Jehu listened to God and to God's prophets only because he wanted to be a great king, not because he loved the Lord.

After King Jehu died, his son became king of Israel, and after Jehu's son ruled a while he died, and Jehu's grandson became the new king. His name was Jehoash. One day he heard that God's prophet Elisha was sick. Elisha must have been a very old man by this time, and when the new King Jehoash went to see him he cried because he knew that Elisha would soon die. Why was he so sad? Did he love Elisha and Elisha's God so much? No: but if Elisha died, the king would have no one to help him when Israel's enemies came to fight them. He **needed** Elisha. But he would not turn to Elisha's God and say he was sorry for his sins and trust God to help him and his people.

Elisha talked to King Jehoash, and even from his bed, the bed on which he would die pretty soon, he made one last picture of the wonder God would do for Israel. He said to the king: "Take bow and arrows."

After the king took his bow and arrows, Elisha said, "Put thine hand upon the bow."

377

As the king put his hand on his bow, Elisha put his hands over the king's hands and said, "Open the window eastward."

Eastward was the direction of Syria: that was the way Israel's enemies came! Then Elisha said, "Shoot." And the king shot his arrow toward the land of Syria. To make sure that King Jehoash understood the picture he was making, Elisha told him what it meant: that arrow was a picture of God's victory over the Syrians.

But there was more to the picture. Next Elisha said, "Take the arrows." When the king had all his arrows in his hands, Elisha told him to throw them to the ground. When those arrows fell to the ground, it was to be a picture of the Syrian armies falling down before Israel, by God's power.

And do you know what happened? King Jehoash failed his test. He threw only three arrows to the ground and stopped. Wouldn't you think he would throw them all down and trust God for many, many victories over the Syrians? He didn't. He did not trust God for His wonder, and he did not obey Him because he did not have God's love and grace in his heart. Elisha was angry. Now Israel would win only three victories over the Syrians.

Very soon after that, Elisha died and was buried in a stone grave, something like a cave. After he had been dead for a while, Israel's enemies, the Moabites, came running over the land, robbing people and taking what they wanted from the Israelites. It happened one day that a man of Israel — we do not know his name — had died, and his sad family was bringing him to a grave. Just as they were passing the cave where Elisha had been buried, they saw the Moabite robbers and they were scared. Quickly they hid the dead man's body in the cave they were passing. They probably did not even know that Elisha's grave was in the cave. When the dead man's body touched the bones of Elisha, he became alive and stood up. God made a wonder: He made the man alive through Elisha's dead body.

After Elisha died, Israel had many more kings. All of them were wicked and most of them ruled only a short while. Sometimes one king would kill another king so that he could sit on the throne. All this time the Israel of the ten tribes became more and more wicked. They learned how to worship more and more idols, and if their idols did not bring them what they wanted, they trusted in witches and in magic charms. When God's prophets came to them with God's words, they poked fun of them.

The last king of Israel was Hoshea. All the years that he was king he had trouble with a strong enemy, stronger than Syria. That enemy was **Assyria.** When Assyria came to fight Israel, King Hoshea needed help. But he went to the wrong place for help. He trusted in the army of the land of Egypt instead of in the arm of God. And Egypt did not help him in his trouble. For three years the Assyrian army surrounded the king's city of Samaria and then Israel gave up. King Hoshea was put into prison and the people of Israel were taken out of their land, to be servants to the king of Assyria. They never came back to their land again.

And what about God's true people who still lived in Israel? Many of them had moved to Judah, the land of the two tribes, where they could worship God with His people.

REMEMBER:

Elisha's bones, which made a man alive, were only a picture. They were a picture of God's power. When we die, we will not be touched by **Elisha's** bones, but by the touch of our **Lord Jesus Christ,** Who was crucified and died, but Who rose and touches us with the touch of His life.

God Calls Jonah

The prophet Jonah lived at the time when the Israelites were having trouble with a very strong enemy, stronger than Syria, the enemy you heard about in our last story — the great country of Assyria. God called Jonah to preach to the people of Israel, to call them to be sorry for their sins, and to show them the worship of Jehovah; and if they would not obey the Lord, He would send the strong armies of the Assyrians to their land.

One day God's word came to Jonah and said, "Arise, go to Nineveh, that great city, and cry against it."

Nineveh was the greatest city in the land of Assyria, and it was a very wicked city. God was calling Jonah to go to a heathen land to tell them that in forty days God would destroy the great city of Nineveh. Poor Jonah was very upset. He did not want to preach to heathen Nineveh. He wanted to be God's prophet to God's own people.

But God had said, "Arise and go," and Jonah went — but not to Nineveh. He went to a city on the seashore, found a ship, paid his money, and set off for Tarshish, in exactly the **opposite** direction from Nineveh. He was going the wrong way! Why? If he didn't want to go to Nineveh, why didn't he just stay at home? He knew he couldn't do that, for he could not live in God's country and be God's prophet and still say no to God. So he ran away. He was saying, "Lord, I quit. I am not going to be God's prophet anymore."

That was very wrong of Jonah. But can't you understand how he felt? He had to preach to Israel's worst enemy. How he hated to do that! And what if the people of Nineveh were sorry and repented of their sins and God saved them alive? Then they would surely come and destroy Israel, the Israel he loved so dearly.

So he sailed in a ship going the wrong way. Before they had sailed far, God sent a terrible storm on the sea, a storm so furious that the sailors thought their ship would break in the towering waves. That storm was a picture of God's holy anger against His disobedient Jonah.

The sailors on the ship were used to storms on the sea. But this one was so much worse than other storms. They were men from heathen lands and they all had different gods. They cried to their gods to save them. Was Jonah praying to his God? No. He was sleeping. By going off alone to sleep, he was saying that he did not care about preaching God's word to Nineveh. He would rather sleep. But he awoke quickly when the sailors shouted, "What meanest thou, O sleeper? arise, call upon thy God."

Next the sailors had to decide who was to blame for this awful storm. So they cast lots. Do you remember that casting lots was a way of choosing? Sometimes they used stones — all white ones and one black one — and the one who held the black one was chosen. We don't know just how they chose. We do know that the lot fell on Jonah.

Then they asked him so many questions: where do you come from; who are your people; why did this storm come upon us? When Jonah told them that he feared Jehovah, the God of heaven, Who made the earth and the sea, and that he was running away from his God, the sailors were terribly afraid. They didn't know what to do. Jonah did. He said, "Take me up, and cast me forth into the sea; so the sea shall be calm unto you." Calm means quiet.

The sailors did not want to throw Jonah overboard. They decided to keep trying to bring the ship to land. They couldn't, no matter how hard they rowed; for God was making the storm more rough and wild. They knew they would have to throw Jonah into the wild waves. First they prayed that the Lord would not put the blame on them, and then they threw Jonah out into the sea. But they did not throw a **disobedient** Jonah out. They threw an **obedient** Jonah, who was offering his own life instead of the lives of the sailors. As soon as Jonah was thrown overboard, the water was calm.

Did Jonah drown? No, for God had made ready a great fish to swallow Jonah. We do not know how a fish can swallow a man whole, nor how a man can live inside a fish three days and three nights. For Jonah stayed in the belly of the fish for three days and three nights. It was a great wonder from God.

What did Jonah do inside the fish? Deep down under the water he prayed. He told his Lord that he was praying from the belly of the **grave,** and he ended his prayer by saying that "Salvation is of the Lord." He knew now that God would save him. The Lord did save him. He spoke to the fish and it spit Jonah out on the dry land.

What a great wonder that was! But it was much more than that. It was a picture, too. As Jonah had sunk into the fish's belly, so our Lord Jesus Who was crucified lay for three days in the depths of the grave. And just as God talked to the fish and made it spit out Jonah alive, so God talked to the grave of Jesus and made it give Him up. And He arose from the dead.

REMEMBER:

Now we can see that Jonah's life was not just a story. It was a beautiful· picture of Jesus' death and of His resurrection after three days. When we think of Jonah, we think of Jesus and how He saves us from our sins by dying and rising again.

Jonah Preaches

After the fish spit him out and Jonah stood on dry land, the Lord called him a second time and said, "Arise, go to Nineveh, that great city, and preach unto it." This time Jonah went to Nineveh, for God had made him an obedient Jonah in the belly of the fish.

Oh, it was a big city! It would take someone three days just to walk from one end of it to the other end. When Jonah came to Nineveh, he walked into the city for a whole day and then found a place where he could preach. This is the message he preached over and over to the people of Nineveh: "Yet forty days, and Nineveh shall be overthrown." That means that God would destroy the city in forty days.

All the people of Nineveh, even the king, heard Jonah's preaching. What did these unbelieving, heathen Assyrians in Nineveh do? Maybe they mocked Jonah and made fun of him. No, they didn't. Maybe they were angry, and killed him. No, they didn't. Maybe they made their armies very strong so they would not be destroyed. No, they didn't.

They repented. They were sorry. They believed God's words and were very sad, so sad that they put on rough, heavy sackcloth and they sat in ashes to show how bad they felt. Even the king wore sackcloth and sat in ashes; and he commanded all the people of this great city and all the animals to stop eating — we call it **fasting** — and to cry hard to God. While they were fasting and praying, he told them to be sorry for their terrible sins and to turn away from their rough, evil ways.

Not everyone in that great city was one of God's own children. Not everyone in the whole city repented. But some did. They turned to God with their whole hearts. And for a while the whole city turned to God with them. Do you know what God did then? He said He would not destroy Nineveh — all for the sake of His own children there, who repented from their sins. The city of Nineveh would be saved.

And Jonah was angry, very angry, so angry that he wanted to die. Jonah **wanted** Nineveh destroyed because Nineveh was a very wicked city and because it was Israel's worst enemy. How could God save such an evil city? Jonah thought **he** was right and **God** was wrong.

While he was angry, he prayed to God and he told God that was the reason he didn't want to go to Nineveh in the first place. He was afraid the people of Nineveh would be sorry. And he told the Lord, "I knew that thou art a gracious God, and merciful, and slow to anger, and of great kindness, and repentest thee of the evil." He was trying to say to God: You were too easy on Nineveh.

All God answered was, "Doest thou well to be angry?"

Then He taught Jonah a lesson. As Jonah sat outside the city, looking at it, the Lord made a very fast-growing plant with big leaves, called a gourd, to grow up beside him. It would shade him from the hot sun that beat down on the city of Nineveh. And Jonah was so glad because of his shady plant.

The next morning God sent a worm to eat it, and the plant fell down and died. Next, God sent a hot wind with the beating heat of the sun, and Jonah thought he would faint. He couldn't stand the heat without the plant! He told God, "It is better for me to die than to live."

God asked, "Doest thou well to be angry for the gourd?"

Jonah answered, "I do well to be angry, even unto death."

Then God showed Jonah the lesson: Jonah felt sorry about the plant which God had made and with which Jonah did not even help and which lasted only a day. Shouldn't Jonah feel much more sorry about that great city which was a much bigger work of God; and shouldn't he feel sorry about the thousands and thousands of little children there whose parents still had to teach them the fear of God? And didn't Jonah feel sorry about all the animals in Nineveh? They were all pictures of how God saves His world; for when God saves His world, He saves a **whole** world.

REMEMBER:

God had to teach Jonah and us how heaven would be. It will be a whole new creation — a new heaven and earth — a perfect heaven and earth for His people. And animals will be there, too.

Trouble in Hezekiah's Time

In this story we are going to meet the Assyrians again. We know that the prophet Jonah preached to them and for a time they were sorry for their sins. But when we had the story of Hoshea we found out that soon they went to the ten tribes of Israel, put their king in prison, and took the people away — out of their own land — and made them live in other countries of the world. And the ten tribes of Israel never came back to their land again.

What was happening all this time to the two tribes of Judah, the people who worshipped God in the beautiful temple King Solomon had made? The people of Judah had many kings who loved the Lord and who taught the people how to obey Him. Hezekiah was a king like that. He taught the people the rules of God's law and how to worship Him with their sacrifices.

But he lived in a dangerous time. While he was king of Judah, the king of Assyria and his armies were capturing all the people of Israel and carrying them away to other lands. What would the king of Assyria do when he finished his war with Israel? Would he attack God's people in Judah next?

Yes, he would. The king of Assyria and his armies started to run over the land of Judah, and they captured some cities. When King Hezekiah saw that the king of Assyria would soon come to Jerusalem, the city of the king and the city of God's holy temple, he told his soldiers to build the walls of the city stronger. Next he asked many people of the city to help him stop up all the fountains of water and the pools and rivers and brooks outside the city so that when the soldiers of Assyria came to fight, they would not be able to find water. He also told his people not to be afraid, for the Lord God would help them and fight for them; and the people rested themselves in his words.

While the king of Assyria took part of his army to fight another city, he sent one of his captains, Rabshakeh, with a very large part of the Assyrian army to fight the city of Jerusalem. Rabshakeh and his army ran into trouble. They had no water. And the walls of Jerusalem were far too strong for them to fight.

Did Rabshakeh give up? Oh, no! He tried to fight another way. He tried to **scare** the people. Standing outside the walls of Jerusalem, he shouted to the people of the city who were on the wide, strong walls and who were listening to what this evil man was saying. He told the people of Jerusalem not to believe Hezekiah's promises that Jehovah God would save them. He told a terrible lie, too. He said, "The Lord said to me, Go up against this land, and destroy it."

Then he promised to take the people to a much better land than Judah, a land of corn and wine and bread and grapes, the land of Assyria. He ended his wicked shouting by telling about all the cities he had already captured; and he said he did not believe that the Lord would save Jerusalem from his soldiers. Oh, what a wicked Rabshakeh!

The people did not answer a word. King Hezekiah had told them not to. The king tore his clothes because he was so sad, and he went to God's temple to pray. He wanted to know what the Lord would do now, so he sent some of his servants to the prophet Isaiah with these words, "This is a day of trouble;" and he asked Isaiah to pray to the Lord for His people. God told Isaiah what would happen: the wicked Rabshakeh would get news that the king of Assyria and his army were in deep trouble, and he would rush off to help them. And that is just what happened. Rabshakeh and the army of Assyria went away.

But King Hezekiah and his people did not have peace very long, for soon the king had a letter from the king of Assyria. The letter told Hezekiah not to let God fool him by saying that Jerusalem would be saved. The letter went on to say that none of the other gods of the other cities saved **them**. The king of Assyria was saying: "I am the strongest." He wanted to fight against God.

King Hezekiah went straight to God's house and spread the terrible letter out before the Lord; and he prayed to the Lord, the God of all the earth, to keep His promise and save His people. God did. He promised His people that they would be safe in Jerusalem; and that very night the Lord sent His angel to the army of the Assyrians and the angel killed one hundred eighty-five thousand of the Assyrian soldiers. Now they could not fight anymore. The king of Assyria went back to his own land. Once again the Lord had saved His people by a wonder.

REMEMBER:

King Hezekiah truly loved the Lord and he loved to pray to Him, too. He called God by such beautiful names: the living God, the God Who made heaven and earth, and the God Who lives with angels. We may call Him by these names when we pray to Him, too.

Hezekiah's Sickness

Poor King Hezekiah had two very bad troubles at the same time. In our last story we learned that the huge army of the Assyrians stood around the city of Jerusalem and were going to try to capture it. Just at the time when the Assyrian army was bothering God's people the most and when Hezekiah thought that God's people needed him very much, he became sick. We do not know what kind of sickness it was, except that he had a very swollen sore, called a boil, and it must have sent poison all through his body.

The prophet Isaiah came to King Hezekiah and said, "Thus saith the Lord, Set thine house in order; for thou shalt die, and not live."

The king was quite a young man yet when these words of Isaiah came to his ears; and he turned his face to the wall and cried. Why did he do that? Was he acting like a spoiled boy? Or was he afraid to die? No, those were not the reasons; for King Hezekiah loved the Lord with all his heart. He was God's dear child, and he knew he would go to heaven when he died. Why didn't he say, "All right, Lord; I'm coming"?

He **couldn't** die. Not yet. That is why he cried. Then he prayed. He begged the Lord to remember His promise to save His people. If King Hezekiah died now, the wicked king of the Assyrians would win the war and would sit on his throne. King Hezekiah's prayer said, "Lord, keep Thy promises! Save Jerusalem! Let me live a while!"

King Hezekiah had another reason for praying so hard. God had made another promise: that all the kings of Judah would have children until it was time for Jesus to be born; for Jesus would be born from the line of the kings of Judah. But King Hezekiah had no children yet. And he was saying to the Lord, "Don't let me die! Jesus must be born! We need a Savior! Let me live so I can have a child so that Jesus can come!"

The prophet Isaiah had gone only a short way when the Lord told him to turn around and go back to King Hezekiah's palace with these words, "Thus saith the Lord, I have heard thy prayer, I have seen thy tears: behold, I will heal thee: on the third day thou shalt go up unto the house of the Lord."

God promised two things more: He would give the Israelites the victory over the Assyrians and He would let King Hezekiah live fifteen more years.

Then Isaiah told the king's servants to lay a lump of figs on King Hezekiah's boil. Figs are dark fruits, something like dates. When they laid the figs on the boil, King Hezekiah got better. Remember, though, the **figs** did not make the king better. **God** made him better. The king had to use the figs because he had faith in his God.

It was wonderful news that the prophet Isaiah had for King Hezekiah. He believed God's prophet, too, because he believed that his God can do great wonders. But King Hezekiah wanted a picture-sign from God that he would really

be well enough to go to God's house in three days. So the Lord gave him one. People in those days did not have clocks as we do. They had sundials. The sun shone on the pointer of the sundial and it made a shadow. The people could tell time by the shadow. Now God asked the king whether the shadow on the sundial in his palace yard should go backward or forward ten degrees.

King Hezekiah chose that the shadow would go backward. That was a picture of God turning back the clock of the king's life. It would be enough time to give the king a son, so that some day Jesus could be born. Now King Hezekiah wasn't crying anymore. Now he was singing. He sang, "The living, the living, he shall praise thee, as I do this day."

All the world heard how God had made King Hezekiah better by a wonder. Even the king from the far-away land of Babylon knew about it. The king of Babylon sent servants with a letter and a present to King Hezekiah because he had been sick and now was better. The king of Babylon told his servants to see how strong the city of Jerusalem was. Maybe, some day, if Babylon became strong enough, he could send armies to capture it.

King Hezekiah felt important when the men from such a far-away country visited him. He showed them all his riches and treasures of gold and silver. He was friendly to them. And all the time he knew they were heathen men from a country which worshipped idols.

Once more the prophet Isaiah had to come to the king to tell him how wrong he was to be friends with those men; for some day the king of Babylon would come with his army and take away all those treasures and take the people of Judah captive to the land of Babylon. Then King Hezekiah was very sorry. All he could say was, "Good is the word of the Lord."

REMEMBER:

What a wonder the Lord made for King Hezekiah! Soon He gave him a baby boy, too, from whose family Jesus would be born. Aren't we glad that King Hezekiah prayed so hard? For Jesus **was** born, and He is **our** Jesus, too. He saved Hezekiah and He saves us.

King Manasseh
Rules in Wickedness

Three years after King Hezekiah was so very sick his baby son, Manasseh, was born. As Manasseh grew up, his father Hezekiah must have told him about all the wonders of God: the wonders He had done to the Assyrian army and the wonder of fifteen more years that He had added to King Hezekiah's life. Don't you think that in those years good King Hezekiah showed his son Manasseh how sinful it was to worship idols and how good and right it was to love the Lord and serve Him?

When Manasseh was only twelve years old, his father Hezekiah died and Manasseh became king. He was not really old enough to become a king. Oh, King Manasseh could have ruled God's people when he was only twelve years old if he had trusted in God and had listened to God's prophets. But he didn't. He did not listen to his father's words, either. Inside he was not strong for the Lord at all, and he listened to the words of wicked men, men who worshipped Baal and all kinds of strange gods. Besides, Manasseh did not have a soft, kind heart as his father Hezekiah had. He had a hard, cruel heart.

What did Manasseh do when he was king over God's people? That question has a sad answer. Manasseh built altars to Baal in the city of Jerusalem. He learned from the Assyrians how to worship the sun, the moon, and the stars; and then he taught the people how to worship them. He even set up an altar to worship the stars in the yard of God's temple. Worse still, inside God's temple he set up a lady idol and the people worshipped her right in God's house. He offered his own son to be burned on the fire of the altar of one of the heathen gods. He trusted in witches and good luck charms, and he taught the people to trust in them rather than in God. Manasseh taught the people of Judah to do more wickedness than the heathen lands around them did.

When Jehovah in heaven sent His prophets to scold King Manasseh and tell him to turn to God, Manasseh would not listen. He killed God's prophets and many of God's people so that he filled the city of Jerusalem from one end to another with their blood.

Then God said, "That's enough." He told His prophets that He would punish wicked King Manasseh and wicked Judah so hard that their ears would ring because they could not believe the hard punishments God would send. God made a picture when He said the city of Jerusalem was like a dish. God said He would wipe Jerusalem as a man wipes a dish, turning it upside down. If a dish is turned upside down, it is empty. When Jerusalem would be turned upside down, it would be empty; for the people would be taken out of it and brought to the land of Babylon. But it was not quite time for that yet.

First God let the Assyrians take hooks and chains, tie up wicked King Manasseh, and carry him out of Jerusalem and make him a prisoner in faraway Babylon. There in prison, with nothing to do, Manasseh had time to think. He thought about his dear, God-fearing father who tried to bring him up to serve the Lord. He thought about his awful sins and about the holy God; and he was sorry. He prayed. He told God how sorry he was for all his wickedness: for all the idols he had made and all the witches he had let the people trust in and all the true people of God he had killed.

God heard his prayer and made the king of Assyria let him go back to the city of Jerusalem as King of Judah again. Oh, Manasseh was busy after the Lord let him be king the second time. He tried to set things right: he threw down the idols and put the heathen gods out of the city; he built up the altars of the Lord and taught the people to worship Him; and he built the walls of Jerusalem stronger. After he came back from prison, Manasseh must have been a sad, humble, sorry king.

Then King Manasseh died. His wicked son Amon ruled only two years and he died, too. Josiah became king next. He was the last king of the two tribes of Judah who feared the Lord. All the years that he was king he tried to bring the people of Judah back to the Lord. Many of the people did not care about the Lord. They liked the idols that King Manasseh had taught them to worship. They did not care that God's temple was broken and nobody had bothered to take care of it.

King Josiah cared. He threw out some of the idol priests who were still living in God's house and he burned the dishes that they used to offer food to their idols. Near the door of the temple King Josiah set a box, and God's people dropped money into it. After they had enough money in the box, the king used the money to pay workers to repair the broken parts of God's temple.

Do you know what the workers found when they were cleaning God's house? His book of the law. King Josiah had never heard it before. Neither had the people. When good King Josiah saw how far from God's law they had been living, he was so sad he tore his clothes. Then he called together all the people and read God's book of the law to them, and they all promised to serve Jehovah God again.

REMEMBER:

King Manasseh's sins were terrible — some of the worst sins a man can do. Were those sins too big for God to forgive? Oh, no! For God is a merciful God and He is ready to forgive all our sins, even our very worst ones, for Jesus' sake.

The Last Days of the Kingdom of Judah

King Josiah was the last God-fearing king of the two tribes of Judah. After he died, some very wicked kings sat on the throne of Judah; and all of them were bothered by their enemies. Nebuchadnezzar, king of Babylon, was becoming very strong, and his armies came to the land of Judah and ran all over it. The kings of Judah did not trust in God and they did not ask Him to help them, so their armies were very weak and could not win any battles against King Nebuchadnezzar's strong armies. His armies fought against the city of Jerusalem, took much of the silver and gold from the city, and carried many of the people away to the land of Babylon.

Zedekiah was the last king of Judah. King Nebuchadnezzar would let him rule over Judah if he would be Nebuchadnezzar's servant. He had to promise not to fight King Nebuchadnezzar nor to get any other kings to help him fight. For a little while King Zedekiah listened but soon he did not want to obey. He made plans with five other countries to fight against King Nebuchadnezzar. He was not keeping his promise.

The Lord sent His prophet Jeremiah to King Zedekiah, and he told the king not to fight but to give in to King Nebuchadnezzar; for it was the Lord's will that the people of Judah would be taken out of their land for a while to live in Babylon. How did the prophet Jeremiah know that? The Lord had showed Jeremiah two baskets of figs — those brown fruits something like dates — one basket of very good figs and one basket of very bad figs that could not be eaten. The good figs were pictures of those people who would give in to King Nebuchadnezzar and who would be taken to Babylon: for while they stayed in Babylon, God would give them new hearts and take them back some day to their own land. The bad figs were pictures of King Zedekiah and his wise men who would not give in to King Nebuchadnezzar nor to God. They would stay in the city of Jerusalem and have war and sickness and death.

Did King Zedekiah listen to God's prophet? Oh, no! After four years he went to the king of Egypt for help and tried to fight to be free of King Nebuchadnezzar. But King Nebuchadnezzar came with his armies and surrounded the city of Jerusalem. Now King Zedekiah and the people of Jerusalem did not know what to do, but they would not give in because they hated God's word which Jeremiah had told to them. In fact, King Zedekiah was so angry with Jeremiah that he put him in prison.

At the same time, it bothered King Zedekiah that he had put God's prophet in prison and one day he called him out secretly and asked whether Jeremiah had any words of the Lord for him. Jeremiah did. He said, "Thou shalt be taken by the hand of the king of Babylon." That meant that the king of Babylon would surely win.

For a little while the king let Jeremiah be free again. But soon the rulers of the city of Jerusalem came to the king and complained about Jeremiah. They said they were so tired of Jeremiah's words: that the king of Babylon would

surely win and that all the people must quietly give in and go along with Nebuchadnezzar to Babylon. They wanted the prophet Jeremiah **dead!** They persuaded the king to let them throw him into a dungeon. That dungeon was a cold, dark pit with deep mud in the bottom. Those wicked rulers let Jeremiah down into that dungeon with ropes. Jeremiah sank down into the mud. The rulers did not care. They wanted God's prophet to die a slow death from cold and hunger.

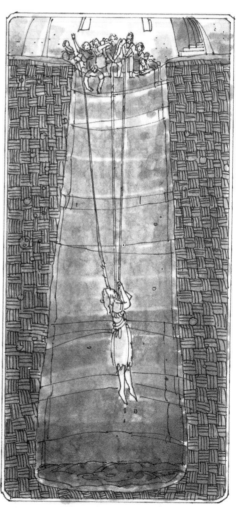

One of the king's servants, called Ebedmelech, heard about it and he begged the king to save Jeremiah. Ebedmelech said, "He is like to die of hunger in the place where he is."

King Zedekiah changed his mind and said, "Take thirty men with thee, and take up Jeremiah the prophet out of the dungeon, before he die."

Ebedmelech and the thirty men gathered rags and worn-out clothes and put them under Jeremiah's arms so that the ropes would not cut into his skin. Then they pulled him up out of the muddy dungeon and saved his life.

Once more King Zedekiah asked Jeremiah what he should do and once more Jeremiah gave him the same answer: give in to the king of Babylon and the Lord will save the city of Jerusalem from being burned. But King Zedekiah was afraid of the rulers and did not dare to listen to Jeremiah's wise words.

After King Nebuchadnezzar's army stood around Jerusalem for a year and a half, the soldiers finally broke into the city. King Zedekiah and his soldiers ran out another gate of the city, but they did not get away. King Nebuchadnezzar's soldiers ran after them, captured them, killed Zedekiah's two boys right before his eyes, and then put out Zedekiah's eyes and carried him away to Babylon.

Nebuchadnezzar took all the treasures out of the city of Jerusalem — from God's temple, too — and carried them to Babylon. He killed many of the people and the rest he carried away prisoners to the land of Babylon. There they would stay for seventy years, until God would call them back to their own land again.

REMEMBER:

Sometimes God's people must suffer and be hurt and be unhappy. Jeremiah suffered. God's people who went to Babylon suffered. Sometimes we must suffer and be hurt, too. But we will always know that even when God brings us suffering, He does it because He loves us.

Daniel Lives in the King's Palace

In our last story we heard that all the kings who ruled after good King Josiah were wicked. We heard that while they were ruling over Judah the Lord let King Nebuchadnezzar bother them. Those poor, weak kings of Judah, who would not trust in Jehovah, could not stop Nebuchadnezzar's armies from running over the whole land of Judah, taking whatever they wanted.

King Nebuchadnezzar was very fussy. He wanted only the **best** of the treasures and the **best** of the people to be taken to Babylon. He told Ashpenaz, one of his servants, to look for the best boys in the land of Judah. These boys had to be good-looking boys with perfect bodies; they had to have very good minds so that they could easily learn whatever the king wanted to teach them.

The servant Ashpenaz looked in the homes of the best families in Judah and there he found the kinds of boys he wanted. One day he found Daniel and Daniel's friends. Daniel was not so very old when Ashpenaz found him — maybe not even fourteen years old yet. It did not matter to King Nebuchadnezzar that Daniel and his friends cried and begged to stay with their own families in their own land. The king ordered Ashpenaz to take them away by force and carry them to Babylon. Poor Daniel and his friends would never see their homes and their families again.

Why did King Nebuchadnezzar want these fine young boys? So that he could send them to school in Babylon. Daniel and his friends had to learn the language of Babylon and they had to learn all about numbers and all about God's world. They had to learn about the idol-gods of Babylon and about how to live, with fine manners, in the palace of a king. Nebuchadnezzar wanted wise, smart young men who would be able to help him and to answer his questions. For Nebuchadnezzar was a great and strong king: his armies had captured all the lands of the world. King Nebuchadnezzar was king of the whole world!

Why did **God** want Daniel and his friends to be taken away from their homes and to live in the palace of Nebuchadnezzar? God wanted Daniel to be a leader of His people in the strange land of Babylon. Remember, they had to stay in Babylon for seventy years. God chose Daniel to show His people that they must be sorry for their wickedness and wait for God to take them back home again. God chose Daniel to live in the palace of King Nebuchadnezzar for another reason. King Nebuchadnezzar had to learn a hard lesson; for he was very proud of himself and thought he was a great and powerful man. He had to learn that he was really **not** great and that he must bow before God, Daniel's God. And God chose Daniel to teach King Nebuchadnezzar that lesson.

When Daniel and his three friends, Shadrach, Meshach, and Abednego, sat down in the palace dining room to eat the king's food, they had a problem. God had given His people strict rules about the kinds of food they might eat and the kinds of food they might not eat. Some of the king's food was the wrong kind. But there was a bigger problem: the food at the king's table had been first offered to idol-gods. That means that the workers in the palace had asked the idol-gods to bless the food. Daniel and his three friends did not want to eat food that had been blessed by heathen idols.

Daniel begged the servant Ashpenaz not to make them eat that food. Ashpenaz loved Daniel and his friends, but did not dare to disobey the king. He did not want **their** faces to be pale and thin and sickly, and the faces of all the other young men rosy and round and healthy. But Daniel had an idea. He asked

the servant to let them try their own plain food — good vegetables and water —
for ten days and then see how their faces looked.

After ten days the faces of Daniel and his three friends were so much
healthier and fatter than the faces of the other young men at the table. That was
a wonder! **God** gave them those beautiful faces and they did not have to eat
food offered to idols anymore. God also gave such good minds to Daniel and his
friends and so much understanding in their hearts that they were ten times better
than all the other wise men in the palace of King Nebuchadnezzar. God gave
Daniel one more gift, the gift of understanding dreams. He would need that gift
to be God's ruler under King Nebuchadnezzar in the heathen land of Babylon.
Our next story tells us about it.

REMEMBER:

Daniel was not afraid to stand all alone in a heathen land and tell everyone
that he trusted in Jehovah God. Do we dare to stand up and tell everyone that we
trust in Him, too?

Nebuchadnezzar Dreams a Dream

The days in which Daniel lived were days of great wonders. Often God did great wonders on the earth by sending strange dreams to the heathen kings of the earth. This time He sent a dream to King Nebuchadnezzar. When the king awoke from his dream, he was upset and troubled by it.

He called all his wise men and asked them to tell him what he had dreamed about. Maybe the king **could not** remember his dream. More likely, he was stubborn and **would not** tell them his dream. The proud wise men had boasted that they knew so much. Now the king was going to test them to see whether they could tell him his dream.

But this test was too hard for them. They begged the king to tell them the dream and they would tell what it meant. They told him no king had ever asked such an unfair thing of his wise men. No one could see a dream in a king's mind.

King Nebuchadnezzar answered them roughly. He said that if they did not tell the dream they would all be cut into pieces and their houses would be pulled down. In hot anger the king ordered all the wise men in Babylon to be killed. That was unfair and cruel of the king, but his soldiers had to obey him. They went out to kill all the king's wise men.

Probably they had already killed some men when Arioch, the captain of the soldiers, came to Daniel. Daniel was one of the king's wise men, and he would have to be killed, too. Daniel asked why the king was in such a hurry to kill all his wise men; and then Arioch told him the story of the king's dream. Daniel went to the king and asked for a little time and he would tell him his dream and what it meant.

Quickly Daniel went to his house and told his three friends, Shadrach, Meshach, and Abednego, all about it. Together they prayed for the mercies of the God of heaven so that He would show them His secret. God answered their prayer. In the night in a vision — a sort of dream — God told Daniel His secret. Oh, how Daniel thanked His great God, Who knows everything, for telling him one of His great secrets.

401

Then Daniel stood before King Nebuchadnezzar. The king asked, "Art thou about to make known unto me the dream?"

Daniel answered him that he was no wiser than the other wise men. "But," he said, "there is a God in heaven that revealeth secrets."

This is what King Nebuchadnezzar saw in his dream: a very large and great image, bright and terrible. The image was in the shape of a man. Daniel told the king what the image in his dream had looked like. Its head was made of shining gold; the top of its body and its arms were made of silver; its belly and the top part of its legs of brass — brass looks something like gold; the rest of its legs were of iron; and its feet partly of iron and partly of clay. In his dream the king had seen a stone cut without hands out of a mountain. That stone rolled and hit the feet of the image and they broke. Then the whole image toppled over and broke into pieces so small that the wind carried them away and no more of the image could be found in the earth. Then that small stone cut without hands grew until it was a great mountain that filled the whole earth.

That was the dream. What did it mean? Daniel told the king what it meant. The head of gold was a picture of King Nebuchadnezzar. He was the golden ruler of the whole world. After he died, another ruler of the whole world would come — the one of the silver body and arms. He would not be quite so strong as King Nebuchadnezzar. The brass belly was a picture of the third ruler over the whole world and the iron legs were a picture of the fourth ruler over the whole world.

Then came the toes of the image, the broken toes partly of iron and partly of clay. It was a picture that the lands of the world would be broken up. No one would rule over the whole world anymore. At that time the stone would be cut out of the mountain. That stone was a picture of **Jesus.** **Then** it would be time for Jesus to be born! When He was born in a manger, He would seem to be a picture of only a small stone. But He is God! He would live and die and rise again and go back to heaven. Soon He is coming again. He will destroy all the wicked kings and take all His people with Him to fill the new heaven and the new earth just as the mountain in the dream filled the whole earth. Jesus will be the Ruler of the new heaven and earth. There He will have all the power and there we will live with Him forever.

REMEMBER:

The stone that became a great mountain is a picture of **our** Jesus. Right now He is getting ready to come again. When He comes, it will be the end of the world. Never be afraid of the end of the world, for Jesus will take us into the new heaven and the new earth.

403

The Three Friends in the Fiery Furnace

The dream of King Nebuchadnezzar about the great image, especially the part about the head of gold, must have given him an idea. If that great head of gold was a picture of **him,** he would make a **real** golden image and put it where everyone could see it. He made the image ninety feet tall, taller than three houses on top of one another. The image probably looked like the head and shoulders of a man, set on a very tall stand; and it was covered from top to bottom with bright, shiny gold.

We don't know whether the image looked like King Nebuchadnezzar. We **do** know that the king was a very proud man and wanted everyone to know how great he was. And we **do** know that King Nebuchadnezzar told everyone that all his power came from his idol-god, Bel. Bel was a picture of the devil and when King Nebuchadnezzar worshipped Bel, he really worshipped the devil.

When the image was finished, the king called all the rulers from all the countries in the world, the great rulers and the lesser rulers, to come to worship the image. After they were all gathered around the great image of gold, an announcer shouted that when they heard the sound of all kinds of instruments playing music, they must bow down to the golden image that King Nebuchadnezzar had set up. If anyone did not obey the king, he would be thrown into a burning, fiery furnace.

Then all the musical instruments started playing: the horns, flutes, harps, and many more. All the rulers from all the countries which King Nebuchadnezzar ruled bowed down to the image — all but Daniel's three friends, Shadrach, Meshach, and Abednego. Daniel must not have been there. The Bible does not tell us where he was. Maybe he was gone on an errand for the king. Some of the rulers ran and told the king that Shadrach, Meshach, and Abednego, the three young men who came from Judah, did not pay attention to the king's command and would not bow down to his image.

Now the king was angry, terribly angry. He commanded his servants to bring Shadrach, Meshach, and Abednego before him. He said, "Is it true, O Shadrach, Meshach, and Abednego, do not ye serve my gods, nor worship the golden image which I have set up? Now if ye fall down and worship the image which I have made; well: but if ye worship not, ye shall be cast the same hour into the midst of a burning fiery furnace; and who is that God that shall deliver you out of my hands?''

What would these three friends do? They were rich and important men in the king's palace. Now would they have to die such a painful, cruel death? Maybe they could bow down on their knees but not worship the image in their hearts. Maybe they could worship Jehovah if they said that Bel was god, too. Oh, no, they couldn't! They knew they could not worship Jehovah and the devil at the same time. They could never say that Bel was god.

They told the king that he did not have to give them another chance to bow down to the image because they were going to obey God, not the king. They were going to choose not King Nebuchadnezzar's riches, but God's riches — the riches of heaven. They told the king that their God could save them from the hot fire and bring them safely out of the furnace. But if it was not His will to save them, they were ready to die and go to heaven.

Those words make **us** happy, don't they? They made **King Nebuchadnezzar** more angry than ever. He was so furious that he ordered the furnace to be heated seven times hotter. That furnace had an opening at the top, and strong men tied up Shadrach, Meshach, and Abednego and carried them to the opening. As they dropped the three friends into the furnace, the hot flames shot out of the furnace and killed those strong men.

Near the bottom of the big furnace was an opening. King Nebuchadnezzar went near to the opening and looked in. He could not believe his eyes! Quickly he called for some of his rulers and asked, ''Did not we cast three men bound into the midst of the fire? I see four men loose, walking in the midst of the fire, and they have no hurt; and the form of the fourth is like the Son of God.''

405

King Nebuchadnezzar was right. God had sent His Son to take care of the three friends in the furnace. When the king called them to come out of the furnace and they came out, everyone crowded around to see the wonder their God had done. They saw that the fire had burned the ropes that had tied them, but that it did not have any power over the three friends at all. Their hair was not burned, their clothes were not burned, and there was not even the smell of fire on them. Now King Nebuchadnezzar blessed their God Who sent His Son to keep them safe, and he commanded that no one might say anything against the God of Shadrach, Meshach, and Abednego. The three friends knew and we know that He is the only God.

REMEMBER:

On that day long ago in Babylon God sent His Son to save the three friends from the fire of the furnace. On the cross He sent His Son to save them and us from the fire of hell.

Nebuchadnezzar Dreams Another Dream

One day King Nebuchadnezzar told a story about himself. He wanted all the people in the whole world to know what happened to him, and he wanted them to give glory to God in heaven for the wonders He did.

King Nebuchadnezzar said that all seemed to be well in the countries he ruled. While he was at rest and peace, God sent him a dream; and this dream bothered him just as much as his first dream had bothered him. His wise men listened to the dream but they could not tell him what it meant. Why didn't the king call Daniel right away? He **knew** that God would tell Daniel the meaning. The reason is that King Nebuchadnezzar did not **want** to know what Daniel's God would say to him. He knew the great God of heaven and earth would make him feel small; and Nebuchadnezzar wanted to be great. But at last he had to call Daniel.

The king told his dream. In his dream he saw a tree, a tall tree that grew until it reached heaven. The tree stood in the center of the earth and its branches spread until they covered the whole earth. Its leaves were so thick that everyone could live in its shade and there was so much fruit on its branches that everyone had plenty to eat. Even the animals rested under this great tree and the birds made nests in it.

In his dream King Nebuchadnezzar saw a holy one come down from heaven and say, "Hew down the tree, and cut off his branches, shake off his leaves, and scatter his fruit: let the beasts get away from under it, and the fowls from his branches." Fowls are birds.

The holy one from heaven said they should leave the stump of the tree standing and put an iron band around it. There the lonely stump would stand, with nothing to cover it from the rain, and with only grass and animals for company. Then in his dream the picture of a **tree** changed to a picture of a **man**: the man's heart would change to an animal's heart, until seven times — that probably means seven years — went past.

After Daniel heard the dream, he sat still for a little while. He felt so troubled. And, oh, how he hated to tell the king the meaning of his dream. Even though Nebuchadnezzar was a heathen king, he had been good to Daniel. Daniel said he wished the dream would happen to the king's enemies.

But the dream **would happen** to King Nebuchadnezzar. He was the great tree in the dream, for King Nebuchadnezzar ruled the whole world just as the tree covered the whole earth. And just as the tree was cut down, the king's mind would be cut down. He would lose his mind. He would not be able to think. Just as the stump of the tree was tied with an iron band, so God would tie the king's mind with chains. He would become crazy, so badly crazy that he would live like an animal of the field, eating grass and being wet with the rain from heaven. For seven years the poor king would live as an animal, without the mind of a man. But, like the stump of the tree, he would grow again. God would give him back his mind and his understanding. After seven years he would be king again.

Daniel begged the king to be sorry for his sins, to be good to the poor people, and to turn to Jehovah and serve Him; for maybe God would give him a little time of peace first.

King Nebuchadnezzar listened to Daniel, but he did not turn to the Lord and he was not sorry for his sins, for his heart was hard. For a year all seemed to go well. Then one day as the king was walking in his palace looking over the beautiful city of Babylon which he had built, a city with beautiful buildings, great temples to idol-gods, and special hanging gardens, he said, "Is not this great Babylon, that I have built for the house of the kingdom by the might of **my** power, and for the honor of **my** majesty?"

While he was still talking about himself, he heard a voice from heaven, the voice of a holy one, with the awful news that his kingdom was taken away from him and that his servants would chase him away from other people and that he would live like an animal.

God's words came true that same hour. The king became a wildly crazy man and they chased him away from his palace. For seven years he lived like an animal. His body began to grow like the body of an animal; his hair became like eagle's feathers and his nails like bird's claws.

Then God gave the king his understanding back. He could think again and rule his people again. Do you know what King Nebuchadnezzar said then? Let him tell it: he said, "I blessed the most High and I praised and honoured him that liveth forever."

He had to say that. For seven years God had made him small, so small that no one would go near him. Then the Lord had made him king again! He knew that only the Lord God rules over the heaven and earth. He knew how great the Lord is. Was he sorry now? Did he turn to the Lord with all his heart? No. He was still the same proud Nebuchadnezzar. It is a terrible thing to be a Nebuchadnezzar — to know all about God's great wonders and power and then to turn away from Him.

REMEMBER:

Only God's grace and love in our hearts, because He has chosen us to be His own, makes us different from unbelieving Nebuchadnezzar. God makes our hearts soft and makes us call Him the God of the wonder and God our Father.

The Fall of the City of Babylon

Sometime after he had his last dream, King Nebuchadnezzar died. Daniel lived on and was still living when Nebuchadnezzar's grandson, Belshazzar, became the ruler of the world. Many things happened in those years. Slowly King Nebuchadnezzar and the kings who ruled after him lost their power. Their armies could not win all their battles anymore. The kings were not strong enough to rule over the whole world; for the Lord was getting the great city of Babylon ready to fall into the hands of the armies of another great country.

Belshazzar was not a strong king of Babylon. He knew his armies could not chase away the armies of the Medes and Persians, the strong new country which wanted to rule the world. So he tried to make the city of Babylon very strong so that the enemy king could never get in. He had two rows of very high, thick walls all around the city. Inside the city there was plenty of room for farms to grow food and many riches for all the people. King Belshazzar thought that the city would be safe for a long time.

Even though his country was in danger and enemies were marching toward Babylon, King Belshazzar held a big party, a party where everyone drank strong drink and became drunk and praised their gods of gold and silver, brass and iron, wood and stone. More than a thousand people came to his party. At the party, King Belshazzar ordered his servants to bring to him the beautiful gold and silver cups which his grandfather Nebuchadnezzar had taken out of the temple of God at Jerusalem; and the wicked people at the party drank their wine from those cups.

In the middle of all their shouting and laughing and praising of their idol gods, a hand appeared on the wall near the candlesticks and the fingers of the hand wrote words on the wall. Can you hear how quiet the party became all of a sudden? Look at King Belshazzar. His face was turning white and he was shaking so hard that his knees knocked together and his bones seemed loose from one another in his body. Why was King Belshazzar so scared? Because in his heart he knew he was doing a very great wrong. He knew it was a great sin to have a drunken party when his city was in danger. He knew he might not use the dishes from God's holy temple to praise his idol gods. And he knew that the hand that wrote the words was the hand of God speaking to him.

King Belshazzar could not read those strange words on the wall and he had no idea what they meant. He called all his wise men to read the writing and tell the meaning, but not one of them could do it. Even when the king promised great rewards to the man who would tell the meaning — a king's robe, a chain of gold around his neck, and that he would be the third ruler in the country — no one could tell him the meaning.

Then the queen, the old grandmother queen, the wife of King Nebuchad-nezzar, heard the frightening news. She knew what to do. She remembered a man who could tell the meaning of dreams and could understand hard things, because the spirit of God was in him to teach him to say what God wanted him to say. That man was Daniel. She told the king to call Daniel.

When servants brought him in a great hurry to the king, Belshazzar showed that he knew all about him. He had heard how Daniel had been taken away from his own country of Judah. But he could never be taken away from his God; for King Belshazzar told Daniel that he heard that God's spirit was in him. The king promised Daniel a king's robe, a chain of gold around his neck, and that he would be third ruler in the country if he could tell him what those words meant.

411

Daniel told the king he did not want those rewards. All he wanted was to tell the truth that came from God. But before he would tell the meaning of the words, Daniel had to scold Belshazzar and teach him a lesson. He told about the king's grandfather, the great Nebuchadnezzar. God had given him so much power and greatness that the whole world trembled in fear of him; but King Nebuchadnezzar did not give God the glory. He gave all the honor to **himself.** And then God had to make him very humble and take away his mind and make him an animal until he would say that God ruled. Now King Belshazzar was doing the same thing his grandfather had done: he praised himself and his idols instead of God and he used God's holy temple dishes for a drunken party.

Then Daniel read the words on the wall: **Mene, Mene, Tekel, Upharsin. Mene** means that God numbered the kingdom of Belshazzar and finished it. **Tekel** means that the king was weighed in God's holy scales and he did not weigh what he should. He weighed **wickedness** instead of **obedience** to God. **Upharsin** means that Belshazzar's kingdom would be divided and given to their enemies, the Persians.

Even though the news was so sad for King Belshazzar, he gave Daniel his reward and then — that very night — the king was killed by his enemies. How did they get into the strong city of Babylon? Not by climbing the walls. But while King Belshazzar was having his party, the enemies must have changed the water of a river that flowed into the city and made it flow another way. Then they crept through the sand of the old river into the city, setting it on fire before the king and his rulers even knew they were in his city. Now a new king, called Darius, would sit on the throne.

REMEMBER:

God weighs us in His scales, too. He tells us that our weight must be heavy with love for Him, kindness to our neighbors, obedience to Him and to our parents. But we can never weigh the right amount on God's scales. Only when Jesus comes and takes away our sins and gives us clean hearts and fills us with His spirit can we weigh the right amount on God's scales.

Daniel is Thrown to the Lions

When King Darius sat on his throne in Babylon and began to rule over the countries of the world, he chose one hundred twenty men, called princes, to help him. These men were something like policemen, who told the people to obey the laws, and they collected tax money from the people for the king. Over these one hundred twenty men were three presidents and the highest president was Daniel.

Daniel's work was much better than the work of the other rulers and the people liked Daniel better than all the others. Why? Because God's spirit was inside him and it showed on the outside. He **acted** like one of God's children and he did his work the very best he could because he did it for **God's** sake. King Darius was even thinking of making him the highest ruler in the land.

Wouldn't it be wonderful to have a man like Daniel ruling over **us?** The other two presidents and the hundred twenty princes didn't like Daniel to rule over **them.** They were jealous of Daniel. **They** wanted to rule instead of Daniel. So they watched him closely to find out the wrong things he did, but they could never find anything wrong. At last they said to one another that if they were going to make trouble for Daniel, it would have to be trouble about the laws of his God.

For quite a while they had been watching how Daniel prayed to God three times each day. He could not pray in God's holy temple, for King Nebuchadnezzar had burned it. He could not even pray in his own dear land of Judah, for he had been taken out of it. But he could and he did get on his knees in front of a window that faced toward his own land and he prayed to the Lord of heaven and earth in the morning, at noon, and at night. Some of those wicked princes and rulers got together and thought of a horridly wicked plan; and then they ran to King Darius with it.

They did not tell the king that their plan was to kill the God-fearing Daniel. Oh, no, that was not what they said. They tried to trick the king. With nice words they told King Darius that all the rulers wanted him to make a new law: they asked that for thirty days all the people in his kingdom might pray to no other god than to King Darius. And they fooled the king. Can't you imagine what he thought? What a wonderful idea! I will be a god! Quickly he made it a law that could not be changed. If anyone would not obey the new law he would be thrown into a den of lions.

What a foolish and wicked king! Now no one could pray to Jehovah. That was a terrible thing for God's people, for they had to obey Jehovah, not King Darius. Do you know that the devil was working in the hearts of the rulers to take away the worship of God from the whole earth?

Let us see what Daniel was doing. He knew how the wicked rulers had tricked the king. He knew that the law said he might pray only to the king. But Daniel obeyed his God. As he bowed on his knees at his window and prayed for God's help, the wicked princes were nearby, spying on him. Sure enough, Daniel was praying! They went into his house and saw him with their own eyes!

Rushing to the king, they asked him, "Hast thou not signed a decree, that every man that shall ask a petition of any God or man within thirty days, save of thee, O king, shall be cast into the den of lions?"

The king answered, "The thing is true."

Then those wicked men told how Daniel would not obey him but prayed to God three times a day. How sorry the king was to hear it. Now he knew that he had been tricked into making that awful law. He felt like an animal in a trap trying to get free — free from the law that he himself had made. But, remember, he could not change that law. All that day he tried to set Daniel free. Maybe he tried to show his princes and rulers what an evil trick it was, but they would not listen. All they wanted was to be rid of Daniel.

Evening came and the king had not been able to set Daniel free. It was time for the punishment. Before they threw Daniel into the den of fierce lions, the king talked to him. He knew that Daniel's God was the God of the wonder and he said, "Thy God, whom thou servest continually, he will deliver thee."

Then they threw Daniel to the lions. They pushed a large stone in front of the opening and sealed it shut, and then night came. King Darius could not sleep. He would not eat and he would not listen to music. All night long he was miserable and restless and troubled, for he had thrown a God-fearing man to the lions.

Very early in the morning he rushed off to the lions' den and in a voice full of sadness and trouble and maybe a little bit of hope he called, "O Daniel, servant of the living God is thy God, whom thou servest continually, able to deliver thee from the lions?"

Would he hear an answer? He listened and heard the happiest sound of his life: Daniel's voice. Daniel said, "My God hath sent his angel, and hath shut the lions' mouths." Daniel had spent a quiet night with his God in the middle of all the lions.

The king ordered Daniel to be taken out of the lions' den; and no one could find any hurt on him, because he believed in his God. Then the king ordered all the wicked princes and rulers, with their families, to be thrown into the den; and the lions tore them to pieces before they reached the bottom of the den. Darius told all his people to tremble and fear before the God of Daniel. God **made** him say that.

REMEMBER:

God's cause always wins. Sometimes He leads His people through trouble — even through a lions' den — but God's cause always wins. For He is the only God. Always trust in Him.

415

Some of God's People Go Back to Their Own Land

King Darius, the king who was so glad that Daniel was saved from the lions, ruled for only two years. Then the great King Cyrus sat on the throne, ruling over the whole world. He was a very important world king. God talked to this heathen world king and made his heart ready to do what God told him. What did God tell him to do? The Lord said it was time to send His people back to their own land.

You remember, don't you, that when King Nebuchadnezzar captured the land of Judah and took all God's people captive to Babylon the prophet Jeremiah told them that after seventy years they would go home again. Now the seventy years were over; and God stirred up King Cyrus inside his heart so that he sent this news to all the countries that he ruled: "The Lord God of heaven hath given me all the kingdoms of the earth; and he hath charged me to build him an house at Jerusalem, which is in Judah." **Charged** means **told.**

How did King Cyrus know all about the God of heaven and earth? Daniel was still living, and he must have told him all the wonderful stories of his great God. Daniel must have been a very old man by this time, for he had lived through all those seventy years of captivity in Babylon. Although Daniel was too old to go back to the land of Judah, how happy he must have been when the king said, "Who is there among you of all his people? his God be with him, and let him go up to Jerusalem, and build the house of the Lord God of Israel."

God stirred up the hearts of many of His people living in Babylon. He made them ready to leave their homes and their gardens and their farms in Babylon and travel the long way to Judah. Many of the people had been born in Babylon and did not know what their homeland of Judah looked like. Not all of the Israelites were ready to go back. Some of them **liked** to live in Babylon. They liked the idol gods of Babylon and had forgotten all about Jehovah. Those were not God's true children.

As some of the people from each of the twelve tribes of Israel were getting ready for the long trip back home, King Cyrus told their neighbors who were staying at home in Babylon to give them gifts of gold, silver, precious things, and animals. And God made the people of Babylon heap their gifts on the people going back to Judah. King Cyrus let them take back to Judah the beautiful gold and silver dishes and bowls, more than five thousand of them, which King Nebuchadnezzar had taken from God's holy temple.

What a lot of excitement there must have been as God's people got ready
to go. Zerubbabel was the leader and Jeshua was the high priest who went along.
At last fifty thousand people were ready for their long march. The Bible does not
tell us anything about how all those people took such a long trip. We do know
that when they came to their own land of Canaan all the people first went to the
cities they had lived in before, but they did not stay long. They were needed
in the city of Jerusalem.

What a pile of ruins Jerusalem was! The walls and the buildings had all been
burned or thrown down and the temple was not there anymore. God's people
knew what they must do first: build God's house. They gave money and food
to the workers and robes to the priests so they could start the work on God's
house. First they all came together and built an altar and offered sacrifices on it.
They were afraid of the heathen people who were living in the land; and as they
worshipped God at the altar, they asked Him to take care of them in this broken-
down city.

For seven months — that's seven pages on a calendar — the people worked hard to finish the foundation of the new temple. The foundation is the floor on which the temple rests. When that part was finished, the priests put on their robes and blew their trumpets and played their cymbals to praise the Lord. God's people joined them with loud singing because the Lord is good and His mercy endureth forever. Then they all shouted for joy. But some of the old people, who had seen the first temple in all its beauty, cried. What a lot of noise there was! Some were crying with loud voices and some were shouting for joy, and no one could tell which was which. So the noise was heard far away.

When they started building the rest of God's house, God's people ran into trouble. The heathen people living in the land began to bother them and tried to stop their work. For many years they bothered God's people, until at last the king of Babylon helped them. He stopped the wicked men from making trouble; and after twenty-one years the temple was finished and it was time for a great celebration.

The people brought seven hundred animals for the priests to offer in thanks to God; and for seven days the people had a great feast with happiness and singing. For they were back in their own land and they could worship the Lord in His own temple once more. The Lord had made them happy again.

REMEMBER:

When God's people are happy, they sing praises to Him. They like to play musical instruments when they sing praise to God, too. What is your favorite song of praise to God?

Esther Becomes Queen

For a while we will leave the happy people who went back to their own land of Judah and we will go to the palace of the king who ruled over the whole world. When we get there we will see that not nearly all the Israelites wanted to go back to their own land. In fact, not very many of them did. Most of them were very happy in their new heathen land, and they were not interested in Jerusalem and God's temple. They did not love the Lord and they liked to live as the heathen did.

We will see, too, that a new king, named Ahasuerus, sat on the throne, ruling the kingdoms of the world. This great and rich king called together all the rulers of his land and the captains of his armies and for half a year showed them how rich and strong his kingdom was. The king wanted to make plans to fight more countries, and he showed his great men that they could easily fight and win. After the half year of planning this war with their enemies, King Ahasuerus gave a feast — a party — which lasted for seven days.

If we could peek into the palace room where the rich king served his feast, we would see big pillars of marble. Between the marble pillars the king hung curtains of white, green, and blue; and the floor had patterns of red, blue, black, and white marble. On the tables were gold and silver cups, all different one from the other. And if we watched the people come into the room, we would see that they did not sit on chairs at the tables, as we do. In those days they lay on their sides on couches which were set at their places. And those couches were made of silver and gold.

Wouldn't you think that would be a beautiful sight? It would look rich and gorgeous, if that is **all** we looked at. But if we watched the men come to the feast, we would know that it was a drinking feast, a feast where they drank wine and tried to become drunk and do all kinds of wicked things. They came to this feast to **try** to be wicked! The wife of King Ahasuerus, Queen Vashti, made a great feast for the women at the same time.

For seven days the feast went on, and on the seventh day, when King Ahasuerus had drunk too much wine, the king called Queen Vashti to come to the feast so everyone could see how beautiful she was. Vashti would not come. Maybe she knew how wild and rough those drunken men were, and she would not let them see her.

That made King Ahasuerus angry. He asked his seven wise men what he should do. They said that Queen Vashti had done wrong by not coming; for if the queen did not obey the king, all other wives would not have to obey their husbands, either. They told the king not to keep Queen Vashti as his wife anymore but to get a new wife. That pleased the king. He let Vashti go away, and he started to look for a new wife. It was very wrong of the king to do that, for Vashti was his wife and God says a man may have **one** wife and he must keep her always. But wicked Ahasuerus did not obey God's laws.

He sent his servants through the land to look for very beautiful girls and to take them to a special house, the house of the women, near the king's palace. For a whole year these beautiful girls had to get ready for the king to see them. They used sweet-smelling oils and perfumes and beautiful things to wear. At the end of the year the king would choose one of the girls to be queen instead of Vashti.

One of the girls who came to the special house was named Esther and she was an Israelite girl whose father and mother both had died. We do not know how. Her cousin Mordecai had brought her up and taken care of her, and he wanted her to be one of the girls who tried to become the next queen. Mordecai told Esther **not** to tell anyone that she was an Israelite, and Esther obeyed him and forgot all about God. She knew better. She was brought up as we are. She knew the stories about all the wonders of God; she knew all about His laws; she knew she must live in God's fear and be sorry for her sins; and she knew that God had promised to send Jesus to take away His people's sins. But she didn't care. She **liked** to live with the heathen girls in that special house and she would like to be the wife of wicked King Ahasuerus, who had many wives and served idols.

After a year each one of the girls took a turn to go to the king. When Esther's turn came, the king liked her best. She became queen instead of Vashti. King Ahasuerus made another great feast, called Esther's feast. Now she was the wife of the great world king, and she still did not tell him the most important thing: that she was an Israelite who should be serving Jehovah God.

One night as her cousin Mordecai sat outside the palace, watching to see that she was all right, he heard two of the king's servants talking. They were angry about something and they were making plans to kill the king. When Mordecai heard them, he told Queen Esther and she told the king. The king found out the story was true, and he killed the two servants. Mordecai had saved the king's life; and the king told his servants to write the story in the book in which they wrote everything that happened. We will hear more about those two servants in another story. Will you remember them?

REMEMBER:

It was very wrong of Esther not to choose for God's people but to choose for wicked idol worshippers. She did not want to be one of God's children. Will this story make us think more about being happy that **we** may act as His own dear children?

Trouble for
the Jews

For five years Esther had been the queen, the wife of King Ahasuerus, who ruled over all the kingdoms of the world, and she still had not told him the most important thing about herself: that she was an Israelite girl, born from the chosen people whose God is King of heaven and earth. Queen Esther was an Israelite girl only on the outside. In her heart she did not want God to be **her** God. If she did, she would not have been able to keep still about all her happiness. She would have bubbled over to the king about God's beautiful world, about His kindness and love, and about Jesus, Who is the Savior. No, Esther did not do that. She lived as a heathen girl in a heathen palace.

One day the king made a man named Haman the most important ruler under the king and he told all his servants to bow down to Haman and honor him when they saw him. Mordecai, Queen Esther's cousin, who sat near the king's gate every day, would not bow down to the great Haman. He should have obeyed the king and he should have showed honor to Haman. But Mordecai was proud and stubborn. Besides, he hated Haman and wished **he** could be the great ruler. He was jealous.

Every day the king's servants asked Mordecai why he did not obey the king; and they begged him to bow to Haman when the great ruler rode past. But Mordecai would not. When Haman saw that Mordecai would not bow down and honor him, he was angry. As he watched day by day and saw that each day Mordecai was proud and stubborn and would not honor him, he became more and more angry. Oh, how angry he was with Mordecai! Haman was a mean, cruel man and in his anger he thought up a cruel punishment. Not only would he kill Mordecai, but he would kill all of Mordecai's people too, all of them in the whole world. Mordecai's people were the Israelites — in the days of Haman they were often called the **Jews.** Can you remember that? When cruel Haman said he would kill all the Jews, he meant he would kill all God's people, those in Jerusalem, too.

First Haman had to find the best day to do his wicked deed. Because he was an idol-worshipper, he believed in magic charms. He also believed that the stars told him what day would be best. And his wise men finally told him that the stars said the thirteenth day of the last month of the year would be best to kill the Jews.

Now it was time for Haman to tell King Ahasuerus about his plan. He told a lie about the Israelites whom he called the **Jews**. He said they were different from all other people and they did not obey the king's laws. He asked the king whether he might kill them all. To make the king say yes, Haman promised the king that he would give him all the money from the people he killed.

King Ahasuerus did not even try to find out whether Haman was telling the truth, and he told Haman to keep all the money for himself. He didn't need it. The king's scribes — they were the men who did the king's writing — wrote letters in the name of King Ahasuerus to every part of his great kingdom telling everyone to kill and destroy all the Jews, young and old, women and little children, on the thirteenth day of the last month of the year. Then the mailmen hurried out to deliver all those letters.

The king sent the letters out in the **first** month and the Jews had to wait until the **last** month to be killed — almost a whole year. Those poor Jews! They were shocked! They didn't know why they had to be killed! They stopped eating! They cried and cried! But the king and Haman celebrated by drinking strong drink.

Mordecai tore his clothes and put on rough sackcloth and ashes and ran

through the city crying a loud and bitter cry, not a cry for help to the Lord, but a loud cry to get the attention of Queen Esther. Then he sat crying and wailing at the gate of the king's house until Queen Esther's servants told her about her sad cousin Mordecai. It made Esther very upset and she sent clothes for him to wear but he would not put them on. Then she called Hatach, one of her servants, and told him to find out what the trouble was.

Mordecai told Hatach about cruel Haman's plan to kill all the Jews, and he gave him one of the letters to show Queen Esther. He also told Hatach to tell Esther to go to the king and tell him she was one of the Jews and to beg the king to save the lives of her people Israel.

But Queen Esther had a problem. She answered Mordecai that the law said that no one might come to the king unless he sent for that person; and the punishment for coming was death, unless the king held out his scepter — his golden staff. Queen Esther did not dare to go. What if the king did not hold out his scepter? She would have to die!

Mordecai sent his answer back to Esther: if you do not beg for our lives, you will be killed with the rest of the Jews. He ended by saying, "and who knoweth whether thou art come to the kingdom for such a time as this?" Mordecai knew that the Jews were God's people and that God would not let them be killed. But he did not trust in **God** to save His people. He trusted in **Esther.**

Once more Queen Esther sent an answer: fast for three days, Mordecai. Fasting means to stop eating. Esther promised that she and her maids would fast for three days, too, and then she would go to the king without being asked. She ended her answer with these words, "I will go in unto the king, which is not according to the law: and if I perish, I perish." **Perish** means **die.**

REMEMBER:

When Queen Esther stopped eating for three days, she did not think about praying to the Lord, the Helper of His people. She trusted in herself, and she was afraid. We never have to be afraid if we are God's children, for He always hears our prayers and helps us.

The King Honors Mordecai

The words which Queen Esther said in the last part of the story we just finished were, "I will go in unto the king, which is not according to the law: and if I perish, I perish."

For three days she and her maids fasted — they did not eat — and on the third day Queen Esther dressed in her queenly robes and stood in the hall of the king where he could see her as he sat on his throne. Esther was a beautiful queen and she must have looked especially nice in her gorgeous robes. King Ahasuerus was surprised to see her. He was happy, too, for he held out his golden scepter to her. The Queen came near and touched the top of the scepter.

King Ahasuerus could tell that she had something important to say. Otherwise she would not have come without being asked. He said, "What wilt thou, Queen Esther? it shall be even given thee to the half of the kingdom."

Queen Esther did not ask for very much. All she said was, "If it seem good unto the king, let the king and Haman come this day unto the banquet that I have prepared for him." A banquet is a dinner party.

The banquet that Queen Esther made ready was a banquet of wine. When the king and Queen Esther and Haman were sitting at the feast of wine, the king asked her again what she wanted. And Queen Esther promised that if the king and Haman came again the next day to a banquet of wine, she would ask her question.

Haman left the banquet with a glad heart. He was as happy as a man who lives without God can be. But his happiness did not last long, for he saw his enemy, Mordecai, sitting at the king's gate. It seems as if Mordecai purposely put himself in Haman's way and then would not move. That was wrong of Mordecai. No wonder Haman was angry.

When he came home, he told his family and his friends about how rich he was, about how many children he had, and about the great honor the king gave to him; for only **he** had been invited to the banquet of wine with the king and queen. And tomorrow he was going again! What a happy face he had when he told them all about it. Then his face changed. It became sad and angry, because none of these great things **really** made him happy as long as Mordecai was in his way.

Zeresh his wife and all his friends had an idea: make a gallows. A gallows was a tall, thick pole with some kind of rope at the top on which people in those days hanged a man until he died. Zeresh thought the gallows should be taller than two houses on top of one another, so that everyone for miles around could see it. What would they do with the gallows? Hang Mordecai on it.

That night King Ahasuerus could not sleep. To pass the time in the night, he asked his servants to read in the book that told everything that had happened in his kingdom. As his servants read to him, they came to the story of the two wicked servants who had planned to kill the king. They read how Mordecai had heard their plan, how he had told Queen Esther, how she had told the king, and the king's life had been saved. Do you remember that little story?

The king did, too, but he had one question: what nice thing had they done for Mordecai for saving the king's life? Nothing, the servant told him. In his mind the king started to make plans to honor Mordecai, but he needed one of his wise men to help him. By this time it was early morning and Haman was already in the palace to ask the king whether he might hang Mordecai on the tall gallows he had made. His servants told the king that Haman had come, and he said, "Let him come in."

King Ahasuerus knew that Haman was a proud, selfish man, and maybe he even knew how he hated Mordecai. The king did not care. He thought of something funny. He would play a little joke on Haman. The king asked, "What shall be done unto the man whom the king delighteth to honor?"

Now Haman thought so much of himself that he said in his heart: whom would the king want to honor more than **myself**? So he thought of the great things he would want for **himself**; and then he had his answer ready for the king: get the robe which the king himself wears and the horse which he rides and the crown that is set on his head and put it on the man the king wants to honor. Then let the man ride on the horse, through the streets of the city, while someone shouts, "Thus shall it be done to the man whom the king delighteth to honor."

Haman was all ready to have those honors for himself. Watch his face as the king said, "Do even so to Mordecai the Jew that sitteth at the King's gate." Oh, Haman's face was sad and angry; for instead of killing Mordecai he had to be the man who shouted, "Thus shall it be done to the man whom the king delighteth to honor."

He obeyed the king, of course; but after he finished leading Mordecai through the streets of the city, he went home with his head covered, a sign of deep trouble. He was afraid, too. His wife and his friends agreed. If Mordecai was one of the Jews whom wicked Haman wanted to kill, **he** might be killed instead of Mordecai. While they were still talking about Haman's troubles, the king's servants stood at the door, waiting to take him to Queen Esther's second banquet of wine.

REMEMBER:

Did you notice in this story that when two wicked men — Haman and Mordecai — fight one another, neither one really wins? Do you know why? God says it is because He puts them on the slippery road to hell. Where does He put His children? On the straight and narrow road to heaven. And He blesses them when they walk on it.

The Jews Are Saved

King Ahasuerus was so curious. He wanted to know so badly what Queen Esther's question was. At the second banquet of wine he asked again, "What is thy petition, Queen Esther?"

Don't you think the king was surprised when Queen Esther begged him to save her life and the lives of her people? She told the king that she and her people were sold to be killed! The king could not wait to ask who her wicked enemy was; and she told him, "The enemy is this wicked Haman." Now the king knew that Esther was an **Israelite**, a **Jew**, one of the people Haman hated.

The king was so angry with Haman that he left the wine-table and stamped out into the palace garden. He should not have been so angry at Haman. After all, it was King Ahasuerus who had sent out the letters ordering all the Jews to be killed. He was just as much to blame as Haman.

But Queen Esther put all the blame on Haman and Haman was afraid. When the king, who was still angry, came in from the garden, he saw that Haman was lying across the queen's couch, begging for his life. Maybe the king thought that Haman would hurt Queen Esther. He did not bother to find out whether Haman was really to blame for wanting to kill the Jews. He just gave the order that Haman must be killed. As his servants came in to get Haman, one of them told the king about the tall gallows Haman had made for Mordecai; and the king said, "Hang him thereon."

So Haman died on the gallows he had made for Mordecai. The king gave all of Haman's riches to Queen Esther and she let Mordecai take care of them.

Now the king was not angry anymore. Did he forget that he had sent those letters all over his kingdom, saying that the Jews must be killed on the thirteenth day of the last month? Queen Esther did not forget. Once more she went to the

king without being asked, this time bowing down with her face to the floor and crying bitter tears. And once more King Ahasuerus held out his golden scepter to her. Queen Esther stood up and asked the king to do something he could not possibly do: she asked him to tell the people not to obey those wicked letters and she asked him to make a new law telling people not to kill the Jews. Oh, the king could not do **that!** In his country, no one might ever change any law the king had made, not even the king himself.

But the king had an idea: Queen Esther and Mordecai were allowed to write another law about the Jews, whatever they liked. He knew that Mordecai would think of **something** to save his people.

Would you like to know what kind of law Esther and Mordecai made to save their people? They sent new letters through the whole kingdom saying that on the thirteenth day of the last month all the Jews might fight back if anyone tried to kill them. If no one tried to kill them, the Jews might go out on that day and kill anyone they wanted to: not only soldiers, but people who could not help themselves, like women and children. And they might take anything the dead people owned for themselves. What do you think of Mordecai and Queen Esther? Were they any better than wicked Haman? No, they weren't.

When the dreadful day came at last there was no fighting. By that time no one dared to kill any Jews. The Bible does not tell about even one Jew being killed. But many of the **Jews** took swords in their hands and killed people who they thought were their enemies. After that awful day when the Jews went out and killed whomever they pleased, the king asked Queen Esther what else she wanted and she asked for one more day in which the Jews might kill their enemies. Do you know how many people the Jews killed in those two days? They killed more than seventy-five thousand people in the whole kingdom.

Why did Mordecai and Queen Esther want their people to kill their enemies for two whole days? Because in their hearts they were no better than cruel Haman or wicked King Ahasuerus. They **liked** to have power over their enemies. King Ahasuerus did not mind that so many people in his kingdom were killed, either; and he made Mordecai a great man in his kingdom. He let Mordecai take Haman's place.

Then Mordecai and Queen Esther ordered that the fourteenth and fifteenth days of the last month would be days of happiness and celebration; and each year the Jews celebrated on those two days because the Jews had been saved alive.

And what did God say about all this? Never forget that He was ruling it all, even the wicked people in King Ahasuerus' palace. **God** put wicked Mordecai and heathen Queen Esther in the king's palace and **God** used them to save the Israelites alive. God had to keep them alive because He had promised that one day Jesus would be born from the Israelites. Esther and Mordecai did not care about Jesus. But God did. He was waiting to send His Son for the most important thing that would ever happen in the world: His Son would die to save His people from their sins.

REMEMBER:

Queen Esther and Mordecai are important to **us,** too. For the Jesus that was born from the Jews is our Jesus, too. If we are His children, we know that He is our precious Savior, Who died to save us.

Ezra and Nehemiah Help God's People

While most of the Israelites were enjoying themselves in the wicked lands where they lived, a few were sad. Only a few were God's true children, who loved Him in their hearts and tried to do His will. That is because God gave them new hearts, hearts that always turned to **Him**. God made their hearts wish to go back to Judah, to the city of Jerusalem, to serve their God in His temple. God even gave them a leader: Ezra.

The king who was ruling the world at that time helped Ezra get ready and he sent letters through his whole kingdom telling every Israelite who wanted to go of his own free will to get ready to travel to Jerusalem; and Ezra began to gather God's people together for the trip. Not many — not very many at all — wanted to go back to Jerusalem. Only six thousand people out of all the thousands and thousands of Jews came to Ezra. They were not nearly so many as those who went back to Jerusalem the first time with Zerubbabel. Do you remember that story?

Before they left, Ezra and the people prayed and fasted together. Why? They needed God's help in a special way. They begged God for a safe trip to Jerusalem. Ezra had told the king that his God would take care of them; and now he was ashamed to ask the king for soldiers to guard them. The people prayed that God would be their Guard. He was. He gave them a safe trip. For three and a half months — that's more than a hundred days — they traveled, safe from robbers and killers — until they came to Jerusalem. What a happy day that must have been, when they could meet God's people who were already living there, and when they could see God's house for the very first time. For three days the tired travelers rested. Then they went to God's house to offer animals for sacrifices. They offered sacrifices because they were sorry for their sins and they offered sacrifices to show how thankful they were that God had at last brought them back to Jerusalem, their true home.

Soon Ezra and his people found out that life in Jerusalem was not so happy after all. God's people who had been in Jerusalem for a long time had fallen into sin. They had married wicked, heathen wives, and some of them were forgetting God. Ezra had to make them put their wicked wives away and live as God's children again. They had more troubles. When they tried to build the city of Jerusalem and put walls around it again, enemies bothered them and they had to stop their work.

Thirteen years went past. Hardly any work had been done in Jerusalem. It was still a broken-down city. Then one day Hanani, one of the men of Jerusalem, went to visit his brother Nehemiah who lived in the palace of the great king. Nehemiah was the king's cup-bearer. A cup-bearer served the king wine and he was an important man to the king. Nehemiah's brother told him the sad stories about Jerusalem: how the enemies of God's people bothered and mocked them and how they suffered a hard life and how they lived in a broken-down city, full of ruins.

Nehemiah was so surprised! He had no idea that the life of God's people was so bad! And he was sad. He cried and prayed to God. When he prayed, he begged God to remember His promise to bless His people and keep them safe and happy. Nehemiah **could not** forget God's poor people in Jerusalem. He thought about them even when he was serving the king wine, and the king noticed how sad Nehemiah's face was.

When the king asked him what was troubling him, Nehemiah was not afraid to tell, for he had a plan. He asked the king whether he might go to Jerusalem to be the leader of God's people there and help them build the walls. The king let him go and gave him servants and soldiers to go with him. Soon after he came to Jerusalem he went out at night, secretly, with a few men, to look at the broken walls of the city and to see how much work it would take to build them up again. All around the city they went that night. Oh, those ruins were bad! But the people could build them again. Nehemiah told his men that God would help them and they answered, "Let us rise up and build."

It was not easy. All God's people had to help. Enemies tried to stop them many times. Nehemiah had to tell some of his people to work as guards, holding spears and bows and arrows, to protect the men who were building the walls. From the early morning until late at night when the stars came out the people worked on Jerusalem's wall. In fifty-two days they were finished. At last the

people could stop working. They had a celebration. They made a parade around their new walls, they offered sacrifices of thanks to God, and they sang praises so loudly that they could be heard a long way off.

Now God's people could settle down in their own land and wait for God's great promise, the very biggest and best promise for them: that Jesus would be born. But God was not ready **yet**. First He led His people through some very sad years, four hundred sad years. In all those years God was quiet. He did not send any prophets to talk to His people, and no one heard His voice. Those four hundred years were very sad, dark years. The Bible does not tell us anything about those awful years; but after those four hundred years were over, it would be almost time for Jesus to be born on the earth.

REMEMBER:

Malachi, the last prophet who talked to God's people before Jesus was born called Him the Sun of Righteousness. Jesus was the bright Sunshine Who would chase away the darkness of those four hundred awful years. He is **our** Sunshine, too, Who chases away the darkness of our troubles and sins and puts the light of His love into our hearts.

The Angel Visits Zacharias

Those sad four hundred years when God was quiet were almost over. During those years there had been many wars in the world. Babylon was not the great world power anymore. Now Caesar, king of the city of **Rome**, ruled the world; and he made Herod, a wicked man, to be king over Judah, where God's people lived. God's people did not **like** to have those heathen kings ruling over them while they were waiting for **the King** to be born, the King Whose name is Jesus. While they waited, they obeyed God's laws and worshipped Him in His temple.

Zacharias and his wife Elisabeth were two of the people who were waiting. Both of them were born in families of priests, and Zacharias had to take his turn to work in God's temple. You remember, don't you, that the priests were God's temple workers. When his turn came, Zacharias had to work for eight days in God's house.

Zacharias was getting old. When he and his wife Elisabeth were young, they had prayed many prayers for a child. They wanted a baby so badly! But as the years went past and they became older and God did not give them a baby, the prayer died in their hearts. They could see that God's answer was no, for Zacharias was sixty years old already — as old as a grandfather.

And now it was his turn to serve the Lord for eight days in His temple. The priests chose the kind of work they would do in the temple by casting lots. You remember, too, that we do not know exactly how they cast those lots, but we do know that Zacharias was chosen for a very special work, a work he might do only once in his whole life. It was to go into the Holy Place in the temple and burn sweet-smelling incense to Jehovah. Do you remember that when a priest burned incense in the temple and when the smoke of the incense went up toward heaven it was a picture of the sweet smelling prayers of God's people? Oh, Zacharias must have been glad that he could do this special work in God's house.

As he burned the sweet incense on the altar, he prayed sweet prayers to God; and all God's people who had come to worship Him were kneeling down in the courtyard praying, too. Suddenly a shining visitor stood next to Zacharias, and he was afraid. He could see it was a heavenly visitor, an angel. God had sent a special angel to Zacharias. His name was Gabriel, the angel who brings words of happiness of God's people.

He said to Zacharias, "Fear not, Zacharias: for thy prayer is heard; and thy wife Elisabeth shall bear thee a son, and thou shalt call his name John."

The angel told him that John would be a special boy who would live **separate** — that means **away** — from the world. John would live in holiness to the Lord. Such a special boy might not cut his hair, might not drink strong drink, and might not touch a dead body. Those were signs that he belonged to the Lord. The angel told one thing more: that John would preach and make the way ready for Jesus; and many people would turn to the Lord when they heard John's words.

What wonderful news! Don't you think Zacharias was excited? No. He didn't believe the angel. His faith in God was not very strong and he asked the angel, "Whereby shall I know this? for I am an old man, and my wife well stricken in years." He was telling the angel that he **couldn't** believe they would have a baby because they were too old. He needed a **sign** that the angel's words would come true.

Now Zacharias needed a scolding. Listen to what the angel said to him: "I am Gabriel, that stand in the presence of God; and am sent to speak unto thee, and to show thee these glad tidings."

The angel Gabriel was telling Zacharias that he did not need a sign. He must believe the angel's **words**. Because he did not believe, Zacharias would not be able to talk until the baby John was born. He wouldn't even be able to tell anyone about the wonderful news of the angel.

Outside in the courtyard, the people waited for Zacharias to come out of the Holy Place. How long he stayed! What was happening? At last he came out. Usually he said a beautiful blessing as he stretched out his hands over them. Usually he said, "The Lord bless thee, and keep thee: the Lord make his face shine upon thee, and be gracious unto thee: the Lord lift up his countenance upon thee, and give thee peace."

But on this day when he came out of the Holy Place Zacharias could only make motions to them to show them he could not talk; and the people knew that he had seen a heavenly visitor in the temple. Zacharias was not able to talk until the baby John was born.

REMEMBER:

Do **you** like to talk? What do you like to talk about? About angels? About Bible stories? About God's face shining on you?

John is Born

The angels in heaven are so interested in knowing all about God's people on this earth. Often, long ago, God sent His angels to earth with good news for His people. Just before Jesus was born, at the most important time there ever was, God sent them to talk to His people more than ever before. The angels had so much good news!

Do you remember that God had promised that Jesus would be born from King David's family? David's family was a family of kings, but all the kings had died. Almost everyone from the family of the kings had died, too: all except Mary, a young girl. The angel Gabriel suddenly came to visit Mary about a half year after he had visited Zacharias in the temple. He came to Mary with the happiest, the most important news that ever came to earth. This is what the angel said: "Hail, thou that art highly favored, the Lord is with thee."

When Mary saw her visitor from heaven and heard his wonderful words to her, she was troubled and afraid. But the angel said, "Fear not, Mary: for thou hast found favour with God."

The angel Gabriel went on to tell Mary the rest of the news: that she would have a baby and she must call His name Jesus. This Jesus would be the Son of God, the King Who would rule forever and ever — not on the earth, but in heaven. What wonderful news! Mary believed it, too, but she could not understand it all. She had a question: "How shall this be?"

The angel explained to her that the power of the Holy Spirit would be like a shadow over her and that her baby would be holy and pure, the Son of God. Mary still could not really understand. Neither can we. For it is a wonder.

The angel had more glad news for Mary. The news was about Mary's cousin Elisabeth. Do you know who Elisabeth was? The wife of Zacharias, who had seen the angel in the temple. The angel told Mary that God had kept His promise and Elisabeth, who thought she was too old to have a baby, would soon have a baby. For God can do all things! Then the angel went away.

He did not **tell** Mary to go to visit her cousin Elisabeth, but Mary hurried to her house. She could hardly wait to tell the news that made her heart almost burst with happiness. All alone she traveled about one hundred miles to see Elisabeth. And such a happy meeting they had! Do you know what Elisabeth called Mary? "The mother of my Lord:" for **Jesus** was her Lord. And Mary answered her by singing about the Baby, the Lord Jesus. It was a song of praise to God. For three months Mary stayed with Elisabeth and then went home.

Not very long afterward, the baby boy that God had promised to Zacharias and Elisabeth was born. When the baby was eight days old, they had a celebration. All their friends and relatives came and they called the new baby **Zacharias** after his father. Elisabeth said, "Not so; but he shall be called John."

The friends and relatives did not agree with Elisabeth. They said, "There is none of thy kindred that is called by this name." Kindred are **relatives**.

And Zacharias could not tell them that the angel had told him to name the baby **John**, for he still could not talk. He could not hear, either. The people made signs to him to find out what the baby's name really should be. Zacharias got a tablet and wrote on it, "His name is John." Suddenly God opened his mouth and loosened his tongue so that he could talk again; and he praised God as he told the story of the angel's visit to him in the temple.

The news of the wonder of the baby John's birth traveled all through the country. Everyone was talking about the special boy who was born and they said, "What manner of child shall this be!" They knew they were seeing a wonder from God.

After God made his tongue loose, Zacharias could not keep still. He kept on singing praises to God. He praised God for Jesus Who was almost ready to be born, and he said, "The dayspring from on high hath visited us." The dayspring is the early morning. When the dayspring comes, it means that the **sun** rises. Zacharias' song made a picture of Jesus as the sun rising in the morning, chasing away the dark night. Jesus is the Sun that chases away the darkness of sin. Zacharias said one thing more: when Jesus, the Sun, gives His people light, He leads them in the way of peace that goes to heaven.

REMEMBER:

The prophet Malachi called Jesus the Sun, too — the Sun of righteousness. God's people like to call Jesus the Sun. When we see the sun shining outside, shall we remember it is a picture of Jesus Who shines the sunlight of His love in our hearts?

Jesus is Born

The ruler of the world, whose name was Caesar Augustus, gave an order to the people in all the countries he ruled. Everyone must go to the city where he had been born and sign his name and then pay money. We call it **taxes**.

God's people who lived in Israel had to obey him, too. Mary and her husband Joseph left the town of Nazareth and together they traveled to the town of Bethlehem. Bethlehem was the town where King David had been born long, long ago. Joseph and Mary came from the family of King David, so they had to go to Bethlehem to sign their names.

It must have taken them at least three days to make the trip and when at last they came to the town, tired after the long ride on their animals, they found it full of people who had come to sign their names, too. No one had room for Joseph and Mary to stay overnight. The inns — we call them hotels — were full already. But Joseph and Mary needed a place to sleep that night. Where would they go? The only place they could find was a sort of cave in one of the hills near the outside of the city, a cave where travelers stopped with their animals. It was a place where **animals** were kept, like a barn. Sometimes it was called a stable.

In the stable, maybe that very night, the Baby Jesus was born. It was a wonder! God came down to earth in the form of a Baby. It was the greatest wonder that ever happened! We would think that everyone would crowd around to see. But in that stable-cave it did not look like a wonder. Only a poor girl called Mary and her husband Joseph were there to see God's wonder. Mary wrapped the Baby Jesus in swaddling clothes. Those were long, thin strips of cloth which she wound around His tiny body. Then she laid him in a manger, a feeding trough of one of the animals.

Why didn't God let His own Son be born in a beautiful palace, in a room fit for a king? Why did Jesus have to be born in a stable, with only animals for company? Because it was God's picture. God's picture said that there was no room for Jesus in the whole wicked world nor in the hearts of any wicked man. Only when God opens people's hearts is there any room for Jesus.

That night in the fields near the city of Bethlehem, shepherds were quietly guarding their sheep. Suddenly a bright, shining light came over them and they saw an angel. Maybe it was Gabriel again. Oh, those shepherds were afraid. Why? Because that light was so pure and heavenly and wonderful, it was too great for their sinful eyes to look at.

The angel told them, "Fear not: for unto you is born this day in the city of David a Saviour, which is Christ the Lord."

Then the angel gave them a sign. He said, "Ye shall find the babe wrapped in swaddling clothes, lying in a manger."

That sign would help the shepherds find the Baby Jesus. But that wasn't all. That sign taught the shepherds that Jesus **could not** be born in the rich palace of a king. He **had** to be born in a poor stable: for Jesus did not come to have the riches of **this** world. He came to show the riches of **heaven:** His love, His grace, and His mercy.

As the shepherds looked up, the sky was filled with angels. Don't you think that the angels asked God whether they might come down on this great night to sing and shout His praises to the shepherds? Many, many angels sang — a multitude of them. They sang, "Glory to God in the highest, and on earth peace, good will toward men." Then they were gone.

The shepherds left their sheep and went to Bethlehem. There they found the Baby and Mary and Joseph. They believed that the Baby was the Lord, the Son of God, and they worshipped Him. They knew they were standing at the door of God's heavenly kingdom. After they left the Baby, they went all over the city. They couldn't keep still. They told everyone about the great wonder of this night, the holy night when Jesus was born. But Mary kept quiet and thought about those great things that had happened, too great for her to talk about.

REMEMBER:

Sometimes we are like Mary. We sit still and think about God's wonder. Sometimes we are like the shepherds. We want to tell everyone that we are so happy that Jesus is our Lord, Who loves us and saves us.

The Wise Men Come

In a country to the east, far away from the town of Bethlehem, lived wise men. We do not know how many wise men there were and the Bible does not tell us very much about them. Men who are wise know a lot and study a lot. These wise men in the faraway country knew about God and they knew very much about God's world, especially about God's sky and His stars.

At night, when they went out to look at the stars, they knew that **God** had made all those shining lights in the sky and that He holds them all in His hands. They knew, too, that God had given His Son Jesus a picture-name long before He was even born: He had called Jesus a **Star** that would be born from Jacob's family. When, one night, the wise men saw a special star in the sky, they knew it was God's picture-sign in the sky that Jesus was born. God had made this special star as a wonder for this special time. The wise men called it **His** star. And they saw it only once.

They knew what to do: they would travel a long, long way and find the Baby Who was the King of the Jews. Remember, the Jews were the Israelites, God's people. So the wise men traveled to Judah, the land of the Jews, and went straight to Jerusalem, the city of the king. Surely, they thought, this Baby would be born in the palace of the king. How disappointed those wise men were when they found wicked King Herod in the king's palace, but no Baby Jesus.

Their first question had been a happy one: "Where is he that is born King of the Jews? for we have seen his star in the east, and are come to worship him."

They thought their King would be born right in the middle of Jerusalem. They thought the people of Jerusalem would be as happy as they were. But when they asked their happy question about the King of the Jews, all the people in Jerusalem looked at them with sad, troubled faces. For they didn't even know that Jesus had been born. Most of them didn't care, either. They wanted a king on **this** earth. They did not want the King from heaven. King Herod had to ask his servants to look up in God's Book where Jesus was supposed to be born; and his servants found the answer: "In Bethlehem." The wise men were in the wrong city!

If we looked at King Herod, we would see that his face was ugly with sin. **He** wanted to be the king of the Jews, and he did not want another King to sit

on his throne. He was jealous of the Baby Jesus. He did not understand that
Jesus was the King Who rules from heaven. In his evil heart, King Herod decided
to kill Jesus.

Now watch that wicked King Herod change his face as he talked to the wise
men. He asked them very carefully what time they saw the star in the sky, and
the wise men told him. It was probably almost two years ago already that they
had seen the star, and Jesus did not live in the stable anymore. He lived with his
parents in a house. King Herod acted very interested in the Baby Jesus. He said
to the wise men, "Go and search diligently (that means **look very hard**) for the
young child; and when ye have found him, bring me word again, that I may come
and worship him also."

445

The wise men started out for Bethlehem with sad hearts and troubled faces. They had hoped to find everyone in Jerusalem happy about Jesus' birth and nobody even knew about it. But suddenly their sadness changed to gladness, for the star that they had seen in the east came back into the sky and it led them right to the house where Jesus lived. What great happiness was in their hearts as they fell down before Jesus and worshipped Him and gave Him the presents they had taken from their own land: gold and expensive spices called frankincense and myrrh.

God talked to the wise men and told them not to go back to wicked King Herod but to go home another way.

After the wise men had gone home, God's angel came to Joseph and told him to take Mary and Jesus and run away to the land of Egypt; for King Herod was going to try to kill Jesus. Joseph did what the angel told him and went away that night to the land of Egypt.

Do you know that the land of Egypt is a picture of sin and death and hell? Do you know that we are such sinners that we live in the picture-land of the Egypt of sin and death? God sent His Son Jesus to the land of Egypt to give us a picture of how He will save us from sin and death and hell. For God is going to call Jesus out of Egypt again! And He calls us out of the Egypt of sin to His heaven of life and happiness.

REMEMBER:

God tells us that many things in His world are pictures of Jesus. He tells us that the Star of Bethlehem was a picture of Him. God made animals to be pictures of Jesus, too: the lamb and the lion are two beautiful pictures of Jesus. The lamb's blood is a picture of Jesus' blood which He gave for us and the lion, who is king of all the animals, is a picture of Jesus Who is King over heaven and earth.

Jesus as a Child

When the wise men did not come back to King Herod with news of the Baby Jesus, he was angry, furiously angry. Through his whole life that wicked and selfish king had killed many people who might want to be king instead of himself. Now the king was very old and sick. Still he wanted to find the new King, the Baby Jesus, Who had been born in Bethlehem, and he wanted to kill Him, too. He did not know that God already had saved Him and that He was safe in Egypt with Joseph and Mary.

In his terrible anger, King Herod decided to kill all the baby boys of the town of Bethlehem. He remembered the questions he had asked the wise men and figured Jesus could not be older than two years old. So he ordered his servants to kill all the baby boys of two years old and under in Bethlehem to make sure he killed Jesus, too. What sadness! What great crying in Bethlehem! And what a cruel king was sitting on the throne! God did not let him live very much longer. He sent the king a terrible sickness and about a year later he died.

Joseph and Mary in Egypt heard the news, for God sent His angel to tell Joseph, "Arise, and take the young child and his mother, and go into the land of Israel: for they are dead which sought the young child's life."

At first Joseph was going to take his family to Bethlehem, but when he heard that King Herod's most cruel son was king instead of Herod, he was afraid to go there. Once more God came to him, this time in a dream, and told him to go back to Nazareth, the city they had come from before Jesus was born.

Jesus grew up in the little town of Nazareth. The Bible does not tell us what Jesus looked like when He was a boy and it does not tell us who His playmates were. It **does** tell us that He was filled with God's grace. His mother Mary must have told Jesus about the wonders that happened when He was born. She must have told Him that He was God's Son. He acted like God's Son, too, for He never sinned. He never disobeyed His mother or father. He never lied or sneaked. He never did anything wrong, for He was perfect.

But the boy Jesus had a body just like ours. He grew taller and stronger just as we do. He could get sick just as we can. As Jesus grew up, He watched everything that happened in His small town of Nazareth: the birds, the flowers, the farmers, and the children playing. Many years later, when He was a man, He talked about these things when He preached to the people.

It was an important time for Jesus when He became twelve years old, for in those days when a boy was twelve years old he was not a little boy any longer. He was a young man. Then he could go along with his father and mother each year to celebrate the passover feast. Do you remember what the passover was? It was the feast that made the people remember how God had led the Israelites out of the land of Egypt long ago. At the passover they killed a lamb and put its blood over their doors. It was a picture of the blood of Jesus that saved them from their sins. Now Jesus could go to see the feast which was a picture of Himself.

Joseph and Mary took Jesus along to the feast when He was twelve years old. Probably it was the first time He went. Many people from the town of Nazareth went, and they all traveled together for the three or four days it took to get to the temple at Jerusalem. There they celebrated the passover feast.

When it was time to go back to Nazareth, Mary and Joseph did not see Jesus, but they thought He was somewhere in the crowd of people traveling with them. At the end of the first day, when they missed Him, they asked their friends and relatives about Him. No one had seen Him. After they had looked for Him, they went back to Jerusalem. Three days later they found Jesus sitting in one of the rooms of the temple, in the middle of all the wise teachers, listening to them and asking them questions. And those wise old teachers were very surprised that the twelve-year-old Jesus could answer all their hard questions!

Joseph and Mary were so surprised to see Him there that probably for the first time in her life, Jesus' mother scolded Him a little bit. She asked Jesus why He had done that to them. She and Joseph had been so sad because they couldn't find Him.

In His answer Jesus tried to help His mother understand. He said, "How is it that ye sought me? Wist ye not that I must be about my Father's business?"

Jesus' Father is God. Jesus had to get ready for His Father's work of teaching His people why He had come to earth. And poor Mary couldn't understand it all. But she kept Jesus' words in her heart and she thought about them.

REMEMBER:

We must be about **our** Father's business, too, for our Father is God. When we do our Father's business, we love Him, sing His songs, talk about Him, and pray to Him.

John Baptizes Jesus

While Jesus was growing up, John was growing up, too; and when he was old enough, God called him to the desert, a hot, dry, lonely place. For a long time John lived in the desert, eating locusts, which look like big grasshoppers, and wild honey. He wore the clothes of poor people: a coat of cloth made from camel's hair, tied with a leather belt.

When John was thirty years old, he started to preach to the people. He stayed out in the desert and the people came out to hear him. This is what he said to the people: "Repent ye." It means you must be sorry for your sins and turn around to love God. Next he told them **why** they must be sorry for their sins: Jesus was coming! John was getting the way ready for Jesus. They must turn their hearts to Jesus and listen to His Words and obey them. Many of the people of Israel listened very hard to John. God touched their hearts and they were sorry for their sins and they **believed** that Jesus was coming. John gave a sign to all those who believed: he baptized them. Nearby was the Jordan River, and John told them to dip in the water of the river. It was a picture of God washing them clean from all their sins. Because John baptized them, the people began to call him **John the Baptist.**

By this time everyone was talking about John the Baptist. More and more of God's people believed his words. The wicked teachers in Israel, called the Pharisees, came to listen to John, too; but they did not believe his words and they were not sorry for their sins. John the Baptist knew they had wicked hearts and he called them snakes — sneaky, poisonous snakes.

All the people — those who believed and those who did not believe — had a question to ask John the Baptist: "Who art thou?" They were wondering whether he was Jesus Christ Whom God had promised. John told them, "I am not the Christ."

He told the people that when he baptized them he could only make a **picture** of the people being washed clean from their sins. All he could do was baptize them in the river. But when **Jesus** came to baptize them, He would put His Spirit into their hearts and make them truly clean from their sins.

Don't you think the people were eager to have Jesus come to preach to them? They were so excited about all the good news. And then Jesus did come. He was thirty years old, and grown up, too. Suddenly, as John the Baptist was busy preaching and baptizing the people, he saw Jesus, but he did not know Him. Probably he had not seen Jesus since he was a little boy. Jesus had to tell him Who He was. The Lord in heaven told him, too. He promised to give John a

picture-sign that this was really Jesus Christ. God's Spirit would come down from heaven in the shape of a dove.

Why did Jesus come to John? He asked John to baptize Him. Oh, John couldn't do **that**. Being baptized is a picture of being washed from ugly, black sins. But Jesus didn't have any sin. He was pure and holy. John said no, he wanted it the other way around: Jesus should baptize John.

But John the Baptist was wrong. He didn't understand. And Jesus had to show him that when He asked John to push Him under the water of the river it was a picture of Jesus dying with the heavy load of all the sins of His people on top of Him. And when He came up out of the water, it was a picture that all of the sins of His people were washed away. When Jesus was baptized, He made a picture of washing away **our** sins, too — for we are His people, aren't we?

After John understood why he had to baptize Jesus, he went into the Jordan River and baptized Him. As Jesus stood up out of the water, the heavens about Him were opened and the Spirit of God in the shape of a dove came upon Jesus. Then God the Father from heaven spoke these beautiful words: "This is my beloved Son, in whom I am well pleased."

What an important day Jesus' baptism day was! It was the beginning of Jesus' work on this earth, His work of saving His people. And it was a picture of Jesus opening the door of His kingdom of heaven. He opened that door for us, too.

REMEMBER:

When you were a baby and the minister baptized you, it was a picture that Jesus washed your sins away and a promise that He will give you a new life when you die and go to heaven. Will you think about that beautiful picture the next time a baby is baptized in church?

451

The Devil Tempts Jesus

After He was baptized by John the Baptist, Jesus was led by the Spirit of God into the desert for forty days and forty nights. Why? So that Jesus could be tempted by the devil. When the devil **tempted** Jesus, it means that he tried to make Jesus fall into sin. Oh, how the devil wished that he could make Jesus sin. But Jesus is God and He can do no wrong. He is perfect. Do you know why **God** wanted the devil to tempt Jesus? To show to the devil — and to us — that Jesus is the **perfect** Son of God and He is not able to do any sin.

During all those forty days and nights Jesus had nothing to eat. At the end of those days He must have looked pale and thin and He was **very** hungry. That is the time the devil chose to come to Jesus to tempt Him three times. Do you remember that the devil is a spirit and we cannot see him? Sometimes he puts on the form of a man so that we can see him. The devil probably came to Jesus in the form of a man and started to talk to Jesus by saying, "If thou be the Son of God. . . ."

Oh, that was a wicked way to start to talk to Jesus. The devil knew better. He knew Jesus **was really** the Son of God. Don't you think he had followed the angel Gabriel when the angel told Mary that her Baby would be the Son of God? The devil had listened to the song the angels sang to the shepherds, and it was the devil who told King Herod to kill all the children of Bethlehem so that he would be sure to kill Jesus, the Son of God. Yes, the devil **knew** that Jesus was the Son of God, but he didn't **like** to know it.

Then the devil went on, "If thou be the Son of God, command that these stones be made bread." The devil meant to say: "If you are God and have as much power as God, use that power to change stones into bread."

Jesus was very, very hungry. If He made stones into bread, He could eat and would not be hungry any longer. And if Jesus could make stones into bread, He could command the hot, dry, sandy desert to grow all kinds of food: wheat and corn and vegetables and fruit trees. If Jesus could make lots of food for everyone in the desert, He could make trees of life so that people could eat the fruit of those trees and live forever. That would be heaven on earth. And then Jesus

would not have to die on the cross to save His people from sin and take them to heaven. That is what the devil wanted: to make a heaven on this earth.

But it is not what God wanted. God said Jesus must suffer and die to take His people to heaven. And Jesus listened to His Father in heaven and told the devil, "It is written, Man shall not live by bread alone, but by every word that proceedeth out of the mouth of God."

The next time he tempted Jesus the devil took Him to the city of Jerusalem where God's holy temple stood. God gave the devil power for a little while to take Jesus and put Him on one of the high towers on top of the temple. It was probably the tower on which the priest stood every morning, blowing his trumpet, to let the people know it was time to offer sacrifices.

Once more the devil started with the word **if**. He said, "If thou be the Son of God, cast thyself down." Cast means **throw**. He **dared** Jesus to throw Himself down from the high tower. He told Jesus that the Bible says the angels would take care of Him and hold Him in their hands so He would not hurt His foot against a stone. The devil was trying to say: "Go ahead! Show me that you trust your Father in heaven."

The wicked devil was tempting the holy God and this was Jesus' answer to him: "It is written again, Thou shalt not tempt the Lord thy God."

The last time he tempted Jesus the devil took Him to a very high mountain. We do not know where. God let the devil have a special power so that from that high mountain he could show Jesus all the lands of the world at the same time. Jesus could see how beautiful these lands of the earth were, how rich, and how many people they had. The devil showed Jesus only the beauty of the land, not their troubles and their cryings and their sins.

Then he made a great promise to Jesus: "All these things will I give thee, if thou wilt fall down and worship me."

The devil **really** does not own the world. God does. But the devil rules the hearts of wicked men in the world, and he wanted to rule Jesus, too. How **easy** it would be for Jesus to be King of the world: just bow down to the devil. Now think how **terrible** it would be: the holy God would worship and obey the wicked devil. He would be the devil's slave!

Jesus had just the right answer for him: "Get thee hence, Satan: for it is written, Thou shalt worship the Lord thy God, and him only shalt thou serve."

Then the devil went away, and God's angels came to Jesus. They knew how hard, how very hard it would be for Him to obey His heavenly Father and to suffer and die for His people. They came to comfort Him.

REMEMBER:

Every time Jesus answered the devil he started by saying, "It is written." Do we know **where** it is written? In the Bible. Whenever we have trouble and we don't know what to do, we can find the answers in the Bible. God's Word is always there to help us.

Jesus Works His First Miracle

After His temptation by the devil, Jesus was ready to start His work on earth. He went first just where we'd think He would go: to John the Baptist who was preaching and baptizing near the Jordan River. When John looked up, he saw Jesus coming toward him and he said to two of his followers, "Behold the Lamb of God." Wasn't that a beautiful name to call Jesus?

The two followers were John and Andrew. As John the Baptist talked, Jesus turned and walked away and John and Andrew followed Him. They wanted to know more about the Lamb of God. Jesus knew they were following Him and He asked, "What seek ye?" That means: "What are you looking for?"

They answered with a question: "Where dwellest thou?" Dwell means **live**.

Jesus knew why they asked that. They wanted to go home with Him and learn all about Jesus Christ, the Son of God; and Jesus took them home with Him. Oh, how they loved to listen to Him! When they left Jesus' house, they ran to tell their friends all about Him. They were **sure** He was Jesus Christ the Savior! First they found Andrew's brother, Simon Peter, and then **he** ran to find Jesus.

Jesus **wanted** John and Andrew and Simon Peter to come to Him, because they were going to be His disciples. Disciples are followers and helpers. Jesus called two more disciples, Philip and Nathanael. Now Jesus had five disciples with Him: John, Andrew, Simon Peter, Philip, and Nathanael. Soon He would call more disciples to be with Him; and they would stay with Him all the time He lived on the earth.

Three days after Jesus had called the five disciples to Him, they went to a wedding in the small town of Cana. We do not know who was being married, but we do know that Jesus' mother Mary was at the wedding, too. In those days a wedding often lasted more than a whole day — sometimes two or three days, or even seven days.

At the wedding feast they ran out of wine. Maybe the people who gave the wedding were poor and could not buy enough or maybe extra people — like Jesus and His five disciples — came. When Jesus' mother heard about it, she said to Jesus, "They have no wine." She knew He was the Son of God and she thought He should show His power and do something.

Jesus answered, "Woman, what have I to do with thee?"

Do you think it was strange that Jesus called His mother "woman"? No, it wasn't. He was trying to make His mother understand that even though she was His mother and He was her Son, He was also the Lord; And she might not ever tell Him how to show His great power. He was Lord of heaven and earth.

Even though Jesus scolded His mother a little, she told the servants to do exactly what Jesus told them to do. She still thought He would show His power. And He did.

In the house were six big empty waterpots. They usually held water for baths or for washing dishes. Jesus told the servants to fill those waterpots with water, and they filled them to the brim. Now Jesus told them to draw some of the water out and serve it. The water was wine.

Usually, when God makes wine, He makes a grapevine grow and get grapes. When the juice is pressed out of the grapes and stands a long while to get strong, it becomes wine. Making wine out of grapes is a wonder of God.

But at the wedding feast Jesus made a special wonder. He did not need to grow a grapevine. In an instant Jesus made **water** into wine. We call it a miracle. The ruler of the feast, who did not know about Jesus' miracle, told the servants they were working backwards: the good wine was supposed to be served **first** and the poor wine **last;** and they were serving the good wine last. The good wine was Jesus' wine.

When Jesus worked His miracle, He wanted it to be a picture of something much better than wine; for wine is a picture of the joy and happiness that He gives to those who believe on Him. It is a picture of the happiness of heaven.

REMEMBER:

When we see a grapevine, we should remember that it is a picture of Jesus, for He said, "I am the Vine." We are the branches of His vine, and He feeds us with His wine of happiness. Isn't that a beautiful picture to think about?

Jesus Goes to the Passover Feast

Every year the people of Israel went to Jerusalem at the time of the passover feast. Now it was time for the feast again and Jesus traveled to Jerusalem with His mother and brothers and sisters. When they came to Jerusalem, they went first to the temple. What a busy place it was! So many people had come to the feast. Many of them had come a long, long way, and had not taken with them a lamb to sacrifice on the altar.

So the store-keepers set up little shops in the yard of God's temple and sold the people the animals for their sacrifices. The yard did not look at all like the yard of God's holy temple. People were pushing, and animals were crying. The yard of God's house was crowded and noisy and dirty. People who were buying animals or selling animals were trying to cheat one another.

What did Jesus do? He found some small pieces of rope lying around and made a whip out of them. With the whip He chased out the store-keepers and the customers. He chased out the animals, poured out the store-keepers' money, and tipped over their tables. Then He told them **why** He did it: they might not make His Father's house a store for buying and selling. Jesus' Father is God. When Jesus called God His Father, He was telling those wicked Jews that He was the **Son of God.**

And all those wicked Jews, the buyers and the sellers, obeyed Jesus. They did not talk back to Him. They did not fight. Why not? Because Jesus showed them that He was the Son of God. He showed to them His power from heaven and they did not dare to do anything. They knew Jesus was right: that God's house was a house where they must love Him and praise Him and pray to Him. Even though they knew that Jesus was right, those wicked Jews obeyed Him only because they had to; and they began to hate Jesus.

All the while that Jesus was at the passover feast, He showed that He was the Son of God; for He worked many miracles. Remember, miracles are wonders. The Bible does not tell us what kinds of miracles He did. It does tell us that many people believed in Him when they saw His great miracles.

One man, whose name was Nicodemus, watched Jesus closely. Nicodemus was a ruler in Israel, a great and rich man. He knew all about God's laws, for he had been learning about them for years and years. And he thought that if he would obey God's laws very carefully, God would save him and take him to heaven. He thought he could go to heaven by making **himself** holy.

But when he watched Jesus' wonders and listened to Him talk, Nicodemus felt troubled inside. How he wished he could talk with Jesus. But he did not dare. The other rulers did not like Jesus, and they would hate Nicodemus if he talked with Jesus. So he went to Jesus secretly, at night, when no one would know about it. This is what he said to Jesus: "Rabbi, we know that thou art a teacher come from God." He knew that Jesus could not do those great wonders unless God was with Him.

Poor Nicodemus was all mixed up. Couldn't he save himself by being good after all? Did he need Jesus, the Son of God? Jesus could see into Nicodemus' heart and He knew what Nicodemus was thinking; and Jesus answered him, "Except a man be born again, he cannot see the kingdom of God."

Nicodemus did not understand Jesus' words at all. How could he be born when he was old? Must he become a baby all over again?

Then Jesus told him what He meant. Jesus meant that God had to put His grace and Spirit into Nicodemus' heart and give him a new heart that believed that Jesus would die on the cross for his sins. When God made Nicodemus believe in Jesus, He was a new person **inside**. He was born again to a new kind of life. Now he could see that Jesus' kingdom was the kingdom of heaven.

REMEMBER:

We are just like Nicodemus. We cannot make ourselves holy for we are sinful, just as Nicodemus was. But when God makes us to be born again, He gives us hearts that believe His promise that Jesus died for us and that we will live in heaven with Him forever.

Jesus and the Samaritan Woman

At the time that Jesus lived on the earth, the land of Israel was divided into two parts: Judea and Galilee. Between the two parts was a land called Samaria. The people who lived in Samaria were people from all kinds of countries and they had a very mixed-up kind of worship. They worshipped Jehovah-God but they worshipped the idols of other lands at the same time. The Jews in Israel hated the Samaritans and their gods and would not have anything to do with them.

If the Jews had to go from one part of Israel to the other, they usually traveled **around** Samaria, not **through** it. Jesus did not do that. He was God and He knew all things. He knew He **must** travel through Samaria. He had a special reason for going there: He came to bring the good news that He was the Savior to the Samaritans, too.

Jesus and His disciples left the passover feast at Jerusalem and all morning they walked under the hot sun toward the middle of the land of Samaria. It was noon when they came to a place called Sychar. At Sychar was a well of water which Jacob had dug many, many years before. Hot and tired, Jesus sat down at the well, probably on a stone wall which was built all around wells in those days, and rested while His disciples went into the town to buy some food.

As He sat there, He saw a woman of Samaria coming to draw water out of the well; and Jesus said to her, "Give me to drink."

Oh, that Samaritan woman was surprised! The Jews hated the Samaritans. They hardly ever said a word to them. She said to Jesus, "How is it that thou, being a Jew, askest drink of me, which am a woman of Samaria?"

It seems as if Jesus didn't answer her question, for He told her if she knew Who was talking to her she would ask Him for living water, and He would give it to her.

But the Samaritan woman did not understand what Jesus was saying. She did not know anything about living water. She kept talking about drawing water from the well that Jacob had dug. She knew that Jacob was one of God's children. Was Jesus greater than Jacob, she wondered?

Once more, Jesus did not exactly answer her question. He started to tell her all about the living water which He could give. He told her that whoever drank of the water from the well — just plain, ordinary water — would get thirsty again; but whoever drank of the living water would never be thirsty again. Do you know what Jesus' living water is? It is being friends with God. It is having His love and His mercy. Without that living water we would all die in hell for our sins. But Jesus came to save us from our sins — because He loves us. We cannot drink that living water with our mouths. We drink it inside our hearts.

Jesus was making the Samaritan woman thirsty for **that kind** of water, His **living water**. She said, "Sir, give me this water."

Then Jesus asked her to call her husband. She had to tell Jesus, "I have no husband."

Jesus showed her that He was God Who knows everything when He told her that she had lived a very wicked life; for she had already had five husbands, and the man who lived with her now was not really her husband. Jesus knew all her secrets.

The Samaritan woman knew that Jesus was a prophet from God. But she did not know how to worship God. She was a Samaritan and worshipped God in Samaria. The Jews worshipped God in the temple at Jerusalem. Where was the **right** place? Then Jesus explained to her that the place does not matter, for God is a Spirit, and God's people can worship Him in their hearts, wherever they are.

The Samaritan woman told Jesus one thing more: that Jesus Christ, the Savior, was coming, and He would tell them everything they must know. Don't you think she was surprised and happy when Jesus said to her, "I that speak unto thee am he"?

I think we would have liked that Samaritan woman. She forgot all about her waterpot at the well and ran into the city to find her friends. She was bubbling over with the good news and kept saying, "Come, see a man, which told me all things that ever I did: is not this the Christ?"

Her friends listened to her and followed her out of the city until they came to Jesus. They begged Him to stay with them and He taught them there for two days. Many of them believed, not because of the Samaritan woman, but because of the words of truth which Jesus taught them. Before Jesus left, they said these beautiful words: "for we know that this is indeed the Christ, the Savior of the world."

REMEMBER:

Jesus made the water that we drink from a glass to be a picture of the living water, the water of His love and mercy, which He pours into our hearts. Aren't we glad that He makes us thirsty for Him?

463

Jesus in Galilee

Our last story told that Jesus left the passover feast in Jerusalem and walked through the land of Samaria on His way to the other part of Israel, called Galilee. When He at last came to Galilee, the people there were glad to see Him. They had been to the passover feast, too, and had seen all the wonders that Jesus had done there. He probably had made many sick people well. Now the people of Galilee were wondering what kinds of miracles Jesus would do next.

The people were glad to see Jesus, but He was not happy with them. He could see into their hearts, and He knew that they were glad **only** because they saw His great miracles. They did not want a Jesus Who had to die on the cross to save His people. And Jesus had to scold them for their wicked hearts.

While Jesus was there in Galilee, a nobleman came to Him. A nobleman is a very important servant of a great ruler. He was so sad and worried that he had come twenty miles to see Jesus. He begged Jesus to come back to his city with him to make his son better; for his son was very sick and had such a high fever that he was ready to die.

This is what Jesus said, "Except ye see signs and wonders, ye will not believe." Why did Jesus say that to the nobleman? Because most of the people wanted to see His great wonders. That is **all** they wanted to see. They would not believe that He was the Son of God. Jesus was saying to the nobleman: you just want a miracle; you don't want to believe my words. Jesus was testing the nobleman. Was he like all the rest of the Jews in Galilee? Oh, no! He didn't give up. He showed to Jesus and all the people that he believed in Him by quietly saying, "Sir, come down ere my child dies."

Jesus knew the nobleman believed and He told him, "Go thy way; thy son liveth." The nobleman believed Jesus' words. He did not need any more signs. He knew his son was better.

It was very early in the afternoon when Jesus said those words to the nobleman. If he hurried, he could ride those twenty miles back home before it became dark. But he didn't hurry. He stayed overnight and went home the next morning. And he **knew** that when he got home his son would be better. Sure enough, his excited servants went out to meet him with the good news that his son was all better. They could tell the nobleman the exact time: very early yesterday afternoon the boy was better all of a sudden. He was sick one minute and the next minute his fever was gone and he was well. The nobleman knew, and we know, that it was exactly the time that Jesus said these words to the nobleman: "Go thy way; thy son liveth." And the nobleman and his family and all his servants believed on Jesus.

As Jesus walked through the land of Galilee, He came to the town of Nazareth, where He had lived when He was a boy. He knew the people of Nazareth and they knew Him. On the sabbath day He went into the synagogue — something like a small church building — and preached to the people of Nazareth. There never was a better preacher than the Lord Jesus, for He is **God!**

When He preached, He told them how He had come to save His people whose hearts were broken because they had sinned so much, whose eyes were blind to God because their wickedness got in their way, and who were tied with chains of sin by the devil. Jesus told them that He came to mend their broken hearts, to give the light of heaven to make them see again, and to break the chains of the devil. He was going to save His people!

Were the people of Nazareth happy? No, they did not believe His words. They called Him the son of Joseph, the son of a man — not the Son of God. Jesus' words made them so angry that they stood up and rushed Him through the city to the sharp edge of a steep cliff and they were ready to push Him off. They wanted to kill God's Son.

They could not do it, of course, for it was not time yet for Jesus to die. By a wonder Jesus walked away from the angry mob of people, and they had no power over Him.

REMEMBER:

There are always two kinds of people in the world and we can't see the difference on the outside. There are those with hard hearts like the people of Nazareth who will not believe Jesus and there are those with soft hearts like the nobleman who love Him and believe in Him. Thank God every day that He has given us soft hearts so that we may believe.

The Miracle of Catching Many Fishes

Jesus left the city of Nazareth where the people had tried to push Him off a high cliff and He went to the city of Capernaum, which was on the shore of a beautiful sea called the Sea of Galilee.

Do you remember that Jesus had called five men to be His followers — His disciples? Those men were Simon Peter, Andrew, John, Philip, and Nathanael. They followed Jesus, but they did not stay with Him **all** the time. Sometimes they went back to the kind of work they did before Jesus called them. Do you know what that was? Fishing. They were fishermen on the Sea of Galilee.

On the day that Jesus was in Capernaum, He went out to the shore of the sea and many, many people followed Him. They were so eager to hear Jesus preach. As the crowd of people got bigger and bigger, they pressed closer to Jesus to see Him and to hear Him better. They were almost pushing Him off the shore into the water.

As Jesus turned around and looked into the water, He saw the empty fishing boats of His disciples. They had been fishing all night and now that it was morning they were on the shore cleaning their fishing nets. In those days the fishermen did not use fishing poles, but they let down large nets into the water to catch the fish. When Jesus saw the empty boats, He stepped into Simon Peter's boat and asked him to row it out a little way from the land; and from the boat on the lake Jesus taught the huge crowd of people on the shore.

After Jesus had finished teaching the people, He asked Simon Peter to row Him to the deep water of the lake and let down his nets into the water. Jesus wanted Simon Peter to go fishing. But Simon Peter did not feel like it. He told Jesus that he had been out fishing all night and had not caught a thing. Besides, morning was a bad time to catch fish. He was tired and sleepy, and he should be on the shore cleaning his fishing nets.

But he said to Jesus, "At thy word I will let down the net." That means that even though he did not feel like fishing, if Jesus said so, he would go.

Andrew was with Simon Peter and Jesus in the boat and together they let their huge nets down into the water. Suddenly they caught so many fishes in their net that it broke. It could not hold so many fishes! They had to call to James and John who were fishing in another boat to come and help them. When they had filled both boats with the fishes they had caught, the load was so heavy the boats began to sink.

When Simon Peter saw what happened, he sank down on his knees before Jesus and said, "Depart from me; (that means **Go away from me**) for I am a sinful man."

Can you see why Simon Peter said that? He and the other disciples were very good fishermen. He knew there were no fish in that place. They had fished there the whole night before. Now suddenly there were too many for them to hold. Simon Peter knew it was a great miracle. Jesus, by His great power from God, brought those fishes there. When Simon Peter saw that He was in the boat with the Holy God, it was too much for him. He felt like such a poor, weak, sinful man. But Simon Peter should not have told Jesus to go away from him. No one may say that to Jesus. He said those words before he thought them through. He should have said, "Be merciful to me, Lord Jesus."

Why did Jesus work the miracle of catching so many fishes? He used the great miracle to teach His disciples that from now on they were going to catch **men**, not fishes, and they were going to catch **men** only through **His** power. They were going to go with Jesus all the time, wherever He went as He preached to the people and put His Spirit into their hearts so that they would believe in Him. They would be fishers of men! Jesus called James to be His disciple, too, so now there were six disciples. They obeyed Jesus and left their homes and their fishing boats and followed Him because He called them.

REMEMBER:

Jesus calls us to be His disciples, too. We do not have to leave our homes to follow Him. He makes us want to leave our sins — all our naughty thoughts and actions — and say to Him, "I will follow Thee."

469

Jesus Heals the Man With a Devil

In this story, Jesus was still in Capernaum, the city on the shore of the beautiful Sea of Galilee. On the sabbath day He went to church — they called it the synagogue — and preached to the crowds of people who came to hear Him. The people had never heard anyone preach the way Jesus preached. When their teachers, called the scribes, preached, they read all the laws over and over to them and told them over and over again to obey those laws. But they never said anything about the love they must have in their hearts. Jesus' preaching was different. He spoke right to their **hearts** and He told their hearts to be **happy,** for He had good news! He was their Savior from sin!

The people were surprised to hear Jesus' words. They listened so closely to Him! They were so interested! Suddenly, in the quiet church, someone shouted and screamed a horrible scream. It was a man who was screaming. He was shouting to Jesus, "What have we to do with thee?"

What was the matter with the man? Why did he scream? He had the most miserable trouble a man can have. A devil, one of the wicked servants of Satan, had forced his way into the man's body. No one could see the devil, for he was a spirit without a body. When Satan gave this devil-spirit power, it was stronger than the man, and when he came into the man, he lived in his body. He even talked for the man. The devil took over his whole body and the poor man had no power to fight him.

When that poor man shouted, it was the devil's voice shouting from inside the man. He could not stop the devil from talking; and the devil went on and said to Jesus, "I know thee who thou art, the Holy One of God."

Jesus did not want the devil to talk to Him, even when the devil called Him the Holy One of God. He told the devil-spirit to keep still. Then He ordered the devil to come out of the man and he had to obey, because Jesus has all the power over the devil-spirits. But this devil was so very evil that he tried to hurt the poor man as much as he could when he came out of him. He threw him and he tore his body, but Jesus did not let him **really** harm the man.

How happy that poor man must have been. He was free from that awful devil-spirit. And how he must have thanked Jesus. In the synagogue, the people were so excited and happy. They were filled with wonder for now they knew that Jesus had power even over the devils.

Right after the church service in the synagogue, Jesus and His disciples went to the home of Simon Peter. But there was sadness in Simon Peter's home. His wife's mother couldn't go to church that morning because she was sick, very sick. She had a very high fever. When they told Jesus how sick she was, He went to her and scolded the fever and the fever left her. It was all gone that very minute. And she did not get better **slowly**, either. Her high fever did not leave her very weak and tired. No, she was all better that very minute. She got right up and started to help serve the food for the meal that they had. How happy she must have been to take care of her Lord Jesus, Who had just done such a great miracle on her sick body.

By this time the whole city of Capernaum was excited. The news about the man who had the devil cast out from him and about Simon Peter's wife's mother just flew through the city. Everyone, but especially those who were sick, wanted to go to Jesus.

That evening, as the sun was going down, Jesus found almost everyone from the city at His door. There were many, many sick people in the days when Jesus lived, and they all wanted to come to Jesus. Maybe He would make them better. He did. He felt sorry for the poor people who were suffering and He put His hands on them and by the wonder of His power He made them better.

That is not all that Jesus did that evening; for Jesus had to teach the people that He was not just a kind of Wonder-doctor Who made people better. Oh, no! He told the people that when He healed all their sicknesses, He was making a picture of healing them from something much worse than their sicknesses — **their sins.** He would go to the cross and take all the sins and the sadness of His people away and make them clean and take them to their perfect home in heaven where there is no sickness and no sin.

REMEMBER:

Jesus tells **us,** too, that these beautiful stories of how Jesus made people's bodies all better are pictures of how He makes our hearts and souls all better from their black and ugly sins. He tells us in the Bible that He has taken all our sicknesses and all our sins upon Himself.

Jesus Heals
Two Men

What a busy day that sabbath day of healing the sick had been for Jesus! Early the next morning, long before it was light, Jesus was up. He went alone to a quiet place where He could get away from all the people and pray to His Father in heaven. His disciples had to look for Jesus that morning, and when they found Him, Jesus would not go back to the city of Capernaum. He wanted to preach in other towns, too.

In one of the towns a man with leprosy came up to Jesus. Remember, leprosy was a terrible sickness. First, sores would come on a person's body, often his hands or face. Sometimes the sores turned his skin white and dead. Sometimes the sores opened up and made his body rot and parts of it fell away. This poor man's body was partly living and partly dead. No wonder leprosy was called a **living death**! People with leprosy had to live separately; and if anyone came near them, they had to shout, "Unclean! Unclean!"

On this day the man whose whole body was full of leprosy, so full that he was almost dying, came running through the crowds to Jesus. And the people must have made a big wide path for him, for no one would come near such a leper. The leper did not care. He had one thing in his mind: to fall down and worship Jesus. He said, "Lord, if thou wilt, thou canst make me clean."

Jesus was so sorry for the poor leper. He touched him. It was against the law to touch a leper. But Jesus' touch was different. His touch was the touch of the wonder of His grace; for He said to the man, "I will: be thou clean."

That very minute the leprosy was all gone and the man was perfectly well again. Then Jesus told him to go to the priests and show them that he was really clean from his leprosy. Before that happy man ran off to the priests, Jesus told him not to tell anyone about this great wonder. But the man **couldn't** obey Jesus. For years he had been walking in a living death. Part of his body was rotted away. Now he was healthy. And he was wildly happy! The happy news just burst from his heart and streamed from his mouth, and he told everyone he saw.

Could **we** keep still if Jesus made **us** better from leprosy? Leprosy is a picture of sin, you know, which makes us dirty and rotten. Sin is a living death just as leprosy is a living death. When Jesus feels sorry for us and touches our hearts with His grace and makes us clean from our sins, **we** are happy, too, aren't we? **We** tell everyone, too, don't we?

A few days later, Jesus went back to Capernaum and was preaching in a house. So many people came to hear Him that not one more person would fit in that house. Many people were standing around the door.

But four men carrying a sick man on a mat **had** to get near to Jesus. The man was so very sick. He had palsy. That means that his body was stiff and paralyzed and he could not use his arms or his legs. He had to be carried around and helped with everything. Oh, that poor, sick man wanted so much that Jesus would heal him.

The four men carrying the man with the palsy would never be able to get through the crowds. So they got to Jesus another way. They climbed a stairway or a ladder on the outside of the house to the flat roof and began to make a hole in the roof right on top of the place where Jesus stood. When the hole was big enough, the four men let the sick man down with ropes right in front of Jesus.

There the sick, helpless man lay, quiet and afraid, and ashamed; for he believed that Jesus was God, and he knew that Jesus knows all things. Jesus knew that the man had sinned especially bad sins and that he needed to be forgiven. So the first thing Jesus said to him was, "Son, thy sins be forgiven thee."

Some of the rulers of the Israelites heard Jesus' words and they were very angry. They did not believe that Jesus was God. They said that only **God** can forgive sins. Jesus had to prove to those wicked rulers that He was truly God. So He asked them a question: "Whether is easier, to say, Thy sins be forgiven thee, or to say, Rise up and walk?"

Then Jesus gave them the answer. He said to the man with the palsy, "Arise, take up thy bed, and go unto thine house."

He proved to them that He could heal sicknesses and forgive sins; for the man who couldn't even move got up, picked up his sleeping mat, and walked away, praising God. And all those who believed thanked and praised God for His wonders.

REMEMBER:

This story tells how happy Jesus made His people. Do you know that God's people are happy people? When He gives us happy hearts, we thank Him and praise Him all day long.

475

Jesus Calls Levi and Heals a Man With Palsy

You remember, don't you, that the people of Israel — the Jews — had no king of their own. For years and years the wicked world power had ruled over them. At the time when Jesus was on earth the world power was in Rome; and the Roman king made all the rules for them. The people of Israel had to pay money, called taxes, to the king of Rome; and the men who collected the taxes were called publicans.

Oh, how the Jews hated the publicans! They hated them because most of the publicans were cheaters who stole the people's money. Most of them charged more money than they were supposed to and put the extra money into their own pockets.

As Jesus was walking from one city to another in Galilee, He saw a publican sitting at his table, collecting taxes from the people. The publican's name was Levi. Jesus said only two words to him: "Follow me." Levi got up, left his tax table, and followed Jesus.

Levi's other name was Matthew. Maybe, before Jesus called him to follow Him and to be His disciple, Matthew had cheated, too, and taken too much money from the people. He must have heard about Jesus and His great wonders. Now he was so glad that Jesus had chosen him.

Because he was so happy to follow Jesus, Matthew-Levi made a great feast — a party — in his home and he invited other publicans to the feast, too. Some of the teachers of the Jews, called the Pharisees, watched the feast. They were not happy. Here was Jesus, sitting down at a feast with the very worst kind of people, the publicans — the lowest of all the people. To His disciples they said, "How is it that he eateth and drinketh with publicans and sinners?"

476

When Jesus heard it, He told them a little story. He said that a man who is very strong and healthy does not call a doctor. He doesn't need one. Only a very sick man calls a doctor. He needs a doctor. Jesus' story to the Pharisees had a meaning. He was telling them that **He** was the Doctor and He came to save the sick, but the Pharisees did not believe that they were sick. The publicans knew that **they** were the sick ones. They were dying in their awful sins. Jesus was the Doctor, Who had to say to them: "Be sorry for your sins! Believe on Me, and I will save you from your sins!" And many publicans believed.

After He called Matthew-Levi to be His disciple, Jesus traveled to the city of Jerusalem to a feast in the temple. Near one of the gates of the city of Jerusalem was a pool, a special pool, called the Pool of Bethesda; and it had five porches around it. Many sick people sat on those porches, waiting. For every once in a while an angel from God came and made the water bubble and ripple, and the first person who stepped into the pool after the angel had rippled the water was made better of his sickness.

One man was lying on a porch, but he could never be the first one in, for he had the sickness called palsy. He was paralyzed and could not move by himself. His sick friends would not help him, either. They were all too busy trying to be the first one into the water. For thirty-eight years that poor man had been lying there, paralyzed.

Jesus, Who knows all things, saw him lying there. He knew how long the man had been there and He knew that the only way the man would get better was through a wonder. He asked, "Wilt thou be made whole?" Whole means better.

The man answered, "Sir, I have no man to put me into the pool; but while I am coming, another steppeth down before me."

Jesus said to him, "Rise, take up thy bed, and walk."

The man got right up, took his sleeping mat, and walked away. By the wonder of Jesus' power he was better. Wouldn't you have liked to see his face? He was walking! He could use his arms! He was all better! And Jesus had done the wonder on a happy day — the sabbath day.

Now watch his face as the teachers of the Jews came and scolded him for carrying his sleeping mat on the sabbath day. They had a rule that no one might do that. The man said that the One Who had just made him all better had told him to carry his mat. He didn't know that the One Who had made him better was **Jesus**. All he thought about was that he could **walk!** But the wicked Jews didn't even care that he was better. They thought only of their silly rule.

The man went into the temple and there Jesus found him and said, "Thou art made whole: sin no more."

Now the man knew that it was Jesus, God's own Son Who had made him better; and he told the wicked Jews. What did they do? They tried to kill Jesus because He worked His great wonder on the sabbath day.

REMEMBER:

The sabbath day is our Sunday. God made it a special day; and when Jesus was on earth He used it to do works for God's glory. So do we. We worship Him and sing to Him and pray to Him and love Him when we go to church.

Jesus Teaches About the Sabbath Day

Shall we leave the city of Jerusalem and travel back with Jesus to Galilee, the other part of the land of Israel? Jesus did not want to stay in Jerusalem any longer. The Pharisees, those wicked teachers of the Jews, were making plans to kill Him because He healed a man with the palsy on the sabbath day. Those Pharisees were jealous of Jesus, and they hated Him, too.

So Jesus and His disciples walked the long, long way back to Galilee. Even then they could not get away from the Pharisees. Those wicked rulers followed Him. They did not follow Him because they wanted to hear His beautiful words or see His great miracles. No, they followed Him to try to find something wrong — to see whether they could find a reason to kill Jesus.

As Jesus and His disciples walked through the fields of Israel on the sabbath day, the disciples picked a few ears of corn from a farmer's field, rubbed the kernels from the corn, and ate them as they walked along. That was not stealing. Remember, Israel was **God's** people, and He told them in His law to love one another and share their fields with hungry people traveling through them.

Those wicked Pharisees were watching every move of the disciples and now they saw the disciples doing something wrong. They were picking corn on the sabbath day. The Pharisees couldn't wait to ask Jesus why His disciples were breaking the law when they picked corn and ate it on the sabbath day.

But the Pharisees forgot something: the disciples were not breaking **God's** law; they were breaking one of the **Pharisees'** laws. Oh, those Pharisees had so many, tiny, silly laws about what they might not do on the sabbath day. And Jesus scolded them. He told them that **He** was the Lord of the sabbath day and that His people must use the sabbath day to worship God, to love one another, and to do good works. The Pharisees could not understand that, for their hearts were hard and stubborn. But we can, can't we?

On another sabbath day, maybe the next one, Jesus and His disciples went into a synagogue and Jesus began to teach the people. Sitting in the synagogue listening to Jesus was a man with a withered, dried-up hand. The Pharisees were sitting in the synagogue, too, spying on Jesus again; and they saw the man with the withered hand. Their foolish law said that a doctor might make a man better on the sabbath day **only** if he were dying. Now, the man with the withered hand surely wasn't dying. They wondered what Jesus would do. Would He make his hand better?

They asked Him a question: "Is it lawful to heal on the sabbath day?" Lawful means **right**.

Jesus answered them by asking a question: if one of your sheep fell into a deep hole on the sabbath day, wouldn't you pull it out? He asked them next whether it was right to do good on the sabbath day or evil, to save life or to kill.

The Pharisees knew the answers to Jesus' questions but they did not want to tell Him it was right to do good on the sabbath day, so they kept quiet and would not answer.

Jesus looked with an angry face at them and yet He had a sad face because their hearts were so hard. He called the man with the withered hand to Him and said, "Stretch forth thine hand;" and He made it better, just like his other hand. Then the Pharisees left and once again made plans to kill Jesus.

After that, Jesus went to a quiet mountain spot and chose the rest of His followers, His disciples. He already had chosen seven of them: Simon Peter, Andrew, James, John, Philip, Nathanael, and Matthew. He chose five more: Thomas, another James, Judas, another Simon, and Judas Iscariot. Now He had His twelve disciples. These disciples were going to stay with Jesus and be His helpers all the time that He was on earth.

REMEMBER:

We are Jesus' disciples, too. We cannot walk with Him on the earth because He has already gone to heaven. But we can listen to His words from the Bible and follow Him with our hearts every day of our lives. Some day we will walk with Him in heaven.

The Centurion's Servant and the Widow's Son

Do you know that there were many soldiers from Rome in Israel? These soldiers did not fight, but they helped to rule over Israel. They kept order. They were heathen men who worshipped idols, and the people of Israel did not like them.

But there was one Roman soldier who was different. He was the captain of one hundred soldiers and was called a **centurion.** This man did not love the heathen idols of the Romans. He loved the people of Israel and had even spent his own money to build them a synagogue where they could worship God. This centurion had heard of Jesus, too.

He had a servant whom he loved dearly. That servant was very sick with the palsy and he had great pain in his body. He was so sick that the centurion knew he was dying. And he wished his dear servant would not die.

When he heard about Jesus' wonderful miracles, the centurion knew what he would do: he would ask Jesus to make his servant better. But he did not dare to come to Jesus. He was not a Jew. He was a heathen. He did not think he was good enough to come to Jesus. So he sent some of his friends who were Jews to ask Jesus to come and make his servant better.

The Jews came to Jesus and begged Him to heal the servant. They told Jesus that the centurion was a good man and had even built them a synagogue. Jesus agreed to go with the Jews, but before they came to the centurion's house, he sent more friends to meet Jesus. These friends had more words from the centurion. He told them to tell Jesus not to trouble Himself to come to his house. His house was a heathen home, not good enough for Jesus to visit. The centurion told his friends to tell Jesus that he, a Roman, a sinner, wasn't good enough to stand next to Jesus. But he asked Jesus to say only a word and his servant would be healed. He believed that Jesus' **word** was the power of God.

Oh, Jesus was surprised that the Roman centurion had such great faith in Him. He told the people that were with him that He didn't find such great faith even in the people of Israel. And Jesus **did** say the word of power. He said, "Go thy way; and as thou hast believed, so be it done unto thee."

The word of Jesus made the servant better that very hour. The word of Jesus did one thing more: it made the centurion believe that Jesus was his Savior. Jesus' word **saved** the centurion.

The next day Jesus and His disciples walked through a little town called Nain. At the gate of the town they met a crowd of people, very sad people. For someone had died and the people were walking with the dead body outside the town to bury it in a grave.

Who had died? A young man, the only son of a widow. A widow is a lady whose husband has died. She had only one son and she must have had to take care of him all alone. Can you think how much she loved her only son? Now, just when he was old enough to help take care of his mother, he had died. No wonder the poor mother was crying and all her friends were crying with her.

When Jesus saw the sad mother, He felt sorry for her and said, "Weep not." He said that because He knew that He was going to take her sadness away. Then He walked over to the coffin where the dead young man lay; and the men who were carrying the coffin stood still. Jesus said, "Young man, I say unto thee, Arise." And the young man sat up and began to talk.

Now a sad day had turned into a happy day. They did not have to go to the grave! What great happiness must have come into that mother's heart! And the crowds of people were so surprised that it made them afraid. This was such a great wonder! A dead man came back to life! They knew that this wonder had flashed down from heaven and they glorified God.

We know that when Jesus took the young man's hand and gave him life, He gave him life out of **Himself**. The Bible calls Jesus the Resurrection and the Life.

REMEMBER:

Some day we will have to die, too, and be buried in a grave. But one day, at the end of the world, Jesus will take us by the hand, too, and raise us to life. Then we will live in heaven forever.

Simon and the Woman

The teachers of the Jews who were called the Pharisees thought very much of themselves. They thought they were very good men. After all, they studied God's Word and obeyed every law that God had made. They made even **more** laws for themselves and the people to obey. They taught the people that if they obeyed those laws they would go to heaven. The Pharisees obeyed God's law on the **outside,** with their bodies, but on the **inside,** in their hearts, they did not love and obey God at all; and they hated Jesus, Who is God's Son.

One of the Pharisees named Simon invited Jesus to his house for dinner. We do not know why such a wicked Pharisee would ask Jesus to come for a meal. Maybe he wanted to ask Jesus some questions. Simon was a **proud** Pharisee. That means he thought very much of himself. He was an impolite one, too. For in those days it was polite to give people a basin of water to wash their hot, dusty feet when they came into a house; and it was polite to greet them with a kiss of friendship; and it was polite to sprinkle some cool perfume over their hair. Simon did not do any of these things to Jesus.

Then the meal started. In those days poor people might come in and stand against the walls and watch the rich people's dinners; and at Simon's feast people were watching as the guests ate.

Suddenly a woman stood at Jesus' feet. All the people in the room must have become very quiet as they looked at that woman. They knew who she was: a bad woman, a woman who lived a wild, wicked life. What was this woman doing? She was standing at Jesus' feet. Remember, in those days, people did not sit in chairs to eat. They lay down on couches. There, at the end of His couch stood the woman, crying. She was crying so many tears that they ran over His

feet. Her tears were washing Jesus' feet.
Then with her long, loose hair she dried Jesus'
feet. Next she poured very expensive
perfume over Jesus' feet.

No one was talking. And Jesus did not
stop the woman. But Simon the Pharisee was
thinking wicked thoughts. He thought to
himself that if Jesus were **really** a prophet,
He would know what kind of wicked sinner
was touching His feet.

Jesus knew what Simon was thinking and He said, "Simon, I have somewhat
to say unto thee."

Simon answered, "Master, say on."

Jesus told him a little story. Two men owed another man some money. One
man owed him only fifty pieces of money but the other man owed him five
hundred pieces of money. Those men were poor. Neither one could pay back the
money they owed. So the rich man said he would forgive them both — they
wouldn't have to pay it.

Then Jesus asked Simon a question: "Which of them will love him most?"

Simon answered, "I suppose that he, to whom he forgave most."

Simon knew that the one who owed him most would love him most; and
Jesus said that his answer was right.

Then Jesus told Simon what His little story meant. He told how He came
into Simon's house and didn't even get water to wash His feet. He got no kiss and
no perfume for His hair. But the woman washed His feet with her tears and
dried them with her hair, she never stopped kissing His feet, and then she put
perfume on them.

What a difference between Simon and the woman! Simon thought he had
hardly any sin. He thought he did not need Jesus. And he knew he did not love
Jesus. The woman knew what an awful sinner she was. Her sins were too big a
load for her to carry. So she went to Jesus and cried about all her sins and Jesus
told her, "Thy sins are forgiven."

The woman loved Jesus the most, for she knew how much Jesus had forgiven her. He had taken her whole load of sins away. Jesus told her: "Thy faith hath saved thee; go in peace."

Very soon after this Jesus did another great wonder. The people brought to Him a man who was blind, who could not speak, and who had a devil in him; and Jesus healed him. The man suddenly could see and talk and the awful devil inside him was gone. When the people saw that Jesus did three wonders in one great miracle, they said, "Is not this the Son of David?" They meant that they believed that this was the Christ, the Son of God, born from the family of David.

The proud and wicked Pharisees did not like to hear the people speak these words. They did not want the people to believe in Jesus. So they made up a terrible story. They said that Jesus could cast a devil out of a man because a devil inside Jesus helped Him do it. Jesus told the Pharisees that those were the worst kinds of words that could ever come from their lips. God would not forgive those words.

REMEMBER:

We are like the woman in our story. We all carry big loads of sin. We must go to Jesus every day to ask Him to take those loads of sin away. When He does, we are so happy and we love Him so much.

The Parable of the Four Kinds of Soil

When Jesus taught the people, He often told stories and these stories were always pictures of heavenly things. We must remember that God made our earth to be a picture of the new heaven and earth; and He did that because He wanted to give us a little look into His heavenly things. We call these picture-stories that Jesus told **parables.**

One day Jesus sat at the seashore. Soon crowds of people came to Him and Jesus did what He had done once before: He went into a boat a little way into the lake and taught them from the boat.

All of Jesus' parables to the people were about things that we see around us on the earth. This parable was about a farmer. Everyone in that huge crowd of people knew how a farmer worked in those days. There were no tractors yet, and no big farm machines. In those days a farmer divided his farm into small fields and each field had a path around it so the farmer could walk to his fields very easily. In the springtime when he planted his seed, he carried a big sack at his waist, took handfuls of seed from the sack, and scattered the seed over his fields. Oh, yes, they all knew how farmers worked in those days.

In His story, Jesus told where the farmer's seed fell:

some fell straight down on the hard path where the farmer was standing;

some fell on a thin layer of soil — soil is dirt — with a thick layer of stones and rocks under it;

some fell on soil where weeds and thorns were already growing;

some fell on good ground, soft and freshly plowed.

That was Jesus' story. What did it mean? Of what were all those things pictures? Let us start with the seeds in the farmer's bag. Each seed had a hard shell around it, but inside it was a **living thing.** It could grow into a plant. That seed was a picture of God's Word. We know, don't we, that God's Word is a **living thing** in our hearts. The farmer who scattered the seed is a picture of Jesus. He preached His Word to the people in Israel. Now He is in heaven and He still preaches His Word to us through the mouths of our ministers.

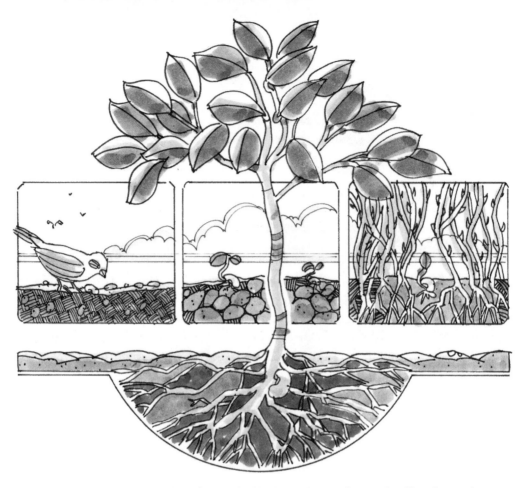

A seed will not grow in a farmer's dry bag. It needs good soil, rain, and sunshine. Now we will talk about all the different kinds of soil where the seeds fell and tell how they are pictures.

The seed that fell on the hard path couldn't grow. People had walked on the path and packed the soil tight so that the seed could not dig in. The birds came and ate that seed. That kind of soil is a picture of a man whose heart does not love God's Word. His heart is hard. If he goes to church, he does not want to listen to God's Word. Maybe he falls asleep. Then the devil, like the birds, comes and takes away the seed of God's Word from the man's hard heart. We call him the **hard-soil** hearer.

The seed that fell on the thin layer of dirt on top of hard stones and rocks dug down into the thin soil and started to grow a little bit. But when the roots hit the hard rocks, it could not grow anymore. The plants withered and died in the hot sun. That kind of soil is a picture of a man who has a happy face and seems very happy to hear God's Word. It **seems** as if God's Word is going right into his heart. But when troubles, like the hot sun, come to the man, he is not so happy anymore. Maybe he wants to live a sinful, wicked life and not be sorry for those sins. He is the man who has a hard heart underneath a thin layer of a little bit of happiness. We call him the **thin-soil** hearer.

489

The seed that fell where weeds and thorns were already growing started to grow along with the weeds and thorns. But the weeds and thorns were so much bigger than the tiny seed-plants because they had a head start; and soon they choked out all the sunlight, and the plants died. That kind of soil is a picture of the man who hears God's Word but who has so much trouble listening to it. He likes to think about all the nice things in his life: his good food, his nice car, and his good times on his vacations. All those thoughts choke out the thoughts of God and His Word. We call him the **thorny-soil** hearer.

These three kinds of hearers, the hard-soil hearer, the thin-soil hearer, and the thorny-soil hearer really do not want to hear God's Word. They have hard hearts and they are not interested.

The seed that fell on good soil that was plowed and soft and fertilized began to grow and kept right on growing into beautiful, tall, strong plants. That kind of soil is a picture of a man whose heart God has made ready for His seed. He has the Holy Spirit of God living in his heart. The Holy Spirit makes him love God's Word, makes him sorry for his sins, and makes him want to obey God with all his heart. He is one of God's own dear children and he grows up to be one of God's plants on the earth. We call him the **good-soil** hearer. We, too, are good-soil hearers, by God's grace.

REMEMBER:

The next time we see a farmer working in his field, shall we remember that God has made it to be a picture of the preaching of His holy Word?

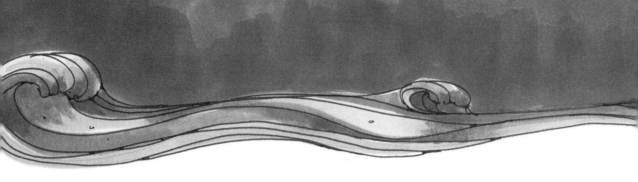

Jesus Stills the Storm and Heals the Man With Devils

For hours Jesus had been teaching the people, telling them parables like the one we had in our last story. He was still in the little ship in the Sea of Galilee, teaching the crowds who sat on the shore. The people never seemed to get tired of hearing Jesus, but toward evening Jesus was very tired. He sent the people home and asked His disciples to row the ship over to the other side of the sea. They took Jesus along with them just as He was, without stopping on the shore for food. A few small ships followed the ship of Jesus and His disciples; and Jesus lay down in the back part of the ship, put His head on a pillow, and fell fast asleep.

Often strong winds and fierce storms came very suddenly on the Sea of Galilee, but Jesus' disciples were not afraid of these storms. They were very good sailors and they were used to the storms. On this night as Jesus lay sleeping in the ship, God sent one of those fierce storms. This storm was so much worse than the other bad storms on the sea. It was so rough and wild that the tall waves covered the ship and the ship was full of water. The disciples had never seen one so bad and those brave sailors were terribly afraid. They thought they would all drown!

They ran to Jesus, woke Him up, and asked Him: "Master, carest thou not that we perish?"

491

Jesus stood up and scolded the storm. He said only three little words, "Peace, be still," and the winds stopped blowing and the sea was calm. In that quick second Jesus' power **as God** shone through Him and His word of power stopped the fierce, wild storm.

Then Jesus looked at His disciples and asked, "Why are ye so fearful? how is it that ye have no faith?"

But the disciples' hearts were almost more afraid of the great wonder than of the great storm. It was almost too much for them to think that Jesus had all power over the winds and the waters of the sea and they asked, in great surprise, "What manner of man is this, that even the wind and the sea obey Him?" We know that He is **God!**

Do you know that this great miracle is a picture of **us?** No, we are not in a big storm on the Sea of Galilee. But we are in a ship. What kind of ship? The ship of the **church** — that's what the Bible tells us. The Bible makes a picture of the church as a ship, with God's people in it. Sometimes God sends storms of troubles to us in the church. Sometimes the devil tries to tip us out of the ship of the church. But Jesus is with us in the ship and He always says, "Peace, be still;" and then we don't have to be afraid.

After the storm the ship landed on the other side of the Sea of Galilee. As soon as Jesus and His disciples were on the shore, a man met them, a man with a terrible storm **inside** of him. This poor man didn't have only **one,** but he had **many** devils living inside of him. These devils made the man their slave. They ruled his whole body, they talked through his mouth, and they hurt him. They made the man act like a wild, crazy man.

The devils would not let the man live with other people. It was not safe to come near him, for he was very strong. He lived alone and ran screaming through the quiet cemetery, where the graves of dead people were. If he was quiet for a few minutes, his keepers tried to keep him quiet by tying him with heavy chains, but he would soon break those heavy chains and run wild again. All the time he knew how miserable he was with those devils in him, and he would cry out loudly and cut himself with stones. Maybe it was the worst suffering Jesus and His disciples had ever seen. We can't even think how terrible it was.

When he saw Jesus, the man knew Who He was, and ran and worshipped Him. But the devils in him didn't want him to do that! They shouted, through the man's mouth, "What have I to do with thee, Jesus, thou Son of the most high God?"

Jesus asked the man his name and he answered, "Legion." That name means **many: many** devils.

Then Jesus said, "Come out of the man, thou unclean spirit."

The devils knew they had to obey Jesus. If they came out of the man, they would have to go to hell and they did not want to go to hell just yet. So they asked Jesus to send them into a herd of swine — swine are pigs — who were eating on the hillside; and Jesus said, "Go." As soon as the devils went into the swine, all two thousand of them ran headlong down the steep hillside and were choked and drowned in the sea.

The news of this wonder traveled like lightning. Soon the owners of the swine came running and they saw that all their swine were gone. They saw more. They saw the man, with clothes on and in his right mind, sitting with Jesus. And the owners of the swine were angry! They asked Jesus to go away. They would rather have their swine than Jesus, Who saves His people from the power of the devil.

REMEMBER:

That poor man was a picture of us. Without Jesus our hearts are all in the power of the devil. But when Jesus scolds the devil and chases him away and puts His own love in our hearts, we worship Him. For He gives us a new life and new clothes. We call those new clothes **robes of salvation.**

Jesus Raises Jairus' Daughter

After Jesus had cast many devils out of the man on the other side of the Sea of Galilee, He and His disciples rowed back across the sea again. There on the shore all the people were standing, waiting for Him. But before Jesus could leave the seashore, a man came running to Him and fell down at His feet. The man's name was Jairus and he was the ruler of one of the synagogues. Most of the rulers of the synagogues were wicked Pharisees who hated Jesus. Jairus was different. He believed in Jesus.

He fell down at Jesus' feet because he had such sadness inside his heart. His only little girl who was twelve years old was dying, and he begged Jesus to come to his house. He believed that if Jesus touched her, she would be better. Jesus went along with Jairus, down the road to his house; and the crowds of people walked along, too.

In the crowd was a very sick woman who had been losing blood for twelve years. She had gone to many, many doctors and had spent all her money trying to get better, but no one could help her. She got worse instead of better. This woman had heard of Jesus and all the wonders He did. She believed that His power to heal was so great that she would not even have to bother Him. If only she could touch Him — or touch His clothes — she knew she would be healed. And no one needed to know about it.

She pushed through the crowd behind Jesus and touched the border — the hem — of His coat. In that instant her bleeding stopped and she felt in her body that she was all better. Before she could go away quietly, Jesus asked a question: "Who touched me?" Jesus knew that power had gone out from Him because the woman had touched Him with a special touch, the touch of **faith**. She **believed** on Him!

No one answered Jesus. Peter and the rest of the disciples tried to tell Him that the people were walking so close to Him, pressing against Him on all sides and how could they know who had touched Him?

Didn't Jesus know who touched Him? Doesn't He know all things? He surely does! Jesus knew, but He wanted that woman to be touched by more than the hem of His coat. He wanted her to be touched by His love. Jesus did not want her to keep her happiness a secret! He wanted her to tell about it.

Now the woman knew that she **had** to tell. Trembling and afraid, she fell down before Jesus and told all the people how she had been healed by touching the border of Jesus' coat. Jesus said her faith had made her better. He healed her body and saved her soul inside her and He said to her, "Go in peace."

While Jesus was still talking to the woman, some servants from the house of Jairus ran up to them with the sad news that it was too late for Jesus to make the little girl better. She had died. They told Jairus not to trouble Jesus any longer. But Jesus kept on walking. He said to Jairus, "Fear not: believe only, and she shall be made whole."

When they came to the house of Jairus, Jesus did not like what He saw. In those days the sad people in whose house someone had died would pay money to men and women who would cry loudly all day long. Jesus did not like that loud crying and He scolded them for all their noise. He told them, "The damsel is not dead, but sleepeth."

Jesus **meant** that she was sleeping the sleep of death. But the people who were making the loud cries stopped crying and laughed and poked fun at Jesus. Jesus ordered them all to go away and they obeyed Him. He is **the Lord**, you know, and they had to obey Him.

Quietly, with only the little girl's father and mother and three of His disciples, Peter, James, and John, Jesus went into the room where the girl was lying. He took her by the hand and said, "Maid, arise;" and she got up and walked. She did not have to stay in bed and wait to get better slowly. No, she was suddenly alive and strong and well. Her mother and father and the three disciples were so surprised by this great miracle that they could hardly believe their eyes. They couldn't understand the power of the Lord Jesus! They acted as if they were shocked. They even forgot that the little girl had not eaten very much when she had been sick; and Jesus had to remind them to give her something to eat.

It was a great wonder. Jesus had just showed to His disciples and the mother and father of the girl that He is the Lord over death. He has power to make alive again.

REMEMBER:

When we die, we sleep, too. We will sleep longer than Jairus' little girl did. We will sleep until the end of the world. At the end of the world, Jesus will touch us and make us stand up and live in the new heaven and earth, where we will never be sick anymore.

Jesus Heals Two Blind Men and Sends Out the Disciples

Soon after Jesus left the house of Jairus, two blind men followed Him and kept calling to Him. They called Him a different kind of name. They kept saying, "Thou Son of David." They knew that Jesus would be born from King David's family and when they cried, "Thou Son of David," they were telling everyone that they believed that Jesus was the promised Christ from David's family.

Yet Jesus did not seem to pay any attention to them. He let them go on calling Him. Why? He wanted them to **show** their faith in Him so everyone could see it. When Jesus went into a house — we don't know whose house it was — the two blind men followed Him inside. Inside the house they said, "Thou Son of David, have mercy on us." They wanted to see so badly! They wanted Jesus to do a miracle on them!

Then Jesus asked them a question: "Believe ye that I am able to do this?" They answered, "Yea, Lord."

When Jesus heard their answer, He touched their eyes and both the men could see. Maybe it was the first time in their lives that they could see. Their faces were so full of happiness and their hearts felt so glad. They weren't blind anymore! That is when Jesus told them not to tell anyone that He had made them see. Oh, how could those happy men keep their mouths shut about such a great wonder?

Why did Jesus ask them not to tell? Because their blindness was a picture of a much worse kind of blindness: a blindness **toward God.** Jesus was thinking of all the people who were walking around with the darkness of sin in their hearts. They were so blind they couldn't even see God. And Jesus had come, not just to heal blind eyes, but to put light into His people's hearts and to save them by dying on the cross. Jesus did not want His people to forget it. They might not think only about blind eyes.

But those blind men couldn't keep still. They were bubbling over with happiness. They told the news in every part of the country. If Jesus made **our** eyes to see and put His light into **our** hearts, could **we** keep still?

Everywhere Jesus went crowds of people were waiting for Him. Some wanted to hear His teachings, his story-parables, and many wanted to be healed of their sicknesses. Jesus felt sorry for the crowds of people. He told the disciples that the people looked like sheep who have no shepherds and He said that they looked like a big field of crops ready to be harvested into barns, but there was no one to cut down the crops.

What did Jesus mean by those two little pictures of the people? He meant that the people needed more **helpers,** more **teachers,** more **leaders.** Who would

498

those helpers and teachers and leaders be? The twelve disciples. They had been watching Jesus and listening to His teachings for a long time. Now Jesus was going to train them to be teachers and preachers and leaders.

Jesus knew that His disciples might be afraid to go alone, so He sent them out two by two. What did they have to preach to the people? They had to tell the people to be sorry for their sins and to believe in Jesus, for the kingdom of heaven was come. Jesus gave His disciples special signs, too, to show that they really did come in the name of Jesus. He gave them special, heavenly power to heal sick people, make lepers better, cast out devils, and even raise the dead. The disciples were only men, and Jesus gave them all these great heavenly powers.

He told them not to pack a suitcase with clothes, not to take an extra pair of shoes, not to take money, and not to take a lunch. Is that a good way to go on a preaching trip? For the disciples it was, for they had to learn to trust that God would give them what they needed. Besides, they were going to preach to God's people and God's people must always take care of their preachers gladly and give them what they need.

Jesus told the disciples that when they came to a city they must **look for** those who believed; and if the people truly did believe, the disciples must bless them with God's peace. But if they could not find believers and no one in the city would listen to their preaching, they must shake the dust of that city off their feet and then leave.

REMEMBER:

Nowadays we still must take care of the preachers who preach the good news of Jesus Christ. When we love them and help them and take care of them, God still blesses us with the best kind of blessing: His peace in our hearts.

The Death of John the Baptist

Quite a long time ago we heard a story about John the Baptist. He was the young man who grew up in the desert and preached to the people to be sorry for their sins. For Jesus was coming! It was John the Baptist who saw Jesus coming and said to the crowds of people, "Behold the Lamb of God, which taketh away the sin of the world."

Do you remember him? He kept preaching to the people for a little while longer and then he did not preach anymore. In this story we will leave Jesus and His disciples and see what had happened to John the Baptist.

He **couldn't** preach anymore because he was in prison. Wicked King Herod, who was ruler over the Jews, had put him there. What had John the Baptist done? He had preached to King Herod and scolded him; for King Herod had left his own wife and married his brother Philip's wife, whose name was Herodias. God's law said that no one might marry another man's wife; and John the Baptist preached the words of God's law to King Herod. The king wouldn't listen to him. In fact, he became angry when he heard John the Baptist's words, so angry that he put him in prison.

For a year already he had been in prison. King Herod was afraid of him, for he knew that John the Baptist was a man of God who told him the truth; and many times he asked John to come out of prison to talk to him and he gladly listened while John told him the way God wanted him to live. But King Herod was never sorry for his sins and he would never walk in God's way. His wife, the wicked Herodias, hated John the Baptist and she tried her hardest to kill him, but King Herod kept him safely in prison.

Then it was King Herod's birthday and he had a great feast for all the important rulers in the land. He loaded his tables with the best food he could find and plenty of wine; and everyone ate until he could eat no more and everyone drank wine until he was drunk. Now it was time for all of them to sit back and have a good time.

King Herod had an idea. He called Salome, the daughter of Herodias his wife, to dance for them. Salome came and danced a very wicked dance and everyone at the feast liked it. King Herod was very pleased with Salome and in a loud voice so that everyone could hear, he promised to give her anything she would ask for. That was a foolish promise, wasn't it?

Salome did not know what to ask for, so she ran to her mother and said, "What shall I ask?"

This was Herodias' chance! That wicked woman had been begging and begging King Herod to kill John the Baptist, and he wouldn't do it. Now Herodias could get Salome to help her. She told her daughter to ask the king for the head of John the Baptist. Back to the noisy feast went the dancer Salome and asked King Herod for the head of John the Baptist on a platter. Can't you hear how still that loud feast became — how everyone stopped talking and laughing as he thought about the awful killing of John? They were all shocked!

King Herod was, too. He didn't want to kill John the Baptist. What was he going to do now? He could choose: either he could say that he would not keep such a foolish promise that he had made after he had drunk too much wine or he could show the guests at the feast that he would keep his promise even though he had to kill a prophet of the Lord. He chose the second one and sent a soldier to go to prison and cut off John the Baptist's head and put it on a platter for Salome. What a terrible ending to a very wicked feast.

When the followers of John the Baptist, who loved him dearly, heard the awful story, they went to the prison and took his dead body and buried it in a grave, with sadness and love. And when the disciples of Jesus told Him about it, He asked them to take Him into a ship to a quiet place in the desert to rest awhile. They needed rest for their bodies and for their hearts and souls inside of them; and while they rested, they prayed that God would give them peace in their sad hearts.

King Herod did not ask God for peace. God did not have any peace for the king who killed His prophet. King Herod knew what a cruel murder he had done and every day it bothered him. He was afraid and all upset. Yet he would not be sorry before God.

When King Herod heard that Jesus was teaching and preaching and when he heard about the great wonders He was doing — how He healed lepers and the blind and how He cast out devils — he thought he knew who Jesus was. He was John the Baptist raised from the dead! **We** know that John the Baptist was in heaven with God; but King Herod did not believe that, and he never had any more peace in all his life.

REMEMBER:

It was good for Jesus and His disciples to come away and rest awhile in a quiet place. It is good for us, too, to be in a quiet place to rest awhile with Jesus — to sing, to pray, or to think about a beautiful Bible story.

Jesus Feeds the Five Thousand and Walks on the Water

When Jesus heard that King Herod had killed John the Baptist, He sent the crowds of people away and went across the sea with His disciples to rest in a quiet place. The crowds of people watched them sail across the Sea of Galilee and they ran along the shore, to meet Jesus on the other side. They would not let Him alone. Jesus and His disciples did not get much rest. Just as they were alone on a quiet mountainside, the crowds of people came running to them.

Although Jesus really wanted to rest with His disciples, He went out to the people because He felt sorry for them. He taught them many things and He healed many sick people. Time seemed to go so fast that day and soon the disciples reminded Jesus that it was getting late in the day and that they were in a lonely desert place without any food. They told Jesus to send the people away before it was too late so they could buy food for themselves in some of the little towns nearby.

Jesus answered them, "Give ye them to eat."

How could the disciples do that? Feed such a huge crowd of people? They didn't have food even for themselves. While they were wondering what they could do, Jesus came to Philip, one of the disciples, and asked, "Whence shall we buy bread, that these may eat?"

Jesus knew how He was going to feed the people, but He wanted to **test** Philip by asking him that question. Philip answered Jesus that two hundred pennies' worth of bread would not be nearly enough and they didn't have so much money anyway. Then Andrew came up and said that a little boy in the crowd had five loaves of barley bread and two small fishes. "Maybe, just maybe," Andrew must have thought, "Jesus will do a wonder." But how? So aloud he said, "But what are they among so many?" Andrew was right. Five loaves of bread and two small fishes would feed only a few people.

Let us stand next to Andrew for a minute on that mountainside, with its covering of fresh spring grass, and watch the sun ready to go down. Then let us watch the crowds of people. Jesus separated them into groups, with fifty people in each group. What a lot of groups of fifty people were sitting on that mountainside; for about five thousand men plus all the women and children were in that huge crowd.

Jesus stood in front of the quiet groups of people and prayed a prayer of thanks to God and then began breaking the bread and the fishes. He gave the food to the disciples and they kept running back and forth to the people, giving them bread and fishes that never stopped coming from Jesus' hands. At last, after everyone had eaten enough, Jesus sent His disciples to gather up the leftovers, and they gathered twelve baskets full. Much more food was left over than what Jesus had started with. That great wonder was a picture of a greater wonder: just as Jesus gave the bread **of this earth** to the five thousand people, He gives the **Bread of Life** to His children when He saves them and feeds them with His goodness first on this earth and then in heaven forever.

Then the miracle was over. Soon it would be dark. Jesus sent His disciples back to the ship and told them to sail across the Sea of Galilee. He stayed on the mountainside and sent away the crowds of people. When they were finally gone, He stayed alone on the mountainside to pray.

You remember, don't you, that storms came up very quickly on the Sea of Galilee. On this night a great wind started to blow and the ship was rocking on the high waves. The disciples were in the middle of a terrible storm. Although they tried very hard to get across, by the middle of the night they were still only halfway. They were helpless in that dangerous sea.

Alone on the mountain, praying, Jesus kept His watchful eyes on His disciples. Then He got up and went to them. We know that He holds even the strong seas in His hand and He made a path for Himself on the stormy waves. He walked right on top of those waves and acted as if He would walk right past the disciples. Those tired disciples, troubled by the fierce storm, looked up and cried out in fear. Oh, they were afraid! They thought they were seeing a ghost.

But Jesus called out, "Be of good cheer: it is I; be not afraid."

Peter, the disciple who was quick to talk, called out, "Lord, if it be thou, bid me come unto thee on the water."

Jesus said, "Come."

With faith in Jesus, Peter climbed out of the ship and walked on top of the waves to Jesus; for Jesus, by His wonder-power, kept Peter up. But then poor Peter looked at the waves towering all around him. He saw what wild, rough waves he was walking on. He forgot to look at Jesus. He began to sink and he cried out, "Lord, save me."

Jesus looked with mercy on him, stretched out His hand and caught Peter. He scolded Peter, too, and said, "O thou of little faith!"

As soon as Jesus and Peter came into the ship, the storm stopped and at that very minute, without rowing the ship anymore, they were at the other side of the sea. That, too, was a wonder.

REMEMBER:

We are just like Peter. When we are in trouble or in danger, we look all around us and we are so afraid. The only thing we can do is look up to Jesus. He will take our hands and keep us safe.

Two More
Miracles

We have heard so often in our Bible stories that the Lord chose **Israel** to be His people. We remember that He sent prophets to preach to the people of **Israel**; and Jesus was born to the **Israelites**. In those days the people of Israel were God's people and only once in a great while did Jesus preach to people from other countries.

In this story we will hear about a woman from another country who was saved by Jesus. As He went from one place to another place in the land of Israel, He came to a house and there He wanted to rest quietly for a while. Jesus did not want anyone to know where He was, but He could not be hidden. The people were so eager to be with Jesus that they always managed to find out where He was; and in that house the crowds found Him.

Along with the people who came to the house was a heathen woman, a Greek, who did not even live in Israel. If you looked at her face, you would see that she was very troubled and unhappy. You would see more on her face. You would see that she had made up her mind to talk to Jesus. If you listened, you would hear her say, "Have mercy on me, O Lord, thou Son of David."

Why? Her daughter had a devil living inside her and that devil hurt her little girl so badly that the mother could hardly stand it. If only Jesus could make her daughter better!

But Jesus did not pay any attention to her. She did not give up but kept calling to Jesus. At last the disciples asked Jesus to make her daughter better so they would be rid of her — she was bothering them. That wasn't a very good reason, was it?

Then Jesus gave the woman what seems to be a hard answer. He told her that He was sent to the sheep — that means the **people** — of Israel. And this woman was not an Israelite. She was a heathen. Did that stop her? Oh, no! She came closer to Jesus and worshipped Him and said, "Lord, help me."

Jesus had another answer for her, and this time it was a picture-answer. He said, "It is not meet to take the children's bread, and to cast it to dogs."

Jesus made a picture of children, the children of Israel, sitting around His table. **They** were the ones He came to save. The dogs in His picture-story were not pet dogs but wild dogs. These wild dogs were the heathen people like this woman. Jesus made a picture of her being a wild dog that everyone hated.

Did those words stop her? Oh, no! She said, "Truth, Lord: yet the dogs eat of the crumbs which fall from their masters' table."

What crumbs did this heathen woman want from the table of Israel? The crumbs of Jesus' love and mercy. She believed in Jesus. She had faith in Him, for God had put His grace into her heart. And Jesus said to her, "Great is thy faith." Her faith in Jesus was so great that **nothing** could stand in its way. At that very instant Jesus cast out the devil and made her daughter better.

Jesus went on, then, and walked to a mountain. When He had walked up a little way, He sat down. On that mountainside the crowds came to Him and He healed blind people, crippled people, crooked people, and all other kinds of sick people. He healed so many that day that the crowds couldn't quite take it all in; and they kept on praising God.

Then a deaf man stood in front of Jesus. Never in his life had he heard a sound. This deaf man could not talk, either, for his tongue was tied down in his mouth. When Jesus saw him, He took the man away from the crowds, all by himself. Why? Because this man had never yet talked with anyone. He had always lived all to himself. Now Jesus wanted the man to pay close attention to Him.

Jesus talked to him in sign language. First He put His fingers into the man's ears. Then He spit on His finger and touched the man's tongue. The man could understand what Jesus was going to do, don't you think? Jesus did one thing more: He made the man look at His lips as He said, "Eph-pha-tha." That means, "Be opened."

The man understood and suddenly he could hear and talk. Jesus told the man not to tell anyone, but the poor man had never in his life talked before. Now he couldn't keep still! And all he could do was praise God.

REMEMBER:

The heathen woman knew that Jesus was the Bread of Life. We know it, too. She wanted the crumbs of that Bread of Life, the crumbs of mercy and of kindness and of love. We do, too.

Jesus Feeds Four Thousand People and Heals a Blind Man

As Jesus walked through the land of Israel preaching and teaching, He came to the very edge of the country of Israel. All around Israel lived heathen idol-worshippers. These people had heard of Jesus, too, and crowds of them left their work to follow Him. For three days they had been with Jesus, walking where He walked, and listening to all His words.

Now it was time for Jesus to send them home, but He had pity on them because their food was all gone. Whatever food they had taken with them they had eaten during those three days; and Jesus told His disciples, "If I send them away fasting to their own houses, they will faint by the way." Many had come a long, long way to hear Jesus. Yes, they **must** have something to eat before they left.

When Jesus talked to His disciples about it, they asked Him, "From whence can a man satisfy these men with bread here in the wilderness?"

They had asked almost the same question just a few days ago, before Jesus had fed the five thousand people. What was the matter with the disciples? Couldn't they remember the great miracle Jesus had done with the five loaves of barley bread and the two small fishes? Of course they could. But their faith in Jesus, Who is the God of the Wonder, was not very strong yet; and when they were in trouble or needed something they tried to trust in **themselves** instead of looking to **Jesus**.

Once more Jesus asked the same question He had asked a few days ago when the five thousand people were in front of Him: "How many loaves have ye?"

They answered, "Seven, and a few little fishes."

Then Jesus told the tired, hungry crowd of people to sit down on the ground. He prayed a prayer of thanks to God and broke the bread and fishes and fed the people until everyone had had enough. The bread and fishes kept coming from his hand. When the disciples picked up the leftovers, they had seven baskets full. And after they had counted the people sitting on the ground, they found out that four thousand men besides all the women and children had eaten the bread and fishes which Jesus' wonder-hand had given them.

The wonders of Jesus feeding the **five thousand** people and the **four thousand** people were quite a bit alike. But they were different, too. Most of the four thousand people were not Israelites. They were heathen people living near Israel and when Jesus fed them with a picture of the Bread of Life, He was showing them that His mercy and His salvation were for **them**, too. Don't you think they were happy that Jesus came to save them, too?

After Jesus sent away the crowds of people, He went to the shore of the Sea of Galilee again; and the people there brought a blind man to Him, begging Jesus to touch him and make him see. Jesus took the blind man by the hand and led him all the way outside the little town, where He and the blind man could be alone.

Then He spit on His fingers and put them on the blind man's eyes. He asked the man whether he could see anything. Looking up, the man answered, "I see men as trees, walking."

He meant that he could not see clearly yet. Everything was still blurred and people did not look like people, but he **could** see that they were walking. Once more Jesus put His hands on the blind man's eyes and then he could see everything clearly.

Why did Jesus put His hands on the blind man's eyes **twice?** Because the man's blindness was so **deep.** His sight had to come all the way through the deep blurs that his awful blindness caused him, all the way to perfect eyes so he could see everything clearly.

His blindness was a picture of the deep blindness of our sins. Jesus has to take us, too, from the deep blindness of our sins and pull us all the way to His perfect sight.

REMEMBER:

Jesus said, "I am the Light of the world." When He puts His Light into our hearts, He saves us from the dark blindness of sin and gives us the bright sunlight of heaven. In heaven we will have perfect eyes to see His light.

The Transfiguration

Jesus had been preaching and teaching and working for two years already; and now He started to talk more and more with His disciples about what was going to happen to Him. He told them that soon He would have to suffer and then He would have to die a cruel, shameful death by hanging on a cross. He told them that he **must** die that hard, painful way to save His people from their sins. But the disciples did not like to hear Jesus talk about those sad things and they didn't understand how it would happen.

It wasn't quite time yet, and before He suffered and died on the cross, a great wonder happened. Jesus left the rest of the disciples near the bottom of the mountain and took three of His disciples, Simon Peter, James, and John up on a mountain with Him. Jesus loved those mountains, where He could quietly pray to God His Father.

As Jesus and His three disciples were praying on the mountain, Jesus' face began to shine brightly as the sun and His clothes were white as the light. Moses and Elijah, who had been with God in heaven for a long time, came down from heaven to be on the mountain with Jesus. They talked with Jesus about the terrible suffering He would soon have to bear at Jerusalem.

512

At first the three disciples with Jesus did not see all this glory from heaven, for they had fallen deeply asleep while they were praying. When they awoke, they saw that they were suddenly getting a little peek into the bright, white glory of heaven. They couldn't understand it all but they thought it was wonderful. As they looked in great wonder at the beauty from heaven God was showing them, they hoped it would not go away. Especially Simon Peter wanted to hold on to this beautiful glory and he said, "Master, it is good for us to be here." He wanted to build three tents, one for Jesus, one for Moses, and one for Elijah. Poor Simon Peter did not know what he was talking about. Could all that heavenly glory stay in tents on the mountain? Oh, no.

Just then a bright cloud came over them all and the disciples were so afraid that they fell flat on their faces. Then they heard God's voice saying, "This is my beloved Son: hear him."

When the disciples dared to lift their heads and look around them, they saw that they were alone with Jesus and Jesus told them not to talk about the glory they had seen on the mountain until after He was risen from the dead. But the disciples could not help **thinking** about it. They must have asked themselves many questions. Why did God send Moses and Elijah to talk with Jesus? We know the answer: to comfort Him and to help Him before He had to suffer so dreadfully for His people. Why did those three disciples have to see the beautiful glory of heaven? We know that answer, too: so that when they saw Jesus dying on that cruel cross they would know that the cross was Jesus' way to His bright, white, heavenly glory.

Then Jesus and His three disciples walked down the mountain. What a huge crowd of people was there at the bottom! There seemed to be something wrong. Sure enough, the teachers of the Jews were having a big argument with the rest of the disciples who had stayed there at the bottom of the mountain. When the crowds saw Jesus, they all rushed towards Him.

513

Jesus asked the teachers of the Jews and His disciples what they were arguing about, but they kept quiet. They didn't want to tell. Then a man, the father of a boy with a devil inside him, came up to Jesus. He told Jesus how that devil hurt and tore the boy's body when he threw the boy to the ground, and how the devil tried to throw the boy into the fire to burn him, or how he tried to drown him in the water. It was too much for the boy. He was wasting away and was almost dead.

The father of the boy told Jesus how he had asked His disciples to cast that devil out of his son and they could not. **That** is why the teachers of the Jews were arguing with the disciples: because they had no power over that devil.

Jesus said to the father, "If thou canst believe, all things are possible to him that believeth."

The father answered, "I believe; help thou mine unbelief."

Then Jesus ordered the devil to come out of the boy and as it left him, it hurt the boy's body so badly that he fell down as if he were dead; but Jesus lifted him by the hand and gave him to his father.

REMEMBER:

When Jesus was on earth He prayed to God His Father very often. He loved to pray to God. God is our Father, too, and we must do what Jesus taught us to do: to pray often. Do you love to pray?

The Tax Money and the Ten Lepers

Many years ago, when Moses was still living, God told him to charge the people of Israel money when they came to God's house. After Solomon built the temple the rulers used that money to repair it. All though the years God's people paid a piece of money for the temple. It was called the temple tax.

Every year the people were supposed to pay a piece of money and every year men from the temple went all over Israel to collect the tax money from the people. When they came to Simon Peter, they asked him whether Jesus paid the temple tax and Simon Peter, without bothering to find out whether Jesus did or not, said, "Yes."

Before he could tell Jesus about it, Jesus showed Simon Peter that He knew all about it already. For Jesus knows everything. He asked Simon Peter a question: where does a king get his money from — his own children or from strangers? Now Peter knew that children do not have to pay money to get into **their own** houses. We don't have to pay to get into our father and mother's house, do we? And kings don't take money from their own children. So Simon Peter answered Jesus that kings get their money from other people, from strangers.

That was the answer that Jesus wanted. Then He went on to teach Peter. He told him that **He** did not have to pay the temple tax because He was God's Son. The temple was **His Father's** house. And Jesus did not have to pay money to go into His own Father's house. No, Jesus did not have to pay any temple tax.

But the teachers of the Jews couldn't understand how God could be Jesus' Father, because Jesus **looked** like a man. Many of them did not even believe that Jesus was the Son of God. Because they could not understand, Jesus told

515

Peter that He would pay the tax money for His Father's house; and to get that money Jesus chose to do a wonder. He told Simon Peter to go to the sea with his fishing pole and throw out his hook to catch a fish. He had to hold the first fish that he caught, open its mouth, and find a piece of money in it. That is the money he had to pay for Jesus and for himself.

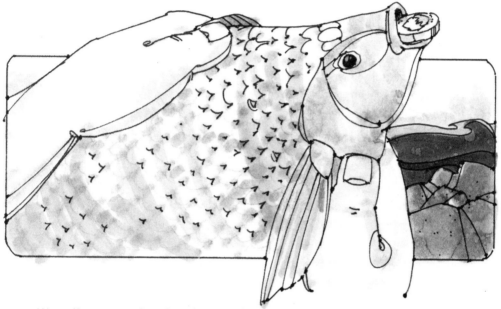

We call our temples **churches** and in our churches we don't have to pay tax money to get in. For when Jesus died, He paid for all His children **with His blood**. That is the greatest price He could pay.

Jesus was thinking so much these days about the death on the cross that He would soon have to die. He talked to His disciples about it, too. He would have to die in the city of Jerusalem; and it was time for Jesus and His disciples to go there. Do you remember that the land of Samaria was between the two parts of the land of Israel? And do you remember that the people of Samaria were not Israelites, but a mixed kind of people, from all different lands? Jesus had to go through Samaria to get to Jerusalem.

Just as Jesus and His disciples came to the edge of the land of Samaria, ten men who had leprosy stood far away from them and called, "Jesus, Master, have mercy on us." They had to stand far away, for leprosy was such a dreadful sickness that they might not come near healthy people. Nine of these lepers were Israelites and one was a Samaritan, whom the Israelites hated. All of them had heard about Jesus and knew He could make them better by the wonder of His power.

When Jesus saw them and heard them cry to Him for mercy, He said, "Go show yourselves unto the priests."

If a leper was made well, he always had to show the priests that he was clean from all his leprosy. As those happy lepers set out to find the priests, they could feel in their bodies that they were healthy again. Their leprosy was gone!

Nine of the lepers kept on running, but one turned back; and he was the Samaritan. Why did he turn back? Watch that Samaritan leper. He was praising and glorifying God with a loud voice. He wanted everyone around to hear what God had done for him. Then he fell down on his face at Jesus' feet and gave Him thanks.

Jesus answered all this by saying, "Were there not ten cleansed? but where are the nine?"

Where were they? Far away, probably still running. Those nine lepers who were Israelite lepers were not God's children and they did not believe in Jesus. They did not thank Him, either.

The Samaritan, from a heathen country, needed much more than a healthy body. He needed Jesus to save his soul from sin. That is why he came back. Jesus told him, "Arise, go thy way: thy faith hath made thee whole."

The Samaritan went away with a new body and a new soul, saved by Jesus; and he had a song in his heart.

REMEMBER:

We need Jesus to take care of us every day and give us healthy bodies. But we need more than that. We need Him to save our souls from the leprosy of sin. That is what we need most of all. When He takes away our sins and gives us clean hearts, we always remember to thank Him, don't we?

Jesus Visits Bethany and Heals a Blind Man

Before Jesus and His disciples went to the city of Jerusalem, they stopped in a little town called Bethany. In this little town lived three of Jesus' dear friends, Mary, Martha, and Lazarus. Jesus liked to stop at their home to talk and to rest. Mary and Martha and Lazarus loved Jesus, too; and when He came they tried to make Him so comfortable.

Mary and Martha gave Jesus and His disciples water to wash their dusty feet and then served them a meal. After the meal, in those days, it was time to talk; and Jesus did the talking. He taught all the people in the house with beautiful words about the kingdom of heaven. Mary wanted to hear those words so badly! She loved Jesus so much! And she believed His words!

So Mary sat down with the rest of the guests to listen to Jesus' words. Her sister Martha loved the Lord Jesus, too. But she had a different kind of nature inside her. She wanted to be busy **doing things** for Jesus. She wanted to have her home neat for Jesus and be ready to serve Him anything He wanted. She was so busy. And her sister Mary wouldn't help her. She just sat and listened.

At last Martha complained to Jesus and said, "Lord, dost thou not care that my sister hath left me to serve alone?"

Jesus had to tell Martha that she was troubled too much about little things and that Mary had chosen the good part — to sit and listen to Jesus. Martha really chose the good part, too, for she loved Jesus and believed on Him, but she let her housework get in her way. Jesus had to teach her that it is better to sit at His feet and listen to Him as Mary did.

After that, Jesus went to Jerusalem and there He saw a blind man begging. His disciples saw the man, too, and asked Jesus why he was blind. Was it a punishment for a sin he had done or a sin his parents had done? Jesus answered them that there was another reason: so that Jesus might do a wonder on his eyes and show that He is the Light of the world.

The blind man could not see Jesus, of course; and Jesus worked His wonder with a sign that the blind man could **feel**. He spit on some clay on the ground and when it was wet He put it on the eyes of the blind man and told him to wash in the pool of Siloam that was nearby. After he washed, the man walked away **seeing**.

The blind man who could see must have had such a different look on his face now; and his friends didn't know if he was the blind man or not.

Some said, "This is he."

Others said, "He is like him."

The blind man said, "I am he."

Then they were all very interested and they crowded around him, asking, "How were thine eyes opened?"

He told them about the man called Jesus Who put clay on his eyes and told him to wash in the pool of Siloam. And then he could see!

519

His neighbors wanted to see Jesus, too. They asked, "Where is He?" But the man did not know.

Everyone was happy until the Pharisees, those wicked teachers of the Jews, asked the man how he could see. So he had to tell the story all over. But the Pharisees were not happy, for Jesus had healed the blind man on the sabbath day. Besides, they did not believe that the man really had been blind and now could see. So they called his father and mother and asked, "Is this your son who ye say was born blind?"

They answered, "We know that this is our son, and that he was born blind."

His father and mother would not talk about Jesus, the Man Who made him see, because they were afraid of those wicked Pharisees. They knew how the Pharisees hated Jesus.

The Pharisees went back to the blind man who could see and asked him once more how Jesus made him better. By this time the blind man was tired of all their questions, and he asked them, "Will ye also be His disciples?"

Then the Pharisees mocked and called Jesus a sinner. Oh, they were wicked men! The blind man wouldn't listen to their wicked words. He told the Pharisees that God would not let a **sinner** do such a wonderful miracle.

Then Jesus met the man and asked him, "Dost thou believe on the Son of God?"

The man answered, "Who is he, Lord, that I might believe on him?"

Jesus said, "It is he that talketh with thee."

Then the blind man who could see said, "Lord, I believe." And he worshipped Jesus.

REMEMBER:

Jesus said we must be like Mary in this story. Mary chose to sit at Jesus' feet and listen to Him. We must choose to sit at His feet and listen to Him in church, in Sunday School, and at Bible story time.

Jesus Raises Lazarus From the Dead

For a little while Jesus left the city of Jerusalem and walked across the Jordan River with His disciples to a more quiet place called Perea. There the people streamed out to Him and He spent many days teaching them. While Jesus was there, a servant came running from the town of Bethany, where Mary, Martha, and Lazarus lived, with this news: "Lord, he whom thou lovest is sick."

It was Lazarus who was sick, and he must have been very sick. Mary and Martha must have expected Jesus to rush right over to Bethany and probably heal him. Jesus answered the servant, "This sickness is not unto death, but for the glory of God." And Jesus stayed in Perea for two more days.

On the third day, when Jesus suggested to His disciples that they go to places around Jerusalem again, the disciples did not want to go. They knew how much the wicked Pharisees hated Him. Just a few days ago, the Pharisees were so angry they had taken stones in their hands to kill Jesus. The disciples were worried. They forgot to trust God to take care of Jesus and themselves.

Before they left, Jesus told them that Lazarus was asleep; and then He said, "But I go, that I may awake him out of sleep."

His disciples answered, "Lord, if he sleep, he shall do well."

The disciples did not understand. Jesus was talking about the sleep of **death**. Then He said plainly to them, "Lazarus is dead." Oh, that made the disciples feel sad.

But what was Jesus saying? "I am glad for your sakes that I was not there, to the intent ye might believe."

Was Jesus going to do a great wonder? Thomas, one of the disciples, didn't think so. He felt so sad and gloomy inside because he was sure Jesus would die in Jerusalem. He said, "Let us also go, that we may die with him."

It took a whole day to walk to the town of Bethany, near Jerusalem, and by the time they arrived, Lazarus had been in the grave four days already. When Martha heard that Jesus and His disciples were coming, she rushed out to meet them. That's the kind of person Martha was: a bustling, busy person. But Mary sat still in the house. That's the kind of person Mary was: a quiet person and a listener.

521

When Martha saw Jesus, she said, "Lord, if thou hadst been here, my brother had not died. But I know, that even now, whatsoever thou wilt ask of God, God will give it thee." Do you think she was hoping that **maybe** Jesus would still do a miracle?

Now Jesus was talking. He said, "Thy brother shall rise again."

Martha knew that he would rise again — at the end of the world. But that is not what Jesus meant. He said to Martha, "I am the resurrection and the life," and He asked Martha whether she believed that.

Then Martha gave Jesus a beautiful answer. She said, "Yea, Lord: I believe that thou art the Christ, the Son of God, which should come into the world."

Jesus wanted to see Mary, too; and when she knew that Jesus was calling for her, she left her house quickly and came to Jesus. When she saw Him, she said the same words Martha had said: "Lord, if thou hadst been here, my brother had not died."

Jesus looked around and saw that many Jews had walked along with Mary. They were unbelieving Jews, men who hated Jesus and who would soon kill Him. And Jesus felt sad and troubled because their hearts were so hard and they were so wicked. They would not believe even when Jesus did His great wonders! Jesus felt so bad about them that He started to cry.

Some people thought He cried because Lazarus was dead. No, that was not why Jesus cried. Watch what Jesus did next. He walked to Lazarus' grave. It was in a cave and a big stone was rolled against the opening of the cave. Jesus asked someone to move the stone away.

Martha argued with Jesus and said, "Lord, by this time he stinketh: for he hath been dead four days."

Jesus told her only to believe and she would see the glory of God. Then He prayed a prayer of thanks to His Father and after He prayed, He cried with a loud voice, "Lazarus, come forth."

Jesus' voice was the voice of power, the voice of God; and Lazarus came out of the grave with the graveclothes still wound around him and the napkin for his head still over his face. Jesus told them to unwrap the strips of graveclothes and let him go. How happy Mary, Martha, and Lazarus must have been, and how they must have praised God.

The wicked Pharisees were not happy. They were afraid that now everyone would want to make Jesus king, and the Pharisees did not want **that!** They hurried to have a meeting, and they decided there was only one thing to do: they must kill Jesus.

REMEMBER:

It is almost too hard for us to understand how Jesus could raise a man from the dead when he had been dead four days already. And it is almost too hard for us to understand how Jesus can raise us out of the grave after we die and then take us to heaven forever.

Jesus and the Children, Jesus and the Ruler, Jesus and Zaccheus

Although the wicked teachers of the Jews were making plans to kill Him, they could not stop Jesus' work of preaching and teaching. One day as He was teaching the crowds, some mothers with little children in their arms came to Him. Those mothers believed in Jesus, but they knew that their babies were too little to understand Who Jesus was and that they were too little to know that He brought forgiveness for their sins. Those mothers **did** know that God's Spirit works even in the hearts of little babies and they were so eager for Jesus to bless their children. They wanted **their** babies to be **Jesus'** babies.

But the disciples thought those mothers were bothering Jesus. Couldn't they see that He was busy teaching? They scolded the mothers and put themselves in the way so the mothers couldn't get to Jesus. Then Jesus had to scold the disciples and call the mothers to Him and say, "Suffer the little children to come unto me, and forbid them not: for of such is the kingdom of God." He took the little children in His arms and blessed them.

That beautiful story happened in the land of Israel when Jesus was still on the earth. Now Jesus is not living on this earth anymore. But do you know that this beautiful story happens to us, too? When we were babies, our fathers and mothers brought us to Jesus to be baptized. And our fathers and mothers still bring us to Jesus every day by reading the Bible and praying with us and by taking us to church and singing His praises. If we are His children, Jesus takes us in His arms each day to bless us.

A young man was probably watching Jesus as He took the children into His arms and blessed them. Suddenly he came running to Jesus and kneeled down at His feet. This young man had a question to ask Jesus, a question that made his heart feel troubled: "What shall I do that I may inherit eternal life?" This is what he meant: what must I do so that I will go to heaven after I die?

Jesus told him to obey God's law — all the commandments: do not steal, do not kill, do not lie, and all the rest.

The young man said he had always obeyed God's commands, ever since he was a young boy. But he knew this was not enough. He felt hollow inside and he did not have any peace inside his soul.

Jesus knows all things. He knew why the young man still had a troubled heart. It was because he was rich. No, it is not wrong to be rich. But this young man loved those riches more than anything else, more than Jesus, too. Those riches were getting in his way. He wanted to hold onto them. That is why Jesus had to give him such a hard test. He told the young man to sell everything he had had — his beautiful house, his furniture, and all his treasures — and give the money to the poor. For he had to learn that to serve God is **much** better treasure than all the money in the world.

And that young man walked away from Jesus still sad and troubled. He didn't want to give away his riches. Later on he must have listened to Jesus and sold his goods, for the Bible says that Jesus loved him, and Jesus loves **obedient** children.

The next part of our story is about another rich man. His name was Zaccheus and he was a publican who collected money for the king of Rome. In fact, he was the head over all the publicans in his city. And he was rich. He did not get his money honestly. Just as Levi had probably done, he charged too much money and cheated the people. And, oh, how they hated him!

Zaccheus heard that Jesus was walking through his city and he wanted to see Jesus. Whenever Jesus went anywhere, huge crowds walked along with Him. How could Zaccheus ever push through those crowds to get close enough to see Jesus? Besides that, he was a very short man and would never be able to see over anyone's head.

But Zaccheus was a quick thinker. He ran ahead of the crowds and climbed into a low, spreading tree called a sycamore tree. From there he could peek down and see Jesus.

525

Right under that tree Jesus stopped and said, "Zaccheus, make haste, and come down."

Don't you think Zaccheus was surprised? He climbed down, full of happiness, and led Jesus to his house. Listen to what the crowd of people were saying: "He is gone to be guest with a man that is a sinner."

Jesus knew that Zaccheus was a sinner but He walked right on to his house; for the house of Zaccheus was a special house, a house of salvation. Jesus had come to his city to look for this lost man and to save him from all his sins. And when Jesus put His love into his heart, Zaccheus was sorry for all his cheating and promised to pay back more than he had taken and follow Jesus.

REMEMBER:

We feel the same way Zaccheus felt when Jesus comes to **us,** don't we? We are sorry for our sins, too, and we promise to obey Him again and then we follow in Jesus' paths.

The Royal Entry

Now it was Friday, just one week before Jesus would suffer and die on the cross. Jesus knew the time was getting near. He had only one week to live on this earth. We call the week before Jesus died **Passion Week**.

Next week in the city of Jerusalem it would be time for the passover feast; and the wicked Pharisees were trying hard to find Jesus to kill Him before the feast. Jesus was not afraid of them because He knew they could not kill Him before it was God's time that He should die. So He and His disciples walked calmly to the town of Bethany to visit their dear friends, Mary, Martha, and Lazarus — the Lazarus whom He had raised from the dead a few weeks before.

Jesus spent the sabbath day with His friends and for the evening meal they were invited to the house of Simon the Leper. Simon was probably a man who once had been sick with leprosy and whom Jesus had made better. Besides the people who were invited to the feast, many other people came just to stand and watch it. They came to see Jesus and they came to see Lazarus whom Jesus had raised from the dead. Everyone was still talking about that great wonder!

If we watched the dinner, we would see Lazarus on an eating-couch near Jesus and His disciples. Martha could not sit still long enough for a whole dinner. She was busy serving her Lord and taking care of Him. Where was Mary? She was standing very quietly behind Jesus with a beautiful box of very expensive perfume in her hands. She poured the perfume first over Jesus' head and then over His feet and wiped His feet with her hair. Soon the lovely smell of the expensive perfume went through the whole house. What a beautiful thing for Mary to do to Jesus. She was showing how much she loved her Lord.

But there was a dark, unhappy face at the table which spoiled the picture of this happy dinner. It was the face of Judas Iscariot, one of Jesus' disciples. Although he was one of the disciples, he did not love Jesus at all, for the devil lived in his heart. Judas said to himself that the precious perfume was worth two hundred pence, as much money as a man earned in a whole year. He would have liked that money because he was a thief and he lived only for money. Aloud he asked why Mary did not sell the perfume and give the money to the poor.

Jesus answered, "The poor always ye have with you; but me ye have not always."

Why did Mary pour the perfume over Jesus? To show that she **believed** that Jesus would suffer and die the next week. It was her good-bye offering.

The next day Jesus and His disciples walked to Jerusalem. Just before they got there Jesus stopped and sent two of his disciples into a tiny town nearby and told them where they would find an ass and her little colt tied up. He told His disciples to untie them and bring them to Him. If anyone asked why they were taking them, Jesus told the disciples to say, "The Lord has need of them."

The two disciples brought the little colt to Jesus, put their coats on the colt, and Jesus sat on it. Sitting on the colt, Jesus started His ride into the city of Jerusalem. Oh, the disciples were so happy! This was just like a parade! Maybe this was the day that Jesus would become king over Israel. The poor disciples didn't understand yet. They thought Jesus would be a great king on earth, in Israel. **We** know that He is King in heaven over the whole world.

Crowds began to gather and they threw their coats under the feet of the colt so it could walk on them. Then they cut down branches of palm trees and laid them on the path of Jesus, too. All the way they sang and shouted hosannas. Hosannas are songs of praise. They sang, "Blessed is he that cometh in the name of the Lord."

That is the way Jesus rode into Jerusalem: on the lowly little colt, a King without a crown on His head; and it was a picture that soon He would become humble and lowly and die. Meanwhile, all the crowds were singing hosannas to the King!

REMEMBER:

Some day Jesus will come riding again. That will be at the end of the world. He will ride on the clouds. Then He will not be humble and lowly, but He will come as the great King to take us to heaven. Then **we** will sing hosannas.

In the Upper Room

Do you remember that we call the last week when Jesus was on earth **Passion Week?** On Wednesday of that week Jesus and His disciples took time to rest and to talk, probably sitting on the side of the Mount of Olives, near to the city of Jerusalem. Jesus told them that in two days, on Friday, He would be hanged on a cross and die. What a sad, quiet day it must have been for the disciples.

While Jesus was telling His disciples how He must suffer and die, Judas Iscariot got up and slipped quietly away. Judas had been listening to Jesus, too; but his heart was not filled with sadness and love for Jesus. He was disappointed. All this time he had expected Jesus to be a great and powerful king — and a rich one — on the earth. Then Judas would be rich and important, too. Now he saw that all his hopes were taken away from him. He did not want a Jesus Who would die. He did not care what happened to **Jesus.** He cared what happened to **Judas.**

Then a plan came into his wicked mind. Maybe he could get some money after all. He would sell Jesus — we call it **betraying** Jesus — to the wicked rulers of the Jews for money. When he thought about it, Satan came into his heart to urge him to betray Jesus. For Satan wanted to kill Jesus, too.

When Judas slipped away from the disciples, he went to the rulers of the Jews and offered to sell Jesus to them; and the Jews were very happy that at last they could kill Him. They gave Judas thirty pieces of silver, about as much money as a slave cost.

The next day Judas was with the disciples again as if nothing had happened. That was a special day: the day of the feast of the passover, when the people of Israel killed a lamb and sprinkled its blood over their doorways. That lamb was a picture of Jesus, the Lamb of God. Jesus and His disciples needed some place to celebrate the feast of the passover that night, and Jesus sent Peter and John into the city. He told them that when they saw a man carrying a pitcher of water, they should follow the man into the house where he went; and they must say to the man, "The Master saith, My time is at hand; I will keep the passover at thy house with my disciples."

The man listened to them and showed them a large upstairs room and the disciples made the passover feast ready there. When it was ready, Jesus and His disciples went to the upstairs room; and after they were all at the table on their eating couches, Jesus stood up, took a basin of water and a towel in His hand. All the disciples knew their feet were dusty from walking on the hot, dirty roads, but there was no servant in the room to wash their feet. They did not even think about washing one another's feet. They did not feel very **lowly** and **humble**. They were always trying to be the **greatest** of Jesus' disciples.

So Jesus started to do the work of a servant. He washed the disciples' feet and dried them with the towel. When it was Simon Peter's turn, he said to Jesus, "Thou shalt never wash my feet."

Poor Simon Peter did not understand that when Jesus washed his feet He was making a picture of washing away the dust and dirt of sin from his heart. And to-morrow Jesus was **really** going to wash away Simon Peter's sins, not with water, but with His blood. That is why Jesus said, "If I wash thee not, thou hast no part with me."

Simon Peter was only starting to understand, for he said, "Lord, not my feet only, but also my hands and my head."

Jesus had to tell him once more that He was making only a **picture** when He washed Simon Peter's feet. It was only a **little** picture. Washing Simon Peter's feet was a picture of his being clean **all the way** from his sins.

There was another reason why Jesus washed His disciples' feet. He wanted to teach them a lesson: to be humble and to serve one another. Jesus was their Lord and Master and He said, "If I then, your Master and Lord, have washed your feet, ye also ought to wash one another's feet."

After Jesus had sat down again, He felt very troubled and said, "One of you shall betray me."

Jesus knew it was Judas and He knew Judas had the thirty pieces of silver in his pocket. Some of the disciples heard Jesus' words and they looked at one another in surprise and in fear. Would one of the **disciples** sell Jesus?

John, who was next to Jesus, asked, "Lord, who is it?"

Jesus told him it was the disciple to whom He would give a piece of bread after He dipped it in the bitter sauce on the table. John and the other disciples saw Jesus hand the bread to Judas Iscariot. Satan came into Judas's heart as Jesus said to Him, "That thou doest, do quickly." And Judas left the upstairs room to betray Jesus.

REMEMBER:

Judas did not want to betray Jesus on **that** night, the night of the passover feast, but Jesus rules over all things and He forced Judas to go out to betray Him. Why? It was time on God's clock for Jesus to die. And Jesus wanted to die, too, to give His people His most precious gift: the washing away of their sins.

In the Garden of Gethsemane

Now there were only eleven disciples in the upstairs room. Judas was gone into the dark night to find the Pharisees and the rulers of the Jews to make plans to kill Jesus. Judas was not happy and the Pharisees were not happy, either. They wanted to kill Jesus **quietly**, in secret, so no one would know about it. They thought this was the **worst** time to kill Jesus, for crowds of people had come to Jerusalem for the passover feast and now they could not kill Jesus in secret.

It was really the **best** time to kill Jesus, for it was **God's** time. And Jesus was obedient to God His Father and went ahead with His plans to die. While they were still sitting at the table in the upstairs room, Jesus tried to explain to His eleven disciples what would happen that night. He told them they would not understand and that they would feel sad and hurt inside and would run away from Him. They wouldn't want anything more to do with Him. We call it being **offended**.

Peter couldn't believe **that!** He said, "Though all men shall be offended because of thee, yet will I never be offended."

Jesus answered him, "This night, before the cock crow, thou shalt deny me thrice." Deny means to say, "I don't know Him!" Thrice means three times.

Peter was **sure** that would not happen to **him**. He told Jesus, "Though I should die with thee, yet will I not deny thee."

Then Jesus told His disciples how glad He was that He could eat this last passover feast with them. After tomorrow they would never need a passover feast again. They would never need a picture of a lamb; for tomorrow the Lamb of God would really die, as He had promised.

Jesus gave His disciples — and us — another kind of feast. It is called the Lord's Supper. He took a piece of bread, gave thanks to God, and then broke the bread and told each of His disciples to eat a piece of the bread. It was a picture of Jesus' body being broken for their sins and for our sins. Next Jesus poured wine into a cup and told the disciples to drink the wine. It was a picture of Jesus' blood which He spilled for their sins and for our sins. In our churches today we still remember Jesus' body and blood with the bread and the wine of the Lord's Supper, don't we?

Jesus and His disciples sang a song and then they left the upstairs room to go to the Garden of Gethsemane, near the Mount of Olives. He left most of the disciples near the gate and took Simon Peter, James, and John with Him into the garden to watch and to pray with Him on this awful night of His suffering. Jesus went still farther into the garden, about as far as you could throw a stone, and fell on His face and prayed to His Father in heaven.

What did Jesus pray about? About a cup. It was not a real cup. It was a cup of **suffering**, an awful cup that was so terrible that our little minds can never know what was in the cup that Jesus had to drink. The Bible gives us a little peek into that cup. It tells us that in the garden Jesus started to feel very heavy and terribly sad. He was shocked! For in that garden it seemed to Jesus that He was standing at the gate of hell. Jesus had to feel all of God's anger for all the sins of God's people and Jesus had to take the punishment that **we** deserved to have. There He had to stand, frightened and lonely. It was so horrible that Jesus' body almost died.

Then Jesus prayed to His Father and said, "O my Father, if it be possible, let this cup pass from me." Jesus was asking God, "Is there any other way I can save My people? If not, I will be perfectly obedient."

After He prayed, Jesus got up and walked to His three disciples and found them fast asleep. He woke them and said, "What, could ye not watch with me one hour?"

Jesus left them again and prayed the same sad prayer to His Father: "O my Father, if it be possible, let this cup pass from me;" and He went to His three disciples again. He **needed** their prayers to give Him strength in this awful hour. But He found them fast asleep. Once more He woke them. Why were they so sleepy? Partly because they were so tired from the work of the day. Partly because they were so sad about Jesus' suffering and their sadness acted like a sleeping pill. Partly because the devil came to tempt them to sleep instead of to pray for their Lord.

One more time Jesus prayed to His Father, but God did not show Him another way to save His people. Now Jesus knew that God's answer was, "No, no other way." It was no wonder that His sweat was as great drops of blood, so much He suffered. And God sent an angel to comfort Him.

REMEMBER:

When He was on earth, Jesus often needed God's angels to help Him. We need them, too. Although we cannot see them, God tells us that they watch over us to care for us and to keep us safe.

Jesus is Captured

In our last story we left the three disciples, Simon Peter, James, and John, asleep in the Garden of Gethsemane. They could not stay awake to pray with Jesus in His darkest night of suffering. After Jesus had prayed to His Father the third time, He went to His disciples and told them, "Sleep on now, and take your rest."

These words made His disciples wide awake; and they were ready to go along with Jesus when He said, "Rise up, let us go; lo, he that betrayeth me is at hand." The last part of Jesus' words meant that Judas, who sold Him to the rulers of the Jews, was there in the garden.

It was dark in the garden, about midnight, when Judas came. With him were many soldiers with their swords ready. The soldiers took lanterns and candles, too, to find their way in the dark, quiet garden. Wasn't that a strange way to capture Jesus? For three years He had walked all over the land, teaching them; and they never tried to capture Him. Now in the dark of the night, they thought they needed an army of soldiers with sharp swords. They expected that Jesus and His disciples would fight them there in the garden.

Judas was the leader of the army of soldiers and he had given them a sign. He said, "Whomsoever I shall kiss, that same is he."

Wasn't that a terrible kind of kiss? A kiss to kill Jesus! And Jesus scolded Judas by saying, "Judas, betrayest thou the Son of man with a kiss?"

Judas stepped back and stood with the soldiers when Jesus asked His next question: "Whom seek ye?" That means: "Whom are you looking for?"

They answered, "Jesus of Nazareth."

Jesus said to them, "I am He."

When Jesus said those three little words, "I am He," all His power as the Son of God shone through Him; and do you know what happened to that army of soldiers and to Judas, too? They all fell over backwards to the ground. It was a wonder there in the dark garden. When Jesus made them all fall backwards, He was telling them something. He was telling them that all those soldiers and swords were silly, for now those soldiers were lying helpless at Jesus' feet. He was telling the soldiers one thing more: that He was the Lord and He was ruling even in the garden of His suffering; and they would not be able to capture Him unless He let them.

As all the soldiers lay on the ground, Jesus asked them once more, "Whom seek ye?"

They answered, "Jesus of Nazareth."

Jesus said, "I have told you that I am he."

Then He let the soldiers get up, and with shame on their faces they tied up Jesus.

Where were the disciples all this time? They were standing with Jesus, watching the things that were happening so fast. When they saw the soldiers tie up Jesus to take Him away, they thought they knew what they must do: fight to save Jesus from His wicked enemies. The disciples had two swords with them and Simon Peter was holding one of them. He would lead the other disciples in fighting for Jesus. He raised his sword and cut off the ear of Malchus, a servant to the high priest. He did not mean to cut Malchus' ear off. He meant to cut his head open! This was a battle!

Then, to Simon Peter's great surprise, Jesus told him to put his sword away, and He touched Malchus' ear and healed him. Jesus talked to His disciples, too, and told them that it was not right for them to fight the soldiers. They must give in. Jesus told them that if He needed help, God would send Him thousands and thousands of angels to save Him.

When those poor, mixed-up disciples still had surprised faces, Jesus told them that this was the most important night that there would ever be. For years and years God's people made pictures of killing lambs. Now it was time for the one great Lamb of God to die for the sins of all His people; and He told His disciples that this was the way it **must** be.

They did not understand why. They loved Jesus. They offered to fight for Him. But Jesus **wanted** to give up and let the mob of soldiers take Him away in the middle of the night. It was too much for the disciples. They all left Jesus and ran away.

Now Jesus was alone with the soldiers. Down the dark streets of Jerusalem they marched, to the house of Caiaphas, the high priest. How do you think Judas and the soldiers felt? They had just seen two great wonders in the Garden of Gethsemane. First Jesus made them all fall down, helpless, and then He healed the servant's ear. Wouldn't you think they would bow down and worship the Son of God? No, they couldn't; for their hearts were hard with unbelief.

REMEMBER:

God gave us, His children, the gift of soft hearts so that we **can** believe in Jesus. We call it **faith.** By faith we know that Jesus suffered that night for **our** sins.

The Trial of Jesus

In the dark of the night the soldiers took Jesus to the house of Caiaphas, the high priest, to have a **trial**. At the trial the high priest would ask Jesus questions to find out whether He did anything wrong and whether He should live or die. All the rulers of the Jews were supposed to come to the trial, too. But it was still night and the rulers were at home, sleeping. Besides, God's law said they might not have a trial in the darkness of the night. Trials had to be held in the daytime.

The high priest and the rulers of the Jews didn't know what to do. They did not want to let Jesus go, but they were not ready to ask Him questions yet. They were all mixed up. Only Jesus was quiet and calm, for He was doing just what His Father wanted Him to do.

Quickly the high priest sent servants to get the rulers of the Jews out of bed so they could come to the trial of Jesus. By the time they were all ready the night was almost over and it was starting to get light. What a strange trial those rulers gave Jesus. No one could think of anything wrong that Jesus had done. They could hardly think of any questions to ask Him. And when they **did** talk, everyone of the rulers said something different. All this time Jesus was quiet. He did not argue. He did not say a word.

Caiaphas was a very wicked high priest, and he had made up his mind that somehow he would find a reason why Jesus must die. So he asked Jesus a question: "Tell us whether thou be the Christ, the Son of God."

Jesus answered, "Thou hast said." It means, "Yes, it is true."

What did the wicked Caiaphas do then? He tore his clothes to show how sad he was because Jesus had said He was the Son of God. And all the rulers said, "He is guilty of death."

Then they began to spit in Jesus' face and to slap Him — Jesus, the Son of God Who had never sinned.

For a moment let us take a look at another part of the house of Caiaphas. His house had an open yard in the middle, with rooms all around it. In the open yard some soldiers had made a fire, for the night was chilly, and they warmed themselves there. Standing there near the fire warming themselves with the soldiers were two of Jesus' disciples, Simon Peter and John. They had followed

Jesus there. A girl, probably a servant-girl, came up to Simon Peter and said, "Thou also wast with Jesus of Galilee." Peter said he didn't know what she was talking about.

Another girl saw him and said, "This fellow was also with Jesus of Nazareth," and Peter answered, "I do not know the man."

A little later one of the servants of the high priest asked Simon Peter, "Did not I see thee in the garden with him?" And Peter cursed and swore that he did not know Jesus.

Then the cock — the rooster — crowed and Peter thought of Jesus' words: that he would say three times that he did not know Jesus. Just at that minute Jesus was walking along the hall around the yard and He looked down at Simon Peter. **Now** Peter knew how greatly he had sinned, and he was so sorry. He went out all by himself, crying bitterly.

Let us go back to Jesus. Caiaphas had said He must die, but Caiaphas was the ruler in the **church** and he could not kill Jesus. He had to send Jesus to the ruler from the **world power, Rome.** This man's name was Pontius Pilate. Pilate did not really want to be Jesus' judge. He had heard wonderful stories of Jesus and he knew that Jesus was no wicked man who had to die.

When Pilate asked Him questions, he could find nothing wrong with Him. Pilate did not want to say that Jesus must die. Yet he was afraid of the rulers of the Jews. If he made them angry, they would make trouble for him.

So Pilate thought of another answer. At the passover feast he always let one prisoner go free and Pilate gave the rulers a choice: let Barabbas go free — a bad man who had robbed and killed people; or let Jesus go free — a Man Who had never done anything wrong. Surely, Pilate thought, the rulers would not choose to let wicked Barabbas go free. But they did. And they wanted to kill Jesus.

Just then Pilate's wife told him that she was very troubled and upset, for God had sent her dreams about Jesus and she suffered in those dreams. She told Pilate not to harm that good Man, Jesus. **God** was talking to Pilate through his wife. Did he listen? No.

He said to the rulers of the Jews, "What shall I do then with Jesus?"

They had the answer: "Crucify Him." That means, "Let Him hang on a cross."

Pilate asked, "Why, what evil hath he done?"

But they kept shouting, "Crucify Him."

Then Pilate took a bowl of water, washed his hands in front of all the people, and said he was innocent of Jesus' blood. That means he was not to blame that Jesus would die. But Pilate was **not** innocent of Jesus' blood. He did not really care what the Jews did with Jesus. He let them lead Jesus away to the cross.

REMEMBER:

God used wicked Pilate and the rulers of the Jews to take Jesus to the cross so He could die for us.

Jesus is Crucified

Judas, the disciple who sold Jesus for thirty pieces of silver, left the hall where Jesus was standing in front of Pilate, the Roman ruler. He stayed long enough to hear Pilate give Jesus to the Jews so they could nail Him to a cross. That is the time Judas ran away to the temple. Now he wished that he had not sold Jesus to die, for he knew that Jesus had done only good in all His life on earth. Judas wished he had not sold Jesus, but in his heart he was not sorry for his sin before God.

He went to the priests in the temple and tried to give them back their thirty pieces of silver, but they would not take them. He threw the money down in the temple, ran out, took a rope, and hanged himself by it until he died. Judas took his own life away, and God put him in hell for betraying the Lord Jesus. The priests did not want the thirty pieces of silver so they bought a piece of land with the money, where they could dig graves to bury strangers who might die in their land.

Meanwhile Pilate gave orders that they should whip Jesus on His back with stinging whips that made deep bleeding scratches over His whole back. Then Pilate let the soldiers mock Jesus. These wicked soldiers took a plant that had very sharp thorns on its stem and bent the stem into the shape of a crown. Then they pressed the sharp, thorny crown onto Jesus' poor, bleeding head, put a robe on Him, and pretended they were bowing down to a king. All the while they slapped Him and spit at Him and mocked Him, and Jesus never answered them a word.

Then they led Him away, outside the city of Jerusalem, to a hill called Golgotha, where they would nail Him to the cross. Some of Jesus' friends, sad and quiet, were walking along with Jesus and the soldiers toward Golgotha. Simon was one of these friends. We do not know very much about him except that he came from a place called Cyrene and that he loved Jesus with all his heart. The soldiers made Simon carry the heavy cross for Jesus; and he must have carried it gladly for His suffering and bleeding Lord.

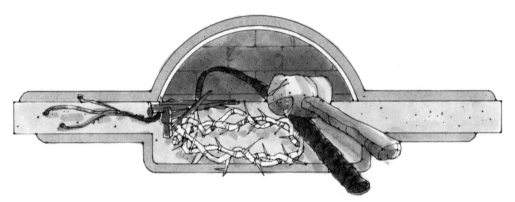

When they came to Golgotha, the soldiers crucified Jesus. They pounded nails into His hands and feet to fasten Him to the cross. The Bible does not tell us much about the cruel soldiers nailing Jesus to the cross, for they were pounding nails into **our Lord**; and we don't have great enough words to make us understand the terribleness and the greatness of it all.

As soon as Jesus was nailed to the cross, the soldiers started to cast lots to see which one would get Jesus' coat, which must have been a rich and beautiful one. Even though they knew in their hearts that Jesus had done nothing wrong, they did not care about Him. They wanted only His beautiful coat. But there must have been **some** people standing there who were different; and Jesus said something for **them**. He said, "Father, forgive them; for they know not what they do."

Jesus was praying for His own children who were there on the hill of Golgotha, His own children who some day would be sorry that they spilled the blood of Jesus that paid for their very own sins.

After Jesus prayed that prayer, the soldiers put His cross into the ground. Now the cross was standing up and Jesus was hanging between the heaven and the earth. The soldiers put up a cross on each side of Him and on these two crosses were hanging two wicked men who were robbers. Jesus' cross was in the middle.

Pilate wrote these words on top of His cross: "Jesus of Nazareth, the King of the Jews."

It was about nine o'clock in the morning when the soldiers nailed Jesus to the cross. Even at that early hour of the morning many people walked past the hill of Golgotha, and those who passed by Jesus wagged their heads and mocked Jesus, saying, "If thou be the Son of God, come down from the cross."

Then the soldiers and the two robbers alongside Jesus joined the people in shouting those mocking words at Jesus. They did not see that Jesus was not interested in coming down from the cross, but in saving His people by dying on the cross. They did not believe in Jesus. That is a terrible thing.

REMEMBER:

We can learn a lesson from the people who wagged their heads and passed right by Jesus. We may never do that to Jesus. What must we do? We must run to Jesus' cross, trust in it, and be saved by that cross. How do we run to Jesus' cross? By praying to Him and believing that He died for us.

Jesus Dies

The day that Jesus died on the cross was probably the most special day that ever was. It was a day when God spoke loudly to the people on the earth, not by a voice, but by sending them many picture-signs.

For six hours — from nine o'clock in the morning until three o'clock in the afternoon — Jesus hung on the cross between the crosses of the two robbers. At first both the robbers shouted at Jesus and mocked Him, but after a while one of them was quiet. He must have been thinking of all the sins he had done in his wicked life; and God's grace came into his heart and he was very sorry for all those sins. He prayed a beautiful prayer to Jesus, hanging there on the cross next to him, saying, "Lord, remember me when thou comest into thy kingdom." Jesus' kingdom is heaven.

God's love and grace had turned that robber to Jesus on the last day of his life; and Jesus answered him, "Today shalt thou be with me in paradise." Paradise is heaven, too.

All that morning the crowds of busy people walked back and forth on the roads around the hill of Golgotha as if nothing special were happening. Suddenly, at noon, the time we usually eat lunch, the brightest time of the day, the Lord sent darkness, black darkness over the whole land. That had never happened before! The people stopped what they were doing and stood frightened before this awful wonder. **God** sent this special picture-sign, and the people knew it. They stopped their mocking tongues and stood near the cross in a strange stillness.

Jesus was quiet, too, for when God's darkness came over the earth, God's dark anger against His people's sins came over Jesus. In that time of darkness Jesus suffered so much! God put on Him all the terrible punishments of all His people's sins. And in the dark quietness Jesus had to bear them all alone.

For three hours the darkness stayed on the earth and then God took it away. Just before it was light again, Jesus called out in a loud voice, "It is finished." He had finished all the work He came to earth to do. He had finished paying for our sins. Then Jesus died.

Many strange picture-signs happened just as our Lord Jesus died. Let us go to the temple to see what happened there. Maybe you remember that between the two rooms in the temple was a heavy doorway curtain. The priests who worked in God's temple might never push that curtain aside and go into the special room, the Most Holy Place. Only once a year the high priest might go in with the blood of a lamb, the picture of the blood of Jesus. What happened to that curtain when Jesus died? It ripped from the top to the bottom. **God** ripped it. He was talking to the people of Israel that they did not need pictures of the blood of lambs anymore. They did not need the temple anymore. Now they could pray to God through the Lord Jesus Who had just paid for their sins.

Next we will go to see what happened in Jerusalem. There was an earthquake! The ground shook and broke open and big rocks broke apart. **God** was talking in that earthquake and telling the people how angry He is with all the sinful, wicked people who will not believe on Him and Jesus Christ, His Son.

Now if we would go to the cemetery at Jerusalem, we would see a beautiful wonder. Just at the time that Jesus died, God opened many graves where His people were buried. Those graves stayed open until after Jesus rose from the dead and then those people rose from their graves, too, and walked through the streets of Jerusalem in special bodies that the Lord gave them. When Jesus went to heaven, they went back to heaven, too. Don't you think those dear children of the Lord were happy that they could be a part of the wonders God showed when Jesus died? And don't you see why God opened some of the graves when Jesus died? It was a picture for all God's people — for us, too — to show us that when **we** die we will not stay in the grave. We will arise and go to heaven where Jesus is!

What was happening on the hill of Golgotha? Jesus and the two robbers were still hanging on their crosses. The soldiers were in a hurry to get them down from the crosses, for soon the sun would go down. When the sun went down the sabbath day in Israel started and the law said that no one might hang on the cross on the sabbath day. Both the robbers were still alive on their crosses and the soldiers cruelly broke their legs so they would die very soon. When the soldiers came to Jesus, they were going to break His legs, too, but to their surprise they saw that He was dead already. God would not let any bone of His Son Jesus be broken! All that the soldiers did was to put a sword into Jesus' side; and blood and water flowed out.

Then Joseph of Arimathea, a rich man who loved Jesus, went to Pilate and begged for the body of Jesus. Pilate said yes. Working very quickly, for it was almost time for the sabbath day to start, Joseph of Arimathea took Jesus' body down from the cross, wrapped it in linen cloths, and laid it in a new grave. Another rich man, Nicodemus, helped him. The grave was a cave and they rolled a big stone in front of the opening. Then they rested on that sad sabbath day.

REMEMBER:

Because we are God's children we do not have to be afraid to die and to go into a grave; for Jesus has promised us that He will never leave us there. He tells us that He will raise us up and take us to heaven with Him.

547

Jesus Arose

At the cross of Jesus His mother and His dear friends had stood with tears in their eyes as they listened to the mocking words of the Lord's enemies. They had watched while He suffered and they had heard Him cry out and they had seen Him die. After Joseph of Arimathea and Nicodemus buried Jesus they thought that this was the darkest, saddest day of their lives. They thought it was the end of all their happiness.

Three days later they heard heavenly words of such wonder and such gladness that their minds could hardly take it all in. We will go with those friends, too, and we will see what happened to bring such happiness that bright morning three days later.

Jesus lay dead in His grave in the big cave all of Friday night, all of Saturday and Saturday night, until very early on Sunday morning, just as the light was starting to color the sky. Then He arose from the dead. The Bible does not tell us **how** He rose up, alive, from the grave. It was such a great and beautiful wonder that no words could make us understand it. Even if we had been standing right next to that cave, we would not have seen Jesus arise from the grave. No one moved the rocks of the cave. No one rolled away the stone. Jesus went **through** the grave to heaven and our eyes could never see such a wonder as that. We would have felt something, though, for at the moment that Jesus arose God sent another earthquake.

Then an angel of the Lord came down from heaven and rolled back the heavy stone from the opening of the empty grave and sat on it. Who were the first people to see the angel come and open the empty grave? Wicked soldiers. The ungodly rulers of the Jews asked the soldiers to guard the grave to make sure Jesus would not rise up out of it. Those wicked soldiers, standing in the quietness of the early morning, felt the earthquake and saw the angel who came from God's holy and pure heaven. They saw that the angel's clothes were so white and bright they looked like lightning. Those soldiers were so afraid they trembled and shook and fell down flat as if they were dead.

At this same time, very early in the morning, some of the women who had helped Jesus and who had loved Him so much were walking to His grave, carrying sweet smelling spices to put on His dead body. They wanted to do one last act of kindness to Jesus by taking care of His body. As they walked to His grave, they probably felt the earthquake but they were so busy talking about their problem they didn't notice it much. What was their problem? The stone in front of the cave was too big for them to move. How could they get that stone rolled away from the opening?

But look! The stone was already rolled away! Running into the grave and looking for their dead Jesus, they had another surprise. The grave was empty. Then they saw the bright, shining angel and his first words to them were, "Fear not ye: for I know that ye seek Jesus which was crucified. He is not here: for he is risen, as he said."

The women were looking for a **dead** Jesus and they had come to the grave of the **living** Jesus! The angel showed them the place where Jesus had lain in the grave and then he scolded them. They **should** have known, for Jesus had told them often that He would arise again in three days. The angel told them one thing more: "Go tell His disciples."

Now the women understood. Now they were happy. They were so happy they started to run to tell His disciples the wonderful news that Jesus was alive. Then Jesus met them and talked with them and those happy women did not know how to tell Him about their great joy. They held Him by His feet and worshipped Him.

One of the women, Mary Magdalene, went with the other women only part of the way to the grave. When she saw that the great stone was rolled away, she thought she knew what had happened. Someone had stolen Jesus' dead body. Without going any farther, she ran to two of Jesus' disciples, Simon Peter and John, and told them that someone had stolen Jesus' body.

Then those two disciples ran to the grave. John ran faster and was there first. He stooped down and looked inside. When Simon Peter came, he went inside the cave and John followed him. There they saw the linen clothes still lying as they had been wound around Jesus, in the shape of His body, with a napkin for His head lying all by itself. When they saw this great wonder, they could not understand it all, but they believed that Jesus rose from the dead.

REMEMBER:

We did not see Jesus' grave as Simon Peter and John did; and even if we had, we would not understand how He could rise out of those linen clothes and go through the walls of the grave. But we believe it! God puts faith into our hearts to make us believe that Jesus is alive and is in heaven now.

Jesus' First Appearances

Do you know to whom Jesus showed Himself first after He rose from the dead, even before He appeared to the other women? To Mary Magdalene. Let me tell you how it happened. Quite a while ago, when Jesus was still preaching on the earth, He had cast out seven devils from her. Before Jesus did this wonder, she had lived a terrible life with those seven devils inside her. Suddenly Jesus had made her well again and after that she spent all her time taking care of Him. She made Him comfortable with food and drink or she gave Him a place to rest. It was her "thank-you" to Jesus. Mary Magdalene listened to Jesus preach, and she loved Him with her whole heart.

Now her Jesus had died on the cross and was buried in a cold grave in a rocky cave. Early on that Sunday morning she had walked with the other women to Jesus' grave with her sweet smelling spices. When she saw that the stone was rolled away and the grave was empty, she was sure someone had stolen Jesus' body. And she cried sad tears.

The two angels who had come down from heaven saw her standing there crying so hard and they asked her, "Woman, why weepest thou?" Weep means cry.

Mary Magdalene answered, "Because they have taken away my Lord, and I know not where they have laid him."

Poor Mary had so many tears she did not even look up and see that she was talking to **angels.** Instead, she turned around and saw a man standing near her who looked like a gardener, a man who took care of the graveyard. She did not know it was Jesus, risen from the dead, Who purposely made Himself look like the gardener. All she could think about was getting Jesus' dead body back to the grave. Through her tears she asked Jesus, Who looked like the gardener, "Sir, if thou have borne him hence, tell me where thou hast laid him, and I will take him away."

Then in His own voice Jesus said, "Mary."

Now she knew Who it was! She said, "Master!"

Jesus said, "Touch me not."

Why did Jesus say that to Mary? To teach her a lesson. Jesus had to teach Mary that He did not have His old earthly body anymore. Now He had a heavenly body that would not need Mary's food and drink anymore. He would not live on this earth anymore, either. He told Mary that He was going back home to **His** Father and to **Mary's** Father.

What a happy Mary Magdalene ran to the disciples! At last she understood why her Lord Jesus had to die. And He was alive again, she told the disciples.

But the disciples were not sure that they believed Mary Magdalene. Maybe she had a dream. This resurrection day was such a strange day to them. Peter and John saw the empty grave. Mary and the women said they had seen Jesus, too. No, the disciples said, those were just stories.

In the afternoon two of the disciples started to walk home, about six miles, to the little town of Emmaus. All the way home they talked and asked one another questions about Jesus; and as they talked, a stranger, a man they did not know, began to walk along with them. They did not know that the stranger was Jesus. He would not let them know Who He was. The two disciples did not stop talking about the only thing there **was** to talk about: Jesus. And then this stranger asked them what they were talking about and why they were sad.

Oh, those disciples were surprised! It seemed as if this stranger walking along with them did not even know about Jesus. So they told the stranger — Who was Jesus — all about Himself. They told Him that when Jesus was on earth they thought that He was the Son of God Who would save Israel. But then everything went wrong. The rulers killed Him on the cross and He was dead and buried. The strangest part was that some of the women said that He was alive.

That is when Jesus scolded them and said, "O fools, and slow of heart to believe all that the prophets have spoken," and then He told why Jesus **had** to die: to save His people from dying in hell. All the way home Jesus taught them how the Bible said He had to die as the Lamb of God. And still they did not know Who was walking with them. When they came to the town of Emmaus, Jesus acted as if he were going on, but they begged Him to come and eat with them. As they were at the table, Jesus opened their eyes and they knew it was Jesus. Then He disappeared.

Those two disciples got right up. Probably they did not even take time to eat their food. Right back to Jerusalem they walked. They couldn't wait to tell the other disciples. But when they found the disciples, they could not even tell their story, for the other disciples were so excited that they shouted their news first: "The Lord is risen indeed, and hath appeared to Simon."

Then the two disciples told their story and now all the disciples believed that Jesus was truly risen from the dead.

REMEMBER:

On Resurrection Day Jesus came three times to people who were especially sad: Mary Magdalene, because she loved Him so much; the two disciples, because they were so mixed up; and Simon Peter, because he had sinned so badly when he said he didn't know Jesus. Then Jesus made them all glad. Whenever we are sad, He makes us glad, too.

Jesus Appears to His Disciples

You remember, don't you, that Jesus arose from the grave early on a Sunday morning? Many, many wonders happened on that day. In our story for today it was still Resurrection Sunday. The disciples (all except Thomas) were together in a room, talking about the Jesus Whom they had thought was dead but Who really was alive. They had locked the doors of the room because they were afraid of the wicked rulers of the Jews. While everyone was trying to tell his story about Jesus rising from the dead, Jesus Himself stood with them in the room. He did not have to unlock a door or a window. He just came into the room and said, "Peace be unto you."

The disciples did not feel very peaceful. They were afraid, terribly afraid. They thought they were seeing a ghost. Didn't they know Jesus? Yes, they did; but this Jesus seemed **different**. This was a **heavenly** Jesus, not the Jesus they knew Who had walked with them for three years through the land of Israel. He asked them, "Why are ye troubled?"

Jesus really knew why they felt so troubled. He explained to His disciples that He was not coming back to this earth to live again. Now He had a heavenly body and in that heavenly body He would soon go to heaven to live forever. But even in His heavenly body Jesus could eat earthly food; for He asked them, "Have ye here any meat?" and they gave Him a piece of fish, and He ate it in front of them.

Then He breathed on them the Holy Spirit and opened their minds so they could understand all about His dying and rising again. Suddenly Jesus was gone.

Those excited disciples ran to find Thomas to tell him the news that Jesus had come to them and had talked with them; but Thomas did not believe them. Oh, he didn't really think the disciples were lying to him, but he was the kind of

man who would not believe unless he saw it with his own eyes. He said to the rest of the disciples, "Except I shall see in his hands the print of the nails, and put my finger into the print of the nails, and thrust my hand into his side, I will not believe."

After eight days the disciples were together in a room again and this time Thomas was with them. Again the doors were locked and suddenly Jesus stood in the room with them saying, "Peace be unto you."

Jesus knew what Thomas had said to the other disciples, and He showed Thomas His hands with the prints of the cruel nails in them. He told Thomas to touch the nail holes in His hand and put his hand into the hole in His side where the soldiers had cut Him with a sword. Jesus scolded Thomas, too. He said, "Be not faithless, but believing."

That was too much for Thomas. Now he knew he did not have to touch Jesus. All he could say was, "My Lord and My God."

Jesus told His disciples to travel to Galilee and wait there for Him. The disciples went to Galilee and waited for many days. At last they were tired of waiting and Simon Peter told the rest of the disciples, "I go a fishing."

Do you remember that Simon Peter was a fisherman before He followed Jesus? Now he decided to go back to his old work of fishing. Seven of the disciples went with him and they fished all night. Toward morning they saw a stranger on the shore but they did not know that the stranger was Jesus.

He called to them: "Children, have ye any meat?" He meant: "Did you catch anything?"

The disciples were unhappy and disgusted, for they had fished all night without catching a thing. They answered Him, "No."

Once more Jesus called to them, "Cast the net on the right side of the ship, and ye shall find."

When they did that, they could not pull their net into the boat because it was too full of fishes — a hundred fifty-three of them. Now they knew Who was on the shore!

John said to Simon Peter, "It is the Lord."

Peter was so eager to get to Jesus that he dived into the sea and swam to the shore to Jesus. Why did Jesus do this wonder? To teach them not to go fishing by themselves. They needed Jesus and His wonder. It was a picture of what the disciples were going to do the rest of their lives: they were going fishing for **men**. They would preach to them and teach them all about God's Word. And they needed the power of Jesus to go with them. From now on they would preach for the Lord.

When all the disciples came to the shore, they saw that Jesus had a fire and had prepared fish and bread. He invited them to eat with Him. How happy those disciples must have been! It was the third time Jesus had appeared to them.

REMEMBER:

When we see a fisherman catching fish, we will know that it is a picture of God's preachers fishing for men by preaching God's Word. Aren't you glad Jesus used the picture of a fisherman?

557

The Day of Jesus' Ascension and the Day of Pentecost

Many times in the forty days after He arose from the grave, Jesus came to His disciples and talked with them and then suddenly disappeared. On the fortieth day after He arose, He came once more to His disciples as they were in the city of Jerusalem and He walked with them to His favorite mountain, the Mount of Olives. There Jesus made them a promise: that He would soon send the Holy Spirit into their hearts. The Holy Spirit is God; and when God was in their hearts, they would understand all the things about Jesus they had not understood before. And then, Jesus told them, they would have power to preach about Him over the whole earth.

As Jesus was talking with them, a cloud — a special cloud — came down and took Jesus into it and lifted Him up to heaven. The disciples stood there on the mountain top watching the cloud that took Jesus away, until they could see it no more. They knew that Jesus would not come back to them. He had gone to another country, to heaven.

They were still standing there, looking up into heaven when two angels in white clothes stood next to them. They asked the disciples, "Why stand ye gazing up into heaven?" Gazing means **looking**.

The two angels promised the disciples that some day Jesus will come back to the earth the same way He went up to heaven: in a cloud. Do you know when that will be? At the end of the world. Then He will take all His people to heaven with Him. We are still waiting for Jesus to come again in a cloud.

Then the angels went back to heaven and the disciples walked to Jerusalem again to wait for Jesus' promise to put the Holy Spirit into their hearts. They waited for ten days. The tenth day was a feast day, a feast of thanks to God for giving them crops in their fields and for making those crops ripe. The people made bread from the wheat that they gathered from their fields and gave the loaves of bread to the Lord in His temple.

After the feast day was over, the believers in Jesus — one hundred twenty of them — were together in one room, praying. Suddenly Jesus kept His promise to send the Holy Spirit into their hearts. He sent three picture-signs when He sent His Spirit.

First the disciples in that room heard the sound of a strong, rushing wind. Think of wind. We cannot see it but we know it is there because we can hear it and we can see the bushes and trees moving. The picture of wind in the room where the disciples were was different. They heard the sound but nothing moved. That kind of wind is a picture of the Holy Spirit. We cannot **see** the Holy Spirit, for He does not work like a big, strong wind in the world. No, the Holy Spirit works like a quiet wind in the hearts of His own children.

The second picture was tongues, or little flames, that looked like fire, which came over every one of the believers in that room. Think of fire. It burns the trash we do not want anymore. It does something else, too. It sterilizes the needle that our mother uses to take out our slivers, so the needle is pure and clean. Those tongues that looked like fire were a picture of the Holy Spirit in the hearts of God's children. The Holy Spirit burns away the trash of sin and makes our hearts pure and clean.

The third picture was a great wonder. All those one hundred twenty people started to talk in other languages. Many people were in Jerusalem for the feast of thanks to God for making their crops ripe and these people came from all over the world. Suddenly they heard Jesus' disciples speaking in their languages, too. Jesus' disciples must have left that room and told all the people about the wonder of the Holy Spirit coming into their hearts. And everyone could hear them speak in his own language!

The wicked Jews who did not believe in Jesus were not happy. They said it wasn't a wonder at all. They said those one hundred twenty disciples of Jesus were drunk and were talking nonsense. Oh, that was a wicked thing to say about God's holy wonder!

Simon Peter answered them and said that it was still early in the morning. People don't drink wine and get drunk early in the morning. Then he preached to the crowds of people. He told them how Joel, one of God's prophets who had lived long, long ago, had said that some day this great wonder would happen. He went on preaching to the crowds of people, telling them that Jesus **had** to die to save His people and He **had** to be buried and rise again and go to heaven.

When the crowds of people heard the wonderful news that Peter preached, God pricked their hearts and they cried, "Men and brethren, what shall we do?"

Peter had the answer. He said, "Repent and be baptized every one of you in the name of Jesus Christ."

That day the Lord made three thousand people sorry for their sins and He made them believe in Jesus. That day was a day of great excitement and happiness for the church, because the Spirit of Jesus Christ gave salvation to so many people. We call that day **Pentecost**.

REMEMBER:

Jesus promises us, too, that "whoever shall call on the name of the Lord shall be saved." That makes us excited and happy, too, doesn't it?

The Healing of the Lame Man

Two of Jesus' disciples, Simon Peter and John, went to the temple one day about the middle of the afternoon, which was the time when many of the people came to pray. Do you know why they chose that time to go? So that they could preach to the crowds of people the glad news that Jesus rose from the dead and was alive in heaven.

As they passed one of the gates of the temple called the Beautiful Gate, they saw a man sitting there who could not walk. We call him a **lame** man. Maybe they had seen him sitting there quite often; for that man had been born lame and every day for years someone had carried him to the Beautiful Gate and he sat there all day, begging for money. Now he was more than forty years old and no one thought that he would ever walk.

When Peter and John walked past him he begged them for a piece of money. Peter stopped and said to him, "Look on us."

The lame man looked up, expecting some money from Peter; but Peter said, "Silver and gold have I none; but such as I have give I thee: In the name of Jesus Christ of Nazareth rise up and walk."

Peter was giving him something **much** better than a piece of money. He was going to make that man's legs better; but Peter could not do that wonder all of himself. Jesus Christ was going to make that man better, Jesus Christ Who rose from the dead and Who gave Peter power to do that wonder. Peter did what Jesus had done so often when He was on earth: he reached down his hand and lifted the man up. It was a picture of Jesus reaching down and healing him.

That lame man did not have to learn to walk as a baby does. He felt strength go into his lame feet and ankles, he stood up, he walked, and then he jumped and praised God.

All the people just stood there in great surprise and watched the wonder that Jesus did through Peter's hands. What excitement there was in the temple! Everyone ran to the porch where that lame man was walking and jumping, happily praising God. Why were they so **greatly** surprised? Hadn't they seen

561

Jesus do many wonders like this one? Oh, certainly, they had. But they thought that Jesus was **dead**. How could a **dead** Jesus work such a wonder?

Peter knew why they were surprised and he told them the answer to their question by preaching a sermon to them. He asked them, "Why look ye so earnestly on us, as though by our own power or holiness we had made this man to walk?"

He told the people that he made this man walk through the power of Jesus Whom **they** killed and Whom **God** raised up from the grave. He preached to the people beautiful words, telling them to be sorry for their sin of killing Jesus and to believe in Him.

While Peter and John were still speaking to the people, the ruler of the temple and the wicked rulers of the Jews heard all the excitement and all the commotion. They were not happy at all. They arrested Peter and John and put them in jail. Why did they do that? Because Peter and John preached that Jesus rose from the dead. All that night Peter and John had to stay locked up in jail.

In the morning all the rulers of the Jews — the same rulers who said that Jesus must die — came together to judge Peter and John. When the rulers had killed Jesus, they thought they were rid of Him forever. Do you think God in heaven was laughing at those foolish rulers? Now those rulers asked Peter and John, "By what power, or by what name, have ye done this?"

Peter answered, "By the name of Jesus Christ of Nazareth, whom ye crucified, whom God raised from the dead."

When those wicked rulers saw the lame man who was healed standing with Peter and John, they **knew** that they were seeing a great miracle. They did not dare to hurt Peter and John nor keep them in prison, so they told them they might never again speak or teach in the name of Jesus.

Peter answered them that they could not obey that rule. They must first obey God; for it was **right** to teach in the name of Jesus. What could those rulers do? With hard hearts they promised them more punishments if they taught in the name of Jesus. Then, because they did not know what else to do, the rulers let Peter and John go free.

REMEMBER:

Peter and John were not afraid to talk about Jesus, for they knew God would take care of them, even in prison. We know that He will take care of us, too, when we speak out for Him.

Ananias and Sapphira Sin

In our last story we learned that the rulers of the Jews put Peter and John into prison overnight because they preached about Jesus. The rest of the disciples and all the other believers knew that Peter and John would not come home that night. They knew that the two disciples were locked up in jail. Anxiously they waited for news. I think they prayed while they waited, don't you?

Then in the morning when the rulers let them go, Peter and John hurried to the rest of the disciples and believers and told them what the rulers had said to them: do not speak in the name of Jesus ever again. When all those disciples heard the story of Peter and John, they prayed and asked God to make them all strong and bold to speak out in Jesus' name and to do many wonders in His name, too.

God answered their prayer in a special way. He shook the room where they were meeting and filled them all with His Holy Spirit so that they would not be afraid of the rulers and would dare to speak in Jesus' name.

We call all those people who loved Jesus **the church**. Just as we go to church with people who love the Lord, so all those who loved the Lord and Jesus Christ His Son came together as a church. They did more than that. For a while they all lived together, too. They felt safer from the wicked rulers when they were all

together. Everyone shared his money and
his food and his furniture and whatever he
had with everyone else. In that way no one
had too much and no one was too poor
and everyone was taken care of very well.
One of the disciples, whose name was
Barnabas, sold a piece of land and brought
the money to the leaders of the church.
We call those leaders **apostles**. The apostles
could give the money to the poor people
in the church. Barnabas did not love his
land. He did not love his money. He
loved God and God's people.

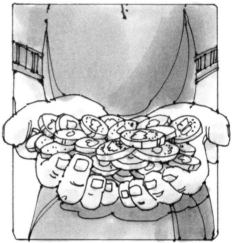

Then a terrible sin came into the church. A man called Ananias and his
wife Sapphira sold a piece of land, too. They kept some of the money for themselves and gave the rest to the leaders of the church, the apostles. That was not
a sin. It was all right for them to do that. They did not **have** to give all the
money to the church. They might even have kept all the money if they wanted
to.

What was their terrible sin, then? They lied. They told Peter and the other
apostles that they were giving **all** the money to the church. They told that lie
because they wanted everyone in the church to think that Ananias and Sapphira
were wonderful people! They **said** the Holy Spirit was in their hearts and that
they loved the Lord but the devil was really working in their hearts.

Ananias and Sapphira did not come at the same time to tell their lies. First
Ananias came and told his lie, that he had given **all** the money to the apostles.
Peter said to him, "Why hath Satan filled thine heart, to lie to the Holy Ghost?"

How did Peter know that Ananias was lying? God told him. Because
Ananias had told a lie to God, he needed a punishment everyone could see.
Peter did not punish him. **God** did. Ananias fell down dead. Some of the young
men had to carry him out and bury him in a grave. Oh, the people who saw it
stood in fear and trembled before God!

Sapphira his wife did not stand in fear. She wasn't there and no one told her what had happened to Ananias. Three hours later she came to the leaders of the church. Peter was ready with a question for her; "Tell me whether ye sold the land for so much."

She told the same lie that her husband had told: "Yea, for so much."

Peter **had** to ask her that question to see whether she was lying. And she was. It must have been with sadness in his heart that he asked her, "How is it that ye have agreed together to tempt the Spirit of the Lord?"

And then Sapphira fell down dead. Some of the young men had to carry her out and bury her in a grave. Once more, great fear of the Lord came over all the people of His church.

REMEMBER:

This story will help us remember what a holy and pure God we have, a God Who hates lies and Who punishes the wicked. We must bow before Him, but we do not have to be afraid, for we are His children, who come to Him very humbly and tell Him about our sins and ask Him to take them away.

The Rulers
Stone Stephen

From now on in our stories we will call the disciples who were the leaders of God's church the **apostles**. Every day the apostles went to the temple and preached to the people about Jesus and they did many wonders in Jesus' name; for He gave them power to make sick people better and even to cast out devils. Such crowds of sick people came to the porch of the temple that most of them could not get near to the apostles. But they did not go home. They waited until it was time for the sun to go down, when the light of the sun made long shadows. When the long shadow of the apostle Peter fell upon them, they were made better. Wasn't it wonderful that God used Peter's shadow to heal sick people? Oh, those people were excited and happy and very many believed in the Lord Jesus Christ.

The rulers of the Jews watched all of these things happen. They were angry, so angry that they were ready to do anything to get rid of the apostles of Jesus. They grabbed them and threw them into the worst kind of jail where all the very evil kinds of men were kept. Then they locked the door. The apostles were not alone in that awful jail. God was right there with them and He sent His angel to open the prison door, to let them out, and to lock it again. The angel told them to go right back to the temple and preach to the people. Early in the morning the apostles went to the temple to preach.

Meanwhile, the rulers of the Jews thought the apostles were safely locked up in jail. When some of them went to get the apostles, they had the surprise of their lives. All the doors were locked but the apostles were gone. They couldn't figure out what had happened! Can you imagine how their faces looked when some-one told them, "Behold, the men whom ye put in prison are standing in the temple, and teaching the people"?

567

To the temple the rulers of the Jews went. Once more they ordered the apostles **not** to speak in the name of Jesus, but Peter said, "We ought to obey God rather than men."

Those rulers did not know what to do. They beat the apostles on their back with whips and then let them go free. Do you think the apostles cried and complained to God because they were whipped so badly? Oh no: they were happy that they could suffer bleeding backs for Jesus' sake.

God was blessing the people in His church very much in those days. He made the hearts of very many people turn to Jesus and trust in Him. The more the Lord blessed His people the more angry the rulers of the Jews became. They especially hated Stephen, a great leader in the church, who preached and who had the power of Jesus to do great wonders. How those rulers hated Stephen! They wished they could kill him! Then some of the wicked rulers had an idea: they would start a fight with Stephen and with God's people. They paid evil men to go around telling lies about him. They told those evil men to make the people of the city all upset so they would not listen to Stephen anymore.

What lies did those evil men tell? That Stephen wanted to break down God's temple and to throw away God's holy law. Weren't those terrible lies?

The rulers brought Stephen to their court to judge him. While the evil men were telling their lies about Stephen, the rulers were watching his face. God made it shine like the face of an angel. It was a wonder. Wouldn't you think that those wicked men would bow before the Lord when they saw His glory shining down on Stephen's face? They didn't. The high priest asked Stephen about those lies. He asked, "Are these thing so?"

To answer that question Stephen preached a most beautiful sermon about how all God's people looked for Jesus for years and years and finally He came, just as God had promised. Suddenly Stephen turned to those wicked rulers and told them that **they** had killed Jesus, the Just One.

Those words made the rulers so angry that they stood grinding their teeth at him, but Stephen looked up and saw Jesus standing at God's right hand in heaven. He cried out, "Behold I see the heavens opened, and the Son of Man standing on the right hand of God."

Those hard-hearted rulers would not look at Jesus and they would not listen to Him, either. They stopped their ears, took Stephen out of the city and threw huge stones at him, to kill him. While they threw the stones, Stephen kneeled down and prayed, saying, "Lord Jesus, receive my spirit." That means **take me to heaven.**"

He prayed one more prayer. He asked the Lord to make those men sorry and forgive them for this awful sin. And then he fell asleep in death and went to be with Jesus. Stephen had died for Jesus' sake.

REMEMBER:

If we are God's children, we do not have to be afraid to die, for when we fall asleep in death we wake up with Jesus.

569

The Story of Philip

After the rulers of the Jews had stoned Stephen until he died, they thought that the apostles and the other believers would be very frightened and stop preaching in the name of Jesus. It didn't turn out that way at all. The apostles remembered the words of Jesus: to preach the glad news of His death and resurrection in all countries of the world; and they kept right on preaching in Jesus' name.

Now the rulers began to **persecute** those who believed in the Lord Jesus. Persecute means to do cruel, painful things to them, to put them in prison, to burn their houses, and sometimes to kill them. One ruler especially, whose name was Saul, did all he could to hurt God's people. When Stephen was stoned, he was the man who held the coats of the men who stoned Stephen. He hated God's people so much he would burst into their houses and drag them to prison. Sometimes he killed them. It wasn't safe for them to live in the city of Jerusalem anymore. Many of them moved to other countries. Oh, they felt so sad and they hated to move away, but God was with them, and He said it was good. Do you know why? When the believers moved away, they took the good news of Jesus along with them in their hearts and preached it in all the countries they came to. Many people in those countries came to believe in Jesus, too.

One of the men who ran away from Jerusalem was Philip. He was a preacher and he went to the city of Samaria, in the land where most of the people worshipped in a mixed-up way. Partly they served idols and partly they tried to serve God. Philip preached the glad story of Jesus to them, how God sent Him to save His people from their sins. And the people of Samaria listened very eagerly to Philip's preaching. The Lord gave Philip power to do many wonders, too. He healed people from the sickness of palsy and many other sicknesses, and he cast out devils. When the people heard his preaching and saw all the wonders, they believed and there was so much joy in their city.

In the city of Samaria was a man called Simon. He called himself a magician and with his magic tricks he made all the people think he was a great man. Everyone in Samaria listened to this great Simon and they said, "This man is the great power of God."

Then Philip had come to Samaria and when Simon had watched the wonders that God did through Philip's hand, he knew that Philip's power was much greater than his magic tricks. Simon kept listening to Philip's preaching and especially he watched the wonders Philip did in Jesus' name. Simon wished he could do that! He would be an even greater man if he could do **such** wonders! So he said he believed, too; and Philip baptized him. But Simon did not really believe that Jesus died on the cross for his sins. No, he wanted only one thing: to be a great man in this world.

When the rest of the apostles heard about the happiness in Samaria, they sent Peter and John to Philip. When they came to him, Peter and John prayed for the believers, that the Holy Spirit might come into their hearts; and when they laid their hands on the believers, the Lord sent the Holy Spirit into their hearts. Simon wished he could have the gift of the Holy Spirit in his heart, too, and he offered to buy it with money.

Peter scolded him sternly for trying to buy God's precious gifts with money and he said to Simon, "Thy heart is not right in the sight of God."

He told Simon to be sorry for his sin, but the Bible does not tell us that he was ever sorry.

Then God called Philip, the preacher, away from Samaria to a place in a lonely, sandy, hot desert. There on the road he met a man, a very important man, from a far country. The Bible does not tell us his name. As this important man was riding, probably in a beautiful covered wagon, he was reading aloud from the Bible. Philip asked him whether he understood what he was reading. The important man answered, "How can I, except some man should guide me?"

Then Philip climbed up into the wagon and read with him the beautiful words which the prophet Isaiah told about Jesus, Who would be killed as the Lamb of God. That poor man did not understand who the Lamb of God was. Then Philip preached to him the whole story of the Lamb Who was born in Bethlehem, Who lived on this earth, Who died on the cross to take away His people's sins, and Who rose again to save His people.

Just then they rode past some water, maybe a river; and the important man begged Philip to baptize him in Jesus' name. Philip said, "If thou believest with all thine heart, thou mayest."

He answered, "I believe that Jesus Christ is the Son of God."

Philip baptized him and the man went on his way to his own country, happy to bring the glad news of Jesus to his own people.

REMEMBER:

Everyone in our story who believed in Jesus was so happy. That is because the story of Jesus is the happiest story in the world.

God Converts Saul

Saul was the ruler who persecuted those who believed in Jesus more than any other ruler. Remember, persecute means to chase the believers, put them into prison, whip them, or kill them. The more wickedness Saul did the more the believers preached in Jesus' name. Saul was so angry with them that he was **breathing murder** against all the followers of Jesus. Murder means **killing.**

Saul heard that many of the believers had run to a faraway city called Damascus, where they thought they would be safe for a while. Saul had a different idea. He asked the high priest, the most important ruler, for letters saying that he might tie up any people who believed in Jesus and take them back to Jerusalem to punish them in prison.

After the high priest had given him the letters, Saul started out with several other men to the city of Damascus. About noon they were coming close to the city. Suddenly a bright light shone down from heaven on Saul and his men. The light was so bright and so heavenly that all of them fell to the ground on their

faces. Then a voice from heaven spoke to Saul, saying, "Saul, Saul, why persecutest thou me?"

Saul asked, "Who art thou, Lord?"

And the Lord said, "I am Jesus whom thou persecutest."

All this time when Saul had been cruel to the believers, he had really persecuted **Jesus!** No wonder Saul was trembling and shaking with fear, hardly daring to look up. When he did look up, he saw **Jesus Himself** through that heavenly light and he said, "Lord what wilt thou have me to do?"

Jesus told him that He had chosen Saul to be a special minister for him, to preach the glad news all over the world. Right now he must go into the city of Damascus, and he would be told what to do. Then the bright light was gone.

The men who were with Saul were so shocked by the wonder they saw that they could not say a word. They had seen the bright light and heard a voice but they could not understand it. When Saul stood up, he could open his eyes but could not see anything. He was blind. His men had to lead him by the hand into the city of Damascus.

In Damascus Saul stayed with a man named Judas. Don't you think Judas was surprised when he saw a sad, quiet, blind Saul instead of a loud, hateful, wicked Saul? For three days the Lord left Saul blind, with nothing to do but think. What terrible thoughts Saul must have had inside him. **Now** he loved Jesus. What had he done to the Jesus he loved? Whipped His dear people, put them in jail, and even killed them! Oh, he was sorry. All he could do in those three days was pray that God would take those awful sins away. He was so sad and so sorry that for all those three days he could not eat or drink.

Then God came to him in a sort of dream and showed him that a man named Ananias would give him back his sight. At the same time God came to Ananias and told him to go to the house of Judas on Straight Street and put his hand on Saul to make him see again.

Ananias was not very happy with what God had told him to do. He said, "Lord, I have heard by many of this man, how much evil he hath done to thy saints at Jerusalem."

God explained to Ananias that He had changed Saul from a hard, cruel man to a soft, humble man who loved Jesus; for God had put His love and grace into Saul's heart. Then Ananias gladly went and when he found the sad, blind Saul, he said, "Brother Saul, receive thy sight."

Scales, like hard skin, fell from Saul's eyes and he could see again. What a lovely picture that was! It was a picture of the blindness of sin falling away from his eyes and the light of God's love shining through them. Ananias baptized Saul — a picture of the washing away of his sins — and Saul went into one of the synagogues and preached in the name of Jesus. What a shock for the people of Damascus to hear Saul preaching in the name of Jesus! How happy the followers of Jesus must have been!

For three years Saul stayed in Damascus, preaching and teaching. By that time the wicked rulers hated him so much they made plans to kill him because he taught the story of Jesus. Saul's life was in danger and Jesus' disciples who lived in the city helped him. Quietly, in the night, they let him down in a basket from the wall of the city and Saul ran away, back to Jerusalem to be with Jesus' disciples there.

REMEMBER:

The light of God's love shone through Saul's eyes after he believed in Jesus. It shines through the eyes of all God's children. How does the light of God's love shine through **your** eyes?

575

The Church Grows and Spreads

In today's story we will find out how God's people were living in those dangerous times when the rulers tried to put all the followers of Jesus into prison. More and more of God's people moved away from the land of Israel and their preachers moved away with them, too. When they came to the faraway lands where they would live, they preached to the heathen people in those lands. Do you know what happened? God turned the hearts of those people to Jesus and they believed that He died to save them. For many years God had saved only His people Israel. Now He opened the doors of His salvation to the heathen people, too. We call them **Gentiles**. And the Gentiles were so glad that Jesus died for them. **We** are Gentiles, too; and we believe that Jesus died for us, don't we?

Far away from Jerusalem was a big city called Antioch. Many of the believers went there to live and to teach the Gentiles in the name of Jesus. It was in Antioch that the followers of Jesus were first called **Christians**. Christian means **Christ-people**. It is a beautiful name. We are called by the name of Christians, too.

Now we will leave the city of Antioch for a little while and go back to Jerusalem. The apostle Peter was still preaching there, but he knew it was not safe for him and the rest of the Christians to preach in the name of Jesus. It was more dangerous than ever, for a new King Herod was ruling now and he had one thing in his mind: to get rid of all those who loved Jesus. When God's people came together for church, they usually met in someone's house and they locked all the doors so they would be safer.

There was one man whom wicked King Herod wanted to kill very badly, a man who **would not** stop preaching about Jesus. That man was Peter. He captured Peter and threw him into prison just at the time of the passover feast. When the feast was over, King Herod planned to take Peter out of prison and kill him. King Herod knew, too, that God often saved His people by a wonder. **This** time King Herod wanted to make sure Peter would not get away, so he tied two soldiers to Peter, one on each side, with strong chains, and he set two soldiers nearby to guard the door. It **seemed** as if Peter would not be able to get away this time. All the time that Peter was in prison the church of Jesus did not stop praying for him.

On the night before King Herod planned to take Peter out of prison to kill him, Peter was sleeping soundly between the two guards who were chained to him. He knew King Herod wanted to kill him, but he trusted in God to take care of him. The guards did not sleep. They kept a watch over Peter. If they ever slept while they were guards, they knew they would die for it.

Suddenly a bright light from God shone into the prison and an angel stood beside Peter. Peter was sleeping so peacefully that the angel had to hit him on his side to waken him. His chains fell off his hands and the angel told him to get dressed. Peter and the angel walked right past the other two guards and out of the prison. What had happened to the guards? Maybe a deep sleep from the Lord had fallen upon them.

Peter and the angel walked to the gate of the city and that big, heavy gate opened for them all by itself. It was a wonder from God, of course. Then the angel was gone and Peter was standing alone. At first he had thought he was **dreaming** that this was happening, but when the angel left him he was surprised to find that he was truly standing in one of the streets of Jerusalem, free from prison. Peter knew then that the Lord had saved him from prison once more.

Although it was the middle of the night, he went to the house of Mary, where God's church met. Yes, God's people were there, praying for Peter. He knocked at the door and a young girl named Rhoda answered it. When she heard Peter's voice outside the door, she didn't unlock it. She was so surprised and so glad she ran to tell everyone that Peter was at the door. The rest of the people didn't believe **that!** Why, Peter was in prison, they told her. While they argued about it, poor Peter stood at the locked door and kept on knocking.

When at last they opened the door with great excitement and joy and talking, Peter had to hold his hand up and make them be quiet, for he wanted to tell them the whole story of God's wonder in setting him free. Then they sent Peter away for a while to a safer place.

Can't you imagine how surprised and angry King Herod was the next morning when the guards were still guarding the prison but Peter was gone? Do you think God in heaven laughed at wicked King Herod?

REMEMBER:

God's people prayed for Peter when he was in trouble. God tells us to pray for His people who are in trouble, too; and He always hears our prayers.

Paul's First Missionary Journey

In our last story about Saul we left him preaching in the name of the Lord Jesus in the city of Jerusalem. He did not stay there long but went to the city of Antioch, the big city where the followers of Jesus were first called **Christ-people**, or Christians. Saul was called by a little different name in Antioch, too. He was called **Paul**.

Barnabas, who was also a preacher of Jesus, was with Paul in Antioch; and God told His people in the church there to send Paul and Barnabas away on a trip. It would be a **preaching trip** and it would last a whole year. We call this trip a **missionary journey**. On this missionary journey Paul and Barnabas would go from city to city, always preaching the glad news of how Jesus came and died and arose to save His people. It would be a dangerous trip, because many of the wicked Jews lived in those cities and they hated Jesus and the men who preached about Jesus. Paul and Barnabas were not afraid to go because they knew that God would take care of them. Before they left on their journey, the leaders of the church at Antioch prayed for them. Then the leaders laid their hands over Paul's and Barnabas' heads. That was a picture of God's blessing over them.

First Paul and Barnabas took a ship across a big sea to an island called Cyprus. On the island of Cyprus lived some Jews and some heathen people called **Gentiles**. Paul and Barnabas preached first to the Jews and then to the heathen Gentiles. In one of the cities they met a man called Bar-jesus who knew how to work all kinds of magic tricks. He did not want Paul and Barnabas to preach about the Lord Jesus and spoil his magic tricks. When the ruler of Cyprus listened to Paul's glad news of Jesus, the wicked Bar-jesus tried, by his magic tricks, to turn the ruler's heart from believing on Jesus Christ.

Paul scolded the wicked magician with very hard words. He said, "O full of all mischief, thou child of the devil. . . the hand of the Lord is upon thee, and thou shalt be blind, not seeing the sun for a season." A season is a **time**. We do not know how long a time.

At that minute darkness came over the eyes of Bar-jesus and he became blind. Someone had to lead him by the hand. But the ruler of the island believed on the Lord Jesus.

Soon Paul and Barnabas left the island and preached in other cities. When they came to Iconium, those who hated Jesus made trouble for them. Those wicked men tried to turn all the people of the city against Paul and Barnabas and they were ready to take up big stones in their hands to kill them.

Do you think Paul and Barnabas were afraid and went back home? Oh, no. They ran away to the next city, called Lystra, and preached there. While Paul was preaching in Lystra, he saw a man, a crippled man who had never walked in all his life, listening so closely to Paul's glad words. The man did not take his eyes away from Paul. When Paul looked at the crippled man's face, he could see that he was **eager** to hear about Jesus. He had happiness on his face. By the Spirit in his heart, Paul knew that the crippled man believed in Jesus. Suddenly, in a loud voice, he said, "Stand upright on thy feet." The man obeyed. And he jumped!

What excitement there was in the city of Lystra. These people worshipped idol-gods and they began shouting, "The gods are come down to us in the likeness of men."

They thought Paul and Barnabas were idol-gods. They even gave them names: they called Barnabas by the name of their idol Jupiter and they called Paul by the name of their idol Mercury. Next they brought animals all decorated with flowers and ribbons to sacrifice to Paul and Barnabas.

Now the two preachers had to show the people that they were all wrong. Paul and Barnabas were not gods! They tore their clothes to show how shocked and sad they felt and they told the people that they were only **men** preachers of the Most High God. At last the people of Lystra understood that Paul and Barnabas did not even believe in idols.

More trouble was on the way. Those wicked haters of Jesus from Iconium followed Paul and Barnabas to Lystra and told the people of Lystra that the two preachers were terrible men. They should not **worship** them. They should **hurt** them. The people of Lystra turned right around and helped throw big stones at Paul until he dropped down to the ground and everyone thought he was dead. Then they dragged him, hard and cruelly, outside the city. Paul must have been hurt very badly. Some of God's people in Lystra stood sadly near his quiet body when suddenly God made a great wonder. He healed Paul and made him stand up and go back into the city.

REMEMBER:

It was not easy for Paul to preach about Jesus to all kinds of people in all kinds of cities. But he remembered one verse from the Bible: "The Lord is thy keeper." That verse is for us, too.

Paul's Second Missionary Journey

After Paul and Barnabas finished their first preaching trip for the Lord — remember, we call it a missionary journey — they came back to the city of Antioch. Soon the Lord sent Paul on another journey and this time a preacher named Silas went along with him. On this trip they went to cities even farther away than those on Paul's first trip.

One of those cities was Philippi. On the sabbath day Paul usually found a synagogue, a church of the Jews, and preached about Jesus. But in Philippi there was no synagogue. It was a heathen city, full of idol-worshippers. Only at the riverside a few women came together to worship God. One of these women was Lydia, who made purple cloth and sold it to very rich people. Lydia was probably a rich woman, too. God had opened her heart and she worshipped Him. When Paul preached to her about Jesus, she and her whole family believed and they were all baptized. She was so happy to know that she was saved by Jesus that she begged Paul and Silas to stay with her for a while.

One day when they were going to the place of prayer, probably at the riverside, a girl followed them. She had an evil spirit, a devil, inside her. Wicked men who owned her told everyone that she could work magic charms and that she could tell them what was going to happen to them in the rest of their lives. We know of course that only **God** knows what is going to happen to us because He rules over our lives. Many people believed that this girl had magic charms and they paid her money to tell what would happen to them. But the poor girl did not get to keep the money. Her owners did. That money made them rich.

When the girl followed Paul and Silas, she kept shouting, "These men are the servants of the most high God, which show unto us the way of salvation."

For many days she shouted those words. It made Paul and Silas sad and Paul turned around and said to the devil, "I command thee in the name of Jesus Christ to come out of her."

And the devil came out of the girl. It was **Jesus** Who made her better, for Paul healed her by **Jesus'** power. What a happy, thankful girl she must have been. Her owners were not happy, though, for now that the devil was gone out of the girl, they could not earn money by her magic. Those wicked men caught Paul and Silas and brought them to the rulers of the city of Philippi, and as they went, they got together a crowd of people who made a big fuss in the city. We call it an **uproar**. The wicked owners of the girl told the rulers that Paul and Silas made a lot of trouble in the city and that they taught a strange worship of God. The whole crowd of people agreed.

The rulers did not give Paul and Silas a chance to talk. They took off their clothes and beat them on their backs with bundles of sticks tied together and then threw them into prison. The rulers made Paul and Silas lie flat on their bleeding backs on the cold stone floor of the prison. Then they spread their feet far apart and fastened each foot into a hole in a wooden post. Paul and Silas could not move with their feet stretched out that way. They could not go to sleep because their backs and their whole bodies hurt too much. Do you think they screamed because it hurt so much? Do you think they cried? Do you think they grumbled? No; at midnight they started to sing and to pray. Their hearts were peaceful and quiet in God's care and they did not mind that their bodies were hurt because they had preached about Jesus. Oh, the rest of the prisoners must have been shocked when they heard songs of praise from the lips of those two children of God, bleeding there on the jail floor.

God heard them singing, too, and He sent an earthquake, a sign of His anger against those wicked men. This earthquake was a special wonder, for it opened the doors of the prison and loosed the iron chains from all the prisoners. They were free! The keeper of the prison was so scared. He thought that all his prisoners had run away, and if they had, he would be killed. That was the law. The keeper of the prison decided that, if he must die anyway, he might as well kill himself. Just as he pulled out his sharp sword, Paul called out in a loud voice, "Do thyself no harm: for we are all here."

Then the keeper called for a light. He ran to Paul and Silas, scared and trembling, and fell down on his face before them. He must have known that Paul and Silas had preached about salvation in Jesus' name, for he asked, "Sirs, what must I do to be saved?"

They answered, "Believe on the Lord Jesus Christ, and thou shalt be saved, and thy house."

The keeper took Paul and Silas out of prison and brought them to his house. They taught the keeper and his family about Jesus Christ; and he and his family believed and were baptized in Jesus' name. Before he believed in Jesus, the keeper did not care at all about the ugly, dirty sores the bundles of sticks had made on their backs. Now he washed their backs and took care of them with love. The sad night was turned into a happy one because the Lord brought salvation to the keeper's house.

REMEMBER:

The Lord put His love and His strength into the hearts of Paul and Silas so that they could sing to the Lord from the prison floor. He puts that same kind of love and strength into our hearts so that even when we hurt or are sad we can always sing songs of praise to Him.

Paul's Third Missionary Journey

Very soon after Paul came back from his second missionary journey, the Lord sent him on a third journey. This time Paul wanted to visit the city of Ephesus. He had visited Ephesus on his second journey and stayed at the home of Aquila and Priscilla, who were his Christian friends. They did the same kind of work that Paul did. Of course, we know that Paul **preached**. But he did another kind of work, too: he made tents. In those days when there were not many places to stay, people often needed tents to take with them on trips. Paul made tents, either of cloth or skins of animals.

On his third missionary journey, when he visited the city of Ephesus again, Paul made tents part of the time to earn some money; and the rest of the time he preached. Soon he found twelve men who believed in God and who knew that God had promised to send Jesus to live on the earth. They even knew that John the Baptist had preached about Him and they were baptized with John's baptism. But they had never heard that Jesus had been born in Bethlehem, had preached and worked miracles, had suffered and died and had risen from the grave. They were still waiting for Jesus! How happy they must have been when Paul told them the whole story of Jesus. Then he laid his hands over them and God sent His Spirit into their hearts.

Those twelve men were Paul's helpers. They preached to the people of the city of Ephesus. Every day for two years Paul taught about Jesus. Many people from Ephesus and from all the cities near there came to hear him and many believed in Jesus. The Lord gave Paul power to do special wonders in the city of Ephesus, too. He made many people better in Jesus' name. If someone was too sick to go to Paul, friends brought him one of Paul's handkerchiefs or one of the aprons that he used for his work and that very sick person was made well. God used even Paul's handkerchiefs and aprons to cast out devils.

The enemies of Paul and the enemies of Jesus were jealous. They wanted to be great, too, and cast out devils just as Paul did. Seven men, the sons of Sceva, tried to cast out a devil from a man by telling him to come out in the name of Jesus Whom Paul preached.

The devil inside the man answered, "Jesus I know, and Paul I know; but who are ye?"

Then the man with the devil inside him jumped on those seven men and fought them so that they had to run away badly hurt and without any clothes on. When the people of Ephesus heard about it, they knew that the wonders Paul did were truly God's wonders; and they held God's name in great honor. Many people came to Paul and said they were sorry for their sins. Do you know what they took with them when they went to Paul? Their books of magic spells and charms. They made a big fire and burned them all. When they counted how much those wicked books had cost, they found it was fifty thousand pieces of silver.

Soon the word of God was spreading all over the city of Ephesus and many people left their idols and turned to worship the only true God. That made Demetrius very worried. He was a silversmith who made tiny silver idols of the goddess Diana. Demetrius talked to all the other silversmiths who made silver idols of Diana. He told them that they had gotten very rich by making these idols and selling them to the people. Now Paul was spoiling it, for he said that gods which are made with hands are no gods. Demetrius was worried that the people of Ephesus would stop buying the silver idols and would stop coming and bringing their money to the beautiful temple of their goddess Diana.

The longer Demetrius and the other silversmiths talked, the angrier they became. They started to cry out, "Great is Diana of the Ephesians!" Ephesians are people of Ephesus.

Crowds of people gathered and helped them shout, "Great is Diana of the Ephesians!" They caught two of Paul's friends and dragged them to a large open place in the city. Paul wanted to go, too, but his Christian friends said it would be too dangerous. More and more people came running and shouting and the noise and the mixed-up shouting were so great that most of the people didn't even know why everyone was running together, shouting. That was rather funny, wasn't it?

When a man named Alexander stood up and tried to talk to the noisy crowd, they shouted all the louder, "Great is Diana of the Ephesians!" They kept up their shouting for two hours.

Then the ruler of the city came and scolded the people. Suddenly the crowd was quiet as the ruler told them that they all knew that the people of Ephesus worshipped Diana. He scolded them for making so much noise and trouble and then sent them all home.

REMEMBER:

When the new Christians at Ephesus burned their books of magic, very much money went up in the smoke of the fire. But they did not care. They were glad, because they traded it for all the treasures in heaven. We do not care about treasures on this earth, either, for we have our treasures in heaven, too.

587

The End of Paul's Third Missionary Journey

Paul left the city of Ephesus after the big uproar there and traveled to many more cities, preaching as he went. On the way home from his third journey Paul stopped at the city of Troas and stayed with the Christians there for seven days. The day before he had to leave was Sunday and on that day Paul preached to the church there. In the evening they had a very long church service. They all wanted to stay because they knew they would not see Paul again. At midnight Paul was still speaking to them and probably answering their questions.

Rooms in those days were built with very narrow windows so that not much air could come in. Can you make a picture in your mind of that room, crowded with people, and lit with many candles? Those candles burned the good, fresh air that people needed to breathe. One man, named Eutychus, was having trouble. Even though he sat in a window sill, he was not getting enough air to breathe. The Bible says he fell into a deep sleep. He was probably unconscious because he did not have fresh air. Farther and farther he sank down and suddenly he fell out of the window three floors down to the ground.

His friends hurried down to see whether he was hurt. Then they had to cry: for he was dead. Paul followed them down and saw that they had carefully taken up his dead body. He laid his own body on the body of Eutychus and put his arms around him. By a wonder of grace, God put life into Eutychus again and Paul said to the people, "Trouble not yourselves; for his life is in him."

Eutychus was alive and stood up. What excitement and happiness there was in the church of Troas that night! No one wanted to go home. They went back upstairs, ate bread together, and talked until daylight came. Those Christians at Troas were so eager to hear God's Word from Paul's lips that they gladly missed a night's sleep.

Then it was time for Paul to leave for his own land. He took a ship across the sea and it stopped at many cities along the way home. One of these cities was Miletus, where they stayed for four days. Miletus was about thirty miles from the city of Ephesus, where he had preached for so long. Oh, how Paul wished he could see some of his dear friends from the city of Ephesus. He sent word to them that he was at Miletus and he asked some of the elders of the church to come to Miletus to see him. Those elders came thirty miles to see Paul and got there the day before Paul had to leave.

Paul talked with them for a long while and he had some sad news for them. The Holy Spirit in Paul's heart told him he must go to Jerusalem and suffer there and be a prisoner because he preached about Jesus. He told his Christian friends always to preach the truth of God's Holy Word to the church at Ephesus.

When it was time for Paul to go back to the ship, they all kneeled down on the beach and Paul prayed. The elders from Ephesus cried many tears, for their hearts were sad. They knew they would never see their dear Paul again. Then they all walked with him to the ship and his sad friends left for Ephesus.

Paul sailed on, and after the ship had stopped at many cities, Paul left the ship and came to Jerusalem. Many of his friends from the cities Paul had visited had come along with Paul. What a happy meeting they all had with the Christians at Jerusalem. But Paul's life did not stay happy in Jerusalem. Wicked Jews, who did not believe in Jesus, started a story which was really a lie. They said that Paul taught the people **not** to obey the laws which God gave to Moses. Of course, that story was not true; but many people believed it.

Paul's friends had an idea. If Paul would make himself clean and go into the temple, the way Moses' law told him, everyone would **see** that the story was a lie; for then they would **see** that Paul was obeying the law which God gave to Moses.

It did not work out that way. Wicked men can always make things go wrong. Some of those wicked Jews had seen a Gentile — a man from a heathen country who had come with Paul — walking with him through the streets of the city. They **thought** that Paul had taken this Gentile into the temple with him. And no Gentile might come into the temple of the Jews. When they thought that Paul had done wrong, they liked that thought. They did not even bother to ask Paul whether it was true. They **liked** to spread a wicked lie.

Their lie worked. They upset all the people of Jerusalem by crying, "Men of Israel, help!"

Then they told that Paul had taken a Gentile, one of his Christian friends from Ephesus, into the temple; and the people believed the lie. Now Jerusalem was in an uproar, and all the people ran together. They took Paul and began to beat him and tried to pull him apart. Before they could kill him, the captain of the soldiers saved Paul, tied him up with chains, and then asked what he had done. Most of the people didn't know what Paul had done, for some said one thing and some another.

The captain led Paul up some stairs to a tower where he would be safe. When they were on the stairs Paul asked whether he might speak to the people, and the captain let him. Paul gave a beautiful talk to that crowd of people. He told how Jesus had changed his heart when He had come to him in a bright light on the way to Damascus and how Jesus had told Paul to be His preacher. But the crowd would not listen. They shouted, "Away with such a fellow from the earth."

REMEMBER:

In this story it seems as if the wicked people were winning. But they weren't! God wanted Paul to be tied up and go to prison. God always does what is best.

Paul's Trial

The next day, the day after the Jews captured Paul in the city of Jerusalem, the captain of the soldiers led him to the rulers of the Jews. The captain did not understand what wrong Paul had done; and we know that he had done **nothing** wrong.

But everything seemed to go wrong when Paul stood before the rulers of the Jews. The rulers argued among themselves and were very angry at Paul because he said he believed that Jesus rose from the dead. And no one could tell what wrong things Paul had done. When the captain was afraid that they would pull Paul to pieces, he took him away again. That night Jesus stood by Paul's bed and told him to cheer up, for He was leading Paul to Rome, the world power, where he would preach.

The next morning forty of the Jews made a promise that they would not eat nor drink until they had killed Paul. They planned to ask the captain to bring Paul to them once more and on the way they would kill him. But Paul's nephew heard about their wicked plans. His nephew was a young man who had to call Paul **uncle**. He told Paul the story about the forty wicked Jews and Paul told his nephew to tell the captain. The captain ordered the soldiers to take Paul out of the city that very night so that the Jews would not be able to find him. Almost five hundred soldiers, some marching and some on horseback, left secretly in the darkness of the night to guard Paul on his trip. What an excitement there must have been in the army! Five hundred men were guarding one prisoner. They did not know that the prisoner was God's greatest preacher living in those days.

All night they traveled and the next day they came to the city of Caesarea. Felix was the ruler there and he kept Paul in a prison in Caesarea. After five days the Jews sent a man to Felix to tell him why Paul was a prisoner and why he should die. He said that Paul was a pest and he upset people. He said Paul was the leader of those who worshipped Jesus. He said that Paul made the temple unholy. Do you think that man was telling the truth about Paul?

Listen to what Paul answered. He told the ruler Felix that he **couldn't** have been a pest in Jerusalem. He was there for only seven days and did not make any trouble. He told that he truly was a leader of those who worship Jesus, but that was not **wrong.** It was **wonderful** to preach Jesus and to believe in Him. He told that he had never made the temple unholy but had obeyed all the laws God had given Moses.

Then Paul told Felix the real reason that he was made a prisoner. He said, "Touching the resurrection of the dead I am called in question by you this day."

The Jews hated the resurrection of Jesus and Paul loved it. Felix knew that Paul had done nothing wrong. He knew it was not right to keep him a prisoner or put him to death. He knew it was right to let Paul go free. But he was afraid of the wicked Jews. Felix treated Paul well but kept him a prisoner for two years, until another man became the ruler. His name was Festus.

Three days after Festus became the ruler, he went to Jerusalem to visit the rulers of the Jews. Those wicked rulers had not forgotten Paul. They still hated him and they hated the Jesus Whom he preached. Even though they had not seen Paul for two years, yet the first person they talked about to Festus was **Paul**. They asked Festus to take him back to Jerusalem and secretly they planned to kill him along the way.

Festus said no: he would keep Paul at Caesarea. Ten days later Festus went back to Caesarea and the rulers of the Jews went with him. Once again they brought Paul to stand before them and the wicked Jews told about the terrible things that Paul had done, but they could not prove that any of their lies were true.

Paul answered once more that he had done no wrong and Festus knew that he should let Paul go free. But Festus did not want the Jews to hate him, so he kept Paul a prisoner.

Suddenly Festus decided to let Paul go to Jerusalem and to let the wicked Jews judge him. Oh, Paul wouldn't go there! He knew the Jews would kill him. He would rather go to a city where the ruler would listen to him and treat him fairly. What city was that? It was Rome. Paul told Festus to send him to Caesar, the ruler of the world power at Rome.

After Festus talked it over with the rest of the rulers, he said to Paul, "Hast thou appealed unto Caesar? unto Caesar shalt thou go." Soon Paul would go to Rome.

REMEMBER:

The difference between Paul and the wicked Jews was that the Jews wanted a dead Jesus and Paul worshipped a living Jesus, Who was the Son of God. That is the difference between us and those who do not love the Lord. They do not want Jesus. We believe that He is living in heaven and we love Him and worship Him.

The Shipwreck

Many ships sailed for Rome in those days and Festus put Paul and some other prisoners on one of them. Two of Paul's dear friends, who could keep him from being lonely and could cheer him up, went with him. Justus, the captain of one hundred soldiers, took care of the prisoners on the ship. He was very kind to Paul. When the ship stopped at a city called Sidon, he let Paul visit with some of his Christian friends there and even have a meal with them.

Then they sailed on toward Rome. Because the ship stopped at many cities on the way and because the winds were so strong that they held back the ship, they could not sail as fast as they liked. In the middle of the sea was a big island. An island is land with water all around it. After much trouble with the strong winds, they got around the island and came to a place called Fair Havens.

It was getting late in the year and the ship did not have many days to sail to Rome anymore, for when winter came the weather on the sea was so wild and rough that no one sailed a ship there. At Fair Havens Paul talked with Justus, the captain, and told him to keep the ship right there at Fair Havens for the winter. Paul had a good reason for saying that. God had told him that if they went on the ship would be broken and their lives would be in danger. But the captain listened to the man who owned the ship rather than to Paul. Besides, Fair Havens was not a very good place to stay for a whole winter. The captain decided to go on.

When a gentle, quiet wind started to blow, they had the kind of weather they needed to sail the ship, and they started out for Rome. Not long after they left Fair Havens, the soft wind suddenly changed to a terribly hard and wild wind. It was a storm-wind. The sailors could not sail the ship against such a strong wind, so they let the wind push the ship toward the little island of Clauda.

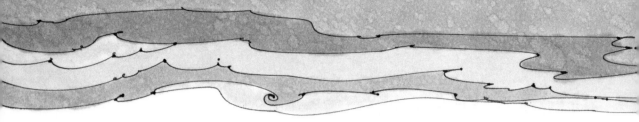

When they were sailing next to the island, the winds did not blow quite so hard and they managed to put chains around the front of the ship to keep it from breaking. They had much wheat on the ship, which they were going to sell in Rome; but the wheat made the ship too heavy, so they dumped much of it into the sea.

After they passed the island of Clauda, the storm became much worse. The sharp winds tossed the ship back and forth over the giant waves. For eleven days they did not see the sun nor the moon nor the stars. It must have been hard to know whether it was day or night. No one could sit down to eat and the cooks could not make any food ready in a ship that rocked and bounced so wildly. Probably many of them were seasick because of the rough storm.

Then Paul talked with the people on the ship. He told them that they should have listened to him while they were still in Fair Havens, but he also told them, "Be of good cheer: for there shall be no loss of any man's life among you, but of the ship."

How did Paul know? God's angel told him. God wanted Paul to get to Rome safely, and He was going to save everyone on the ship, two hundred seventy-six people, for Paul's sake. For three days more the storm rocked the ship on the huge waves. Then at midnight the sailors knew that they were near

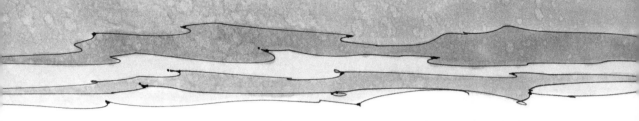

land because the water was getting shallower. They dropped anchors to hold the ship still and waited for daylight to come. While it was still dark, some of the sailors secretly put the small lifeboat into the water and were going to get into it and row away in it. Paul saw what they were doing and told Justus that **everyone** had to stay with the ship in order to be saved, and Justus made the sailors cut the little boat loose and stay with the big ship.

When daylight came, Paul urged everyone on the ship to eat. They hadn't eaten for so many days and now it would be good for them. Paul took bread, asked God's blessing, and ate. Then all the rest ate, too. Nearby was a creek and they sailed into it, toward shore; but two seas met there and the water was pushing and pulling the ship so hard that it broke. It was shipwrecked! The soldiers were ready to kill all the prisoners before they ran away; but the captain did not want **Paul the prisoner** killed, and therefore he would not let them kill any of the prisoners. Some swam and some floated on broken pieces of the ship until they all came safely to land.

REMEMBER:

When they were in the middle of the storm, Paul told the people on the ship, "Be of good cheer; for I believe God, that it shall be even as it was told me." Wherever we are, we can always say that with Paul.

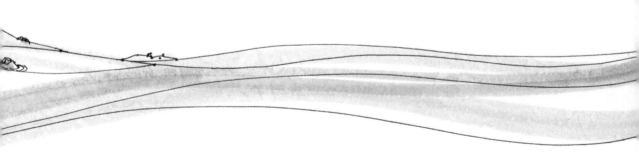

Paul Comes to Rome

Do you remember that the ship in which Paul was sailing was shipwrecked? It lay in the cold water near the shore, broken to pieces. Every person on the ship made it to land safely as Paul had said they would and they found out that the name of the island was Melita.

It was a cold, rainy morning and all the two hundred seventy-six ship-wrecked people were soaking wet and shivering. The people who lived on the island were very kind to them and built a huge fire to warm the shivering people and dry their clothes. Paul helped with the fire. He gathered sticks to burn. In his bundle of sticks was a dangerous, poisonous snake, which he didn't even see because it was stiff and still with cold. As soon as the snake came near to the fire, it came back to life and fastened itself on Paul's hand. It bit him! Paul shook the snake from his hand into the fire.

The people who lived on the island stared at Paul and shook their heads. They said to one another that this Paul must be a terrible sinner, probably a murderer, who was saved from the shipwreck but who would die now for his terrible sins. For not one who was bitten by such a poisonous snake would live. His hand would get swollen because of the poison and soon he would fall down dead. After those people from the island had watched Paul for a long while and when they saw that the snake bite did not even hurt him, they changed their minds and said he was a god. The island people worshipped idols and that was the only thing they **could** think. We know that God worked a wonder: He made the snake bite Paul so that everyone would notice him; for God wanted Paul to **preach** on that island.

Everything always works God's way. He used the wonder of the snake which bit Paul to bring him to Publius, the ruler of the island. Everyone on the island must have been talking about the great wonder and many people must have run to Publius with the story! He asked Paul to come to see him and Paul stayed with him for three days. The father of Publius was very sick with a bad fever that probably came from drinking goat's milk which was not pure. Paul prayed, laid his hands on him, and made him better. The news of this miracle spread very quickly over the whole island and people with all kinds of sicknesses came to Paul to be healed. For three months they stayed on the island of Melita, until the nice spring weather came. Paul prayed in Jesus' name, he healed the people in Jesus' name, and he preached in Jesus' name on the island.

When the shipwrecked people left, the island people gave them whatever they needed for their trip. They found another ship which was going to Rome and sailed on that ship. One of the stops was at the city of Puteoli. Paul got off the ship and found Christian friends, believers in Jesus. He stayed with them for seven days. He did not go back to the ship but walked the rest of the way, with many other prisoners, to Rome.

The Christians in Rome heard that Paul was coming and they were so eager to meet him that some of them walked as far as Appii Forum — fifty-six miles — to meet him. When Paul met these new Christian friends, he thanked God and felt braver to go ahead on his trip.

When he came to Rome, Paul was treated very well. He was allowed to live in his own house. The only sign that he was a prisoner was that he had a little chain around his wrist. The other end of the chain was on a soldier who guarded him. Do you think that the Jews who hated him so much came to Rome to tell the great Caesar what a terrible man Paul was and that he ought to die? No, they never came.

Paul called the Jews who lived in Rome to his house and told them that he had not done anything wrong. He was a prisoner because the Jews hated to hear him preach about Jesus. He was a prisoner for Jesus' sake! Then Paul taught the Jews all about Jesus. For two years he preached in his house to all who would listen. Some believed and some did not.

After two years Caesar let Paul go free again for a while and Paul traveled to many places, preaching in Jesus' name. But once more he was put in prison for Jesus' sake and then he was never free again. Soon Caesar made him die. Then God gave Paul his wish: he went to heaven to be with the Jesus Whom he had preached all over the world.

REMEMBER:

In all his life, Paul's only comfort and happiness was that he belonged to Jesus. Our only comfort and happiness is that we, too, belong to Jesus. Paul went to live with Him forever. If we are His children, we will go to live with Him forever, too.